ECONOMICS FOR ENGINEERING STUDENTS

ECONOMICS FOR ENGINEERING STUDENTS

Second Edition

SEEMA SINGH
Department of Humanities
Delhi Technological University
New Delhi

I.K. International Publishing House Pvt. Ltd.
NEW DELHI

Published by

I.K. International Publishing House Pvt. Ltd.
S-25, Green Park Extension
Uphaar Cinema Market
New Delhi – 110 016 (India)
E-mail: info@ikinternational.com
Website: www.ikbooks.com

ISBN 978-93-84588-08-3

10 9 8 7 6 5 4 3 2 1

Published by Krishan Makhijani for I.K. International Publishing House Pvt. Ltd., S-25, Green Park Extension, Uphaar Cinema Market, New Delhi – 110 016 and Printed by Rekha Printers Pvt. Ltd., Okhla Industrial Area, Phase II, New Delhi – 110 020

Foreword to the First Edition

Engineering and technology has a direct bearing with well being of the society and is directly related to the growth of the economy. The knowledge age, in which we have already entered, is the beginning of the new millennium. Advances in Science and Technology create both the knowledge Power as well as Economic Power of the nations around the world. As such, it is important for the students of engineering and technology disciplines at degree and postgraduate degree levels to understand the role of Economics and Business development in transforming the Knowledge Power into the prosperity of the people. This is the best way in which the Power of Science and the Might of Technology are effectively utilized to strengthen the national and global economies.

I am indeed very happy that Dr Seema Singh, who has taught economics to engineering students at DCE for last eight years and has a close encounter with the excitement and joy of engineering created by the power of innovations in engineering institution campuses, has taken the initiative to bring out this book on "Economics for Engineering Student". Besides discussing Microeconomics, Dr Singh has provided an insight into International Economics and Economic Development and Project Planning. She has given a special emphasis on Indian Economics to highlight the salient features, often unique to economic planning and development in a country like India.

I am sure the publication shall the young, creative and innovative minds of engineering students to understand the role of Economics and Economic Planning while practicing their profession of Engineering and Technology. It goes without saying that engineering and technology are playing a predominant role in shaping the economic system and business development around the world. The rapid pace of development of the India Economy requires a greater appreciation of the role of Financial Engineering as well as engineering aspects of economic planning and development. The all pervasive nature of engineering and that of economics shall bridge the gap between the planners and policy makers of the nations and the innovative and creative genius of the engineering and technology professionals. I hope this book shall create an urge for integration of Economics and Engineering in the coming years.

I congratulate Dr Seema Singh for bringing out this book for the benefit of young students of Engineering and Technology in India and abroad.

Prof. P. B. Sharma
Vice Chancellor
Rajiv Gandhi Technological University Bhopal, MP
pbsharma48@yahoo.co.in, vc@rgtu.net

Preface to the Second Edition

Second edition of the book is itself a proof that the book has been well received by the students and teachers for which I am very happy, thankful and ready with the improved second edition which has also eleven chapters. The seventh chapter of the first edition has been merged with second and sixth chapter and thus, made ten chapters. I have also tried to explain some of the concepts as rent, inferior goods, inflation, etc., in a better way than the first edition. Input-output analysis has been deleted from the eighth chapter due to two reasons. Engineering students are already learning this topic in their engineering subjects and second, the treatment was very simple. A new section on interest formula and their application and an altogether new chapter on Engineering Economics with new topics, have been added. I do hope that the second edition also will be well appreciated by students and teachers, both. However, I am open for any feedback, correction and suggestion for improvement. I am giving my email address here and the readers are welcome to approach me with their queries.

Dr. Seema Singh
seemahumanitiesdtu@gmail.com
seemasinghdtu@gmail.com

Preface to the First Edition

Engineering, in general, is apply scientific laws and principles in economic activities of the human being for enhancing efficiency and productivity. So each engineering activity must be judge on two grounds. First, is the process or product technically feasible? Second, is it economically viable? The second point has become even more important in the era of liberalization and opening up of the economies when geographical boundaries have lost its significance and economic boundaries are continuously being blurred under various norms of WTO and other agreements. As markets are becoming increasingly competitive, firms are opting for cost-effective upgraded technology as a survival strategy to exist in the global market. The engineers need to have an understanding of economic principles to be able to apply them for judging economic viability of an engineering project as well as they must be able to understand broad economic environment under which they have to operate.

Arthur M. Wellington, a civil engineer, was a pioneer to introduce economic analysis in the field of engineering. In the later part of the nineteenth century, he specifically addressed the role of economic analysis in engineering projects. His particular area of interest was-road construction in the United States. Since then, ecnomics is being taught in one form or the other to the engineering students throughout the world. In India also, economics is being taught at many institutions under the guidelines laid down by the All India Council for Technical Education (AICTE) for Humanities and Social Science Component of Bachelors level Engineering Course. However, the course structure of Economics has not been developed yet. Different topics of Economics are being taught or it has been clubbed with some other subject such as Management or Accountancy. In this scenario, it is very difficult to write a book which can be used as a textbook in all such institutions where Economics is being taught.

Overview of the book

Engineering students have no prior knowledge of Economics (some of them may have read Economics at school level). But, they need to know Economics to be able to apply to their engineering problems. This book is designed for one semester course to familiarize engineering students with fundamental concepts of economic theories. The book has been, broadly, divided in three sections. First section is on 'Introduction to Economics' which introduces engineering students to Economics and its relevance in the field of engineering. Second section discusses 'Topics of Economics' that provides basic knowledge from different branches of Economics which a beginner needs to have. Third and last section is on "Topics on Applied Economics'. Application of Economics and other subjects as Operational Research, Accountancy have been discussed in this section which are used to judge economic viability of engineering projects such as forecasting, decision making analysis, price determination in monopoly and perfect competition etc.

SEEMA SINGH

Acknowledgements

I would like to acknowledge all my teachers and friends from whom I have learnt and discussed Economics, whatever little I may be knowing and its application in engineering. I would also like to acknowledge all those paper writers and authors in Economics whose articles and books have given me an understanding of Economics and even though proper reference has been given in the book, I may have used, inadvertently, something from their writing without referring them. I would like to make special mention of my students of Delhi College of Engineering. By teaching them, I have learnt about their requirements and expectations of an engineering student from the subject, which has certainly helped me in writing the book. I would also like to acknowledge the emotional support given by my husband, son and other members of my extended family throughout the process of writing the book. I am thankful to my publisher also for their support and for being patient with me.

At the end, I cannot resist myself from admitting that the book needs many modifications to suit the requirement of an engineer to face present global economic environment. But at present, I have compromised with market forces, i.e., the syllabus of various institutions which is being followed at present. The syllabus of several College and Technological University spread all over India which I have scrutinized before writing the book calls for changes and improvement in the book. Efforts to standardize and formalize the syllabus may be made from that side too. I would appreciate being informed of errors. Suggestion for inclusion or exclusion of any topic or any other comments about the book is always welcome.

SEEMA SINGH

Contents

Part I
Introduction to Economics

1

Introduction

Purpose of this chapter is to acquaint the reader with:

- Scope, Nature Approach and Definition of Economics
- Subject matter and method to study Economics
- Various concepts which are used in Economic Analysis
- Why engineering students should study Economics
- Role of Science, Engineering and Technology in Economic Development
- Managerial Economics: Scope, Definition and Nature

SCOPE OF ECONOMICS

A human being has unlimited needs. Take example of yourself and think about the number of goods you have required since morning. Then multiply it with 63 years (average age of an Indian). It will run in thousands. Do not panic, the case is not unique for you only but it is almost same for all of us. We have unlimited needs. Popularly it is said that even all the resources of the world cannot satisfy all needs of a single human being. Some needs can be satisfied easily because sources to satisfy them are abundantly available (supply > demand). These resources are known as free goods. Example of free goods are air, sunrays, etc. Wait a moment, do not say that fresh air is also not free today. We will discuss it under the topic 'goods' in the next chapter. However, many of the needs cannot be satisfied easily as sources to satisfy them are less in supply than the demand (supply < demand). These goods are exchanged between persons according to their demand and supply. Even intangible goods, as quality of a teacher to teach the students or a lawyer to plea in the court or even beauty of a model, can be considered goods because an advertising company can use it for enhancing sale in exchange of money. All these goods, which have exchange value, are called economic goods.[1] Resources to exchange economic goods are scarce. At the same time, these scarce resources have alternative uses. They are capable to exchange a lot of economic goods. As the needs differ in their intensity, some wants are more urgent in comparison to others. A rational human being,[2] therefore, tries to satisfy maximum of his wants from available resources on the basis of his intensity for consumption. In order to satisfy maximum wants, he always tries to maximize the benefits he receives from a particular good to the sacrifices he makes to acquire that good. Scope of Economics revolves around activities of a rational human being as well as production, distribution and consumption of economic goods. Behaviour of a saint or a priest is not considered in Economics who devotes all his life in public service without expecting anything in return. A rational human being always tries to distribute his limited resources in such a way that he derives maximum benefits from those goods and services, which yield him satisfaction. So, economic problem is essentially a problem of choice between various alternatives. As a consumer, each one of us tries to distribute our limited income between different goods and services in a manner to derive maximum satisfaction. As a producer also, each firm takes decisions about what is to be produced, how to be produced and how much has to be produced, which will fetch maximum benefits for the firm.

DEFINITIONS OF ECONOMICS

Issues, which are discussed in Economics, revolve around unlimited needs and limited resources to satisfy them for individual or society as a whole and how they strive to maximize them. These issues have always remained crucial and have been discussed, but the first problem which leads to the development of Economics as a subject of study (earlier it was called Political Economy) was concerned with international trade. The Mercantilist School, which flourished along with the growth of British overseas trade in the 17th and 18th centuries, had one clear doctrine—the export brings wealth to the nation. Its proponents supported and advocated devices by which the government could protect the balance of trade. Adam Smith mocked them by saying that they mistook gold for wealth (Robinson & Eatwell, p. 5). Despite their often brilliant insight, the British philosophers did not formulate a coherent body of logical economic analysis. The first writers to do so were French philosophers and social scientists who belonged to Physiocrat School of Thought. They discussed for the first time, the system of social classes. In the 18th century, economy was feudal in France. Share of land as rent and peasants' contribution in the produced crop was source of funding for the army and other administrative works. Physiocrats based their doctrine on the idea that land only yields rent, as it is the only source of net output. The growing importance of manufacturing industry made the Physiocrats' vision obsolete. The formal beginning of Modern Economics as a subject of study may be marked by emergence of their successors, the Classical School. It was propounded by Adam Smith.

Since then, various definitions have been put forward by various economists but they are not unanimous. Different economists have defined 'Economics' differently. Not only definitions but neither subject matter nor its name has remained same in last 250 years. Various topics have been included and excluded in the subjects matter of Economics from time to time depending upon the economic environment of that era. From this point of view, it is one of the most lively subjects, which is continuously growing. In order to understand the evolution of Economics, definitions of Economics have been classified in the following manner:

Wealth Definitions

Adam Smith (1723-1790), who is known as the Father of Modern Economics and propounded 'Classical School of Economic Thought'. In his famous work, "An Enquiry into the Nature and Causes of Wealth of Nations" (published in 1776), he has discussed that great object of political economy of every country is to increase the riches and power of the country. He advocated for *laissez-faire* economy where the market will have free hand to operate. Producers will produce if the goods are in demand and consumers will purchase those goods that are available in the market. He proposed to enrich both the people and the sovereign. Smith's wide ranging ideas were formalized and developed within a tight analytical framework by David Ricardo (1772-1823). Some of the other classical economists are J.B. Say (1767-1832), J.S. Mill (1806-1873), and T. R. Malthus (1766-1834). Classical economists discussed Economics as a science of production of wealth and its distribution. In this way, they tried to develop an economic mechanism based on class to provide an analysis of dynamism of the new industrial society. Hence, classical economists made a valuable contribution to the science of Economics.

Important elements

(i) Wealth creation and its accumulation are very important for both individual and country.

(ii) It provides physical subsistence to human beings.

(iii) It also raises standard of living.

(iv) Main objective of political economy of every country is to increase the standard of living of its people.

Criticism

(i) As society of that time was very much influenced by religious and ethical thoughts, importance given by classical economists to wealth and riches were not accepted in right manner.

(ii) Economics as science of wealth was sharply criticized by people of that time.

(iii) It was criticized by Neo-Classical and Modern Economists both. Robbins criticized for restricting the scope of Economics by considering only material wealth. Irrespective of the fact whether material or immaterial, if it satisfies human needs and is scarce in supply, it makes subject matter of Economics. Even skill of an engineer or a singer is required to satisfy human needs and is short in supply. Hence, it should be included in the subject matter of Economics. Similarly, in course of excluding immaterial goods, they did not consider role of education or health in economic development. However, both these factors play a significant role in economic development of a country.

(iv) Neo-classical economists criticized the definition for giving undue emphasis on wealth and wealth-producing activities in the definition. It completely ignored welfare aspect. Both human welfare and social welfare are important indicators and absence of these indicators makes wealth definition incomplete.

(v) They did not see any conflict in the individual good and the general social good. According to them, "individual self-interest is compatible with the interest of society". But in real life, there is conflict between the good of an individual and the social good. Thus, pursuance of individual self-interest is not always in the interest of the society as well. Moreover, apart from wealth, man is also motivated by other feelings such as kindness and love.

In view of these shortcomings, material welfare definition of Economics was propagated in place of wealth definition in the latter half of 19th century by Neo-Classical Economists.

Material Welfare Definitions

Alfred Marshall (1842-1924) was one of the pioneers to shift the emphasis from 'wealth' to 'welfare', by discussing "Economics is a study of men as they live, move and think in the ordinary business of life". This shift in the emphasis initiated a new school known as Neo-Classical School of Economic Thought. This definition examines that part of individual and social action, which is most closely connected with the attainment and the use of the material requisites for well-being. Thus, it is on the one hand, a study of wealth, on the other and important side, a part of the study of men. Marshall laid greater emphasis on Economics being a social science, by using the term 'Economics' in place of the narrower term 'Political Economy', which was earlier being used. Some of the other Neo-Classical Economists were Prof. E. Cannan (1861-1935) and Prof. A.C. Pigou (1877-1959).

Important elements

(i) Study of mankind in the ordinary business of life.

(ii) Production and consumption of material goods.

(iii) Discusses welfare rendered by material goods.

Criticism

(i) Material welfare definition as propounded by A. Marshall and developed by other Neo-Classical economists, was sharply criticized by Robbins for restricting the scope of Economics as production and consumption of material goods only as classical economists did. Neo-Classical economists also excluded non-material goods from the scope of Economics. Thus, according to them, services rendered by a doctor or an architect do not form subject matter of Economics. Robbins, however, regarded all goods and services, which command a price and enter into exchange as subject matter of Economics, irrespective of whether they are material goods or non-material services. Thus, Robbins has criticized definitions developed by Neo-Classical economists as being classificatory rather than analytical.

(ii) Robbins has argued that it is not proper to relate Economics to welfare. Many goods like wine, cigarettes, etc. are produced and sold in the market, which does not yield any welfare to individual or society, yet it forms a part of subject matter of Economics because these are scarce. Again, human welfare is a subjective matter and it varies with person and time. It is very difficult to measure welfare objectively. Above all, money is not an adequate measure of welfare.

(iii) Robbins has argued that Economics is neutral with regard to ends. If we relate Economics to welfare, the economists will have to pass a value judgment as good or bad effects of a particular commodity. In those circumstances, Economics will become a normative science. However, Economics is a positive science, which analyses situation as they are, and not as they should be.

Scarcity Definitions

Robbins (1898-1984) was very scientific in approach towards defining 'Economics' as the science, which studies human behaviour as a relationship between ends and scarce means, which have alternative uses.

Important elements

(i) Human needs are unlimited.

(ii) Means to satisfy these needs are less in supply than the demand.

(iii) Limited resources have alternative uses. Therefore, there is always a problem of choice with respect to the use of resources. According to Robbins, wants differ in intensity and on the basis of its intensity, we decide as to which wants are to be satisfied first and which one later. At this point, we should clearly remember that problem of choice arises because of the presence of all these wants together. So one tries to satisfy maximum wants with limited resources.

This definition of Economics is being used by engineers also in their endeavour.

Criticism

(i) According to Prof. Robbins, economic problem arises due to scarcity but sometime, it arises due to abundance also e.g. under conditions of depression.[3] Aggregate supply[4] is greater than aggregate demand[5] and, therefore, there may be over production.

(ii) The definition gives too much emphasis on the phenomenon of scarcity. However, at present the focus has shifted from scarcity to the question on how to overcome the problem of scarcity and thus, shifted towards Economics of Development and Growth.

(iii) The definition does not take into account the social aspects of economic activities. It is only concerned with the behaviour of an individual either as a consumer or as a producer. However, Economics as a social science, is concerned with the study of economic activities of human being as a member of society. So, the definition must have some social concerns also.

Development and Growth Definition

In the later part of 19th century and beginning of 20th century, economists such as Prof. Samuelson[6] (1915-2009) brought phenomenon of development and growth under the scope of Economics. Economic development of a country is the result of conscious and deliberate efforts of planning of the national economy. It involves two aspects. First is the optimum utilization of limited resources, which the country has. Second is the deliberate structural change in the economy by introducing technological or managerial advancement. These advancements lead to an increase in the production capacity of the economy. Prof. Samuelson has defined, "Economics is the study of how men and society end up choosing, with or without the use of money, to employ scarce productive resources that could have alternative uses, to produce various commodities and distribute them for consumption, now or in the future, among various people and groups in society. It analyzes the costs and benefits of improving pattern of resource allocation".

Important elements

(i) Economics deals with efficient allocation of limited resources.

(ii) It is concerned with the allocation of its limited resources in a manner, which will ultimately lead to economic development of an economy.

(iii) Economics is also concerned with an equitable distribution of fruits of economic development among all segments of the society.

Thus, Samuelson's definition adapts Robbins's definition by incorporating the growth and equity-oriented concepts in it. This is high time when engineers should also consider and adopt this definition in their professional decisions.

Criticism

(i) This definition is being criticized on the ground of equitable distribution of fruits of growth and development. In reality, equitable distribution does not take place in a society. There is skewed distribution of income in the society.

(ii) There are aspects as gender, scheduled caste and scheduled tribe, poor, which also may be regarded important for inclusive growth.

Among the Indian economists, Chanakya is one of the earliest names who discussed topics of Economics in general and public finance in particular in his famous book *Arthsastra* during reign of Chandra Gupta Maurya.

NATURE AND APPROACH OF ECONOMICS

There is debate among several scholars over nature and approach of Economics. Regarding nature, it is debated that whether it is a subject of science or social science or both and regarding approach, it is normative or positive. First, we will discuss its nature. The term science means a systematic body of knowledge, which tries to explain cause and affect relationship. It has its own methodology by which cause and effect may be measured. From that point of view, Economics is a science because it is s systematic body of knowledge. Again, variables in Economics are liable to quantify in terms of money. It has a proper methodology to discuss. As a law of physics or chemistry holds good at given pressure and temperature, similarly, law of demand in Economics also holds good if other things such as taste and income of consumer, fashion and season remain same. However, there is a substantial number of scholars who consider it a subject of social science because economists differ in their approach and opinion on any economic issue as a subject of social science. Economic behaviour of a human being is highly unpredictable and value of the measuring scale of Economics, money does not always remain same.

Economists differ on the approach of Economics also—whether it is normative or positive. Normative approach of Economics attempts to prescribe what ought to be done. For this, we need to use a set of value judgments. Thus, normative economics is based on ethical, moral, philosophical and religious beliefs of the people. Alfred Marshall has discussed normative approach of Economics. He was the pioneer who pointed out that the promotion of human welfare is the ultimate aim of Economics. However, Robbins was of the opinion that if Economics will become normative, it will become unscientific. Robbins was of the opinion that approach of economics is positive, which involves explanation and prediction of economic behaviour as it is and not what it ought to be. He said that the role of economists is to say what consequences could follow of certain action, but it cannot judge the desirability of ends.

So far, engineers have also taken positive approach. A firm or even a country may be using or have used in the past a technology, which may be cost effective or more productive but, in the long run, the technology may adversely affect the environment. Nowadays, there are growing concerns about consequences of using unsustainable technology. Eco-friendly technology or sustainable technology is being innovated and promoted.

SUBJECT MATTER OF ECONOMICS

Subject matter of Economics is vast and is still growing. Many topics have been included and excluded in last 250 years. However, these topics may be grouped into two for convenience of discussion. They are Microeconomics and Macroeconomics.

As 'micro' means small, Microeconomics deals with economic behaviour of small entity; it may be a consumer or a firm. How a rational consumer distributes his limited income over various commodities, which together gives him maximum satisfaction or how a firm decides quantity and price for its product to establish synergy with the industry[7] are covered under Microeconomics. Thus, Microeconomics focuses on the behaviour of the Individual actors in the economic framework, i.e., firms, individuals and their interaction in the markets. As Microeconomics discusses how limited resources are distributed over large number of alternative uses in order to maximize returns, it has great theoretical and practical significance. Most significant of all is its ability to give an understanding of how a free enterprise economy operates. For engineering students, knowledge of Microeconomics helps to understand the forces which operate during production in a firm. How best to use the available scarce resources between various activities of the firm and to select the best production function to become technically as well as economically efficient, etc. Microeconomics helps engineers to understand the forces, which operate on adoption of a particular technology and forces, which are under control of a firm. Some of the topics covered under Microeconomics are as follows:

(i) Consumer Behaviour

(ii) Law of Demand

(iii) Production Function
(iv) Factor of Production
(v) Product Pricing
(vi) Market

The word 'macro' means large and Macroeconomics deals with the study of the aggregate or average covering the entire economy, viz. national income, aggregate production, general price level, etc. It can also be referred as looking at the economy from above. It needs to be understood that the decisions of a firm are always made within the broad framework of an economic environment under which the firm operates. The economic environment is known as macroeconomic conditions. It includes techniques for analyzing changes in total output and also addresses question about the effect of changes in investment. Some of the issues which Macroeconomics deals are as follows:

(i) National Income and Employment
(ii) Saving and Investment
(iii) Trade Cycle
(iv) General Price Level
(v) Inflation
(vi) Development and Growth
(vii) Distribution of National Income between Factors of Production
(viii) Monetary and Fiscal System of an Economy

However, there is one basic difference between them. While all the Microeconomic variables are under control of the firm like what to produce or how much to produce or from where to purchase raw material. For a consumer also, decision about what to purchase and from where to purchase is under control of the consumer but Macroeconomic variables are not under control of the individual who is going to be affected by the Macroeconomic variables as tax rate of a country may affect the firm but the firm does not take decision about the tax policy of the country.

Table 1.1 Comparison between Microeconomics and Macroeconomics

SN	*Microeconomics*	*Macroeconomics*
1.	It deals with economic behaviour of small entity as consumer or firm.	It deals with economic behaviour of large entity as industry or a nation.
2.	Economic decision taken under Microeconomics is under control of the individual regarding whom the 'dicision has been taken as, how much has to be purchased' is under control of the customer.	All of us are affected by Macroeconomic decisions but it is not under control of any one of us as, we all are affected by Income Tax Policy of the Government of India but none of us can change it according to convenience.

Knowledge and understanding of Macroeconomics is very helpful in formulation and execution of government's policy. Also modern theory of income and employment greatly helps in forecasting business conditions. However, it must be taken into consideration that both Microeconomics, and Macroeconomics are relative terms. They may be used to refer smaller and bigger concepts in comparison. In case of discussing income of a firm and Gross National Product (GNP) of India, GNP of India becomes Macroeconomic issue but when discussing global economy, GNP of India becomes Microeconomic issue in comparison of GNP of all the developing economies, taken as one.

Relationship between Microeconomics and Macroeconomics

Microeconomics and Macroeconomics are interdependent on each other. Every Microeconomic problem has Macroeconomic dimension and vice versa. For example, the determination of general price level which is a subject matter of Macroeconomics basically depends on the theory of relative price of products and factors, which is a Microeconomic concept. On the other hand, profit of a firm is a Microeconomic concept but it cannot be understood unless one has complete knowledge of aggregate demand and general price level. Large aggregate demand implies that the profit of a firm is going to be huge. Both Microeconomic and Macroeconomic are used as relative terms. Some of the goals at macro level are merely extension of the goal at micro level and each one of them is complimentary to each other as employment of the individuals leads to high level of employment for the whole economy or economic goal at micro level is to maximize benefit of an individual and economic goal at macro level is to maximize benefit of the whole nation. However, some of the goals of microeconomics and macroeconomics are contradictory also. For example, any move for significant reduction in unemployment through monetary policy may lead to an increase in inflation.

METHOD OF ECONOMIC ANALYSIS

In economic analysis, economic data are subjected to scientific treatment to find out pattern of economic activity. Thus, scientific economic analysis requires clearly defined terms, methods for objective treatment of data and logical reasoning. Generally, two types of logical reasoning are used in economic analysis. They are in deductive reasoning and indeductive reasoning. In deductive reasoning, new conclusion are deduced from already established fundamental assumptions. First step in deductive reasoning may be formulation of assumption on the basis of facts which are to be analyzed. Next step may be analysis of facts through the process of logical reasoning till we arrive at conclusion. Last step is verification of conclusion. If the conclusion confirms with the observed facts, the hypothesis is verified. Deductive reasoning can be applied to all economic problems. Suppose the problem is to find out how a firm maximises its profit. Assuming that the firm is operating under conditions of monopolistic competitions, we shall apply the general principle, which gives maximum profits under this condition. If the firm fulfils the criteria, we shall conclude that the firm is maximizing its profits. The deductive method can be both mathematical and non-mathematical. However, the conclusion derived from deductive reasoning has limited applications. Conclusions obtained by this method in one situation may not be applicable to another situation or place. For example, the general theory of income and employment and price theory are applicable to developed economies, but they do not hold good when applied to a developing economy like India. Economic feasibility of a technology may also be analyzed by deductive method because technology is time and place specific. A technology, which has been developed for a capital surplus and labour scarce country, may not be appropriate in a labour surplus and capital scarce country.

In inductive reasoning, we start from the general and arrive at the particular conclusion. First step is collection of data. The data size must be large for a theory to be true. For example, if we intend to study expenditure on technology by firms after liberalization, we will have to collect data of expenditure on technology acquisition from technology intensive firms after liberalization. Next step will be placing the data in usable form. Tables, graphs, charts are common methods of summarizing data. From the summarized data, next step is to find out uniformity and to find out, if possible, cause and effect relationship. The next step involves the formulation of hypotheses from the observed relationship. After testing of hypothesis, a researcher will be in a position to generalize and formulate a theory. After thoroughly evaluating a theory by applying to all conditions and taking care of all available facts, a final conclusion can be derived.

Earlier, only deductive method was used in economic research. However, modern economists have emphasized that both inductive and deductive reasoning methods are required for proper development of economic theories and principles. In short, Economics is a broad-ranging discipline both in terms of its scope as well as in terms of methods it uses.

VARIOUS CONCEPTS USED IN ECONOMIC ANALYSIS

Like any other subject science, economics is concerned with the explanation and prediction of observed phenomena, which can only be done on the basis of theories. However, economic theories like theories of any other subject are applicable only under certain circumstances. Following concepts are useful in explaining and predicting economic phenomena:

(i) Assumption

Economic analysis explains economic behaviour of a human being, which depends on several factors. These factors are highly unpredictable and uncertain. Thus, each individual behaves and responds differently under particular circumstances. Not only that, each factor is dependent on several other factors. In that circumstance, no linear or non-linear relationship can be established between two variables. However, when two variables are considered keeping others as constant, they show certain relationship. As in case of demand and price, they are inversely related, when other variables are assumed constant. If any of the variables change, the inverse relationship does not hold good. For example, if income of the household increases, demand for a particular product increases even if its price also increases. Similarly, during winter season, demand for woollen clothes increases even if its price also increases.

(ii) Stock Dimension and Flow Dimension of an Economic Variable

In case of stock dimension, value of a variable has no time dimension. Physical quantities, which exist at any point of time, are measured through stock dimension. Some of the examples of stock dimensions are stock of finished product of a firm, and stock of raw material with a firm. On the contrary, value of variable, which has time dimension, is considered under flow dimension. It is discussed in reference of time, generally a year. Requirement of raw material per year by a firm or national income of a country during a year are some of the examples.

(iii) Equilibrium: Statics and Dynamics

Equilibrium refers to a market condition where demand of and supply for the product are same. Once the equilibrium is achieved by a firm or an industry, it tends to persist. Equilibrium is achieved by balancing of the market forces. In comparative static studies, equilibrium and other positions are considered without discussing the transitional period and process in between these two situations. On the other hand, dynamics deal with the time path and the process of adjustment in course of achieving equilibrium. In this book, only static equilibrium has been discussed.

(iv) Model

Model in economics may be a representation of a theory or a part of a theory with the application of statistical and mathematical techniques. It is used to gain an understanding in cause and effect relationship between variables and to measure the phenomena more accurately. It is similar to a situation where an automobile engineer makes a model of a car before making the actual car. The model may be similar to the actual car but simple in comparison to the actual car. The engineer may use the model to do experiment regarding various performance indicators of the actual machine. Similarly, models in Economics are very helpful in understanding the situation and to make appropriate decisions to deal with arising situation.

WHY ENGINEERING STUDENTS SHOULD STUDY ECONOMICS?

Engineering, in general, is an application of science, which is used in development or improvement of products and services, which ultimately benefit the society. It improves the efficiency and the productivity, that means getting same output with less input or more output with same input which is subject matter of Economics. Thus, engineers also confront with the problem of choices in their professional life as economists do. Again, all engineering activities are performed in certain economic environment and an engineer need to be familiar with such economic environment to work efficiently. A pioneer in this area was Arthur M. Wellington, a civil engineer, who in the later part of the 19th century specifically addressed the role of economic analysis in engineering projects. His particular area of interest was rail-road building in the United States. However, the social and economic role of engineers received prominence when Herbert Hoover, an engineer, became President of the United States in 1929. Hoover called attention to the unplanned effects that the technology was having on society due to waste and inefficiencies in industry and plundering of the natural resources that were occurring as a result of industrial development (Gupta, 1987). Eugene Grant published *The Principles of Engineering Economy,* in 1930. It was a milestone in the process of development of engineering economics as a subject. He placed emphasis on developing an economic point of view in engineering and (as he stated in the preface) "this point of view involves a realization that a definite body of principles governs the economic aspects of an engineering decisions as governs its physical aspect". This does not mean that in the beginning costs were usually overlooked in engineering decisions. However, the perspective that economy is a prime concern to the engineers and the availability of sound techniques to address this concern differentiate this aspect of modern engineering practice from the past (Sullivan, 2001).

In the era of liberalization and opening up of the economies, when geographical boundaries have lost their significance and economic boundaries are continuously being blurred under various norms of WTO and other agreements, markets are becoming increasingly competitive. Firms are opting for cost-effective upgraded technology as a survival strategy in the global market. Consequently, economic aspect of engineering projects has become more important than ever before. The engineers need to have in-depth understanding of basic technologies as well as its recent development to cope with the technological advances, but equally important is an understanding of economic theories to achieve break-even and maximize profits for the new ventures as well as to understand global economic environment under which they have to operate. Career of a practising engineer is going to be significantly affected by his ability to deal with economic aspect. Understanding of economic principles and their application in engineering activities is crucial for engineers of a developing country like India, which is reeling under low labour productivity. Some of the basic characteristics of the Indian economy are significantly large informal sector, inaccessible and remote rural areas, subsistence agriculture, etc. After liberalization and opening up of the economy, these sectors also have to face international competition. Appropriate technology may ameliorate these problems up to a certain extent. Even if one per cent of the engineering students are sensitized towards these crucial issues, the impact will be overwhelming (Singh, 2004).

ROLE OF SCIENCE, ENGINEERING AND TECHNOLOGY IN ECONOMIC DEVELOPMENT

Generally 'Science', 'Engineering' and 'Technology' are used as synonyms. However, these words have different connotations. While Science is regarded as an area of study in which basic principles of different physical systems are observed, designed and tested, Engineering and Technology are applications of Science. In Engineering, theories of mathematical and natural science are applied to use materials and forces for the benefit of human beings. Technology refers to application of Science to enhance efficiency and productivity of systems and devices. Both Engineering and Technology produce more and better products and services, which ultimately improve efficiency and productivity. Hence, both of these have important bearing on economic development. In fact, they are seen as an essential precondition for economic development. In strictly economic terms, development is the capacity of a country to higher annual growth rate of its gross domestic product (GDP) or gross domestic income (GDI). Alternatively, it is the ability of a nation to expand its output more than its population growth. Before 1970s, economic development was seen as planned alteration in the share of agriculture, industry and services in terms of GDP and employment. Generally, underdeveloped countries have larger dependence on agriculture and as the country develops, its share of agriculture share in terms of both GDP and employment declines and that of the industry and service increases. Development strategies of developing economies were, therefore, usually focused on rapid industrialization, often at the expense of agriculture, and rural development. It was perceived that "rapid gains in overall and per capita GNP growth would either 'trickle down' to the masses in the form of jobs and other economic opportunities or create the necessary conditions for the wider distribution of the economic and the social benefits of the growth" (Todaro, 2000). However, the recent growth trend of India shows that shift was from agriculture to tertiarty sector by-passing industrial sector. Again, after 1970s it was observed that many developing countries were able to achieve their GDP growth targets which coexisted with large-scale poverty and unemployment. Consequently, limitations of traditional measure of economic development were realized replaced by development index, which includes economic parameters such as reduction in poverty and unemployment as well as non-economic parameters such as education and health system and availability of potable water. However, in whatever way economic development is measured, technology plays an important role in it. In other words, better infrastructure, connectivity and communication can only be achieved through state-of-the-art technology. Hence, engineering and technology may be taken as an index of economic development of country.

The importance of technology in achieving rapid economic development has always been realized by one and all. However, due to variations in socio-politico-economic condition, all countries of the world are not at same level of technological development. Countries of Europe, USA and Japan have taken a lead in terms of technological development. These countries have grown faster and are called developed countries[8]. Countries of Asia, Africa and Latin America, which boarded the train late and preferred to import technology rather than developing technology of their own, constitute developing countries. However, technology is time and place specific. A technology which may be very effective at one place may not be so effective at other place. For example, after independence, India mainly relied on import of technology from those countries which were labour scarce and capita surplus. Though India is a labour surplus country, application of these technologies has provided employment to highly skilled small group of workers which has ultimately resulted into large-scale unemployment and widened the gulf between haves and have-nots. A technology can only be effective in an economy when it is able to develop forward, backward and lateral linkages with the local resources. In the era of liberalization and opening up of the economies, technology plays even more decisive role and appropriate technology has become important than ever before. Hence, to reap the optimum return in the short run and sustainable high rate of return in the long run, it is necessary to undertake R&D activities and to adapt imported technologies according to the local requirements. Also, rapid industrialization without taking care of environment as well as increase in number of vehicles on roads have generated alarming level of pollution. Developing ecofriendly technologies is a challenge before engineers. Again, a large number of workers have low level of education and skill endowment, which creates a vicious circle of low income. Low level of skill endowment causes low/inferior production. It, ultimately, leads to low income for the workers. Due to low level of earning, they are not able to maintain a healthy living and ultimately, not able to work to their optimum capacity. Science and technology has a Herculean task to provide low cost housing, potable water, sanitation etc. for the masses. These facilities will help the have-not segment of the society to be able to maintain their optimum level of efficiency and come out of the vicious circle of poverty.

Advent of Information and Communication Technology (ICT) has provided opportunities to perform a part of the production process to a far off place even in a different country where it can be performed in a cost-effective manner. As India has a large pool of scientific and engineering manpower, through application of ICT, they are playing effective role in the global production process.

MANAGERIAL ECONOMICS: NATURE, DEFINITION AND ITS SCOPE

Managerial Economics is a branch of Economics, which uses tools of Economics to organize and evaluate various alternative courses of action available. It is the science to manage scarce resources cost-effectively (Ivan, 2002). Instead of abstract Economic Theories, it discusses those theories of Economics which are used in managerial practices. It selects those theoretical tools, which are applicable to a real-world situation. Managerial Economics draws results from case studies.

Topics both from Microeconomics and Macroeconomics are subject matter of Managerial Economics. Beside Economics, Managerial Economics draws from Accountancy, Mathematics, Statistics and Operational Research. Managerial Economics deals with the problem of profit optimization where Operational Research comes in picture. Tools of Statistics such as average, regression analysis, probability etc. and tools of Mathematics as set theory, calculus are used to express economic variables and economic phenomenon in Managerial Economics. As in accountancy, business transaction of a firm is recorded and organized, which are used for future decision making. A manager needs information regarding financial operation for decision making. It has led to the development of a new branch of Accountancy, which is known as Management Accountancy. Generally, the following aspects are discussed in Managerial Economics:

(i) Demand Analysis and Forecasting
(ii) Decision Theory under Conditions of Risk and Uncertainty
(iii) Capital Budgeting and Investment Decision
(iv) Cost Analysis
(v) Pricing Policies and Practices
(vi) Production Management
(vii) Profit Management

Main objective of any firm is to earn maximum profit which can be only managed if deliberate attempts are made from the very beginning in the production cycle. Analysing existing demand and assessing future demand is the first step in this direction. Assessing future demand depends on many economic and non-economic variables which are discussed under (i) decision theory under condition of risk, and condition of uncertainty. What should be the level of production for a particular firm, how much finance is required and what may be the source of these finance, etc., are discussed under 'capital budgeting and investment decision', 'cost analysis' and 'production management'. Deciding price for the product in the market is real challenge for any firm. It is a 'make' or 'break' kind of decision for any firm. Issues related to pricing policies are discussed under 'Pricing policies and practices'.

In general, Managerial Economics is used by a goal-oriented manager in two ways. First, given an economic environment, the principles of Managerial Economics provide a framework for evaluating whether resources are being allocated efficiently within a firm. For example, tools of Economics can be helpful to the manager in determining if profit could be increased by reallocating labour from a marketing activity to the production line. Second, these principles help managers to respond to various economic signals. For example, given an increase in the price of output or development of a new low-cost technology, the appropriate managerial response would be to increase output or to shift to the low-cost technology. Alternatively, an increase in the price of one input, say labour, may be a signal to substitute other inputs, such as capital for labour in the production process (Petersen & Lewis, 2001).

Notes

1. Economic goods have the following characteristics:
    - They have the capacity to satisfy human wants.
    - They are always less in supply than demand (Supply < Demand).
    - They can be exchanged.
2. Rational human beings have the following characteristics:
    - Unlimited wants.
    - Means to satisfy these wants are scarce.
    - He always wants to maximize his profit by giving least and expecting most in an exchange.
3. Depression: If in a country, production, national income and employment level decline consistently, it is known as depression.
4. Aggregate supply: It is the sum total of goods and services produced in an economy. Export is deducted and imports are added to it.

5. Aggregate demand: It is that part of national income which is spent by consumer and the government on consumer and investment goods.
6. Paul A. Samuelson was one of the most influential Economist of modern times. Economic historian Randall E. Parker has called him the "Father of Modern Economics". He was Professor of Economics at Massachusetts Institute of Technology (MIT) and won Nobel Prize for Economics. Samuelson was instrumental in the initial development of Indian Institute of Management, Calcutta
7. Lateral summation of all firms producing similar product makes industry (Industry = Σ firms).
8. World Bank has divided countries as developed and developing. Those counties which have very high per capita income are considered developed and those countries whose per capita income is almost half of the per capita income of USA are considered developing.

EXERCISES

A. Objective

Write true or false for each of the following: **(For 1/2 mark each)**

(i) Positive Economics is about what ought to be and Normative Economics is about what it is.

(ii) Macroeconomics tries to figure out what makes the economy boom in some year and slump in others.

(iii) Air has value in exchange.

(iv) Economic goods are more in supply than demand.

(v) Human wants are limited.

(vi) Microeconomics focuses attention on the behaviour of the economy as a whole.

(vii) Microeconomics focuses attention on the behaviour of individual economic units such as household or firms.

(viii) Microeconomics is concerned primarily with achieving equilibrium.

(ix) Modern Economics is growth centred.

(x) Economics provides tools of analysis, but not the readymade solutions for business decision making.

Ans. (i) False; (ii) True; (iii) False; (iv) False
(v) False; (vi) False; (vii) True; (viii) True
(ix) True; (x) True.

B. Subjective

1. What is Economics? Why engineers should study it?
2. 'Economic Problem is a problem of choice'. Discuss.
3. Discuss application of basic economic theories in solving problems faced by engineers.
4. Discuss role of engineering and technology in economic development.
5. Distinguish between:
   (i) Positive Economics and Normative Economics.
   (ii) Wealth definition of Economics and Development definition of Economics.
   (iii) Microeconomics and Macroeconomics.
6. Discuss differences between Economics and Managerial Economics.
7. Discuss difference and similarity between Engineering problem and Economics problem.

References and Suggested Readings

1. Gupta, Madhu S. (1987), Teaching Engineering: A Beginner's Guide. Volume in the IEEE Press Selected Reprint Series, published under the sponsorship of the IEEE Education Society with the co-operation of the American Society for Engineering Education, The Institute of Electrical and Electronics Engineers, Inc., New York.
2. Ivan, P. L. Png (2002), Managerial Economics. Blackwell Publishers Ltd., Great Britain, p. 2.
3. Marshall, Alfred (1956), Principles of Economics. Macmillan & Co. Ltd., Eighth edition, London.
4. Petersen, H. Craig and W. Cris Lewis (2001), Managerial Economics. Pearson Education Asia, Fourth Edition, India, p. 4.
5. Robinson, Joan and John Eatwell (1974), An Introduction to Modern Economics. Tata McGraw-Hill, TMH Edition, New Delhi.
6. Samuelson, Paul A. (1973), Economics. McGraw-Hill Book Company, New York.
7. Singh, Seema (2004), Role of Engineering Institutes in Making Micro and Small Manufacturing Enterprises Sustainable. *University News*, 42 (46), pp. 124-127.
8. Sullivan, William G., James A. Bontadelli and Elin M. Wicks (2001), Engineering Economy. Pearson Education Asia, Delhi, p. 4.
9. Todaro, Michael P. (2000), Economic Development. Addison Wesley Longman (Singapore) Pvt Ltd, Indian Branch, Delhi-92, p. 14.
10. Balasubramanyam, V.N., (2002), Conversations with Indian Economists. Macmillan India Ltd, Delhi.

11. Stoneman, Paul, (2003), The Economics of Technological Diffusion: Blackwell Publishers, New Delhi.
12. Sowell, Thomas (2007), Applied Economics: Thinking Beyond Stage One. Viva Books Private Limited, New Delhi.
13. Wills, Ian (2007), Economics and the Environment: A Signalling and Incentives Approach. Allen & Unwin.

Part II
Topics of Economics

2

Microeconomics

Purpose of this chapter is to acquaint the reader with:

- Goods different type of goods
- Utility different type of utility
- Laws of Utility, Laws of Demand, Elasticity of Demand
- Indifference Curve Analysis
- Production, Factors of Production, Production Process, Production Function
- Factors which affect Price Determination
- Market, different type of markets

As discussed in the previous chapter, Microeconomics deals with the economic behaviour of individuals and their economic relationship with market. Individual may be customer or producer and their interaction for exchange of goods. What is a good? Why is it demanded by a consumer and produced by a producer? What price the consumer will be willing to pay and what price the producer will ask in exchange of the product? What will be the ultimate price on which the consumer and producer will be ready to exchange? Is the price of exchange affected by number of consumers or producers in the market? These are some of the issues which have been discussed in this chapter.

GOODS

Anything, commodity or service, which gives satisfaction to human beings on consumption is called good. Goods give satisfaction either directly, as bread is consumed to satisfy hunger or water to satisfy thirst or indirectly, as grinding machine is used to make flour from wheat, which is ultimately used to make bread and then consumed to satisfy hunger. Goods can be differentiated on the basis of various criteria. Some of them have been discussed here:

Free Goods and Economic Goods

Free goods do not bear a price because their supply is more than the demand (S > D). So, the customer does not exchange for consumption. As sunrays are in abundance, they are not exchanged. So, it is a free good. Free goods are also called non-economic goods. Economic goods are less in supply then the demand (D > S) and so, they are exchanged. Even intangible goods such as beauty of a model and technical skill of an engineer are economic goods because they are less in supply than the demand and they can be exchanged. Some goods become economic or free depending on person, place or situation. If a mother looks after her child it is a non-economic or free good because mother is not going to get anything in return but if a child is looked after by a nanny, it becomes an economic good because she is going to get money for her services. Sand is a free good near river beach but becomes an economic good near construction site.

Capital Goods and Consumer Goods

Those goods, which help in the production of other goods, are termed capital goods. For example, machine and raw materials. Consumer goods are directly consumed by human beings. For example, bread and milk. A particular good can become capital or consumer depending on the type of use. Milk is a consumer good for those who drink it and capital good for a producer of milk-processed goods.

Consumer goods can be further divided as perishable goods and non-perishable goods. Perishable good has very short shelf life as vegetables, milk, etc. Another differentiation is durable goods and non-durable goods. Durable goods have very long working life and can be used for several years as refrigerator, air-conditioner, etc. The other type of consumer good is Veblen goods which violate the law of demand. Demand for Veblen goods increases as their prices increase. A designer dress would be an example of a Veblen good as customer perceives them to be of higher quality.

Transferable Goods and Non-transferable Goods

Land or building of an individual, which can be transferred to another person, are transferable goods and a person's qualities such as beauty of a model, knowledge of a teacher and technical skills of an engineer are non-transferable goods.

Complimentary Goods and Substitute Goods

When two or more goods are required together to satisfy a single want, they are known as complementary goods. For example, ink and ink pen. Both are required together to satisfy single want, writing. However, when two or more goods satisfy similar wants and they can be used in each other's place, they are known as substitute goods. For example, tea and coffee or wheat and rice.

Material Goods and Non-material Goods

All those goods like land, water, agricultural products, mining and fishing or goods like building, machinery and implements which are tangible and has physical existence are called material goods. On the other hand, goods which are intangible as one's own qualities and abilities; are called non-material goods. Non-material goods may be internal such as muscular strength, business ability and professional skill, or external, such as beneficial relations with other people, goodwill and business connections of traders.

Normal Goods, Inferior Goods and Giffen Goods

Demand for normal goods increases with the increase in income. For example, clothes, pens and pencils. However, demand for inferior goods decreases with increase in income. For example, commodities used by poor households. As income of those households increases, they switch over to superior goods. So, demand for inferior goods decreases. One of the examples is millet, which is an inferior type of cereal which is consumed by poor households. When income of the households which are using millet increases, they switch over to superior substitutes, and consequently demand for millet decreases.

In consumer theory, a Giffen good is one which people paradoxically consume more as the price rises, violating the law of demand. Giffen goods are named after Scottish economist, Sir Robert Giffen who discussed the paradox. In case of normal good, price elasticity of demand is negative but in case of both inferior goods and Giffen goods, it is positive. However, in case of inferior goods, substitution effect is more prominent while in case of Giffen goods, income effect is more prominent.

Public Goods and Private Goods

A public good is both non-excludable and non-rivalrous as no individuals can be excluded from its use and use by one individual does not reduce its availability for others. Examples of public goods include air, road, river, etc. Many public goods may at times, be subject to excessive use resulting in negative externalities affecting all users; for example, air pollution and traffic congestion. On the other hand, a private good is owned by a person who gets its benefit and can prevent others from using or consuming it. It is rivalrous as consumption by one necessarily prevents others.

	Excludable	Non-excludable
Rivalrous	*Private goods*: Food, house, property	*Common goods*: timber, mineral
Non-rivalrous	*Club goods*: Library, theatre	*Public goods*: Air, road, river

WHY DOES A CONSUMER DEMAND A GOOD?

Human being needs all those goods, which satisfy his physical, mental, intellectual or spiritual need; in any way. In other words, goods have utility for the human being. Utility may be defined as the power of a commodity or a service to satisfy human need. It can also be defined as the satisfaction, which a person derives from the consumption or use of a good. Utility can be enhanced by adding value to the product in following ways:

Form Utility

Utility may be enhanced by changing form of the product. A person is said to create form utility when he changes the form of the matter in order to make it more serviceable. For example, students can sit on wooden log in the class-room but it would be more comfortable and convenient, if wooden bench and desk are made out of wooden log.

Place Utility

Utility of a good can be enhanced by transporting it from a place where it is in surplus to a place where is in short supply. For example, bringing agricultural crops from rural areas to the urban areas.

Time Utility

Utility of a good may be enhanced by storing a product when it is surplus for the time it will be needed and valued more. For example, vegetables and fruits are stored in cold storage when they are in surplus and are sold when they are in demand during the lean season.

Possession Utility

Utility can also be enhanced by transferring or changing ownership of a good from a person who has little use for it to a person who has more use for the same. For example, selling a table by a carpenter to a person working in an office. Carpenter has little use for the table. But when it is transferred to a person working in an office, its utility increases.

Service Utility

Abilities of doctors and teachers is more for patients and students respectively than any body else. They provide services to their respective clients.

Marginal Utility

Marginal utility is the utility derived from the last unit consumed. Mathematically:

$$MU = \frac{d(TU)}{dx}$$

(Differentiation of total utility with respect to number of units consumed)

where TU = total utility
x = number of unit consumed

A person likes to consume all those goods which yield him utility. However, intensity of utility of a good decreases as he consumes successive units of the product. Even at same point of time, intensity of utility for various goods for a consumer differs from each other. A rational consumer will like to consume the good whose intensity is more than the good whose intensity is less. The concept of marginal utility is used to discuss Law of Utility for successive units consumed by him.

LAW OF DIMINISHING MARGINAL UTILITY

The law states that as a person consumes more units of a good, the marginal utility with the successive units of consumed good decreases while the total utility increases at a falling rate, if other things remain same. When marginal utility is zero, total utility becomes highest and beyond that point, total utility starts falling and marginal utility becomes negative.

The law has the following implicit assumptions:

(i) All units of the good are homogeneous.
(ii) There is no change in taste during consumption of good.
(iii) There is no time gap between consumption of successive units of the good.
(iv) Consumer is rational and he will not do anything, which will reduce total utility.

The law has been illustrated as below:

Table 2.1 Utility Schedule of a Commodity of an Individual Consumer

Units of Commodity	*Total Utility (TU_X)*	*Marginal (MU_X)*
0	0	-
1	4	4
2	7	3
3	9	2
4	10	1

Contd...

Contd...

5	10	0
6	8	–2

Table 2.1 illustrates that the total utility increases upto unit 4. However, there is limit to increase in total utility. Beyond unit 4 it starts falling.

Relation between total utility and marginal utility:

(i) As long as marginal utility is positive, total utility rises (up to unit 4).

(ii) When marginal utility is zero, total utility is maximum (at unit 5).

(iii) When marginal utility is negative, total utility declines (from unit 6 onwards).

The law is represented in Fig. 2.1.

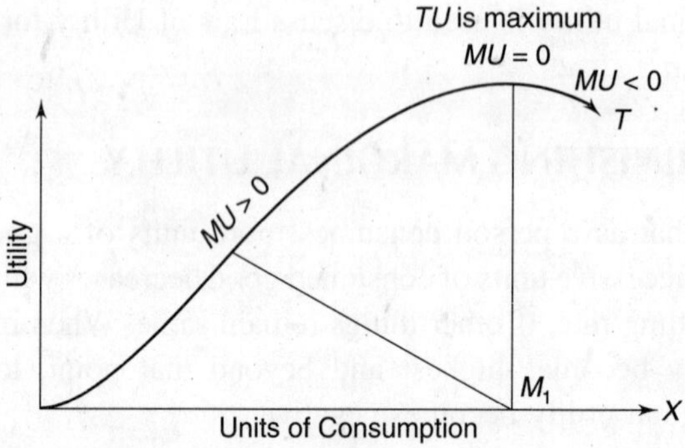

Fig. 2.1

Resources to derive utility, may be considered in terms of money, which is limited with all individuals and organizations. Thus, as a rational entity, one prefers to spend money in order to derive maximum utility from his expenditure. It has been discussed as law of equi-marginal utility.

LAW OF EQUI-MARGINAL UTILITY (CONSUMER'S EQUILIBRIUM)

The law is based on the following assumptions:

(i) Consumer is rational as he wants to maximize his total utility.

(ii) Utility is cardinally measured as one, two, three and so on.

(iii) Marginal utility of money is constant. and

(iv) As more and more units of a commodity are consumed, the utility from each additional unit falls.

Conditions for consumer's equilibrium:

A rational human being spends his total income over a broad spectrum of goods in such a way that marginal utility derived from the last unit of each good is equal. It can be expressed mathematically as,

$$\frac{MU_L}{P_L} = \frac{MU_M}{P_M} = \frac{MU_N}{P_N} = MU \text{ per unit of money}$$

Subject to the constraint that

$$P_L Q_L + P_M Q_M + ... = Y \text{ (individual's income)}$$

where MU_L = Marginal utility derived from the product L

P_L = Price of L

Q_L = Quantity of commodity L and so on.

Marginal utility diminishes as the consumer uses successive units of a good. A consumer transfers resources from the product where marginal unit is less to the product where marginal utility is more till marginal utility per rupee spent on all the goods becomes same.

In marginal utility theory, utility has been discussed cardinally as 1, 2, 3, and so on. However, it has also been measured as high, low, etc. ordinal measurement in indifference curve analysis, which has been discussed as follows.

INDIFFERENCE CURVE ANALYSIS

Indifference curve is the locus of points which represent combination of two commodities M and N which yields equal satisfaction to the consumer.

Characteristics of Indifference Curve

Indifference curve is negatively sloped and convex to the origin. Two indifference curves do not cross and are usually parallel to each other. Indifference curve to the right side refers to higher level of satisfaction. In Fig. 2.2, IC_3 shows higher level of satisfaction than IC_2 and lower level of satisfaction than IC_4.

Marginal Rate of Substitution

The marginal rate of substitution of M for N (MRS_{MN}) refers to the amount of N that a consumer is willing to forego in order to gain one additional unit of M (and still remain on the same curve which means same level of satisfaction). On moving down on indifference curve, the MRS_{MN} diminishes. In Fig. 2.2, MRS_{MN} is more at the point E than at the point F.

$$MRS_{MN} = -\frac{MU_M}{MU_N}$$

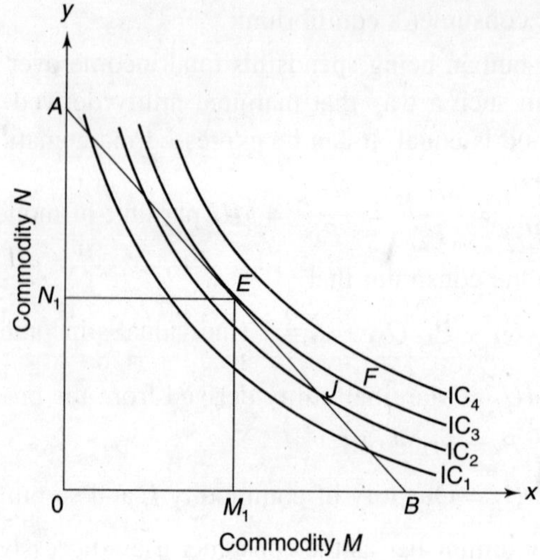

Fig. 2.2

Budget Constraint Line

The budget constraint line shows the different combinations of the commodities that a consumer can purchase, given his money income and prices of the commodities. AB is the budget line in Fig. 2.2. All points within ΔAOB, are within the purchasing capacity of the consumer but any point beyond AB is beyond the purchasing capacity of the consumer.

Consumer Equilibrium

A consumer is in equilibrium when his budget line reaches the highest possible curve. From Fig. 2.2, it is clear that all the combinations of two commodities at IC_4 are beyond the buying capacity of the consumer. On the other hand, IC_1 and IC_2, which cut the budget line at two places are attainable but none of them gives highest level of satisfaction which the consumer can attain. The consumer equilibrium is achieved at the point E of IC_3 as it is tangent to the budget line AB.

Price Effect

Price effect is the impact of change in the price of the commodity M on the consumer's demand and its consumption while keeping the price of commodity N, the consumer's taste and money income constant. We can derive the consumer's price consumption curve (PCC), which is the locus of points of consumer's equilibrium resulting when only the price of commodity M is varied. The consumer's demand curve for commodity M shows the amount of M a consumer would purchase at various prices of commodity M *ceteris paribus* (when other things remain same).

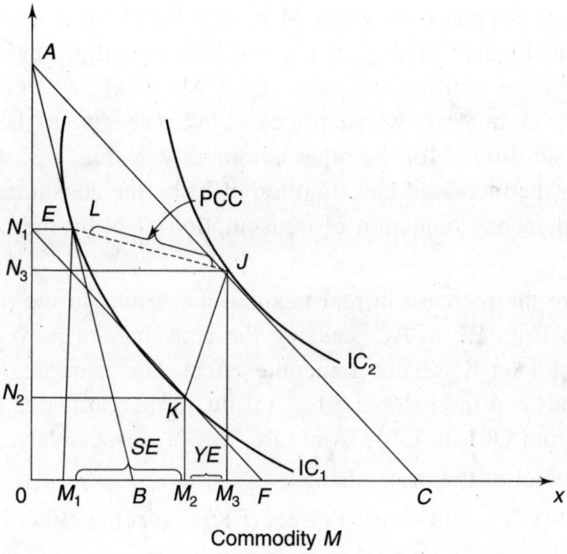

Fig. 2.3

In Fig. 2.3, when price of M falls from B to C and the new budget line is AC, the equilibrium moves from point L to point J and commodity M increases from OM_1 to OM_3. Since M is a normal good, the income effect reinforces the substitution effect in causing the rise in demand for M.

Price effect = Income effect + Substitution effect

We can separate income effect from the substitution effect of the price fall by reducing the consumer's money income sufficiently to keep the real income constant.

As shown in Fig. 2.3, draw a budget line EF, parallel to AC, to neutralize the effect of rise in income while keeping the consumer on the new price ratio. It is tangent to indifference curve IC_1. Since EF is parallel to AC, it has the same slope as AC and hence represents the same price ratio $\frac{P'_M}{P_N} = P'_M$. By making EF tangential to the previous IC_1, the consumer has brought back to the original level of satisfaction, where he would have been if his real income had not increased with a fall in the price of M, but at different point K. The consumer has been brought back to his original level of satisfaction by taking away AE amount of money income from the consumer. This reduction in consumer's income is termed a compensating variation in his income.

With the budget line AB and its slope $P_M/P_N = P_M$, the consumer was in equilibrium at L where the slope and hence, Marginal Rate of Substitution of M for N, (MRS_{MN}) of $IC_1 = P_M$ (slope of the budget line AB). With new budget line EF, the consumer is no longer in equilibrium at L. For the equilibrium to be restored, the slope of IC_1 and hence the MRS_{MN} must fall to the level of

P'_M too. This can happen only when M is substituted for N along IC_1, till the point K is reached where $MRS_{MN} = P'_M$ and hence equilibrium is restored. The movement along the indifference curve from M_1 to M_2 will give substitution effect, where the commodity whose price has fallen relative to the price of other commodity, is substituted for the other commodity. In Fig. 2.3, the substitution effect results in the increased consumption of M by the consumer from OM_1 to OM_2 and simultaneous reduction of consumption of N by the consumer from ON_1 to ON_2.

Now restore the increase in real income that results in the parallel shift of the budget line from EF to AC, causing the consumer to move from point K on IC_1, to point J on IC_2. This is income effect. For example, both M and N are normal goods and the income effect results in the purchases of both M and N increasing, from OM_2 to OM_3 from ON_2 to ON_3 respectively.

The total effect of the price change,

Price effect (EJ) – Substitution effect (EK) = Income effect (KJ)

Application of Indifference Curve

Concept of indifference curve may be used to find out elasticity of demand or nature of products in following way:

(i) Indifference curve analysis may be used to calculate price elasticity of demand for the product which has numerous close substitutes. It will have large substitution effect.

(ii) Indifference curve analysis may be used to differentiate goods as luxury and necessity. Luxury goods will have a strong income effect.

(iii) The concept may be used to differentiate substitute and complementary goods. Substitution effect will be very high in case of substitute goods and not so high in case of complementary goods.

WHAT IS TO BE PRODUCED?

As it has already been discussed, a person can wish to have an aeroplane, a pen, a notebook, a chocolate or any other product which gives him physical, mental, intellectual or spiritual utility. But if he has only 100-rupee note, either he can have a pen, a book or a chocolate but cannot have an aeroplane. So his wish of having a pen, a book or a chocolate becomes want but having an aeroplane does not become a want. It means a wish becomes want only if it is supported by ability to fulfil it. Wants can be of three types: necessaries, comforts and luxuries. Necessaries are basic for our existence. It can again be of three types as necessaries for existence, necessaries for efficiency and conventional necessities. There are wants to enhance comfort, which ultimately enhances efficiency and productivity. Along with necessaries, there are luxuries which are wanted for pleasure. Though they are neither must for our existence nor enhance productivity and efficiency but give pleasure on consumption.

In the previous example, a person can purchase any of the articles worth Rs. 100, i.e., a pen, a book and a chocolate. However, he cannot purchase all of them. He will rank all the good which can be purchased with hundred rupees on the basis of his intensity of consumption and the ranking may vary with the variation in the prices of these products. One will like to fulfil that want first whose intensity is more than that good whose intensity for consumption is less. At the same time, he will like to have more of the good if the price is low and less if the price is high. Consequently, if a wish is supported by ability to fulfil as well as willingness to fulfil, it becomes demand. That is why, demand is always expressed in relation to given price.

LAW OF DEMAND

When price of a product increases demand for that product decreases and vice versa. But if price of a product as well as income of the household also increases, the household may or may not demand more or less of the good. Therefore, if income of the household, fashion, season, etc. remain the same, demand of a product is inversely related to its price. So, in normal circumstances, when price of a good increases, demand for the product decreases and vice versa when other things remain the same.

This is called law of demand.

$$D \propto \frac{1}{P}$$

where, D = Demand for the product

P = Price of the product

The demand curve has negative slope and the sum total of the demand by all the individuals (or a household) is called market demand.

Demand of a good depends on many other factors. Some of them are price of the product itself, taste, preference, income and urgency of demand and price of related goods. Consumer's income and consumer's expectations of future income also influence demand for a product. Size of population as well as social values of the society also influence demand of a good. When price of a good remains same but demand for that good decreases or increases due to change in any other factor, then that is known as 'contraction' or 'expansion' in demand.

Exception to the law of demand

(i) Giffen goods: It has already been discussed under goods. In case of normal goods, when price increases demand decreases and vice versa. However, in case of Giffen goods, when price falls demand also falls and vice versa. This happens because when price falls, purchasing power of the household increases, with which they switch over to its superior substitutes.

(ii) Conspicuous consumption or prestige goods (Veblen effect): Some luxury goods such as sophisticated video or music system and sports car are bought because they are high priced and whose consumption can be shown off conspicuously to boast about the consumer's position in the society.

(iii) Price expectation: If there is expectation of further rise in price, an initial increase in price results in higher demand.

If there is no exceptional situation, there is inverse relationship between demand and price. But million rupees question is, by which magnitude? With one unit change in price, magnitude of change in demand is called price elasticity of demand.

PRICE ELASTICITY OF DEMAND

Ratio between proportionate change in demand of a commodity with proportionate changes in price of that commodity is called price elasticity of demand.

$$e_d = \frac{dQ}{dP} \times \frac{P}{Q}$$

where, dQ = Change in demand

dP = Change in price

Q = Original demand

P = Original price

e_d so calculated is known as the price elasticity coefficient. The sign will be either negative or positive and the value of elasticity coefficients will vary from zero to infinity. The interpretations of these cefficients are shown in Table 2.2.

Table 2.2 Interpretation of Price Elasticity Coefficient

S.No	*Elasticity*	*Type of Elasticity*	*Implications*	*Graphical Representation*
1.	$e_d = 0$	Perfectly inelastic	Change in price leaves demand totally unchanged	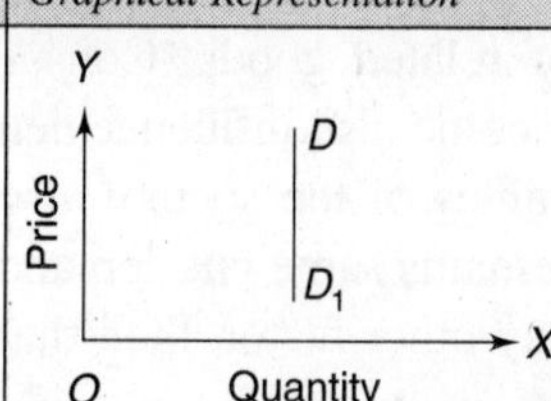
2.	$e_d < 1$	Less than unit elastic	Percentage change in demand falls short of the percentage change in price	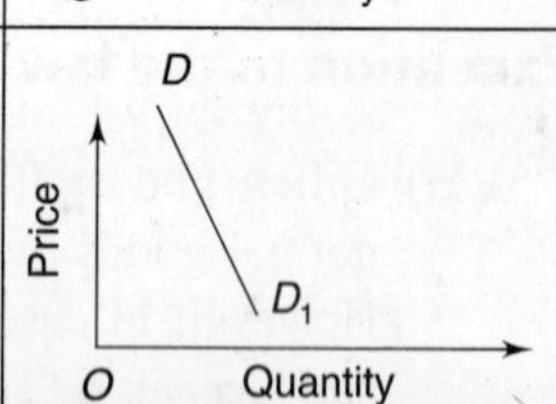

Contd...

Contd...

3.	$e_d = 1$	Unit elastic	Percentage change in demand equals the percentage change in price	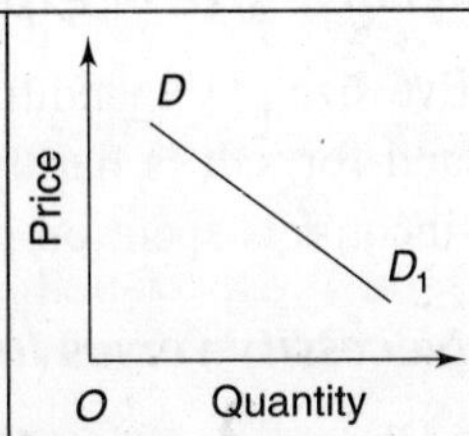
4.	$e_d > 1$	More than unit elastic	Percentage change in demand exceeds the percentage change in price	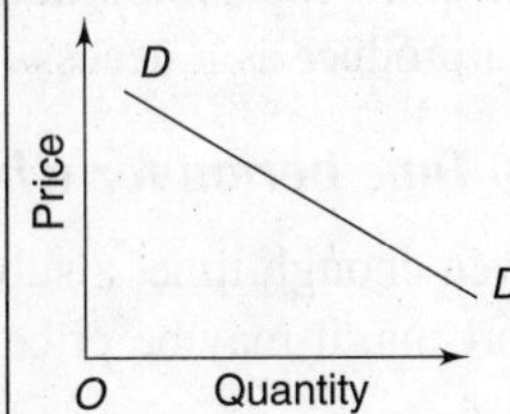
5.	$e_d = \infty$	Perfectly elastic	Any change in price causes infinite change in demand	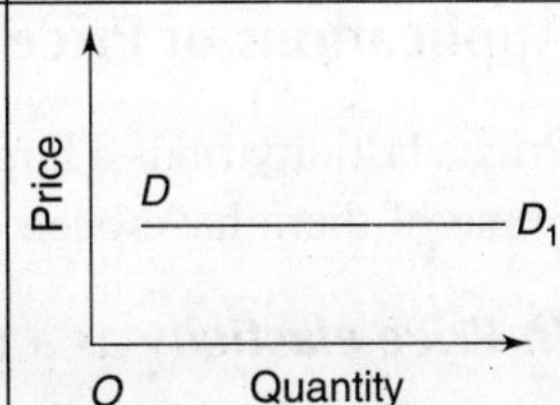
6.	e_d = Negative	Normal good	With increase in price, demand decreases and vice versa	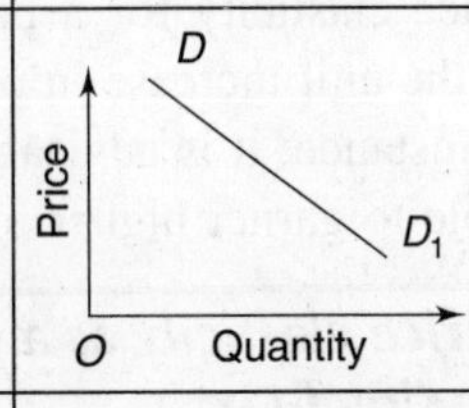
7.	e_d = Positive	Giffen good	With increase in price, demand also increases and vice versa	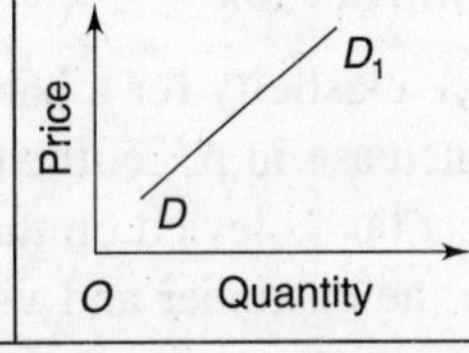

Determinants of Price Elasticity

(i) Substitutability

If more substitutes of a product are available, the demand will be more elastic. Along with the substitution effect, multiple use effect also influences elasticity. If a product has only one use or a very limited number of uses, then the effect of a change in price is relatively limited. But if there are many ways in which the product can be used, then the effect of a price change is more pronounced. Therefore, products with many uses may have higher price elasticity than single use goods.

(ii) Relative size of expenditure on the product concerned

Relative size of expenditure on the commodity is a very important determinant. Demand for salt is hardly affected by its price because very small amount of total income is spent on purchase of salt.

(iii) Necessity versus luxury

One of the most important determinants of elasticity is the consumer's perception of a product as a necessity or as a luxury.

(iv) Time period for which the demand curve pertains

Given enough time, a substitute can be found for almost any product. So in the short run, it may be price inelastic but price elastic in the long run.

Applications of Price Elasticity

Price elasticity finds a large number of applications in business decision making. Some of them have been discussed below.

(i) Price elasticity as a guide for setting prices

If price elasticity for a particular commodity is more than unit, it means that with the unit increase in price, the demand will decrease more than unit. In that circumstance, it is advisable to keep the price low. Ultimately lower prices will be able to garner higher total turnover and vice versa.

(ii) Price elasticity as a guide for shifting tax burden in case of indirect tax

If price elasticity for a particular commodity is less than unit, it means with the unit increase in price, the demand will decrease less unit. In that situation, if an indirect tax is levied on that product, the producer can shift larger burden of the tax to the customer and vice versa.

(iii) Discount sales

While giving discounts, firms take into consideration price elasticity of demand for the good. Whether discounts would attract enough additional customers to offset the lower revenues per unit.

Measurement of Price Elasticity

The price elasticity of demand can be measured by following methods.

Total Outlay or Expenditure Method

If a given change in price does not cause any change in the total outlay or expenditure on the commodity, the price elasticity of demand is said to be equal to one. However, if a given change in price leads to an increase in total outlay or expenditure, elasticity of demand is said to be greater than one and if a given change in price leads to decrease in total outlay, the elasticity of demand is said to be lesser than one. All these results are summarized in Table 2.3.

Table 2.3 Price, Total Expenditure and Elasticities of Demand

Effect of increase in price	*Nature of Change in Total outlay or Expenditure*	*Value of Coefficient*	*Nature of e_d*
	Increase	$e_d > 1$	Elastic
	Decreases	$e_d < 1$	Inelastic
	Remain same	$e_d = 1$	Unit Elastic

Arc Method

Arc elasticity is a measure of the average responsiveness to price change exhibited by a demand curve over some finite stretch of the curve as AB in Fig. 2.4 for which we can find out the absolute change in price ($\Delta P = P_1 - P_0$) and the absolute change in quantity ($\Delta X = X_1 - X_0$).

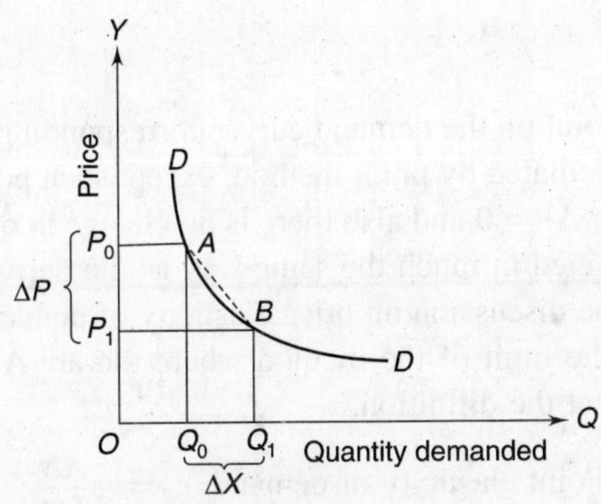

Fig. 2.4

As, exact values of X and P cannot be calculated. Any value may occur between X_0 and X_1 and between P_0 and P_1 respectively. No unique value of X and P can be calculated by the arc method. It is customary for this purpose to use the average of the two end values

$$Q = \frac{Q_1 + Q_0}{2}, P = \frac{P_1 + P_0}{2}$$

Absolute change in demand and price are as

$$\Delta X = X_1 - X_0, \Delta P = P_1 - P_0$$

Hence, the Arc Method is defined by the following expression:

$$e_d = -\frac{\Delta Q}{\Delta P} \cdot \frac{P}{Q}$$

$$= -\frac{Q_1 - Q_0}{P_1 - P_0} \cdot \frac{(P_1 + P_0)/2}{(Q_1 + Q_0)/2}$$

$$= -\frac{Q_1 - Q_0}{P_1 - P_0} \cdot \frac{P_1 + P_0}{Q_1 + Q_0}$$

$$= -\frac{Q_1 - Q_0}{Q_1 + Q_0} \cdot \frac{P_1 + P_0}{P_1 - P_0}$$

where, X_0 = Original quantity

X_1 = New quantity

P_0 = Original price

P_1 = New price.

Point Method

For each particular point on the demand curve, corresponding value of elasticity of demand can be calculated by point method, except such points where there is no change in price, or $\Delta P = 0$ and also there is no change in quantity, or $\Delta Q = 0$. Point elasticity is defined in much the same way as the derivative concept used at the beginning of the discussion on price elasticity of demand. So, we take the point method to be the limit of the method where the arc AB is made smaller and smaller to arrive at the difinition.

so,

$$\text{Point elasticity of demand, } e_d = -\frac{AN}{MA}$$

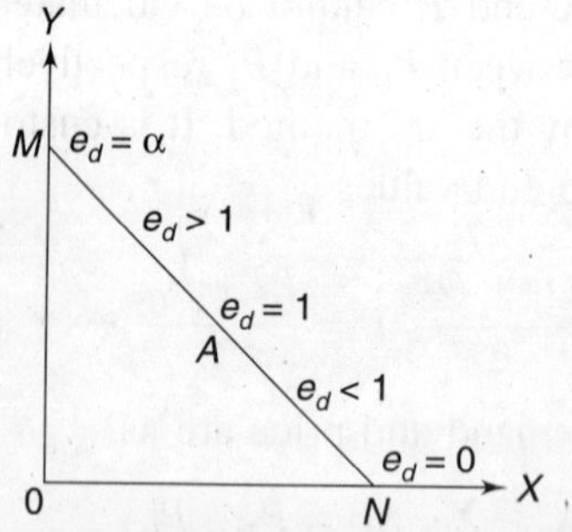

Fig. 2.5

INCOME ELASTICITY OF DEMAND

Ratio between proportionate change in demand due to proportionate change in income is called income elasticity of demand (e_Y).

$$e_Y = \frac{dQ}{dY} \cdot \frac{Y}{Q}$$

where, Q = Original demand of a commodity

Y = Original consumer's income

dQ = Change in demand

dY = Change in income

If, $e_Y < 0$, it is inferior good.

$e_Y > 0$, it is normal good.

$e_Y > 1$, it is luxury good,

$e_Y < 1$, it is necessity good.

Significance of income elasticity of demand:

(i) Goods with low income elasticity of demand are 'recession proof' in the sense that their sales are stable in an economic downturn and firms producing such goods can never expect robust sale.

(ii) If a product is regarded as an inferior good by the market as a whole, the firm must expect the quantity demand of the product to decline as economy grows and income rises.

(iii) Management of firm also wants to consider information about the income elasticity of demand for its products in planning for location and expansion of firm as well as advertising and promotion of product.

CROSS ELASTICITY OF DEMAND

Proportionate change in demand of commodity M due to proportionate change in the price of another commodity N is called cross elasticity of demand.

$$e_d^* = \frac{dQ_M}{dP_N} \cdot \frac{P_N}{Q_M}$$

where Q_M = Original demand of a commodity M

P_N = Original price of commodity N

dQ_M = Change in demand of commodity M

dP_N = Change in price of commodity N

If E_d^* = +ve, then commodities are substitute.

E_d^* = –ve, then commodities are complementary.

E_d^* = 0, then commodities are not at all related.

Significance of Cross Elasticity of Demand

The concept of cross elasticity of demand is particularly useful at two different levels of business. At the level of firm, knowledge of cross elasticity of demand helps in the formulation of marketing strategy. Firms need to know how the demand for its products will react to price changes of either substitute or complementary goods. At the industry level, the cross elasticity of demand indicates whether or not a substitute exists for that product.

ADVERTISEMENT ELASTICITY OF DEMAND

Proportionate change in demand of product X due to proportionate change in expenditure on advertisement is called advertisement elasticity of demand.

$$e_A = \frac{dQ}{dA} \times \frac{A}{Q}$$

where, Q = Original demand of a commodity
A = Original advertisement expenditure
dQ = Change in demand
dA = Change in expenditure on advertisement

If e_A is more than one, sale will increase more than the amount spent on advertising in the given situation. In the present era of electronic and print media, this type of elasticity plays a significant role. However, in treating sales as a function of advertising expenditure, following points must be taken into consideration:

(i) How developed is the product's market?
(ii) Reaction of the rival firms to the company's advertising, either to their own advertising campaign or to the increased merchandising.
(iii) The time lag between expenditure on advertisement outlays and sales response is difficult to find out because such intervals depend, in part, on the type of product and in part, on the type of advertisement.
(iv) The influence of the "investment effect" of the past advertisement of the company and the extent to which this may affect current and future sales, through delayed and cumulative buying, is difficult to find out.

SUPPLY

Price is an important indicator for determining demand of a product. Not only that, it plays a decisive role in deciding what is to be produced, i.e., supply side. In other words, price is determined at the intersection point of demand and supply. Supply of a commodity refers to the various quantities of a commodity, which a seller is willing and able to sell at different prices in a given market at a given point of time, if other things remain same.

LAW OF SUPPLY

According to the law of supply, 'as the price of a commodity increases, its supply also increases'. Thus, there is a directly proportionate relationship between supply and price, i.e., higher the price, larger will be the supply or vice versa, when other things remain same.

$$S \propto P$$

where, S = Supply
P = Price

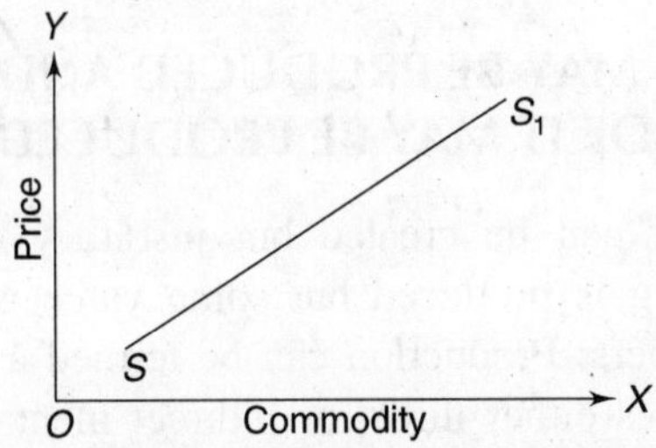

Fig. 2.6

Contraction or expansion of supply means a change in quantity supplied without any change in price. Therefore, a shift in supply curve to the right refers to expansion in supply and shift in supply curve to the left refers to contraction in supply.

The elasticity concept is a simple way of measuring the effect of a change in an independent variable on the dependent variable in any functional relationship.

PRICE ELASTICITY OF SUPPLY

Proportionate change in supply due to proportionate change in price is called price elasticity of supply.

$$e_s = \frac{dS}{dP} \times \frac{P}{S}$$

where, S = Original supply of a commodity
P = Price of the product
dS = Change in supply
dP = Change in price

The determinants of elasticity of supply are as follows:

(i) Nature of the commodity: The elasticity of supply depends upon the nature of the commodity, whether it is a perishable, consumable or durable good. Perishable goods cannot be stored for long, so their supply is relatively inelastic. On the other hand, durable goods can be stored for long, so supply of these goods is more elastic.

(ii) Chances of increasing output: Availability of inputs and at which stage of return-to-scale, production is being carried out, have important bearing on the elasticity of supply.

(iii) Techniques of production: If the technique of production is less time consuming and easy, then the supply will be more elastic. But if the technique of production is more time consuming, very complex and requires heavy investment, then the supply will be less elastic.

HOW A PRODUCT MAY BE PRODUCED AND WHAT QUANTITY OF IT MAY BE PRODUCED?

As in Physics, nothing can be created but just they change their form, in Economics also, nothing is produced but some value is added to it to make more useful for consumers. Production can be termed a sequence of technical processes, which requires either direct or indirect mental or physical skills of the workers who ultimately change shape, size or even, properties of materials to make it more useful for human being.

Production Process

Through production process, a set of input is transformed into a set of output. The concept has signficance for engineers. Through introduction of some technology, engineers are capable of changing the required input mix, less input requirement or smaller gestation period or can make the production process more efficient. Advant of information and communication technology (ICT) has made production process even more flexible. Through ICT, a part of the production process can be digitally shifted to a far off place where it can be performed in a cost effective way.

Production Function

There is an exact relationship between physical input and physical output. With knowledge of production function, maximum output, which can be obtained at a given input at a particular state of technology, may be found out. The production function can be represented by a simple mathematical equation,

$$Y = f\,(L, K \text{ etc.})$$

where Y = units of output, which is a function of the quantity of two or more inputs with L units of labour and K units of machinery. Some inputs are assumed as fixed, i.e., do not change with change in output. Such quantities are never entered in the equation.

A popular production function derived by Cobb and Douglas is as follows:

$$Y = bL^{a} K^{1-a}$$

where, Y = Total output

L = Lobour input (the total manhours worked in a year)

K = Capital input (the monetary worth of all machinery, equipment and building)

b = Total factor productionty

a and $1-a$ are known as production elasticities of labour and capital and measured as percentage. The Cobb-Douglas function for USA is represented by

$$Y = 1.01\, L^{0.75}\, K^{0.25}\, R$$
$$= 0.9409$$

The above function shows that 1% change in labour input (L) is associated with 0.75% change in output, when capital (K) is fixed. Likewise, by 1% change in capital (K), when labour (L) is constant, there is change of 0.25% in output. The coefficient of determination (R) shows that 94% of the variation in the dependent variable (Y) were due to variation in the independent variables (L and K).

As production function tells exactly how much input is required, knowledge of production function helps to:

(i) avoid wastage of raw material in production, and
(ii) helps in managing inventory effectively.

Factors of Production

Generally, inputs used in production can be grouped in four categories and these have been discussed as below.

Land

Generally, contribution of earth in production is regarded as land in Economics. Besides geographical space on earth, land includes everything given free by the nature and is not capable of being produced by human agency. It is a significant factor of production in agriculture sector but less for manufacturing and service sectors. In the age of information and communication technology (ICT), it has become even less significant. Land gets rent[5] for its contribution in production.

Labour

Any exertion of mind or body undertaken by a person for producing a product or service is labour. Labour is different from management. Labour obeys orders but does not take any decision. However, in modern-day production, just to involve labour more in the production process, sometimes, they are given shares of the company or management seeks their suggestions on important issues. Labour is a unique factor of production. It is one of the factors of production and at the same time, production also takes place for them. Again, performance of labour depends on some non-economic factors such as climate, language or custom, etc. In the liberalized environment, labour has become a very significant factor of production. They get wages or salaries for their contribution in production.

Capital

Capital is defined as a part of wealth other than land, which is used for further production of wealth. Anything which is not included in land or labour and contributes in production is regarded as capital. It generally consists of hard cash, raw materials, tools and machinery. Capital gets interest in return to its contribution in production. After liberalization and opening up of the economy, capital has become mobile and ultimately, has created opportunity to grow fast for the developing economies like India.

Entrepreneur

It is the most crucial factor of production. It brings other three factors together for production and takes risk. It gets profit in return of its contribution in production. As India is a labour surplus economy and capital is also available after globalization, importance is being given to inculcate entrepreneurship among young people to alleviate unemployment.

Factors such as labour and capital can be substituted for each other up to a certain extent. Production process, which requires more capital and less labour is called a capital intensive production process and the production process, which requires more labour and less capital is called a labour intensive production process. Developing economies like India, which are generally labour surplus and short of capital, may adopt labour intensive production processes.

A producer will like to know how much of a factor of production function will replace one unit of other factor of production function. That can be depicted on Isoquant curve. Isoquant curves are like indifference curves of utility analysis. On two axes of the curve, two factors of production say, labour and capital are taken. Each point of an Isoquant curve gives equal level of output. The Marginal Rate of Technical Substitution (MRTS) for a product for another one at a point on the Isoquant curve can be known from the slope of the isoquant at that point.

Table 2.4 Various Factors Combinations Which Gives Equal Level of Output

Factor Combination	*Labour*	*Capital*	*$MRTS_{LK}$*	*Output*
A	1	16	–	100
B	2	12	4	100
C	3	9	3	100
D	4	7	2	100
E	5	6	1	100

Note: $MRTS_{LK}$ – marginal rate of tecnical substitution of labour for capital.

Efficiency or Productivity

Efficiency is the output per unit input. It is regarded as an important indicator for maximization of profit. An efficient system will ultimately earn more profit. Efficiency can be classified into technical efficiency and economic efficiency.

Technical Efficiency

It is the ratio between output to input of a physical system. The system may be a machine of a wristwatch or an aeroplane engine. Technical efficiency can be measured as:

$$TE\ (\%) = \frac{O}{Q} \times 100$$

where, O = Output

Q = Input

Technical efficiency of an aeroplane (%)

$$= \frac{\text{Heat equivalent of mechanical energy produced}}{\text{Heat equivalent of fuel used}} \times 100$$

In practice, technical efficiency can never be more than 100%. This is mainly because of the frictional loss and incomplete combustion of fuel, which is considered to be unavoidable phenomena in the working of an engine.

Economic Efficiency

Economic efficiency (EE) is the ratio of value of output to the cost of input of a business system.

$$EE(\%) = \frac{\text{Value of output}}{\text{Cost of input}} \times 100$$

Where value of output and cost of input are in terms of rupees. In practice, it will be always more than 100% for a growing economy.

There are factors which have significant bearing on efficiency or productivity of a system. It may be divided into two as external factors and internal factors. They may be discussed as follow:

(i) External factors

One must keep external factors in mind from the stage of planning because proper planning is very crucial for optimization of return.

(a) Extent of market competition.

(b) Availability of capital.

(c) Structure of taxation.

(d) Government laws and restrictions concerning business.

(e) Availability and mobility of natural resources.

(f) Technical education and training facilities.

(ii) Internal factors

Following internal factors are very important. They should be planned and designed properly at the time of inception and throughout the production system.

(a) Production planning and control
(b) Plant layout
(c) Material handling
(d) Product design
(e) Quality control
(f) Mechanisation
(g) Computerisation
(h) Inventory of input and finished product

LAW OF RETURN

In normal circumstances, a firm will like to adjust its production according to the market demand in the short run[1] as well as in the long run[2]. Behaviour of physical output when only one input is changed while other inputs are kept constant, has been discussed under the law of return. A firm experiences law of return in the short run. In the long run, a firm can adjust its physical output by changing all inputs. This is discussed in Return to Scale.

When one input is increased while other inputs are kept constant, the resulting output increases first at increasing rate, then at a constant rate and after that, at decreasing rate. These three different situations lead to formation of three different stages of the law the of return as shown in Table 2.5.

Table 2.5 Different Stages of Law of Return

Relation between% Output and % Input	*Stages of Law of Return*
% Increase in output > % increase in single input	Law of increasing return
% Increase in output = % increase in single input	Law of constant return
% Increase in output < % increase in single input	Law of decreasing return

In the stage I, which is a stage of increasing return, all three, i.e., Total Product (TP), Average Product (AP) and Marginal Product (MP) increase. TP increases at increasing rate as rate of increase of MP is more than AP. In the stage II, which is a stage of constant return, MP starts declining. MP cuts AP from above and becomes zero at the end of stage II. In the stage III, which is a stage of decreasing return, MP becomes negative and still continuously decreases. TP and AP decline.

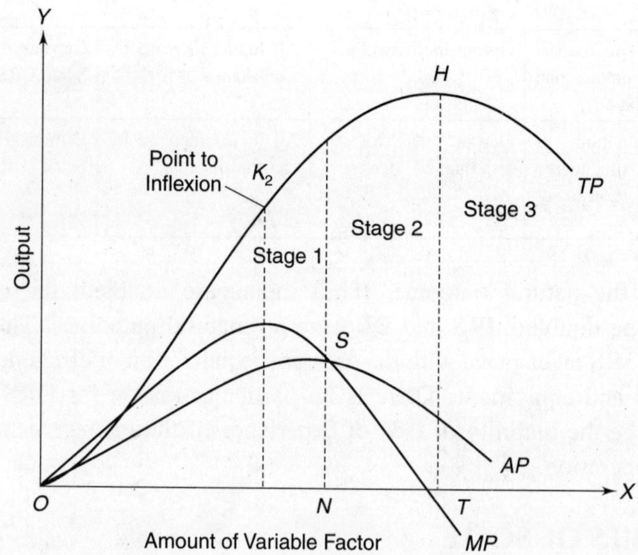

Fig. 2.7

Suppose labour and capital are variable and fixed factor respectively. When the first labour is applied to fixed amount of capital, his efforts are quite inadequate to optimally utilize capital. If second labour is applied, his efforts are quite inadequate to optimally utilize capital. If second labour is applied, both of them work together to utilize the capital in a better way so that MP_L rises. This explains the first phase. Successive unit of labour uses the capital in a better way up to the point where capital is utilized optimally. Beyond that point, if labour is added, MP_L starts declining and ultimately, it becomes negative.

RETURN TO SCALE

In the long run, the firm tries to adjust its output according to the change in demand. As it has already been discussed that behaviour of output with change in all inputs, has been discussed in Return to Scale. In other words, relationship between all inputs and the resulting output is examined in Return to Scale. However, it is assumed that all inputs vary in the same proportion under Return to Scale.

Table 2.6 Different Stages of Return to Scale

Production Function	*Change in Output*	*Change in all inputs*	*Stages of Return to Scale*
Production function is homogeneous of degree two (non-linear homogeneous)	Output increases by λ^2	All inputs increase by a constant λ	Increasing Return to Scale (IRS)

Contd...

Contd...

Homogeneous production function is of degree one (linear homogeneous)	Output increases by λ	All inputs increase by a constant λ	Constant Return to Scale CRS)
Production function is homogeneous of degree less than one (non-linear homogeneous)	Output increases by less than λ	All inputs increase by constant λ	Diminishing Return to Scale (DRS)

CRS is the natural outcome. If all inputs are doubled, the outcome is expected to be doubled. IRS and DRS are not natural outcomes. They need an explanation. IRS takes place with the greater specialization or efficient utilization of machines and equipment. There is no particular reason for DRS. Common reason may be the inability or lack of experience of the management to handle such a big operation.

ECONOMIES OF SCALE

When large scale production is carried out, a single firm as well as the whole industry avail certain benefits which are known as economies of scale. Increasing return to scale is the reason for economies of scale. They arise on account of increase in the size of the firm. Economies of scale, which is reaped by a firm is called the internal economies of scale and the economies of scale which is reaped by the whole industry is called the external economies of scale which happens due to expansion of the industry.

Some of the reasons for internal economies of scale are as follows:

(i) **Expenditure on advertisement:** As a firm increases its production, it does not increase its expenditure on advertisement proportionately. So, cost of production for these additional units is less.

(ii) **Division of labour:** When large number of workers are employed, they are asked to perform specific jobs in which they may have speciali zation. It ultimately increases productivity.

(iii) **Indivisibility of fixed factors of production:** Till fixed factors of production are optimally utilized, increasing production gives economies of scale.

(iv) **Expenditure on transportation:** Till full capacity is utilized, transportation of additional unit does not have any additional expenditure.

Firms derive some external economies of scale also when large number of firms are located at one place. They have been discussed below:

(i) **Co-operation due to concentration of firm at one place:** All firms derive benefits from each other. Most common may be establishing some common facilities such as common transport facility, ancillary firm supplying specialized machinery and marketing organization, which will benefit all firms. Common R&D facilities have been developed by some of the local pharmaceutical companies in India to face the challenges posed by multinational pharmaceutical companies.

(ii) **Fiscal benefit by the government :** Government of that state may give some fiscal benefit for the whole sector if many firms are set up together. The government in Karnataka has given benefits to the software sector.

(iii) **Benefit of information:** Firms need information regarding demand of the product, raw material, name of suppliers of various inputs, etc. If many firms are located at the same place, they can share this type of information with each other.

(iv) **Advantage of disintegration:** If many firms are located at one place, many ancillary firms also establish in the same area and provide some specialized services to the firms. At present, China is reaping the economics of scale in manufacturing sector.

Along with economies, there are diseconomies of scale also. They have been discussed below:

(i) Sometimes, increase in size of firms becomes unmanageable for the management of the firm, which cause internal diseconomies for the firm.

(ii) Large number of firms at one place causes hike in wages for labour and prices of other raw materials, which ultimately, causes external diseconomies of scale.

(iii) Large number of firms at one place create pollution, which may have an adverse impact on health of local people.

(iv) Large number of workers employed in these firms increase demand for consumer products. Hence, cost living index also may go up.

MARKET

Market is an interface between consumer and producer. In general, it may be discussed as a geographical space where producer and customer of a product or service interact and negotiate for exchange. Traditionally, geographical space was important for exchange to take place and market was divided on the basis of geographical extent of market as local markets, regional market, national market or international market. However, with the advent of information technology, geographical space has lost much of its significance in discussion of market. In recent years, emergence of business process outsourcing is a fine example of blurring of distinction line among different geographical areas for completion of business processes. Labour intensive work from the developed countries like UK and USA are being digitally transmitted to developing countries like India,

Philippines and China where the quality of work may be similar but at a very low cost.

There may be many other criteria to divide market but here, we will discuss division of market on the basis of number of producers in the market only. On the basis of number of producers, market may be classified as discussed below.

Monopoly

In this type of market, supply is under control of a single producer, the monopolist. So, law of demand and supply does not work freely. Due to its unique situation, a monopolist derives super normal profit. In deciding price of the product, the monopolist has following two possibilities before him:

(i) He may fix a particular price for the product and leave the quantity to be decided by the forces of demand.

(ii) He may decide a particular quantity to be sold for the product and leave the price to be decided by the forces of demand.

The monopolist will go on producing as long as the marginal revenue is more than marginal cost ($MR > MC$)[3] and will stop producing it before the point where marginal revenue is equal to marginal cost ($MR = MC$) is reached. However, supernormal profit of monopolist attracts other players in the industry. So, under normal circumstances, monopoly cannot exist for long. In the long run, monopoly can exist only if:

(i) Monopoly is legally created as monopoly status to the Indian Railway has been given under an act of Parliament. No other player can operate in this sector. Earlier, Indian Airlines and Indian Postal Department had similar status. However, now other parties are also operating in these sectors.

(ii) Monopoly status is obtained through patent. For example, Microsoft has patented its products. So, no other company can produce the same. After liberalization and imposition of World Trade Organization (WTO) norms, patent laws have become more stringent.

(iii) Monopoly status is obtained through control over raw material supplies. For example, petroleum oil wells are situated only in some countries and most of the diamond mines are in South Africa which gives monopoly status to these countries in their respective areas.

(iv) Market demand is not enough to accommodate two firms. It is called natural monopoly.

Sometimes, monopolist sells its product at discriminated price. Price discrimination means selling a good to different buyers at two or more different prices for reasons not associated with difference in cost. However, it is only possible if price elasticities are different in different markets, it is possible to segregate markets and it is profitable to discriminate. Price will be lesser in more elastic market and higher in less elastic market.

Perfect Competition

Perfect competition is other extreme of market structure where number of sellers[4] is so large that no single firm can influence price. All firms are producing homogenous products. Both buyers and sellers have all information and there is no transportation cost. Buyer will go anywhere the commodity is available at cheaper price and the seller will go anywhere the commodity is costly. In that ways, price will become same in the whole market.

Perfect competition is a hypothetical and not a real situation. It is because of following assumptions:

(i) All units are exactly identical to each other, i.e., they are homogeneous goods. In real world, it cannot happen. Even if goods produced by two different producers are same regarding shape, size and colour as musical tapes produced by Sony and a local producer but the customer would be ready to pay higher price for the musical tape produced by Sony because of the goodwill of the company to provide quality product.

(ii) In the era of information and communication technology (ICT), the customer and seller may have knowledge of prices prevailing in different markets. But movement of customer or seller depends upon the amount of product to be purchased/sold due to existence of transportation cost. If small amount has to be purchased or sold, the buyer or seller will like to buy or sell in the nearby area.

Between extreme market structures, there exists real-world market situations. Now, we are going to discuss two such market situations.

Oligopoly

Oligopoly is a market situation where number of producers in the industry is small and produce heterogenous product. Since, there are small numbers of producer, each one of them knows not only of their own market share but also about the market share of their rivals. So each one of them does not work only to retain its own customer but also works to attract customer of its rival companies, Mobile phone in India is an example of oligopoly. Oligopoly can be of three types:

Cartel

If all the member firms of the industry join hands together and make a cartel for selling their products. They start behaving like monopolist. For example, the main oil producing countries of the world have made a cartel named Organization of the Petrolium Exporting Country. They assign quota to each member country to extract oil from the oil wells and also decide price of the oil in the market. The marketing arrangement gives them chance to earn Supernormal Profit and to maintain stability price of oil in the market.

Price war

If a producer decreases price which is reciprocated by other to attract customer by decreasing their price further. In that way sometimes, they decrease price which is even less than the average cost and may sell at the price which only covers average variable cost. They expect that their competitors will not be able to sustain in the market at such a lower price and eventually will quit the market. The firm in question will be able to earn more or larger market share in the long run. For example, soft drike industry in India. Price wars can be prevented through strategic price management (with non-aggressive pricing), through under standing of the competion.

Price of the leader

If one producer captures larger share in the market, he will decide the price. All the other players will have to accept the price set by the leader. If any one of them will not be able to sustain in the market at lower price set by the leader, it will quit the market.

MONOPOLISTIC COMPETITION

There are large number of buyers and sellers in the market. But the product, which they produce is heterogeneous. So, the customer is ready to pay even higher price for a better product. The example of monopolistic competition is the car industry or toothpaste industry in India. Each firm is producing car but they all are quite differentiated from each other. So, customer is paying differentiated price for the product. As the number of sellers is large, they do not have knowledge about market share of their rivals. So, they concentrate on their own market share and try to enhance it.

Table 2.7 Classification of Market Structure

No. of Firms	*Nature of Product*	
	Homogeneous	*Heterogeneous/Differentiated*
Many	Perfect competition	Monopolistic competition
Few	–	Oligopoly
One	Monopoly	–

MODERN SYSTEM OF INDUSTRIAL ORGANIZATION

Business may be termed an activity in which an enterprise is engaged in production and distribution of goods for sale in market or rendering services for a price. The way by which a business is owned, is called business organization. There are several types of business organizations. Following are some of the main types of business organizations.

Partnership

It is a form of business organization where two or more people come together to combine their resources, i.e., capital, labour, skill and ability, and share the risks and profits equally. It may be of two types: (i) General partnership—Partnership where the liability of each partner is not limited and (ii) Limited partnership—It may be registered business where the liability of the partners is limited to the amount of the capital they each have provided to the business and where the partners may not take part in the running of the business. Every partner is liable and responsible for the acts of other partners in that business. To avoid any complication at a later stage, the constitution of the company may be written on an agreement form. For the best partnership, the number of partners should not be more than six, the lesser the better. It generally happens that persons with a goods idea and experience of a business make partnership with moneyed persons.

Advantages

(i) It can be formed without much legal formalities and without heavy expenditure of organization and stamp duty.

(ii) It enjoys more freedom and is not subject to strict government supervision.

(iii) Due to large number of owners, the amount of capital that can be collected is more than the sole trade organization.

(iv) In this type of organization, person possessing different abilities and skills are chosen and brought together. Therefore, the managerial ability of the firm as a whole would be much greater than that of a sole trader.

Disadvantages

(i) Due to unlimited liability, risk involved is more.

(ii) After the death or retirement of any partner, the partnership organization may come to an end.

(iii) In comparison with joint stock, it raises less capital. So, not suitable for a project, which requires large amount of capital.

(iv) All the partners are responsible for the management of business activity.

Joint Stock Companies

A joint stock company is voluntary association of individuals for profit earning. Capital is contributed by a large number of persons as transferable shares of different value. Here, the liability of a shareholder is limited to the extent of the amount of shares held by him and he is free from the responsibility of the debts and claims on the company beyond the value of shares.

There are two types of joint stock companies:

(a) Private Limited Company: In this form of company, transfer of shares is limited among members only and general public is not invited to subscribe the shares.

(b) Public Limited Company: Such companies can offer their shares to general public through a prospectus.

Advantages

(i) The liability being limited, the shareholders bear no risk and, therefore, more and more persons are encouraged to invest capital. Thus, more amount of capital can be collected to run modern company.

(ii) Such company is not affected by death or retirement of the shareholders.

(iii) It has great potential for expansion.

Disadvantages

(i) Lack of personal interest on the part of the salaried managers can lead to inefficiency and waste.

(ii) As the directors and other members of the management have all the knowledge regarding financial position of the company, they can purchase or sale the share for their own benefit.

(iii) It requires large number of legal formalities to be observed.

Co-operative Enterprises

It is a voluntary organization of any number of persons. A member can continue his membership as long as he desires. Its management is based on democratic basis of equality. Therefore, every member can cast only one vote, whatsoever number of share he has.

Advantages

(i) It sells the product at cheap rate.

(ii) Expenses for bookkeeping and auditing are kept minimum, as members provide honorary service for such tasks.

(iii) There is no question of profiteering, hoarding or black marketing.

(iv) Profits are shared equally.

Disadvantages

(i) As its members do not have much surplus money to invest, it may not be able to raise large amount of money.

(ii) Management may be inefficient and ineffective.

Multinational Companies/ Corporations (MNCs)

An MNC is an enterprise of huge size. It operates in many products, which is completed through many processes and spread over many countries to achieve cost efficiency. MNCs usually grow in a spontaneous manner through mergers and takeovers. In course of time, acquire awesome power and giant size. It makes MNCs oligopolistic in character. Exxon, with estimated value-added of $63 bn, is about the same size as the economy of Pakistan and larger than Peru. It is estimated that the world's top 300 MNCs now control over 25 per cent of the $20 trillion stock of productive assets. Transnational Corporations (TNCs) are very much similar to MNCs. But most significant difference is about control. In case of MNCs, national headquarters controls all its other units, wherever it is, with globally standardized operating procedure laid down in a universally applicable policy manual. In contrast, a TNC favours foreign semi-autonomous units with only reports and income repatriation flowing back to base. An MNC facilitates a multilateral transfer of resources. Usually this transfer takes place in the form of a package, which included foreign capital machinery, technical know-how, raw materials, finished products, managerial services, and so on.

Liberalisation and opening up of economies as well as decline of socialism have facilitated growth of MNCs. They are expanding far and wide to optimize return on their investment. Their movement is benefitting developing economies as these MNCs are bringing with them foreign capital, sophisticated technical know-how, access to superior global distribution and marketing system. They have technology and skills required for diversification of the industrial base and for the creation of backward and forward linkings. However, so far experience of MNCs is not very appreciable for developing economies. To achieve cost effectiveness usually they violate some of the norms, if these norms are not implemented very strictly. As environmental rules are not very stringently applied in developing economies, MNCs violates these rules. In case of some untoward incidence, they move to other countries. It happened in case of Union Carbide at Bhopal in India. After a major accident in 1992, which affected health of large number of people, mainly, from poorer section of society, Union Carbide moved away from India

Advantages

(i) Volume of their production is huge. So they reap economies of large-scale production.

(ii) They have large amount of capital, which they most efficiently use for production.

(iii) They use state-of-the-art technology.

Disadvantages

(i) Volume of their production is large, so sometimes, they face diseconomies of large-scale production

(ii) They, very often, violate national laws.

E-Business

Information and communication technology (ICT) has provided additional mode for interaction between the buyer and seller where geographical space is not required. In fact, it is very popular among educated tech-savvy segment of the society residing in far off places. However, e-business needs a lot of strategic planning to succeed. Development of an e-business initiative may be divided in following four phases:

Phases	*Area*	*Description*
I	Knowledge building	Understand nature and characteristic of prospective customer,
		How value can be added for the customer
		Assess the economic environment and industrial trend
		Assess the priorities in the supply chain, know about the real competitors and their business model. Concentrate upon the advantage of the competitors as well as their drawback.
II	Capability evaluation	It makes no sense for a business to select its future direction without first assessing its capabilities.
		Assessing core competency involves two questions: (i) What capability the company has today? (ii) What capabilities and resources does the company need to acquire quickly? Human resource, production scheduling and distribution network are the area of assessment.
III	e-business design	By considering profit for the firm and benefits for the customer, business model need to be selected
		Provide desired level of responsiveness convenience, variety and information example- Jabong.
		Service and support should cater to end- user.
		Use the Internet to provide end-to-end process of searching, comparing, selecting and paying on line example—Microsoft Expedia and ebay.
		Brand or image positioning that include the company's offering must be shown with greater appeal.
		No vagueness should be on price front. Price with available rebate should be very clearly available.
IV	e-business design refinement	To be at top, periodically refinement is required according to latest technology, change in nature and taste of customer, etc.

Notes

1. Short run is a comparatively small period of time but not a fixed period of time for all production processes. During this time period, the firm can improve its production by adjusting its variable factors of production only.
2. During long run, the firm can adjust its variable factors of production, i.e., raw material as well as fixed factor of production, i.e., machine.
3. MR = Revenue earned from the last unit; MC = Cost incurred on producing last unit.
4. For convenience of discussion, very simple model has been taken where seller and producer is the same person.
5. Rent in Classical Economics was the income derived from the ownership of land and other natural resources in fixed supply. Neoclassical Economics extends the concept of rent to include factors other than natural resource rent. According to them it was the difference between what a factor of production is paid and how much it would need to be paid to remain in its current use.

EXERCISES

A. Objective

Fill in the blanks:

(i) If land gets rent for its contribution in production, capital gets ______.

(ii) Elasticity of demand for rice will be ______ elastic than elasticity of demand for coca cola.

(iii) In case of giffen goods, demand ______ with decrease in price.

(iv) There are ______ producers in case of oligopoly.

(v) Marginal utility ______ with consumption of successive unit.

(vi) ______ of an MNC controls all other units.

Ans. (i) Interest; (ii) Less; (iii) Decreases; (iv) Few; (v) Decreases; (vi) Headquarter

State whether following statements are True or False:

(i) Securities of a public company is listed in any recognized stock exchange.

(ii) Those companies, which operate under the special act passed by the State Legislature or Parliament, are called statutory companies.

(iii) Headquarters of an MNC controls its all other units.

Ans. (i) False; (ii) True; (iii) True;

B. Subjective

1. Differentiate between:
   (i) Monopoly and Perfect competition
   (ii) Capital goods and Consumer goods
   (iii) Land and Labour
   (iv) Price elasticity of demand and Cross elasticity of demand
   (v) Monopoly and Oligopoly
   (vi) Partnership Company vs. Joint Stock Company
2. Discuss Law of Equi-marginal Utility. How is it different from Law of Diminishing Marginal Utility?
3. Discuss Law of Demand. Are there any exceptions to it?
4. Discuss characteristics of different forms of market.
5. Discuss significance of Price Elasticity of Demand.
6. Discuss Income Elasticity of Demand.
7. Discuss Law of Supply. What are the determinants of elasticity of supply?
8. Discuss production process. How advent of information and communication technology (ICT) has affected the production process?
9. What do you mean by Production Function? How does technology affect it?
10. How labour is a unique factor of production?
11. Discuss Return to Scale.
12. Discuss advantages and disadvantages of internal and external Economies of Scale.
13. Discuss significance of co-operative for a developing country like India.
14. Many MNCs have started their base in India. Discuss its expected advantages and disadvantages for the Indian economy?
15. Develop an e-business plan for an automobile company.

References and Suggested Readings

1. Dominick Salvatore, Schaum's Outline Series Theory and Problems of Microeconomic Theory, McGraw-Hill, Inc., Singapore.
2. Gregory C. Chow, "Dynamic Economics: Optimization by the Lagrange Method," Oxford University Press, New York.
3. I. G. Patel, "Economic Reform and global change", Macmillan India Ltd., New Delhi.

4. Ronald A. Wykotra, "Introductory Economics", Harper & Row Publishers, USA.
5. William Fellner, " Modern Economic Analysis", McGraw-Hill Book Company, Inc. Tokyo.
6. William J. Baumol & Alan S. Blinder, "Microeconomics" Principles and Policy," Harrot College Publisher, USA.

3

Macroeconomics

Purpose of this chapter is to acquaint the reader with:

- Money, Functions of Money, Quality of a Good Money
- Money Moves in Circular Flow
- Value of Money, Index Number, Supply of and Demand for Money
- Inflation and Deflation, Stagflation Recession Business Cycle
- Money Market and Capital Market, Stock Exchange, Speculation
- Bank, Central Bank and Commercial Bank, Credit Creation by Bank
- Monetary Policy
- National Income

The term 'macro' derives from the Greek word '*makros*', which means large. Macroeconomics studies economic behaviour of the big economic entities. That is why, it is termed aggregative economics. It does not consider individual demand but the aggregate demand, not the individual supply but the aggregate supply and not the output of a single firm but the national output of an economy. Macroeconomic variables are beyond the control of individual, consumer or business enterprise. They are exogenous to the business enterprises but business decisions are taken after considering macroeconomic variables such as income tax, corporate tax structure, the monetary controls like the bank rate, various lending rates of bank and financial institutions, inflation and general price level. These macroeconomic indicators offer certain economic and business climate, which influences and regulates investment decisions at corporate levels. Generally, macroeconomics deals with

(i) the theory of income and employment,
(ii) the theory of general price level and inflation,
(iii) the theory of economic growth, and
(iv) the macroeconomic theory of distribution.

Study of macroeconomics helps the engineering students to understand broad economic environment in which they operate. Engineering students even get an overview of complex economic system. Study of macroeconomics also helps to understand the reason and logic formulation of economic policies by the government.

EXCHANGE

A very small part of a man's want can be produced by him. Far greater parts of his requirement are fulfilled by exchange. A human being cannot produce everything he wants to satisfy his numerous needs. So, he likes to exchange those goods which he is not able to produce with his surplus. In ancient times, when requirements were limited, people used to practise *barter system*, i.e., exchange products. For example, the person who had wheat in surplus and wanted clothes in exchange, would search for the person who might have clothes in surplus and wanted wheat in exchange. However, there are some limitations of this system. Most significant limitation is lack of double coincidence of wants. In the previous example, it was very difficult for both the persons to meet each other. Another problem is the measurement of value. Different commodities have different units of measurement. It is very difficult to decide the rate at which quantities of two products to be exchanged. Another problem is of indivisibility of product. For example, if a carpenter in a village takes two months to make a bullock cart, he would like to exchange everything else he requires by his bullock cart but bullock cart may not be divided for exchange. In the course of economic development, exchange of goods becomes even more complex, which eventually brought money into existence.

MONEY

In order to avoid inconvenience of barter system, money was brought into as a medium of exchang. Various commodities were successively thought of and employed for this purpose. In the beginning, cattle are said to be used as unit of exchange though it must be very inconvenient one. Yet in old times, we find things were frequently valued according to the number of cattles, which have been given in exchange of it. Over the period, pebbles, precious stones, metals were eventually preferred because of their convenient size.

METAL MONEY

Iron, copper, gold and silver are metals, which have been used for metal money at various points of time. At first, unstamped bars were used to stamped but later on, show their fineness and weight. In the beginning, coins were called by the turm to express their weight. Later on, they were having picture of kings and queens. However, carrying them from one place to other was inconvenient. To overcome the inconvenience of transportation, paper money came into existence.

PAPER MONEY

Introduction of paper money was a milestone in the process of evolution of money. As of now, paper money is being issued in different denominations of currency notes i.e., 1, 2, 5, 10, 20, 50, 100, 500 and 1000 in India. As they are made up of paper, it does not have any intrinsic value but since it is signed by a responsible authority, it is acepted by all within the jurisdiction of that authority. In India, all currency notes of two rupees and above denominations are issued by Reserve Bank of India. However, one rupee note and coins are issued by the department of finance the Government of India itself. Paper money may be of two types. They may be convertible paper money and non-convertible or inconvertible paper money. Convertible paper money is 100% backed by precious metals like gold or silver. However, now, convertibility has been given up. Inconvertible paper money is in practice which is not 100% backed by metal but still it circulates and commands value as its issue is regulated by a responsible authority.

CREDIT MONEY

With further development of economies, business transactions became even more complex. Paper money alone was deficient in entertaining all transactions. Thus, it was supplemented by credit money such as cheque, draft, travellers cheque, and credit card[1] which is the most popular form of money today. It is also called Bank Money. It is backed by deposits, which a depositor is having in the bank. The bank promises to honour all the credit money, which is issued by the depositors. Creation of money by banks will be discussed in detail later in the chapter.

In short, money may be defined as anything, which has general acceptability and passes freely from hand to hand as a medium of exchange and can be used as a measure of value.

Function of Money

Money performs several functions. Some of the main functions have been discussed below:

Medium of Exchange

Money is essentially a medium of exchange because of its general acceptability. Everyone accepts it in exchange for goods and services, and uses it for purchasing goods and services of his choice. In this way, money promotes specialization among individuals, firms and regions. They work in the area in which they have advantage and exchange them with money and ultimately, exchange everything else with money. It is a unit of account for the purpose of calculating exchange values.

Measure of Value

The value of goods can be expressed in terms of money. Therefore, it is used as a basis of measurement and comparison of values of the goods and services. This feature of money facilitates the exchange of goods. However, it has limitation in measuring value. Its own value is subject to change, as it keeps on fluctuating from time to time.

Standard of Deferred Payment

In most of the transactions, instant payments are not made. The debtors make a promise to the creditors that they will make the payments on a particular future date. It is customary to measure the promise of future payments or debts in terms of money because money has general acceptability rather than any other goods or services. However, even in this role the main limitation of money is instability in its own value which keeps on fluctuating from time to time. As a consequence, debtors and creditors both are affected when value of money changes. For example, if the value of money depreciates on account of a price rise, the creditors lose while the debtors gain.

Store of Value

The most economic and convenient way of storing wealth is money. Stored money can be used in future as and when needed because of its liquidity and purchasing power. Liquidity of money ensures that goods and services can be purchased by money at any time in future without delay and loss of value. Furthermore, it has made possible capital accumulation, which is an essential prerequisite of economic growth.

Distribution of National Income

In a modern economy, production is the result of the collective efforts of different factors of production such as labour, capital, land and entrepreneur. Money facilitates the distribution of income among them on the basis of their marginal productivities and ultimately, distribution of national income in a country.

Basis of Credit

In recent years, credit is being used in every country throughout the world. Money is the basis of credit. Without money, credit cannot be created and circulated. For example, a depositor can make use of cheques only when there are sufficient funds in his account and a bank also creates credit on the basis of amount of money deposited with it.

Qualities of Good Money

Good money should possess the following qualities:

(i) **General acceptability:** It is very important that good money should have general acceptability.

(ii) **Durability:** Good money should not deteriorate easily either in itself or as a result of wear and tear. Paper money may not fulfil this criterion.

(iii) **Portability:** Good money should be easily portable. It needs to possess high value in small bulk.

(iv) **Homogeniety:** All units of a particular denomination should have same quality so that equal weights (in case of coin), shape or size will have exactly equal values.

(v) **Malleability:** The material used for making money should be capable of being stamped with intricate designs.

(vi) **Stability of value:** Material used as money needs to have stable value over a considerable period of time.

Money Moves in Circular Flow in an Economy

Modern economic life may be characterized by continuous flow of money. It moves very frequently from one person to other. Individuals and household,[2]

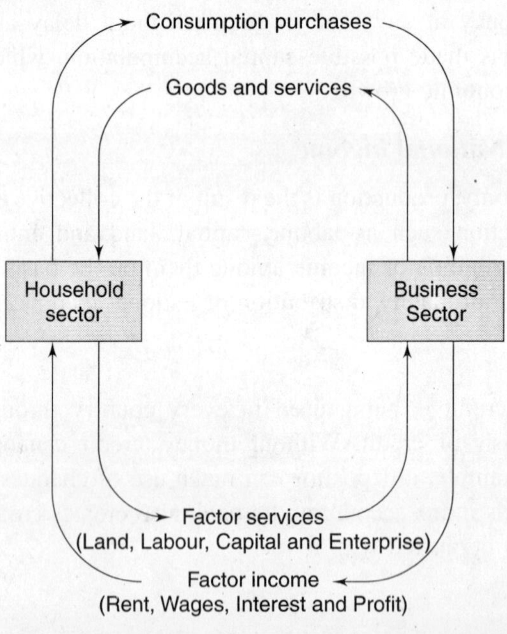

Fig. 3.1

in different capacities, participate in production of goods and services and at the same time, also consume product either made by them or someone else. Figure 3.1 shows how business enterprises make payments of various types to individuals and households for the supply of services for the production of goods. Ultimately, the individuals and households, purchase goods from the money they receive for their contribution in production.

Value of Money

Money, at least paper money, in itself can be quite valueless. For example, intrinsic value of 500 rupees note may be zero as it is just a piece of paper. However, its capacity to purchase goods and services worth Rs. 500 makes its value as Rs. 500. Thus, value of money lies in its purchasing power, i.e., what it can buy. In other words, the amount of goods and services, which one unit of money can purchase is regarded as the value of money. However, value of money does not remain stable. It keeps on fluctuating. Change in the value of money can also be measured in terms of goods and services it can purchase. The value of money is said to have fallen, when with one unit of money one can purchase lesser quantity of goods or services than one could have purchased earlier. But the difficulty here is that, if the value of money is expressed in terms of all commodities, there will be several values of money, since there are several commodities and each one of them may have various prices even within the country. To overcome this difficulty, it is measured by means of a statistical device known as Index Number.

Index Number

Index number may be defined as a series of figures by which changes in the size of an economic phenomenon are measured from time to time. Prices of all goods and services cannot rise or fall simultaneously. Even if the direction is same, the magnitude of change cannot be same. Index number considers the average of the changes in prices of various goods and services. If the index number registers a rise, it is an indication that the general price level has gone up. In other words, increase in prices shows that the value of money has fallen. On the contrary, if the prices of goods and services have decreased, it means that the value of money has gone up. Price index number compares the price level at two points of time. Merely saying price index number for a particular point of time is meaningless unless this figure is compared with the figure of some preceding period. Index number for many variables such as consumer price index[3] etc. is being calculated but the basic principle is same for all—a group of commodities is selected, their prices are noted in some particular year, which becomes the base year for the index number and number 100 is assigned to it. If the prices of these commodities rise by 1% during the 12 months, which has been taken as reference, the index number for the next year will be 101. A fall in the price of 1% would be shown by an index number of 99. Beside price index number, index number is employed to measure changes in certain other economic phenomenon such as changes in the level of production, changes in the levels of imports and exports also.

Supply of Money

In the preceding sections, value of money and how changes in value of money are measured with the help of index number have been discussed. However, more pertinent question is how value of money is determined. Like any other commodity, it is determined at a point of cross section of demand for and supply of money. However, there is one difference between money and any other commodity. Changes in the value of money do not reflect itself in change of any price but of all prices taken together or general price level.

Total money supply refers to aggregate amount of money in circulation, which is owned by public[4] in a country which comprises (i) notes and currency money, which is issued by the central government and (ii) demand deposits (subject to withdrawal by cheques) held by public with the commercial banks. Time deposit is also a constituent of supply of money. Time deposit may be regarded as quasi-money but not full-fledged money. It functions as a store of value but not as mode of payment. The cash balance held by the central and the state government with the central bank or with the treasury or the cash reserves owned by the commercial banks are not in circulation. Thus, they are not included in "money supply" on the ground that they are not in actual circulation.

The total money supply bears a certain variable proportion to the national income of the country. For example, if the money supply constitutes 25 per cent of its national income, this means that the income velocity of money is 4, or in simple words, every rupee circulates four times to facilitate commercial transactions in the country.

Following three monetary institutions are responsible for change in the money supply in a country:

(i) The state is the most important agency influencing the total money supply. State treasury, generally, issues notes of small value which constitutes legal tender money and helps to facilitate smaller transactions. At the same time, state or central government controls supply of money through fiscal policy. If, for example, the central government pursues a policy of deficit financing during war or depression, that will definitely cause an increase in the currency money in the hands of the public.

(ii) The commercial bank creates money through bank deposits. It does not keep its deposits idle but grants loans and advances to the customers. To give loan, bank opens an account in the name of the customer and credits the loan money to that account. The customer is then allowed to withdraw the money by cheques as per requirement. Thus, when the commercial banks expand their loans and advances, they create demand deposits in the bargain.

(iii) The central bank, exercises central control over the entire monetary system of the country. It enjoys a monopoly of note-issue and keep a check on credit creation by commercial banks. As such, it may be looked upon as the most important money-creating agency in the country.

Demand for Money

Money may be demanded for the following three reasons:

Transaction Demand for Money

It refers to the amount of money, which is required for carrying out exchanges to satisfy various demands. It directly depends upon the level of income, employment and the general price level in an economy. As the level of income increases, the size of fresh balances of money with public also increases for transactions.

$$L_t = f(Y, E, P)$$

where, L_t = Transaction demand for money
Y = Level of income
E = Employment
P = Price level

Precautionary Demand for Money

In addition to transaction demand for money, individuals and firms keep some money to meet unexpected expenditure resulting from uncertain and unforeseen events. It depends on income of an individual or a firm.

$L_p = f$ (business conditions, access to credit market and the ease with which the other securities can be converted into money when emergency arises)

So, L_t and L_p are income elastic but interest inelastic.

Speculative Demand for Money

People speculate about the future level of prices of various assets and securities. They would like to hold those securities whose prices are expected to rise and they would dispose of those securities whose prices are expected to fall.

Speculative demand for money is interest elastic.

$$L_s = f(r)$$

where r = rate of interest

The total demand for money can be obtained by adding the transaction demand for money, precautionary demand for money and the speculative demand for money. It can be represented as,

$$L_t + L_p + L_s = L_D$$

INFLATION

Inflation refers to a monetary phenomenon where price rises due to increase of money in circulation and is not accompanied by such an increase in output. Economists like Pigou and Keynes have discussed it as full employment phenomenon. However, later on, it was realized as a global phenomenon. In a developed economy, inflation, generally, occurs after stage of full employment. However, in a developing economy, inflation may coexist with under-employment of resources. This may be on account of shortage of capital, equipment, inefficient transport system, poor power facilities, inappropriate technical know-how, etc. Due to these bottlenecks, increase in the price level may not raise output beyond a certain level even though some of the inputs remain unemployed.

Classification of Inflation

Inflation may be classified on the basis of its cause as (i) Demand Pull Inflation and (ii) Supply Push Inflation, or on the basis of rate of inflation as (i) Creeping Inflation, (ii) Running Inflation and (iii) Galloping Inflation or Hyper Inflation. They have been discussed in detail below:

Demand Pull Inflation

The most common cause for inflation is the pressure of ever-rising demand on a stagnant or less rapidly increasing supply of goods and services. The process may initiate like this. If there is an increase in money supply, it will soon be followed by a fall in the interest rate. The fall in the rate of interest leads to an increase in the investment in the economy which will be followed by an increase in money income of the factors of production. With increased money incomes, there is an inevitable increase in the expenditure on consumption goods. It will further increase investment and money income of the factors of production. Since the economy is already operating at the level of full employment or the output cannot be increased due to some unavoidable reasons, an increase in investment expenditure will lead to demand inflation. General shortage (of goods and services), lengthening queues, increasing imports, rising wages, increasing employment and rising profit margin are some of the indicators of the presence of demand inflation in the economy.

Cost Push Inflation

Cost push inflation is caused by an increase in production cost, which may be due to following three factors:

(i) an increase in wages,

(ii) an increase in profit margin, and

(iii) imposition of heavy commodity taxes.

When cost inflation arises in a particular industry, it soon spreads to other sectors of the economy as well. The reason being that the various sectors of the economy are closely-linked with each other.

On the basis of Rate of Inflation

When prices increase slowly, without increase in supply of products (up to 03% per annum) it is called creeping inflation. Walking inflation is between 03% to 09% per annum. Prof Samuelson has clubbed them together as moderate inflation and did not consider it as a serious economic problem. In fact's single digit inflation is regarded as good for developing economy. But in course of time, the rise in price level becomes more marked. If the price rises at the rate of 10-20 per cent per annum, it is referred as 'running inflation'. If it exceeds that figure, it may be described as 'galloping inflation'. Inflation of higher denomination is not considered desirable for any economy. It causes economic distortions and disturbances. Indian economy has experienced some spats of "running" and "galloping" inflations to some extent (not exceeding 25%) since the second plan period. However, Argentina, Brazil and Israel have experienced inflation over hundred per cent during eighties. Though impact of galloping inflation is really disastrous but even running inflation is also a serious problem. Hyperinflation refers to a situation where the price rise at an alarming high rate which is very difficult to measure. However in quantitative term, rate of price rise is above 1000% per annum. In such situation, value of national currency reduces almost to zero. Paper money becomes worthless and people start trading either in gold or silver. Two examples of hyper-inflational in the world history are of Hungary in year 1996 and Zimbabwe during 2004-09 during Robert Mugabe's regime.

Control of Inflation

Government takes several monetary and fiscal measures to control inflation. Of the two types of inflation, cost push inflation is much more difficult to control than demand pull inflation. To control the demand pull inflation the target is to mop up surplus purchasing power from the hands of the public. Main monetary policy is to increase in the tax rate and decrease in subsidies. But cost push inflation cannot be easily controlled through monetary and fiscal measures. Reason is quite obvious. Any attempt to cut down wages by the authorities will be met by strong resistance on the part of the workers. Balancing act by the central government is crucial. The central bank also plays an important role in maintaining a fine balance between controlling inflation without hampering economic growth. If not controlled effectively, price rise becomes extremely rapid. Persistent inflation has disastrous impact on the economy and a country should avoid it at any cost.

DEFLATION

If prices are abnormally high, it is indeed desirable to have a fall in prices. Such a fall in the price level is good for the society and it does not lead to a fall in the level of production or employment. The process or the technique to reverse the inflationary trend in prices, without creating unemployment, is generally known as "disinflation". So, it is a situation when inflationary rate decreases but does not reverse. Disinflation is considered a normal and healthy part of the business cycle. However, deflation is a situation where there is decrease in the general price level of goods and services. During deflation, the inflation rate falls below 0% (a negative inflation rate) while real value of money increases. There may be fall in aggregate level of demand so, consumers delay purchases until prices fall further leads to increase in idle capacity, unemployment, and lower disposable income. Economists generally believe that deflation is a problem in a modern economy because it may aggravate recessions and lead to a deflationary spiral. It can be controlled by stimulus by the central bank in the form of reduction in interest rates and expanding money supply by printing more money or taking similar actions. Deflation occurs when a recession is so severe that prices are reduced to inspire demand. This often leads to further economic decline. "Reflation" marks an attempt to increase money supply to increase spending in an attempt to spur growth.

During deflation, the fall in the price level may be due to contraction in money supply. Two main causes of deflation are deficient demand and excess supply of goods and services. Deflation may be thought of as opposite of inflation, but it is not. While inflation is rise in prices unaccompanied by increase in employment, deflation is fall in prices accompanied by increasing unemployment. Inflation distorts the distribution of income between different groups of people in the country in a way that rich gain at the expense of poor; but it does not reduce the real income of the society. On the contrary, deflation reduces national income through contraction of production and increases unemployment. Each segment of the society is adversely affected. For the last five decades, there is hardly any country, which has passed through a period of persistent fall in the general level of prices.

STAGFLATION

A situation of slow down or stagnant economy coupled with rising prices is called stagflation. As economy does not exhibit growth, hence, employment and consumption are negatively affected. Economists offer two principal explanations for occurrence of stagflation. First, stagflation can result when the productive capacity of an economy is reduced by an unfavourable supply shock, such as an increase in the price of oil for an oil importing country. Such an unfavourable supply shock tends to raise prices which ultimately, slows the economy by making production more costly and less profitable.

Both stagnation and inflation can result from inappropriate macroeconomic polices. For example, central bank can cause inflation by permitting excessive growth of the money supply, and the government can cause stagnation by excessive regulation in goods markets as well as labour markets. Either of these factors can result into stagflation. Excessive growth of the money supply taken to such an extreme that it must be reversed abruptly can clearly be a cause. Both types of explanations was discusssed for the global stagflation of the 1970s. It began with a huge rise in oil prices, but then continued as central banks used excessively stimulative monetary policy to counteract the resulting recession, causing a runaway price/wage spiral.

Experts have analysed situation of stagflation in the Indian economy as a combination of slower real GDP (gross domestic product) growth of around 6.5 per cent and higher wholesale price inflation (WPI) ranging from 8.8 per cent to double digit. However, India has a substantial growth potential hence, stagflation may not be such problem, as it may be for the economiecs with lower growth rates.

Recession

In economics, recession is regarded as a contraction phase of business cycle. A general slowdown in economic activity. Macroeconomic indicators such as GDP, employment, investment spending, capacity utilization, household income, business profits, and inflation fall, while the unemployment rises. Recessions generally occur when there is a widespread drop in the spending (an adverse demand shock). This may be triggered by various events, such as a financial crisis, an external trade shock, an adverse supply shock or the bursting of an economic bubble. Governments usually respond to recessions by adopting expansionary macroeconomic policies, such as increasing money supply, increasing government spending and decreasing taxation. Recession has a very powerful psychological confidence aspect. For example, if there is expectation about slowdown of the economic activity, consumers do not want to spend and firms may decide to reduce employment levels and save money rather than invest. Such expectations can create a self-reinforcing downward cycle, bringing about or worsening of recession. In economics, the words **recession** and **depression** are used to refer to economic downturns. One could say that while a recession refers to the economy "falling down," a depression is a matter of "not being able to get up." An economic contraction when GDP declines for two consecutive quarters, is usually called a recession and a **depression** refers to a *sustained* downturn in one or more national economies. It is more severe than a recession.

BUSINESS CYCLE

Business cycles are rhythmic fluctuations of an economy, i.e., periods of prosperity followed by periods of depression. Industries are so interconnected that fluctuations in one will be passed on to others. Thus, cyclical fluctuations move from one industry to other. And from one country to another through foreign trade. The fluctuations like the swing of a pendulum automatically generate movement in other direction with equal momentum. Periods of prosperity contain in themselves seeds of depression. However, the waves of prosperity and depression need not always be of the same length and amplitude.

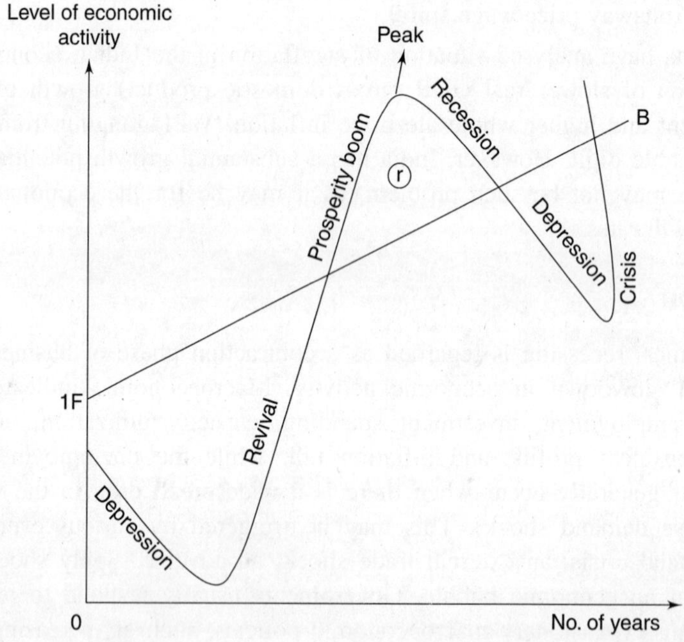

Fig. 3.2

Generally, there are five phases of trade cycle. In monetary terminology, the same phases correspond to depression, recovery, full employment, inflation and recession.

(i) **Depression:** During depression, there is pessimism in the market, which is reflected in the persistent lack of demand. To adjust with the decreased demand, management introduces economic measures like stoppage of waste, introduction of greater efficiency, cutting of wages or even retrenchment of staff to reduce cost of production per unit. Thus, ultimately they will be able to reduce prices. Lower prices reduce profit margin. Workers with the previous salary were demanding many other products and services in the market but after retrenchment, they do not have salary to demand goods and services, which they were demanding earlier. So, it will have cascading effect on other sectors and ultimately, these sectors will also have lack of demand. Large changes in total output and employment and the price level are normally accompanied by large changes in currency, credit and velocity of circulation of money in the same direction. Total output and employment fluctuate by a larger percentage in durable and capital goods industries, which then pass over to non-durable and consumption goods industries.

(ii) **Phase of recovery:** Depression gives place to recovery. Here engineers have a very significant role to play. To create demand, they add value to the exishing products through technological innovations. For example, when there was less demand for normal colour television sets, many other features have been incorporated through technological innovations to enhance its demand. Gradually, pessimism gives way to optimism. There is greater demand for goods and services and consequently, there is increased production. Prices start rising, so, wages, interest and profits too. Employment and income increases which ultimately leads to increase in national income. There is increase in investment, bank loans and advances, increase in the velocity of circulation of money due to more brisk trade. The wave of recovery once initiated soon begins to feed upon itself.

(iii) **Phase of full employment:** The cumulative process of recovery continues till the economy reaches full employment. It means all the available resources are fully employed. Wages, interests and profits are high, output and employment is highest under the given technological circumstances. There may be some voluntary and frictional type of unemployment.

(iv) **Phase of inflation:** Beyond a level of full employment, rise in investment may lead to increased pressure on resources. If any of the resources fails to deliver at the existing price and asks for higher money, it distorts the cost calculation and then management realizes that they have over-invested. The over-optimism paves way for pessimism, which leads to recession.

(v) **Recession:** The over-optimism of the boom gives way to pessimism characterized by feeling of doubt and fear. Though the process of revival is generally very gradual but crash of the boom is always sudden and sharp. Business expansion stops, orders are cancelled and workers are laid off. This period is painful because of widespread unemployment.

MONEY MARKET AND CAPITAL MARKET

Both these markets are interrelated and provide finance to manufacturers and traders for the purpose of production and exchange dealings. Discount houses, private bankers, bill brokers, etc., all are taken as the constituents of a money market. Capital market may be divided into two parts, viz., market for old capital and market for new capital. Market for old capital refers to stock exchange in which stocks and shares of companies are bought and sold.

There is a close relationship between the money market and the capital market. Firstly, the capital market, particularly the old capital market, depends upon the money market for finance. Secondly, both markets provide funds for production. For example, the commercial banks lend funds both for short period as well as for long periods. Thus, the two markets are intimately related to each other. However, there is one important difference between money market and capital market. In money market, short term funds are borrowed and lent. The money market does not deal in cash or money, but with promissory notes and government papers, which are drawn for short periods. These short term bills are known as near money. The capital market provides capital in financial form for medium and long terms. However, some of the institutions deal both with the money market as well as with the capital market.

STOCK EXCHANGE

Stock exchange is a constituent of capital market where dealing in stocks and shares takes place. It is through the agency of stock exchange that people invest their money into joint stock companies. Those who desire to buy stocks and shares come in contact with those who want to sell because money cannot be withdrawn from the company directly. It may be obtained through the transfer of shares, debentures, etc., from one holder to another at rates existing in the market. If there were no stock exchanges, one could not have been able to dispose of his shares at the time of need, and thus, very few people would have dared to invest their capital into loans floated by either the government or other organizations. The price at which a security can be bought or sold in the stock exchange depends, as in other markets, on the relative strength of the demand for and the supply of that particular share at a particular time. If the business prospects are good, the prices of shares will generally, be high and if prospects are poor, prices will be low. Company's balance sheet affects the price of its shares favourably or adversely, as the case might be.

SPECULATION—BULL AND BEAR

It has been discussed under demand for money that people hold money for speculative reasons. They invest in stock and securities because of the following two reasons:

(i) Some people buy for the sake of investment, i.e., with the intention of holding the securities. They look for a regular normal income from their capital.

(ii) Some people try to earn maximum income from the securities. They study growth trends of securities and sell them when they believe prices are near the peak in order to make profit for themselves. Such profits are known as capital gains. Whenever a speculator foresees a rise in prices, he buys with the intention of selling afterwards at a profit and when he anticipates a fall in prices, he sells with a view to buy in future at the lower prices. People who buy securities hoping that their price will rise in future are known as Bulls and people who sell expecting fall in prices are known as Bears. If the market is keen to buy, it is said to be bullish and if it is keen to sell, it is said to be bearish. Thus, speculation helps to make securities more liquid.

BANK

Bank is a German word which means a joint stock fund. In common parlance, it is generally used for a financial institution which deals in money and credit. With growth of economy, these institutions have become important stakeholders in the business activities of any economy. Today, they have started performing several functions but their main functions are: (i) to accept deposit from people who want to keep their money safely and earn profit on them, and (ii) lends money to the needy people and organizations through advances and loans of various types. Actually, bank's main motive is to earn profit. It pays interest to people who deposit their money and charge interest from those whom banks give loans and advances. However, interest they pay to depositors is less than what they charge from those whom they have given loans and advances and the balance is the profit of the bank. Such banks are known as commercial banks. To control and regulate money, banking and credit policy of a country, each country has an apex monetary and banking institution which is known as central bank. All the commercial banks keep reserve with the central bank and the banking policies in the country are also framed by the central bank.

In commercial banks, customers can leave their cash with the bank in saving account, current account or a fixed deposit account.

- Customers deposit their money in Saving Account to save a part of their current income to meet their future needs and also intend to earn an income from their savings (bank interest). For the depositor, the number of withdrawals over a period of time and total amount of money in one or more withdrawals on any date are, however, limited.

- A Current Account, on the other hand, is a running account, which may be operated upon any number of times during a working day. There is no restriction on the number and the amount of withdrawals. The bank does not pay any interest, rather in some cases it takes incidental charges from the depositor on such accounts.
- In a Fixed Deposit Account, the deposits are made for a fixed period from 45 days onwords and a higher rate of interest is paid to the depositor for parting with liquid money for fixed period of time. Depositors get higher rate of interest for longer duration of a fixed deposit. The commercial banks do not keep money idle; rather they lend that money at higher rate of interest to the needy persons and organizations.

Along with the above-mentioned activities, a bank is involved in several subsidiary activities. A few of which are as follows:

(i) Collection of cheques drawn for other banks.
(ii) Acceptance and collection of bills of exchange.
(iii) Dealing in foreign exchange to assist the settlement of overseas debts.
(iv) Stock Exchange trustee and executor of business.
(v) Bank locker facilities.
(vi) Making standing order payments.
(vii) Supplying change and assisting the central bank in keeping the note issue in good condition.
(viii) Selling of application forms for several national examinations.
(ix) Collection of bills on behalf of any organization.

The differences between commercial bank and central bank are shown in Table 3.1.

Table 3.1 Comparison between Commercial Bank and Central Bank

Sl. No.	*Commercial Bank*	*Central Bank*
1.	Objective of a commercial bank is to earn profit.	Objective of a central bank is to stimulate economic growth of the country.
2.	There can be several commercial banks in a country.	There will be only one central bank in a country.
3.	There can be private as well as nationalized commercial banks in a country.	Central bank is an autonomous institution.
4.	Commercial banks perform general banking and agency services for general public.	Central bank performs general banking and agency services for the government.
5.	Commercial bank deals with public directly.	Central bank deals with commercial banks; other financial institutions and the government of the country.

Contd...

6.	Punjab National Bank, State Bank of India, Indian Bank are some of the nationalized commercial banks in India. Yes Bank, Kotak Mahindra Bank, H.D.F.C. Bank are some of the private banks and City Bank, Standerd Chartered Bank are two of the foreign banks.	Reserve Bank of India is the central bank in India.

CREDIT

In cash transaction, cash is paid at the time of purchase of the commodity or service whereas in a credit transaction, the buyer promises to pay for the commodity to the seller at a future date. Thus, credit implies the postponement or deferring of a payment. However, the seller must have confidence in the buyer that the buyer has the intention to pay and he will pay the price of the commodity at a later date as promised by him. Credit is organized through the credit institutions and instruments. As then currency has certain limitations as problem in transportation and fear of theft, credit overcomes then and plays an indispensable role in all transactions in modern industrial economy. It facilitates production by allowing the flow capital, formed by collecting small personal savings, into the hands of entrepreneurs to carry on their business. It also enables to tide over temporary financial difficulties. A good credit policy minimizes fluctuation in prices. However, the greatest danger of credit is chances of over issue as it happened in case of global financial crisis 2008-09 which started with turbulance in the sub-prime segment of the U.S. housing market.

Mechanisms of Operating Credit

The credit can be operated by following mechanisms:

(i) A cheque is a written order by the depositor to a specified bank to pay a certain amount to a person who possesses the cheque or in whose name the cheque has been drawn. It may be of three types:

(a) A bearer cheque is made payable to the person whosoever presents it at the bank for encashment.

(b) An order cheque is made payable to the person only in whose name cheque has been drawn. It is the responsibility of the bank to see that the payment is made to the right person.

(c) A crossed cheque cannot be encashed at the bank counter. It can only be deposited in the bank account of the person in whose name the cheque has been drawn. Crossed cheques are highly safe.

(ii) A bank note is the promise by the bank or a currency note by the government to pay a sum of money written on it on demand to the bearer of the note. When issued by a bank, it is known as bank note and when issued by a government, it is known as currency note.

(iii) A bill of exchange is an order from a creditor to the debtor to pay the stated amount of money to himself or to a specified person or to the bearer after a definite period of time. A bill of exchange differs from a cheque in the sense that cheque can be encashed on demand while bill of exchange is payable after a period of time.

(iv) Under the Negotiable Instrument Act, promissory note is a promise made by the debtor to the creditor, promising to pay a certain amount of money to a person whose name is written on it or the bearer, after stated period of time. A promissory note is perhaps supported by the guarantee of some third person in whom the lender may have confidence.

(v) A bank draft is a kind of cheque. It is an order to pay money, drawn by one office of a bank upon another office of a bank for an amount of money payable to order on demand, inside or outside the country. However, there are two main differences, Cheque is issued by a depositor for the bank in which his bank account is. However, draft can be made from any bank by paying required fee for it. A cheque can bounce when there is not sufficient fund available in the account whereas draft is always backed by required fund and cannot bounce. Therefore, a bank draft has more acceptability than a cheque.

(vi) Hundies are an indigenous credit instrument, which is operating in India for a long time. It is accepted, endorsed and transferred just like a bill of exchange. Written in local language and regulated by local custom and traditions, hundies are issued by the borrower in the name of the creditor with the promise to return his money on demand or after the stated period of time. The interest is paid to the creditor on the very day the money is borrowed at the rate mutually decided by the two parties. A small amount of money is paid to the broker as commission.

Credit Creation

Credit creation is an important function of a commercial bank. All those who want to keep their surplus money safely and earn profit too, deposit their surplus with banks. Banks do not keep deposited money idle with them but safely extend loans and advances on the basis of deposited money and charge interest from the debtors to earn profits. Banks provide interest on deposited money also. But the interest on deposited money is less than interest charged on loans. The amount which a bank gets after deducting administrative cost from the difference between interest charged and paid, is its profit. In this way, a bank creates credit money. However, a bank keeps a certain minimum percentage of its total deposit liabilities as cash to meet its cash demand by the depositors. This is called Cash Reserve Ratio (CRR)[5] and it depends upon the conditions at which an individual bank functions. But, it should never fall below the minimum legally prescribed limit which is decided by the central bank of the country. Lending of a bank may be, in fact, a multiple times of the value of its original cash reserves. When a borrower takes a loan from the bank, the amount of sanctioned loan is credited to his account. The borrower is free to withdraw the amount in the way he likes. The borrower is, however, not expected to withdraw the entire amount as cash. The reason is that cash is not needed for its own sake, but for the facility it provides in purchasing goods and services or for settling debts. In either case, instead, cheques could be used. The sellers of the goods or creditors may, in turn, deposit these cheques with the same bank, or with some other banks. The bank, in turn, may lend to some other borrowers after keeping certain minimum cash reserves to meet the liabilities. These borrowers may again issue cheque to the creditors or seller of goods in connection with their business transactions. The deposits with one or the other bank will increase, when the cheques are deposited. The process may continue and the total deposits created by the banking system would be more than the initial amount of deposits created by the original bank. This power of commercial bank to expand deposits through expanding its loans and advances or investments is referred as credit creation. Since every loan creates equivalent deposits, credit creation by banks implies a multiplication of bank deposits. It depends upon the ratio of cash reserves to deposits.

MONETARY POLICY

There are two tools in the hands of a government for financial administration. They are monetary policy and fiscal policy. We will discuss fiscal policy in the chapter on Pubic Finance. Monetary policy refers to measures taken to control and regulate money and credit supply in the economy. It has a bearing on volume of money. Rate of interest is a very important constituent of it. If there is inflationary trend in the economy, it means that there is more money in the circulation than goods and services available. To control volume of money in the circulation, the government decides to increase rate of interest on bank loan, which leads to reduction in demand for bank loan and ultimately, decreases volume of money in circulation. On the other hand, if there is large-scale unemployment in the economy, the government decides to decrease the rate of interest on bank loan, which leads to larger demand for loan and advances and ultimately eradicates unemployment upto certain extent. By regulating Cash-Reserve Ratio[5], and Reverse Ratio Rate[6], supply of money in the market is regulated by the central bank.

NATIONAL INCOME

National Income refers to total national output or value of a nation's output during a specific period (usually one year). It is an important indicator of a country's level of development. There are three different ways of looking at the value of a nation's output, viz., Gross[7] National Product (GNP), Gross National Income (GNI) and Gross National Expenditure (GNE). They can be explained as follows:

(i) Gross National Product of a country is the monetary value of all final goods and services produced by a country during a given period of time, generally a year. While domestic product emphasizes the total output, which is raised within the geographical boundaries of a country, national product focuses attention not only on the domestic product within the country but also on goods and services produced outside the boundaries of a nation. Gross National Product of a country includes monetary value of all the goods and services produced during a specified period of time and Net National Product is calculated after subtracting depreciation from Gross National Product.

Therefore, Gross National Product (GNP) = Σ Monetary value of final goods and services produced within the country + Σ Monetary value of final goods and services produced outside the country by citizen of the country – Σ Monetary value of final goods and services produced by nationals of other countries working within the country.

And, Net National Product (NNP) = GNP – Depreciation

(ii) Gross National Income (GNI) is the total of all payments received by factors of production such as labour, capital, land and organization for their contribution in production. After subtracting taxes from GNI, Net National Income (NNI) can be obtained.

Gross National Income (GNI) = Σ Payment received by the factors of production for their services in production.

Net National Income (NNI) = Σ Payment made to the factors of production for their services in production-taxes.

(iii) The incomes received by various factors of production are either spent by the factors of production or are saved. So, one way of calculating national income may be by adding total consumption expenditure and total investment expenditure in the country together during a specific period of time.

Gross National Expenditure (GNE) = Σ Expenditure on Consumption + Σ Expenditure on investment[8].

Net National Expenditure (NNE) = Σ Expenditure on Consumption + Σ Expenditure on investment – Expenditure on financial investment which is only transfer of rights – Expenditure on repair of existing good.

However, whichever way national income is calculated, it will be same.

Thus, Gross National Product (GNP) = Gross National Income (GNI) = Gross National Expenditure (GNE).

At the time of calculation of National Income following points must be taken into consideration:

(i) Values of resold goods need not be included in GNP. However, commission of the used car dealer it will be part of GNP since it is a currently produced service.

(ii) Final goods and not the intermediate goods need to be considered.

(iii) Only recently produced goods are considered for calculation. For example, if a car is manufactured in 2001 but it could not be sold till 2002, then it should not be calculated in GNP of 2002.

(iv) Gifts are not included in national income.

(v) People receive old age pension, unemployment relieves, social security payments, etc. Such receipts will constitute income of the individual but they will not be counted in the national income as no corresponding product or service has been created.

Notes

1. Credit card is also called plastic money.
2. Household: All people who eat from the same kitchen are part of a household.
3. Consumer price index (CPI) measures changes in the price level of consumer goods and services purchased by households.
4. Public include private individuals and business firms operating in the economy, but it excludes from itself the central government, the central bank and the commercial banks.
5. Cash-Reserve Ratio (CRR) is a specified minimum fraction of the total deposit with commercial bank which they have to hold as reserve either in cash or as deposits with the central bank. CRR is devided by the central bank.
6. Repo rate and reverve repo rate–

   Repo rate is the rate at which the central bank of a country lends money to the commercial bank if there is any shortfall of funds. Reverse Repo rate is the rate at which the central bank of a country borrows money from commercial banks within the country.
7. Gross: Total, without subtracting any quantity, and net is obtained after subtracting whatever has to be paid. For example, net national product is obtained after deducting depreciation from gross national product.
8. Investment: It is the net increase in the existing stock of real capital assets such as machinery, building, plant and equipment. It also includes the increase that takes place in the inventories.

EXERCISES

A. Objective

1. Fill in the blanks: (For 1/2 mark each)

(i) Money occupies a central position in a modern day economy because it serves as the medium of ______.

(ii) In a modern economy, money constitutes an important form of ______.

(iii) Money does not produce anything but without ______ nothing can be produced.

(iv) There may be ______ commercial bank in an economy.

(v) Value of money ______ during inflation.

(vi) The speculative demand for cash balance varies ______ with the rate of interest.

(vii) A ______ interest rate is an inducement to people to hold more speculative cash balances.

(viii) As the rate of interest rises, people would be tempted to hold ______ earning assets and hold ______ money.

(ix) Money market is a market for ______ funds while the capital market is market for ______ funds.

(x) Full employment is a relevant objective for a ______ economy while economic growth is the dominant objective for a ______ economy.

Ans. (i) exchange; (ii) wealth; (iii) money; (iv) many; (v) decreases; (vi) inversely; (vii) lower; (viii) more, less; (ix) short term, long term; (x) developed, developing

Write true or false for each of the following: (For1/2 mark each)

(i) Money is needed in a socialist economy.

(ii) GNP is the money value of all goods and services produced in a country during a year.

(iii) National income is the money value of goods produced during a period of one year.

(iv) Central bank is called banker's bank.

(v) Objective of a commercial bank is to earn profit.

Ans. (i) True; (ii) False; (iii) False; (iv) True; (v) True

B. Subjective (For five or seven marks)

1. Define Money. Discuss its significance.
2. Discuss the concept of money supply with the public. What are the factors which determine the supply of money in an economy?
3. What are the three motives for holding money? Is the demand for money a function of the level of income or the rate of interest?
4. Define Inflation. Discuss monetary measures to control inflation.
5. What do you mean by Business Cycle? Discuss different phases of business cycle.
6. Differentiate between Money Market and Capital Market.
7. Explain the role and importance of the Commercial Banks in the modern economy.
8. Discuss major functions of a Commercial Bank.
9. Define a Central Bank. Distinguish between Central Bank and Commercial Bank.
10. Discuss role of Central Bank in liberalized economy.
11. Discuss the methods of credit creations adopted by Commercial Banks.
12. How monetary policy may be used to eradicate unemployment among youth in India?
13. Bring out the difficulties in the measurement of National Income in a country.

References and Suggested Readings

1. Smith, Adam (1937), An Inquiry into the Nature and Causes of the Wealth of Nation. The Modern Library, New York.
2. Elliott, Jan Walter, Macroeconomic Analysis. Winthrop Publishers Inc., Massachusetts.
3. Wykstra, Paul A., Introducing Economics: Harper & Row Publishers, USA.
4. Brown, A.J., Applied Economics. Aspect of the World Economy in War and Peace. George Allen & Unwin Ltd., London.

4

Indian Economy

Purpose of this chapter is to acquaint the reader with:

- Salient features of the Indian Economy
- Five-Year Plans
- Liberalization, Privatization and Globalization

At the dawn of independence, India inherited almost a stagnant economy with low per capita consumption and income, low agricultural productivity and a very small industrial base. Aftermath of the partition aggravated the already miserable situation. Immediate requirements of millions of people were shelter and livelihood. To tackle these issues and to achieve higher rate of economic development, India opted to be a mixed economy based on basic ideology of self-reliance, equity and disrtibutive social justice and managed quite well during all these years. Now, in today's economic environment, the real challenge is to enhance growth rate, make it sustainable[1] and inclusive[2]. Engineers are expected to play a very constructive role in this endeavour.

SALIENT FEATURES OF INDIAN ECONOMY

Distinction between developing and developed economy is relative and not rigid. In general, developed countries have high per capita income. On the other hand, countries, which have real per capita incomes less than a quarter of the per capita income of the United States, are developing economies. By that standard, India is a developing economy[3] with specific characteristics. However, after having nominal GDP growth rate in the early years after independence, GDP growth rate took a huge leap and was 9.0% during 2005–2006 and 9.4% during 2006–2007. The country was holding a huge reserve of foreign exchange that was rather unprecedented. At that time, everything was looking bright. After that, the global financial meltdown happened which had disastrous impact throughout the globe. Even then, the situation is better than many other countries and it is being regarded as a potential superpower along with China. Some of the salient features have been discussed below.

Large Population Pressure

India is second only to China in terms of size of population. However, population density in India is more than China due to its smaller geographical area (1079.7) than China (1296.2). India, at present, is going through the second phase of demographic transition.[4] The rate of growth of population, which was about 1.31 per cent per annum during 1941–1950, has risen to 2.0 per cent per annum during 1981–1990. The chief cause of this rapid population growth was steep fall in death rate due to increased medical facilities while birth rate remained very high due to prevalent social values. Though, average annual population growth rate decelerated in 2000 to 1.7 per cent per annum and again, 1.5 per cent per annum during 2000-2010, but even now with this rate, India is going to become largest in terms of population by 2035.

Table 4.1 International Population Dynamics

Country	*Population 2010*	*Average annual population growth 2000-10*	*Population age composition*					
			2004			*2010*		
			0-14 yrs	*15-64 yrs*	*65+*	*0-14 yrs*	*15-64 yrs*	*65+*
Switzerland	81.8	−0.1	16.8	67.6	15.7	13	66	20
USA	309.3	0.9	20.9	66.8	12.3	20	67	13
UK	62.2	0.6	18.2	65.9	15.9	17	66	17
Japan	127.5	00.0	14.1	66.7	19.2	13	64	23
Germany	81.8	−0.1	14.6	67.2	18.2	13	66	21
China	1338.3	0.6	20.2	71.6	8.2	19	72	9
India	1224.6	1.5	22.0	70.5	7.5	31	64	5
Pakistan	173.6	1.8	32.5	62.3	5.2	35	60	4
Bangladesh	148.7	1.4	38.9	57.3	3.8	31	64	5

Source: World Development Indicator, World Bank, 2006 pp. 46-47 and 2012 pp. 42-43.

In Table 4.1, age composition has been compared between 2004 and 2010. It is evident that size 65+ segment of population is growing not only in developed countries but in China also. Not only that, 0-14 years segment is also decreasing in China but it is growing in India. If India has to get benefit of the demographic dividend[5], it has to concentrate on education and health to its young population. Instead it will have to face demographic burden.

Income and Trade

Underdeveloped economies are marked by the existence of low per capita income. The per capita income of India in 2010 was $ 3,400 which is less than half of the per capita income of China. The per capita income of USA is fourteen times more than the same for India[6]. During 1960–1990, developed economies grew at a faster rate than the Indian economy but beyond 1990, Indian economy has grown at a faster rate than the developed economies. Though, foreign direct investment is significantly lower than China but is quite comparable to other countries. There is sense of relief as average annual per cent growth of Gross Capital Formation (GCF) has increased by almost double in India between 1990-2000 and 2000-2010. Though it is lower than China but better than the developed countries where it is decelerating and in fact, it is negative in the USA and Japan as listed in Table 4.2. Even then the difference in per capita income between India and developed economies is very large. Moreover, per capita income may not depict the real story as distribution of income is not equal among all segments of the society.

Table 4.2 International Comparison on Income

Country	*Purchasing power parity gross national income*			*Gross Capital Formation average annual % growth*		*Foreign direct investment*
	US $ in billion 2010	*Per capita US $ 2010*	*Rank 2010*	*1990–2000*	*2000–2010*	*Net inflow % of GDP 2010*
Switzerland	5.7	5,430	134	6.6	5.4	4.1
USA	14,635.6	47,310	16	7.6	−0.6	1.6
UK	2,230.6	35,840	33	5.0	1.6	2.3
Japan	4,411.7	34,610	35	−0.8	−1.6	0.0
Germany	3,115.4	38,100	29	1.1	0.2	1.4
China	10,221.7	7,640	120	10.8	13.3	3.1
India	4,159.7	3,400	157	6.9	12.9	1.4
Pakistan	484.4	2,790	164	1.8	5.0	1.1
Bangladesh	269.7	1,810	182	9.2	7.7	0.9

Source: World Development Indicator, World Bank, 2012 pp. 20-22, 246-248, 366-368.

High Dependence on Agriculture

Though contribution of agriculture to the overall Gross Domestic Product (GDP) of the Indian economy has decreased from about 30 per cent in 1990-91 to less than 15 per cent in 2011-12, agriculture yet forms the backbone. Roughly, half of the workforce is still engaged in agriculture for its livelihood. Being both a source of livelihood and food security for a vast majority of low income, poor and vulnerable sections of society, its performance assumes greater significance in view of the proposed National Food Security Bill and the ongoing Mahatma Gandhi National Rural Employment Guarantee Act (MGNREGA) Scheme. The experience from BRICS (Brazil, Russia, India, China and South Africa) countries indicates that a one percentage growth in agriculture is at least two to three times more effective in reducing poverty than the same growth emanating from non-agriculture sectors. Given that India is still home to the largest number of poor and malnourished people in the world, a higher priority to agriculture will achieve the goals of reducing poverty and malnutrition as well as of inclusive growth quicker than any other sector. Since agriculture forms the resource base for a number of agro-based industries and agro-services, it would be more meaningful to view agriculture not as farming alone but as a whole value chain, which includes farming, wholesaling, warehousing (including logistics), processing, and retailing. Further, it may be noted that in the last two Five Year Plans, it is clearly mentioned that for the economy to grow at 9 per cent, it is important that agriculture should grow at least by 4 per cent per annum (GoI, 2011).

Employment has not decreased in the same proportion as share in GDP. From time to time, several technological packages have been introduced in agriculture as Green Revolution[7], Yellow Revolution[8], White Revoulution[9], Blue Revolution[10] and now it is 'Biodiesel Plant'[11]. However, benefits of all these revolutions have remained limited due to poverty of farmers at the micro level and inadequate credit facility, depletion in ecology, intensive use of inputs, lowering of underground water table, insufficient supply of electricity, poor storage facility, inadequate rural connectivity, etc. Under such dismal scenario, Indian agriculture is facing multiple challenges. Firstly, diversification in the structure of food demands as a result of economic growth as well as population growth. Secondly, opening up of the economy, WTO and ratification of many other protocols related to biological diversity have opened the rural sectors to the international communities. Multinational corporations (MNCs) are coming with genetically modified seeds which may have disastrous impact on the poor and the subsistence farmers. Therefore, there is a need to carefully examine the protection of the agriculture from disastrous consequences. More recently, nano-technological experiments in agriculture are being done. Even after examination and getting approval by the authorized bodies, farmers need help of experts in case of some operational problem specific to a particular geographical situation (Singh & Kumar, 2003, Singh 2012).

Education

In an increasingly complex knowledge-driven economy, education is the foundation for transforming a person to human capital. Realizing the necessity, Government of India has emphasized on education and has made huge strides in this area since independence. It has a large network of public-funded education facility but being one of the youngest country of the world, Government of India has given reemphasis on education and skill formation in recent years. Number of schools, colleges and universities has increased phenomenally. Percentage of gross enrolment ratio in primary education is very good in fact comparable to developed countries. Regarding performance in higher education, even though, status of tertiary education is far below than the developed countries, but the achievement is reflected in large pool of English-speaking professionals and university pass-outs. Indian engineers and management graduates are very much in demand throughout the world.

Table 4.3 International Comparison of Educational Parameters

Country	*Educational Expenditure as % of GNI*		*Gross Enrolment Ratio % of relevant age group in 2010*				*Adult literacy rate % 15 and older 2005-10*
	2004	*2010*	*Preprimary*	*Primary*	*Secondary*	*Tertiary*	
Switzerland	5.0	6.9	102	102	95	51	–
USA	4.8	4.8	69	102	96	95	–
UK	5.3	5.1	81	106	102	59	–
Singapore	2.7	3.0	–	–	–	–	95
China	2.0	1.8	54	111	81	26	94
India	4.0	3.1	54	118	60	16	63
Pakistan	2.3	1.6	–	95	34	05	56
Bangladesh	1.9	1.8	13	103	49	11	56
Peru	2.9	2.1	78	109	92	–	90

Source: World Development Indicator, World Bank, 2012 pp. 86-88, 254-257, 94-96.

Many MNCs are establishing their base in India to exploit engineering talents besides many other things (Singh, 2005). However, there are two challenges before the education system. First is its increasing cost. Looking at soaring cost of providing education in recent years, and, in fact, visulizing shrinking government funding, government has encouraged private funding to supplement the public one. The private initiative, whatsoever, is charging higher fees from the students. However, accelerating fee structure has led to the fear of making education, at least higher education, out of reach of the common man. Another area of concern is the quality of education and challenge to enhance employability among the educated unemployed.

Health

Health is another crucial area, which needs to be taken care of by the Government. Total expenditure on health in India as percentage of its GDP in 2010 is also comparable to developing countries but far below than USA and UK.

Indicators such as access to improved source of water and sanitation facilities which have bearing on general health, have been discussed here. Percentage of population with both parameters has increased over last twenty years. However, apart from numbers, the issue is of quality also which must be given emphasis. Access to improved water sources is important but availability of water for the whole year is another issue which is equally important. Same applies to other parameters also such as number of doctors per million populations, etc. Birth per women has shown deceleration in the developing countries including India and increasing trend in USA.

Table 4.4 International Comparison of Health Parameters

	Health Expenditure Total % of GDP 2010	*Total Access to an improved water source % of population*		*Access to improved sanitation facilities % of population*		*Total fertility rate births per women*	
		1990	*2010*	*1990*	*2010*	*1990*	*2010*
Iran	5.6	90	96	79	100	4.8	1.2
USA	17.9	99	99	100	100	2.1	2.1
UK	9.6	100	100	100	100	1.8	1.9
Peru	5.1	75	85	54	71	3.8	2.5
Sri Lanka	2.9	67	91	70	92	2.5	2.3
China	5.1	67	91	24	64	2.3	1.6
India	4.1	69	92	18	34	3.9	2.6
Pakistan	2.2	85	92	27	48	6.0	3.4
Bangladesh	3.5	77	81	39	56	4.5	2.2

Source: World Development Indicator, 2012 pp 100-102, 108-110, 112-114.

Employment

India has a large reservoir of labour force, second only to China but rate of growth of the labour force is more in India (15.44) than China (10.39) between 2000 and 2010 but less than Pakistan and Bangladesh which has grown by 38.9 and 26.2 respectively.

Young Dependency Ratio (YDR)[12] is also very high in all, India, Pakistan and Bangladesh which shows significant young segment in the total population.

Second is the coexistence of employment in formal and informal sectors. Formal sector employment is protected by law but only makes 7% of the total employment. Rest 93% of employment is generated in the informal sector. Low female labour force participation is another significant characteristic. In China, the female labour force participation is more than double as compared to India. Lastly, emergence of information and communication technology (ICT) has created several atypical forms of employment such as tele-working, outsourced work and part-time work. In these types of work, employer-employee relationship is not well defined.

Table 4.5 International Comparison of Labour Force

	Labour Force Total in millions		*Dependency Ratio % of working-age population*		*Female in the labour force as percentage*		*Labour productivity GDP per person employed % growth*	
	2000	*2010*	*Young*	*Old*	*2000*	*2010*	*1990-92*	*2008-10*
Russian Federation	73.3	75.5	21	18	48.6	48.9	−7.9	−1.4
USA	29.5	31.8	30	20	45.8	46	1.7	2.3
UK	147.1	157.5	26	25	45.2	45.9	6.1	−0.9
Brazil	83.7	101.6	38	10	41.2	43.7	−0.3	1.8
Sri Lanka	7.8	8.6	37	12	33.1	32.2	5.5	4.8
China	724.5	799.8	27	11	45.0	44.6	6.8	8.8
India	409.4	472.6	47	08	27.8	25.3	1.0	5.6
Pakistan	43.0	59.7	59	07	15.3	20.7	6.4	−0.1
Bangladesh	57.3	72.3	49	07	37.5	39.9	2.3	3.4

Source: World Development Indicator, World Bank, 2012 pp. 42-44, 46-48, 54-56.

Labour productivity, in general, is low which is both a cause and an affect of low level of living and working conditions. Low labour productivity is the result of low level of health, education and training of workers, motivation for work and lack of institutional set-up, etc.

Even though, modern technology exists but majority of the productive units and a major part of the output is produced with the help of techniques, which can be described as inferior in terms of productivity. Since, the new techniques are expensive and require skilled manpower for their application, appropriate amount of capital and trained manpower is required. But as developing countries are deficient in physical capital and human capital, they are not able to scrap off the old techniques and install the up-to-date and modern techniques.

However, growth rate of labour productivity increased almost six times in India between 1990-92 and 2008-10 while it was very low or negative in developed countries during the same period.

Prevalence of Large Scale Unemployment and Underemployment

In developed economies, unemployment is cyclical in nature and occurs due to lack of effective demand but in developing economies, widespread unemployment is prevalent due to scarcity of full employment for entire working population. In India, open unemployment is low because poor people cannot afford to remain unemployed. Open unemployment is more for educated persons due to lack of employability.

Before liberalization, unemployment was generally due to deficiency of capital. The Indian economy was not having sufficient capital to expand its industrial base to such an extent that the entire labour force could be absorbed. However, after liberalization there is no lack of capital, so there may be lack of entrepreneurial skill or employable skill among educated youth.

Table 4.6 International Comparison of Vulnerability & Deprivation

Country	*Vulnerable Employment Unpaid family workers and own-account workers in 2007-10*		*Children in Employment*		*Female-headed Households % of Total 2007-10*
	Male as % of male employment	*Female as % of Female employment*	*Male % of male between age 7 to 14*	*Female % of Female between age 7 to 14*	
Russian Federation	06	05	–	–	–
Malaysia	23	20	–	–	–
UK	15	8	–	–	–
Brazil	27	22	6.9	3.5	–
Sri Lanka	38	44	17.0	20.4	–
South Africa	08	12	27.7	29.0	–
India	–	–	4.2	4.2	14
Thailand	50	55	15.1	15.7	30
Pakistan	59	78	–	–	10
Turkey	28	48	2.6 3.3	3.3	–
Bangladesh	–	–	25.7	6.4	13

Source: World Development Indicator, World Bank, 2012 pp 54-56, 62-64, 78-80.

Even though many are employed but the quality of their employment is very bad. Table 4.6 gives a statistic about vulnerable employment, children in employment and female headed households. Capturing this type of employment is very difficult and that is why reported data is low. But field level experience says that incidence of such employment is more than recorded.

Environmental Pollution and Degradation

Growing environmental pollution may be the result of non-sustainable technology or production process, wreckless use of natural resources and existence of poverty. Table 4.7 reveals that though developed countries have controlled up to certain extent the emission of organic water pollutants in last twenty years. But carbon dioxide emissions in total million metric tonnes have increased both in developed and developing countries. Natural resource rent may be used to finance development of such technologies.

Table 4.7 International Comparison on State of Environment

Country	*Carbon Dioxide Emissions Total Million Metric Tonnes*		*Emissions of Organic Water Pollutants thousand kilograms per day*		*Motor Vehicles per 1,000 People 2009*	*Total natural resources rents % of GDP 2010*
	1990	*2008*	*1990*	*2007*		
Russian Federation	2,220.7	1,708.7	1,521.4	1,381.7	271	19.9
USA	4,879.4	5,461.0	2,307.0	1,850.8	802	1.0
UK	570.2	522.9	599.9	521.7	523	1.5
Brazil	208.9	393.2	–	–	209	5.3
Sri Lanka	3.8	11.8	–	266.1	47	0.5
China	2,460.7	7,031.9	–	9,428.9	47	4.0
India	690.6	1,742.7	–	–	18	4.0
Pakistan	68.6	163.2	–	153.7	13	3.9
Bangladesh	15.5	46.5	250.8	303.0	03	3.3

Source: World Development Indicator, World Bank, 2012 pp 170-172, 158-160, 194-196, 204-206.

Business Environment

Globalization and opening up of the economies have enhanced cross boundary business operations. Business houses are expanding their activities throughout the world to achieve cost effectiveness or to expand their markets.

Table 4.8 International Comparison on Business Environment in June 2011

Country	*Starting a business*		*Registering property Time required days*	*Dealing with construction permits Time required to build a warehouse days*	*Getting Electricity Time required days*	*Enforcing Contracts Time required days*	*Protecting Investors Disclosure index 0–10 (least to most disclosure)*	*Resolving Insolvency Time required years*
	Time required days	*Cost % of per capita income*						
Russian Federation	30	2.0	43	423	281	281	6	2.0
USA	6	1.4	12	26	68	300	7	1.5
UK	13	0.7	29	99	109	399	10	1.0
Sri Lanka	35	4.7	83	217	132	1,318	6	1.7
Brazil	119	5.4	39	469	34	731	6	4.0

China	38	3.5	29	311	145	406	10	1.7
India	29	46.8	44	227	67	1,420	7	7.0
Pakistan	21	11.2	50	222	206	976	6	2.8
Bangladesh	19	30.6	245	201	372	1,442	6	4.0

Source: World Development Indicator, World Bank, 2012 pp. 292-294.

Table 4.8 discusses indicators which show countries efficiency in initiating a business activity. India has improved its efficiency in most of the parameters but time taken in contract enforcement is grey area which needs proactive action.

Science and Technology

After liberalization and opening up of the economy, the geographic boundaries of the countries has blurred and the economic boundaries has become insignificant. Market has become very competitive. Companies are relying on improved technology as a survival strategy. In this scenario, developing technology is going to be one of the prerequisite for any country, which wants to develop rapidly. Though, India has large pool of scientific and technical manpower but it is far behind in terms of R&D and innovation, not only from the developed countries but also from China.

Table 4.9 International Comparison on Research and Development (R&D)

Country	*Scientific and Technical Journal Article*		*Expenditure for R&D (as % of GDP)*		*Patent Application Filed*			
					Residents		*Non-Residents*	
	2001	*2009*	*1996-2002**	*2005-09**	*2002*	*2010*	*2002*	*2010*
Switzerland	8107	9,469	2.57	3.00	–	1,622	–	533
USA	200870	208,601	2.60	2.79	198339	241,977	183398	248,249
UK	47660	45,649	1.89	1.87	33671	15,490	251239	6,439
Japan	57420	49,627	3.15	3.45	371,495	290,081	115411	54,517
Germany	43623	45,003	2.50	2.82	80661	12,198	230066	74,339
China	20978	74.019	1.31	1.47	40346	293,066	140910	98,111
India	11076	19,917	0.85	0.76	220	7,262	91704	27,025
Pakistan	282	1,043	0.22	0.46	58	170	0	1,375
Bangladesh	177	260	–	–	–	–	–	–

• Data is for the most recent year available

Source: World Development Indicator, World Bank, 2012 pp 332-334.

Poverty and Malnutrition[13]

Poverty is defined as the situation in which an individual fails to earn sufficient income for his survival. It is, generally, calculated in terms of money. The World

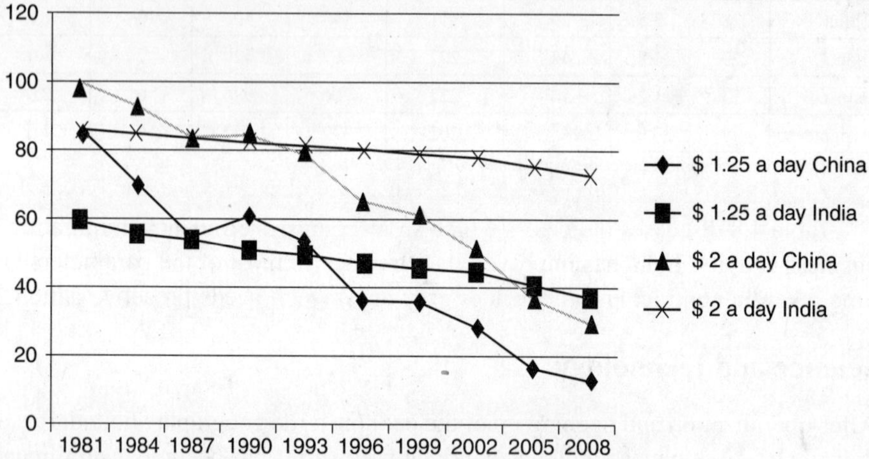

Graph: 4.1 Poverty levels in India and China

Source: World Development Indicator, World Bank, 2012 pp 72.

Bank's estimate of percentage of people staying below $1.25 a day and $2 a day in China and India, gives very interesting trend which has been shown in the graph 4.1 above. In 1981 less percentage of people were below poverty lines [14] of $1.25 and $2 a day in India than China. In both the countries measures were taken which is reflected in downward trend of the curve for both the countries. But the rate of decrease was more in China than India. Both in India and China the proportion of people living below the poverty line is more or less same between 1987 and 1993. After that there is clear sign that poverty dips more in China than India.

At present, existing poverty in India is a combination of natural[15] and artificial[16] poverty. The recent high growth rate of the Indian economy will take care of natural poverty but special care will have to be taken of artificial poverty.

Poverty statistics given in Table 4.10 shows that poverty is decreasing in all the reported countries and urban poverty is less than rural poverty. Malnutrition is reflected from the indicator such as percentage of birth of low weight babies which is quite high in India. The National Food Security Act 2013[17] may be able to solve the problem up to certain extent.

Table 4.10 International Comparison on Poverty and Malnutrition

	Population below National Poverty Line						*Low- weight birth of babies % of births 2005–10**
	Year	*Rural %*	*Urban %*	*Year*	*Rural %*	*Urban %*	
Russian Federation	2005	22.7	8.1	2006	21.2	7.4	06
Peru	2009	60.3	21.1	2010	54.2	19.1	08

Contd...

Contd...

Sri Lanka	2007	15.7	6.7	2010	9.4	5.3	17
China	2004	2.8	–	2005	2.5	–	03
India	2005	41.8	25.7	2010	33.8	20.9	28
Pakistan	2005	28.1	14.9	2006	27.0	13.1	32
Bangladesh	2005	43.8	28.4	2010	35.2	21.3	22

• For the nearest year data is available

Source: World Development Indicator, World Bank, 2012, pp. 66-67, 120-122.

Status of Information and Communication

Advent of information and communication technology (ICT) has revolutionized the means of communication. Average annual growth rate of user is very high. However, number of users of different means of Information and Communication can also be taken as an indicator of economic development. From Table 4.11, it is clear that these sources of information are used more aggressively in the developed countries than in the developing countries.

Table 4.11 International Comparison of Status of Information and Communication

	Daily Newspaper per 1,000 people 2000–05	*Households with television % 2010*	*Computers Users per 100 people 2010*	*Internet Users per 100 people 2010*	*Information and communications technology trade*		
					Goods		*Service*
					Exports % of total goods exports 2010	*Imports % of total goods imports 2010*	*Exports % of total services exports 2010*
Switzerland	420	–	–	82.2	1.6	5.9	–
USA	193	–	–	74.2	10.5	14.2	4.6
UK	290	–	86.7	84.7	5.9	9.3	8.8
Sri Lanka	26	–	–	12.0	0.5	2.9	14.1
Peru	–	77	–	34.3	0.1	7.4	3.1
China	74	–	–	34.4	29.1	20.4	6.1
India	71	60	–	7.5	2.0	6.6	47.0
Pakistan	50	68	–	16.8	0.2	3.3	6.6
Bangladesh	–	36	–	3.7	–	–	13.0

Source: World Development Indicator, World Bank, 2012 pp 328-330

India has achieved competency in software development which makes a lion's share in its total service export.

Infrastructure

Infrastructure is the prerequisite for the development of an economy. It provides support to the factors of production, which ultimately contributes to the development of an economy. Long strides have been taken after Independence. However, from the comparison given in Table 4.12, it is clear that India has to go a long way. Public-private partnership is becoming appropriate mode for construction and operation of infrastructure services such as highways and airports. However, not much investment is coming from the private sector as return from investment is quite slow. Fiscal measures may also be taken for attracting private initiatives. Some other measures such as infrastructure surcharge can be imposed for financing infrastructural projects. Bharat Nirman Programme, a new programme for rural infrastructure in the 11th five year plan of India, has been launched by the goverment of India.

Table 4.12 International Comparison of Infrastructure

Country	*Electric power Comsumption per capita kWh 2009*	*Total road network km 2000-09*	*Rail lines total route km 2000-10**	*Port container traffic thousand TEU 2010*	*Air carrier Passeengers carried thousands 2010*	*Telephones Subscriptions per 100 people*	
						Fixed Telephone 2010	*Mobile Cellular 2010*
Switzerland	8,021	71,371	3,543	99	21,477	56	122
USA	12,914	6,545,839	228,513	42,190	707,426	49	90
UK	5,692	419,665	31,471	7,389	123,972	54	130
Peru	1,136	126,500	2,020	1,534	6,130	11	100
Sri Lanka	408	97,286	1,463	4,080	2,800	17	83
China	2,631	3,860,823	66,239	129,611	267,691	22	64
India	571	4,109,592	63,974	9,753	64,144	3	61
Pakistan	449	258,350	7,791	2,149	6,012	2	57
Bangladesh	252	239,226	2,835	1,356	2,177	1	46

* Data are for the latest year available in the period shown

Source: World Development Indicator, World Bank, 2012 pp. 320-322, 324-326

Five-Year Plans of India

India opted for planned development through five-year plans after independence. Planning Commission was set up in 1950 to develop, execute and monitor five-year plans. With the Prime Minister as the ex-officio Chairman, the Commission has a nominated Deputy Chairman who is of the rank of cabinet minister.

As India has accepted economic philosophy of socialist pattern of society, main objective of five-year plans are to achieve self-sufficiency and self-reliance in agriculture, industry and services with equity and social justice.

First Five-Year Plan (1951-1956)

In 1951, India was facing three main problems—influx of refugees, severe shortage of food items and very high rate of inflation. So, the main objective of the first-five year plan was rehabilitation, rapid agricultural growth and control of price rise. Consequently, agriculture was accepted as a thrust area in the first plan. Out of its total budget of Rs. 206.8 billion, almost half of it was allocated to agriculture-related activities, i.e., irrigation and energy (27.2 per cent), agriculture and community development (17.4 per cent), and land rehabilitation (4.1 per cent). Many irrigation projects were initiated during this period, including Bhakra Dam, Hirakud Dam, and Mettur Dam. Transport and communications were allocated 24 per cent, social services were allocated 16.64 per cent and 2.5 per cent were kept for others.

From the very beginning importance of industrialization in economic development was realized by the policy planners. The first industrial policy resolution was announced by Government of India in 1948. It was the belief of the government that the main motive of the private sector was profit earning. So, they may not be able to provide quality products at reasonable prices and thus, this task was entrusted to public sector. However, in the First Five-Year Plan (1951–1956), no big effort was contemplated for industrialization but the emphasis was to build basic services like power so that the process of industrialization is facilitated. Industry was allocated 8.4 per cent of the total plan outlay with an emphasis on complete public sector industrial projects such as locomotive (Chittranjan), machine tools (Bangalore), rail coaches (Perumbur) and fertilizer (Sindri). It also laid ambitious foundation for establishment of basic industries such as steel, machine and chemicals. Memorandum of Understanding (MoU) were signed to start three steel plants in public sector; however, these plants did not come into existence until the middle of the next five-year plan. Economy responded well to the stimulus of this first plan—introduction of a new dynamic element in a long static situation. Investment in the economy rose from Rs. 45,000 million in 1950–1951 to Rs. 67,500 million in 1955–1956. Incremental Capital Output Ratio (ICOR)during the plan was 3.27. The actual GDP growth rate was 3.6 per cent during the same period. Lower increase of per capita income as compared to national income was due to rapid population growth.

The Indian government addressed children's health and hence, reduction in infant mortality, which further contributed to population growth. The Indian Institute of Technology (IIT) at Khargpur was, started as Technical Institute of National Importance. University Grants Commission was set-up to take care of funding and to take measures to strengthen the higher education in the country.

Second Five-Year Plan (1956–1961)

The Second Five-Year Plan was initiated in an environment of optimism. Target fixed for agricultural growth during the first plan was achieved. Price level registered a fall during the period. Consequently, it was felt that industry needs to be given emphasis to give desired push to the economy. The plan followed the Mahalanobis[18] model. It attempted the optimal allocation of investment between productive sectors in order to maximize long run economic growth. The plan mainly focused on heavy industries. Domestic production of industrial products in the public sector was encouraged.

At the same time, Industrial Policy Resolution 1956 was announced, which classified industries into three groups. Group A consisted of all those industrial products which are crucial for the development of the economy. Only public sector was supposed to operate in Group A. In Group B, less important industries were kept. In this group, both private and public sector were allowed to operate to give each other a healthy competition. In the Group C, least important industries were kept. Only private sector was supposed to operate in this group. An outlay of Rs. 938 crore was kept for the industrial sector. Most significant achievement of the plan was setting up of three steel plants of one million tonnes ingot capacity each in the public sector at Bhilai, Rourkela and Durgapur. There was also rapid expansion of machine building industries for use in agriculture and transport. Good progress was also recorded in modernization and reorienting important industries such as jute, cotton and textile. Rate of investment increased by 8% to 11%. Coal production was increased. More railway lines were added in the north-east.

The Atomic Energy Commission was formed in 1957 with Homi J. Bhabha as its first chairman. The Tata Institute of Fundamental Research was established as a research institute. In 1957, a talent search and scholarship programme was started to find talented young students to train to work in the nuclear power sector.

Table 4.13 Statistics on Five-Year Plans in India

Five-Year Plan	*Aggregate GDP Growth rate*	*Total Outlay (in Rs. Crore) (at 2000-2001 prices)*	*Incremental Capital Output[19] Ratio (in %)*	*Annual Industrial Growth Rate (in %)*
First	3.60	1960	3.27	5.7
Second	4.21	4600	4.28	7.2
Third	2.72	8580	5.29	9.2
Fourth	2.05	15900	5.28	4.5
Fifth	4.83	39430	6.21	5.3
Sixth	4.54	109290	4.23	3.5
Seventh	6.02	218730	3.82	8.5

Contd...

Contd...

Eighth (1992–1996)	6.68	434100	4.24	8.0
Ninth	5.35	–	–	4.3
Tenth	6.78	–	3.73	9.4
Eleventh	7.9	Rs. 3644718*	4.37	–
Twelfth (target)	8.0	–	4.04	9.6

Source: Plan Documents, Planning Commission (Government of India) Economic Survey, Downloaded on 26/6/2014
* at 2006-07 prices

Main difficulties encountered during the second plan were rise in prices and production cost, foreign exchange crisis. To overcome such situation, the Indian currency was devalued during next plan and the value of money went down by 20%.

Third Five-Year Plan (1961–1966)

Results of the Second Five-Year Plan was quite encouraging. The Indian planners felt that Indian economy has entered the 'take-off stage' and the first two plans have generated an institutional structure, which is required for rapid economic development. Second Five-Year Plan had also shown that the agricultural growth rate was the main limiting factor in India's economic development.

The third plan, accordingly, gave top priority to agriculture and construction of dams but development of basic industries, i.e., fuel, power, steel, machines and chemicals, were also taken care of. It was planned that machine building capacity from country's own resources, in particular, will be established within 10 years, which will further pave the way of industrialization. Efforts were made to optimally utilize country's manpower resources and ensuring substantial expansion in employment opportunities. Importance was given to make the economy self sustaining in capital goods industries such as steel and machine building so that, the quantum of external assistance needed for production could be reduced. It was during this period that a fairly sound base for future industrial growth was laid through the completion of projects of the Heavy Engineering Corporation to manufacture machinery and equipment for steel plants and Bharat Heavy Electicals for power generation and transmission equipment. Many primary schools were started in rural areas. States were made responsible for secondary and higher education. State secondary education boards came into existence. State electricity boards were formed. State road transport corporations were formed and local road building became a state responsibility. In an effort to bring democracy, panchayat elections were started and the states were given more development responsibilities. But the third plan could not fulfil all objectives as India experienced China's aggression in 1962, which further weakened the economy and shifted the focus towards defence measures.

National income increased at the rate of 2.5% in the first year, 1.6% in the second year, 3% in the third year and 7.6% in the fourth year, It declined to 4.2% in the fifth year due to unprecedented draught conditions and Indo-Pak war. The agriculture output in the 1964–1965 was an all-time high as 89 million tonnes, but dropped to 72 million in 1965–1966. Employment was provided to approximately 13 million persons but left a backlog of 10 million unemployed.

Annual Plans

The original draft outline of the fourth plan was prepared in 1966 under the stewardship of Ashok Mehta but it had to be abandoned for the three consecutive years because of the pressure exerted on the economy due to drought, devaluation of the rupee and the inflationary recession. It had to be delayed by three years and in the meantime, three annual plans (1966–1967, 1967–1968, 1968–1969) were formulated within the framework of the draft outline of the fourth plan. Highlights of these three years are as follows:

(i) Most significant achievement of the period was implementation of Green Revolution.

(ii) Due to acute shortage of raw materials, equipment and accessories, many industrial establishments were not able to perform to their full capacities.

(iii) Due to high prices, cost of living and wide spread tax evasion, financial position of the country was in a bad shape.

(iv) In spite of devaluation of the currency and measures adopted for promoting exports and restricting imports, the balance of payment position remained bad.

Fourth Five-Year Plan (1969–1974)

This period was very significant from economic and political points of view as the Fourth Five-Year Plan was implemented after a gap of three years. Some of the other majer decisions were nationalization of 19 major Indian banks and implementation of Monopolies and Restrictive Trade Practices (MRTP)[20] act. From the political point of view, privy purse of erstwhile princely states were stopped by the Government of India and the Vietnam War was fought in South East Asia. In addition, the situation in East Pakistan (now Bangladesh) became bad to worse because of Indo-Pak War. In 1971, more than 10 million East Pakistani refugees fled to India during the Yahya Khan regime who was the military dictator of Pakistan. India sent 30,000 troops to surround East Pakistan and liberated it in 15 days. The new nation, Bangladesh, was declared in December 1971. Pakistan's 93,000 troops surrendered to the Indian Army. These prisoners of war were later released after the Simla Agreement (1972).

Main objective of the Fourth Five-Year Plan was to promote rapid rate of growth with stability and self-reliance. The fourth plan aimed at an average 5.5 per cent rate of growth in the national income. Initiatives were taken for import substitutions and export promotions. Three-fourths of the total investment was made in the core sector, viz., iron and steel, non-ferrous metals, petroleum and petrochemicals, coal and iron ore. Production of fertilizers, insecticides, tractors, diesel engines and agricultural implements were given top priority to maximize agricultural production to increase income of the rural people. Maximum attention was given for developing human resources. Efforts were also made to provide greater employment opportunities.

The first two years of the fourth plan were quite promising with record food-grain production and equally rising industrial production. But the next three years of the plan proved to be a great disappointment with successive failure of monsoon, decline in foodgrain production coupled with failure on industrial front due to power breakdown and load shedding, transport bottlenecks, industrial unrest, etc. The performance in industry was far short of even the modest target set out. On an average, the growth rate in industry was around 4.5%, which was much below the targeted growth rate of 8% envisaged in the plan. The inflation rate increased to an alarming level.

Fifth Five-Year Plan (1974–1978)

In the beginning, it was perceived that high rate of GDP growth will automatically eradicate poverty. However, gradually it was realized that benefits of growth rate was not reaching poor people. So, direct attack on poverty was envisaged in the Fifth Five-Year Plan. The overall guiding principles were:

(i) Maximum use of available capacity.

(ii) Creation of additional capacity in the core sector on which accelerated future growth depends.

(iii) Special programme was designed for poor and deprived people. As inequality and underdevelopment are the main causes of poverty; so, creation of productive employment opportunity were planned to eradicate productivity. Aim of employment policy was expansion of both wage employment and self-employment. Creation of additional employment in the non-agricultural sector was also envisaged. Enhancing productivity of labour was also given priority.

(iv) National Programme for Minimum Needs was initiated, which covered elementary education, drinking water, medical care in rural areas, nutrition, home sites for the landless labour, rural electrification and slum improvements.

During the fifth five-year plan, it was targeted to achieve higher production of cotton and oilseeds, fertilizers, petroleum products, steel, non-ferrous metals, crude oil, basic chemicals, engineering ancillaries, etc. The total public sector outlay was fixed at Rs. 13,528 crore, out of which 62% was central sector outlay. The bulk of investment was made for building industrial capacity. However, funds earmarked for the industrial development had to be used for defence purpose. India performed the Smiling Buddha underground nuclear test in 1974. The fifth plan took many bold steps such as removing the restriction on the private sector, monopolistic undertakings and foreign concerns seeking investment in India. Despite all these incentives, the average annual industrial growth was 5.3% during 1974–1975 to 1977–1978, which was much lower than the target 8%. Main difficulties encountered during Fifth Five-Year Plan were sharp increase in the prices of foodgrains, fertilizers and oil, which upset all cost calculation. The sluggishness of demand, shortage of basic inputs, labour unrest and low capacity utilization were mainly responsible for poor performance of industrial sector.

For the first time in the history of independent India, emergency was declared, which became the main cause of defeat of the Indian National Congress at centre. In 1978, the then elected Morarji Desai government terminated the plan.

Sixth Five-Year Plan (1980–1985)

Called the Janata government plan, the Sixth Five Year Plan (1978–1983) was based on the concept of rolling plan in which a perspective plan is made for 10 years or more. This overall period is bifurcated in smaller periods, may be for one, four or five years with fixed objective. After completion of small period, stock of the performance is taken into consideration and appropriate corrective measures are taken to fulfil the objective of perspective plan. Such planning process is practised in Poland. However, when Indian National Congress led by Smt. Indira Gandhi again came to power in 1980, it rejected the model of growth which was in operation and brought back Nehruvian Model of growth in the Sixth Five-Year Plan (1980–1985) which targetted at the problem of poverty in an expanding economy. In a review of the industrial development over the 30 years of planning, the sixth plan noted that though industrial production increased by about five times during this period, the structure of industrial development was not sufficiently guided by cost considerations. Thus, the industries produced to its sub-optimal capacities, leading to a high cost industrial structure. The sixth plan also noticed that the public sector had failed to generate enough resources and that the problem of regional disparities in industrial development was as serious as ever. In fact, new industries tended to gravitate towards the existing centres and the backward areas remained stagnant and almost untouched from the growth process.

It emphasized optimum utilization of existing capacities and improvement of productivity, enhancement of manufacturing capacity. Special attention was given to the capital goods and electronic industries. Not only that, to meet foreign exchange requirement, export of engineering goods and industrial products was also emphasized. To enhance the quality of product, a judicious blend of permitting import of contemporary technology and promoting indigenous know-how through domestic research and development was advocated. The industrial growth rate during the sixth plan achieved was only 3.5 per cent. This was lower than the trend growth rate of six per cent witnessed in the earlier three decades. Promoting policies for controlling the growth of population through voluntary acceptance of the small family norms was propagated.

Seventh Five-Year Plan (1985–1989)

When Rajiv Gandhi became prime minister, he aimed at rapid industrial development, especially in the area of information technology. It was realized that progress made so far was slow, because of the lower productivity of labour. To survive in the competitive international market, the seventh plan (1985–1990) stressed upon improving productivity along with social justice. To improve the productivity and quality of the product, the upgradation of technology was stressed upon, so that the needs of the large domestic market can be met along with the creation of external market for the domestic products. The main objectives of the seventh plan were:

(i) Rapid removal of infrastructural constraints by placing greater emphasis on efficient use of existing resources.

(ii) Encouragement to modernization and technological upgradation of industries.

(iii) Specific targets of productivity for major industries.

(iv) Export promotion will be made an integral part of production in the domestic market.

(v) Encouragement of 'sunrise industries' such as telecommunications, computers, microelectronics and ceramic composites.

(vi) Installation of pollution control system by large and medium industries.

During the seventh plan, annual growth rate of the industrial sector including mining, manufacturing and electricity generation was 8.5 per cent, which was much higher than the growth rate achieved during the previous plan. However, balance of payment position was very bad. There was political instability during this period; the government could not take care of the borrowing to ease the balance of payment position.

The construction of national highways was introduced for the first time and many roads were widened to accommodate the increasing traffic. Tourism in India also expanded. After the devaluation of the rupee, visiting India became cheaper for foreigners. Family planning programmes were also expanded to control population growth. However, in contrast to China's one child policy, Indian policy was not aggressively and uniformly implemented. More prosperous areas of India adopted family planning more rapidly than less prosperous areas, which continued to have a high birth rate.

Period between 1989 and 1992

During Mr. Rajiv Gandhi's tenure as prime minister, large amount of foreign reserve was spent to import technology with the aim of making Indian industries competitive. However, Indian industries could not bring back foreign reserve by increasing exports which led to acute foreign reserve crisis. The 1989–1991 was a time of political instability in India and hence, no five-year plan was implemented. Between 1990 and 1992, there were only Annual Plans. In 1991, India left with reserves of only about US $1 billion, approached International Monetary Fund (IMF)[21] for funds to reform the economy. The IMF agreed to give loan but under the condition of liberalizing the Indian economy. P.V. Narasimha Rao, who was the 12th Prime Minister of India and the Head of Congress Party, led one of the most important administrative reform in India's modern history. At that time Dr. Manmohan Singh (a noted economist and later, Prime Minister of India), the then Finance Minister of India and popularly known as the Father of the Indian Economic Reforms, launched India's free market reforms that brought the nearly bankrupt nation back from the edge. It was the beginning of liberalization, privatization and globalization in India.

Eighth Five-Year Plan (1992–1997)

This was the first five-year plan, which was revised four times from 1987 to 1992 because of political changes. Under this plan, Indian economy opened up gradually to fund the burgeoning deficit and foreign debt. Main objectives of the eighth plan were:

(i) Growth and diversification of agriculture to achieve self-sufficiency.

(ii) Generation of adequate employment to achieve higher growth.

(iii) Stregthening of infrastructure (energy, roads, irrigation, etc.) in order to support the growth process on a sustainable basis.

(iv) Control in population growth through people's cooperation.

(v) Universalization of elementary education and complete eradication of illiteracy.

(vi) Provision of safe drinking water and health facility.

Meanwhile, India became founder member of the World Trade Organization (WTO)[22] on 1st January, 1995. Role of government changed in the new economic environment. Now the government was supposed to play as facilitator rather than active participant in the economic activity. Efforts for modernization of industries were major highlights of the eighth plan to enhance its efficiency and competitiveness. Overall annual growth rate was envisaged as 6.68%. Greater involvement of private sector was experienced in more areas and public sector moved out from certain non-essential areas. Thus, under the eighth plan, the principle of market economy was accepted as the main operative principle except for those commodities and services which were meant for protecting the interests of the weaker sections of the society. Investment in public sector and private sector were made to the tune of Rs. 3,61,000 and Rs. 4,37,000 respectively.

The eighth plan critically examined the role of public sector. Though public sector units (PSUs), in general, significantly contributed to the development of the Indian economy but, many PSUs made substantial losses and became continuous drain on the exchequer. These PSUs were closed after giving suitable social safety to their employees. Industries grew at a rate of 8% per annum during the eighth plan. At the end of the eighth plan, foreign exchange reserves were to the tune of US $20.48 billion.

Ninth Five-Year Plan (1997–2002)

The ninth plan observed that government was overactive in industry and was underactive in the area of social development, which reflected slow pace in the implementation of critical social indicators. Thus, special emphasis was given on social indicators in this plan. Main objectives of the ninth plan were as follows:

(i) Accelerating the growth rate of the economy with stable prices

(ii) Generation of adequate productive employment and eradication of poverty

(iii) Ensuring basic minimum security to all, particularly to the vulnerable section of the society

(iv) Measures to control population growth rate

(v) Ensuring environmental sustainability of the economic development, viz., strengthening efforts to build self-reliance

(vii) Promoting and developing people's participatory institutions like Panchayati Raj institutions, cooperatives and self-help groups

(viii) Empowerment of women and socially disadvantaged group as an agent of socio-economic change and development

The public sector outlay for the Ninth Five-Year Plan was placed at Rs. 8,59,200 crore at 1996–1997 prices. It is an increase of 33% over the approved eighth plan outlay. However, the private sector was assigned more crucial role. The ninth plan noted high underemployment among the labour force. Not only that even the employment, which is being generated, are in the informal sector. So, policies for strengthening informal sector should be initiated. The actual growth rate was just 5.35 per cent, more than a percentage point lower than the target GDP growth of 6.5 per cent. During the Ninth Five-Year Plan (1997–2002), the growth rate for 1997–1998, 1998–1999, 1999–2000, 2000–2001 and 2001–2002 were 6.7%, 4.1%, 6.6%, 5.7% and slumped down to 2.7% respectively due to world recession. Foreign Exchange Reserve with the country was of the tune of US $39.26 billion.

Tenth Five-Year Plan (2002–2007)

The main objectives of the Tenth Five-Year Plan were as follows:

(i) Providing gainful and high-quality employment at least to the addition to the labour force.

(ii) Reduction of poverty ratio to five per cent by 2007

(iii) All children in school by 2003; all children should complete five years of schooling by 2007

(iv) Reduction in gender gaps in literacy and wage rates by at least 50% by 2007

(v) Increase in literacy rates to 75 per cent by 2007

(vi) Increase in forest and tree cover to 25 per cent by 2007 and 33 per cent by 2012

(vii) Access to potable drinking water to all villages

(viii) Cleaning of all major polluted rivers by 2007 and other notified stretches by 2012

The annual growth rate experiencing continuous increase ended with 8% by 2006 bringing the overall GDP growth rate during tenth plan to 6.78%. Total investment of more than Rs. 1.2 million crore at 2001–2002 prices was made. At the end of the Tenth Five-Year Plan, Foreign Exchange Reserves had reached an staggering height of US $121.69 billion.

Eleventh Five-Year Plan (2007–2012)

In "Towards Faster and More Inclusive Growth: An Approach to the 11th Five-Year Plan", the Planning Commission stressed on achieving faster and more inclusive growth. Following are important indicators showing the extent to which the eleventh plan succeeded in fulfilling the objective of inclusive growth:

- GDP growth in the eleventh plan 2007–08 to 2011–12 was 7.9 per cent compared with 6.78 per cent in the tenth plan (2002–03 to 2006–07) and only 5.35 per cent in the ninth plan (1997–98 to 2001–02). The growth rate of 7.9 per cent in the eleventh plan period is one of the highest of any country in that period which saw two global crises.
- Agricultural GDP growth accelerated in the eleventh plan, to an average rate of 3.3 per cent, compared with 2.4 per cent in the tenth plan, and 2.5 per cent in the ninth plan.
- The percentage of the population below the poverty line declined at the rate of 1.5 percentage points per year in the period 2004–05 to 2009–10, that was twice the rate at which it declined in the previous period 1993–94 to 2004–05.
- The rate of growth of real consumption per capita in rural areas in the period 2004–05 to 2011–12 was 3.4 per cent per year which was four times the rate in the previous 1993–94 to 2004–05.
- The rate of unemployment declined from 8.2 per cent in 2004–05 to 6.6 per cent in 2009–10 reversing the trend observed in the earlier period when it had actually increased from 6.1 per cent in 1993–94 to 8.2 per cent in 2004–05.
- Rural real wages increased 6.8 per cent per year in the eleventh plan (2007–08 to 2011–12) compared to an average 1.1 per cent per year in the previous decade, led largely by the government's rural policies and initiatives.
- Net enrolment rate at the primary level rose to a near universal 98.3 per cent in 2009–10. Dropout rate (classes I–VIII) also showed improvements, falling by 1.7 percentage point per year between 2003–04 and 2009–10, which was twice the 0.8 percentage point fall between 1998–99 and 2003–04.

Twelfth Five-Year Plan (2012–2017)

With the objective of "Faster, More Inclusive and Sustainable Growth", the 12th Five-Year Plan (2012-17) has to reverse the observed deceleration in growth by reviving investment as quickly as possible. This calls for urgent action to tackle implementation constraints in infrastructure which are holding up large projects, combined with action to deal with tax related issues which have created uncertainty in the investment climate. From a longer term perspective, the plan must put in the policies that can leverage strength of the economy to achieve average growth rate of 8 per cent during the Twelfth Five-Year Plan (2012-17), generate 50 million new jobs and increase investments in infrastructure sector.

The government intends to reduce poverty by 10 per cent during the Twetfth Five-Year plan. Moving away from previous practice of presenting single growth projection, the Planning Commission has come out with three different economic scenarios for the Twelfth Five-Year Plan.

LIBERALIZATION, PRIVATIZATION AND GLOBALIZATION (LPG)

Liberalization, privatization and globalization are most frequently used terminology in the present-day economic scenario. They can be better understood only after discussing economic philosophy and economic environment in independent India. Keeping the spirit of socialist pattern of society enshrined in our constitution, the government was supposed to play a key role in the economy. In all those areas, which were considered crucial for development of the country, the government sector was given the responsibility to provide quality products at reasonable prices.

Firstly, private producers were only allowed to venture in the areas, which were not so important for the development of the nation or products and services which, in general, were not used by the common man. Some of the areas of production were reserved for small-scale sector only, so that small producers will not have to face the competition of the large producers. To protect the domestic producers from the international competition, many tariff, and non-tariff restrictions were imposed on imports. However, performance of public sector was not upto the desired level. Quantity as well as quality of the products in this sector was not of international standard, and thus, could not fetch enough foreign reserves. At the same time, there are some compulsory imports like import of petrol.

Secondly, some of the technologies which were not appropriate for India such as for enhancing productivity, in place of enhancing efficiency of coal-driven engine which is locally available in abundance, diesel-driven engines were introduced. One time import was made of the engines and then continuously, precious foreign reserve is being spent to import diesel.

Thirdly, we generally export primary goods and import finished goods. All these were having a toll on our balance of payment position. India was continuously having adverse balance of payment position. Realising it, the Government of India during the regime of Mr. Rajiv Gandhi, allowed import of technology which could be a catalyst in improving quality of the product and ultimately, the product will be able to garner international demand. However, finished products were largely sold in the national market and not in the international market. Later half of the eighties was also politically not smooth and so, condition of adverse position of balance of payment was also not taken care of well. Consequently, in 1991 India was left with very small stock of foreign reserve and had to approach International Monetary Fund (IMF). IMF agreed to help but on the terms and conditions of accepting philosophy of privatization, liberalization and globalization.

Many sectors, earlier reserved for public sector, were opened up for the private sector. This is called privatization. Liberalization means reducing government control and restrictions in the economic activities and encouraging privatization. According to Industrial Policy, 1991, only 18 industries were kept for public sector. Rest were opened up for private sector also. Within a firm, the producers are free to increase their production and decide whatever they want to produce. The investment limit of the industries was also raised, i.e., the investment limit of the small-scale sector was increased to three crores. The industrialists are free to buy foreign exchange from the open market and make necessary imports. Initially, the government emphasized to disinvestment[23] their share in loss making PSUs, but gradually they have considered some profit making PSUs also which has been severely criticized in Parliament as well as in the public.

Objectives of Liberalization

(i) To remove control and restrictions imposed by government in the process of economic development.

(ii) To increase the competitiveness among Indian industries in order to enter the international market.

(iii) To widen the scope of private sector.

(iv) To ensure the development of agricultural sector.

(v) To stop inefficiency and misuse of resources.

(vi) To develop better money and capital markets.

(vii) To solve the basic problems of the economy.

Globalization

Globalization means reduction of trade barriers so as to permit free flow of capital as well as goods across the world and creating an environment, which allows free flow of technology. Globalization has integrated the Indian economy to the world economy. Because of this process, we have become economically independent at the global or international level.

Advantages of LPG

(i) Production process is being carried out in many countries on the basis of comperative cost adventage. Many multinational companies are establishing their production units in India to exploit India's talented knowledge workers at reasonable prices.

(ii) It helps in equalization of prices throughout the market.

Disadvantages of LPG

(i) Small and micro enterprises find it difficult to face the competition.

(ii) As capital has become mobile, labour is losing its say in the production process

Effect of LPG on the Indian Economy

Result of LPG during past two decades in India is mixed. Share of private sector has increased manifold and public-private partnership has become most acceptable norm to carry out developmental activities. India's trade share has increased, indeed it nearly tripled over this entire period, but still remains well below 2 per cent, and the average for the three years 2009 to 2011 was less than 1.5 per cent which was just 0.53 per cent in 1990-91. One of the significant achievement is the major export in the field of software. Foreign investment in Indian capital market grew fourfold and has become Rs. 1.63 lakh crore in 2012, with the financial services and software sectors cornering bigger pie. However, despite sound fundamentals and no direct exposure to the subprime assets, India could not remain unaffected by global financial crisis due to globalization. However, the inpact was comparatively mild because of tight fiscal and monetary policy. Under the influence of global crisis, employment scenario also got changed. About half a million workers lost their jobs during October-December, 2008. The most affected sectors were gems & jewelleery, transport and automobiles. The major impact of the slowdown was noticed in the export oriented units.

Notes

1. Sustainable rate of economic development: The country is able to maintain economic development without harming to the environment.
2. Inclusive development: Development which encompasses all sections of society and not a particular segment of society.
3. World Bank classification of economies: For operation and analytical purposes the World Bank's main criterion for classifying economies is GNI per capita. Each economy is classified as low income, middle income (subdivided into lower middle and upper middle), or high income. Low income economies are those whose GNI per capita is less than $825, middle income economies are those whose GNI per capita is more than $825 but less than $10,066. High income economies are those whose GNI per capita is $10,066 or more. The 12 participating member countries of the European Monetary Union (EMU) are presented as a subgroup under high income economies.

4. Demographic transition

   First stage : High birth rate and high death rate

   Second stage : High birth rate and low death rate

   Third stage : Low birth rate and low death rate
5. As fertility rates fall during the transition, it changes the age distribution in favour of young population. If countries act wisely before and during the transition, a special window opens up for faster economic growth and human development.
6. One of the important features is low income and trade. Another feature is its high dependence on agriculture. As it develops, its dependence on agriculture in terms of contribution in GDP and employment decreases.
7. Green revolution: A technological package introduced during sixties; it was a combination of high yielding varieties of seeds, chemical fertilizers and extensive use of water. In the short run farmers reaped huge benefit. However, it was region specific as Punjab, Haryana, Maharashtra, etc., and crop specific as wheat, maize, etc.
8. Yellow revolution: Related to oilseed production.
9. White revolution: Related to milk production.
10. Blue revolution: Related to fish production.
11. Biodiesel plants: Oil can be extracted from seeds of these plants.
12. Dependency burden (DB): The proportion of the total population aged 0 to 15 and 65+, is considered to be economically unproductive and therefore, considered dependent population. So, DB = (population < 15 yr + Population > 65)/ Total population.
13. Malnutrition: A state of ill health resulting from an inadequate or improper diet, usually measured in terms of average daily protein consumption.
14. Poverty line has been defined where a person is not able to get 2400 calories in rural area and 2100 calories in urban area.
15. Natural poverty occurs in a situation of underdevelopment.
16. Artificial poverty is, in most cases, system generated.
17. The National Food Security Act is a bill passed in 2013 by the Indian Parliament which aims to provide subsidized food grains to poor and deprived section of society.
18. An economic development model developed by the Indian statistician Prasanta Chandra Mahalanobis in 1953. He also founded Indian Statistical Institute at Kolkata.
19. On the basis of a simple Harrod-Domar framework, the Incremental Caital-Output Ratio (ICOR) is calculated as dividing the investment ratio by the growth rate of GDP

ICOR = i/g

where, $i = Inv/\text{GDP}$

and g = Growth rate of GDP/sectoral value added.

In other words, A metric that assesses the marginal amount of investment capital necessary for an entity to generate the next unit of production. Overall, a higher Incremental Caital-Output Ratio (ICOR) value is not preferred because it indicates that the entity's production is inefficient. The measure is used predominantly indetermining a country's level of production efficiency.

$$\text{ICOR} = \frac{\text{Annual investment}}{\text{Annual increase in GDP}}$$

20. MRTP Act: In order to curb the monopolistic behaviour of large business houses, the Government of India, in 1969, adopted MRTP Act and set up MRTP Commission in 1970.
21. See IMF in the chapter 5 "International Economics".
22. See WTO in the chapter 5 "International Economics".
23. Disinvestment: In the present context in India, the government is selling its share in PSUs to private parties.

EXERCISES

A. Objective

1. Fill in the blanks:

(i) India is passing through the _______ stage of demographic transition.

(ii) Engineers Day is celebrated on _______ which is the birthday of _______.

(iii) Green Revolution is function of _______, _______ and _______.

(iv) Health and education are _______ factors.

(v) Population Density = _______/_______.

(vi) Labour productivity = _______/_______.

(vii) Capital productivity = _______/_______.

(viii) _______ Five Year Plan is in progress in India.

Ans. (i) second;

(ii) 15th September, Bharat Ratna Mokshagundam Visvesvaraiah

(iii) High Yielding Varieties of Seeds, Chemical Fertilizer and Water;

(iv) basic;

(v) Geographical area, total population;

(vi) Total production during given time, total number of labour employed during that time;

(vii) Total production during given time, total amount of capital employed during that time period;

(viii) 12th

2. Calculate the following on the basis of economic statistics for the two countries given below (1 mark each).

Indicators	*Country X*	*Country Y*
Geographical area in km^2	1,72,00,000	3,87,26,300
Population (million)	83,40,000	98,87,000
Population employed in industry (million)	12,10,000	5,08,50,000
Total capital employed in industry (Rs)	2,00,000	3,87,00,000
Total industrial output (Rs)	25,00,00,000	5,25,00,00,000

(i) Population density in county _______ is more than country _______.

(ii) Industrial labour productivity in country _______ is less then country _______.

(iii) Capital productivity in industry is more in country _______ than country _______.

Ans (i) (population density = Population per km^2) country Y, country X,

(ii) country Y, country X,

(iii) country X, country Y,

B. Subjective

(For two marks each)

1. What is green revolution?
2. Discuss second phase of demographic transition?
3. What do you mean by liberalization, privatization and globalization?

C. Long answer questions

(7 marks)

1. Dicuss salient features of the Indian economy.
2. How Twelfth Five-Year Plan of India is different from the previous plans?
3. Dicuss impact of liberalization, privatization and globalization on the Indian economy.

References and Suggested Readings

1. http://www.investopedia.com/terms/i/icor.asp#axzz2NJtr FgtW dated 12/3/2013.
2. http://planningcommission.gov.in/aboutus/committee/wrkgrp12/wg_invest 1807.pdf dated 12/3/2013.
3. Plan Documents, Planning Commission, Government of India.
4. Press Information Bureau of the Government of India, http://pib.nic.in/newsite/ docpage2.aspx?docid=181aaa downloaded on 10/3/2013.
5. Press Trust of India (2013), "FIIs invested Rs 1.63 lakh cr in 2012", http://www. financialexpress.com/news/-fiis-invested-rs-1.63-lakh-cr-in-2012-/1080175 downloaded on 14/3/2013.
6. Singh, Seema (2012), "Achieving Second Green Revolution through Nano-technology in India", Agricultural Situation in India, LXVIII(10), pp. 545-553.
7. _______ (2005), "MNCs Effect on Employment of Engineers" Indian Journal of Technical Education 28(2) pp. 38-44.
8. Singh Seema and Anil Kumar (2003), "Information Technology: An Effective Tool for Managing Sustainable Agriculture" Agricultural Situation in India, Vol LIX No. 11 pp. 717-721.
9. The World Bank (2012). "World Development Indicators." Development Data Centre, Washington, D.C., USA.
10. C.T. Kurien, "Global Capitalism and the Indian Economy": Tracts for the times. Orient Longman, Hyderabad.

5

International Economics

Purpose of this chapter is to acquaint the reader with:

- Meaning of and Gain from International Trade
- Theories of International Trade
- Terms of Trade, Free Trade vs. Protection, Balance of Payment
- Dumping, Devaluation, Rate of Exchange
- International Organizations, e.g., IMF, World Bank and WTO

Almost all countries of the world exchange goods and services with each other through international trade to optimize their return as a producer as well as a consumer. If every region and every nation can produce every commodity equally cheap, there will be no advantage in exchange. Exchange of goods and services is beneficial only due to difference in efficiency in the production.

INTERNATIONAL TRADE

International trade takes place due to difference in efficiency which arises due to the following reasons:

(i) Climatic and geographical conditions differ widely between regions and nations, which result into difference in efficiency in the production of different goods and services.

(ii) Human capabilities are different in different countries; while some races are physically sturdy, others are intellectually alert. Some possess great dexterity and organizational skill. Even knowledge endowment among human resource may be different among countries. Nowadays, many countries are facing shortage of skilled manpower.

(iii) Difference may arise due to difference in the accumulated capital. Countries are of two types, i.e., developed and developing. Developed countries are richer in terms of capital endowments than the developing countries.

International trade is different from interregional or national trade on the following grounds:

(i) The degree of difficulty in movement is more in case of international trade.

(ii) Different national policies such as national rules, regulations and policies relating to taxation, labour standards, health, sanitation, factory organizations, social insurance, trade union, education and public utilities are more or less uniform for different regions of a country but may differ among countries.

(iii) Access to national markets is much easier than access to international markets.

GAIN FROM INTERNATIONAL TRADE

International trade is beneficial to all participating countries. It enables a country to export commodities to other countries and thus, secure a better market for them and import commodities which it cannot produce at all or can produce only at a high cost. Due to these reasons, Adam Smith and the classical economists advocated trade between countries so that the gain to all countries could be maximized. Thus, it is clear that international trade takes place due to which international specialization leads to the best utilization of the resources among all countries of the world. International trade also helps to equalise prices within all the trading countries. A commodity is cheap or costly depending on its supply and demand. In the absence of trade, the commodity in question will have two sets of prices, low price in the producing country and high price in the country where it is not produced. Through trade, the price in the producing country will increase and will decrease in the country where it is not produced. Thus, international trade equalizes prices in both countries.

THEORIES OF INTERNATIONAL TRADE

Classical Theory of International Trade

The assumptions of classical theory of international trade are as follows:

(i) Labour is the only productive factor which is measured in terms of per mandays.

(ii) Factors of production are assumed to be perfectly mobile within a country but immobile among countries.

(iii) Transportation costs are completely ignored.

(iv) Only two countries and two commodities have been considered which was later extended to more countries and more commodities.

(v) International trade was assumed to be free from all obstacles and barriers.

(vi) Two countries should have common monetary standard.

According to the classical theory of international trade, countries involved in international trade must have cost difference otherwise they will not involve in trade. This is discussed below.

Equal Cost Difference in Production

If cost ratios of production are same in two countries, international trade cannot take place as the basis of trade is the difference in the cost of production.

Example of two countries, Country A and Country B, and two commodities, wheat and cotton, have been taken to illustrate different types of cost difference.

10 days of labour in Country A can produce	100 units of cotton
	or
	80 units of wheat
10 days of labour in Country B can produce	80 units of cotton
	or
	64 units of wheat

In Country A,

100 units of cotton = 10 days of labour = 80 units of wheat

or, 1 unit of cotton = 0.8 units of wheat

In Country B

80 units of cotton = 10 days of labour = 64 units of wheat

or, 1 unit of cotton = 0.8 units of wheat

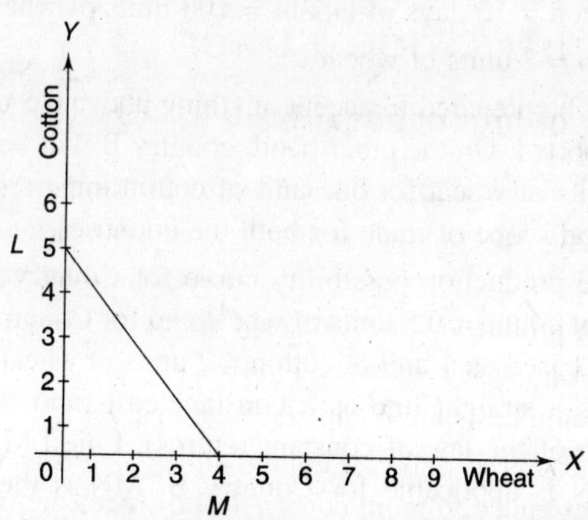

Fig. 5.1 Production-possibility curve under equal cost difference for Country A and Country B

As Country A can get 0.8 unit of wheat for every one unit of cotton within the country so, it would like to get more than 0.8 units of wheat for every unit of cotton exported. Likewise, Country B will be happy to specialize and export wheat, provided it can get more than one unit of cotton for less than 0.8 units of wheat. Thus, there is no possibility of trade to take place between Country A and Country B because the rate of exchange does not coincide.

In Fig. 5.1, line LM is the production-possibility curve prepared on the basis of 1 unit of cotton = 0.8 units of wheat. As the cost ratio for both the countries is same, none of the countries will have advantage. So, no trade will take place.

Absolute Cost Difference in Production

International trade is bound to take place under absolute cost differences, but then, it is neither easy nor necessary to have absolute cost differences.

The following imaginary example illustrates comparative cost differences in production.

10 days of labour in Country A can produce	100 units of cotton
	or
	50 units of wheat
10 days of labour in Country B can produce	50 units of cotton
	or
	100 units of wheat

In Country A,

100 units of cotton = 10 days of labour = 50 units of wheat

1 unit of cotton = 0.5 unit of wheat

In Country B,

50 units of cotton = 10 days of labour = 100 units of wheat

1 unit of cotton = 2 units of wheat

Country A will be prepared to accept anything above 0.5 units of wheat for one unit cotton exported. On the other hand, country B will be prepared to give as much as two units of wheat for one unit of cotton imported. Thus, there are advantages and good scope of trade for both the countries.

In Fig. 5.2, the production-possibility curve for Country A is prepared on the basis of 1 unit of cotton = 0.5 units of wheat and for Country B's production-possibility curve is based on 1 unit of cotton = 2 units of wheat. The production-possibility curve is a straight line as a constant cost ratio has been assumed (on the assumption of the law of constant returns). Line LM is applicable for Country A and LN is applicable for Country B. MN is the amount of pure surplus, which can be shared by two countries, in case trade takes place. Any rate of exchange between M and N will be beneficial to both the countries.

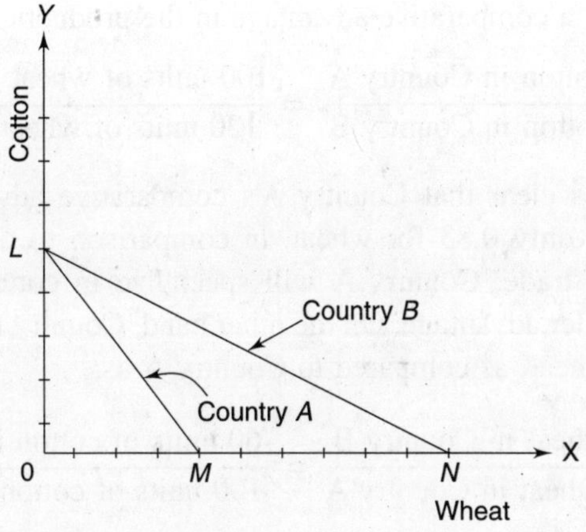

Fig. 5.2 Production-possibility curve under absolute cost difference

Comparative Cost Difference in Production

It is sufficient to have comparative cost differences, that means one country has comparative advantage over the other in the matter of one commodity and the other country has comparative advantage in the matter of the other commodity.

The following example illustrates comparative cost differences in production:

10 days of labour in Country A can produce	100 units of cotton
	or
	100 units of wheat
10 days of labour in Country B can produce	60 units of cotton
	or
	120 units of wheat

In Country A,

The cost ratio is

100 units of cotton = 10 days of labour = 100 units of wheat

or

1 unit of cotton = 1 unit of wheat

In Country B,

The cost ratio is

60 units of cotton = 10 days of labour = 120 units of wheat

or

1 unit of cotton = 2 units of wheat

These differences in cost ratio will enable the two countries to benefit from trade.

Country A has a comparative advantage in the production of cotton, as:

$$\frac{100 \text{ units of cotton in Country A}}{60 \text{ units of cotton in Country B}} = \frac{100 \text{ units of wheat in Country A}}{120 \text{ units of wheat in Country B}}$$

From this, it is clear that Country A's comparative advantage to produce cotton is 1.67 and only 0.83 for wheat, in comparison to Country B. If there is no international trade, Country A will specialize in cotton in which it has comparatively greater advantage. On the other hand, Country B has an advantage in production of wheat, as compared to Country A as:

$$\frac{120 \text{ units of wheat in Country B}}{100 \text{ units of wheat in Country A}} = \frac{60 \text{ units of cotton in Country B}}{100 \text{ units of cotton in Country A}}$$

It implies that Country B has an advantage in the case of wheat and if international trade takes place, Country B will specialize in wheat and export the same, to pay for its imports of cotton.

Figure 5.3 illustrates the principle of comparative advantage. Line LM illustrates the production possibility curve for Country A and is based on the cost ratio of 1 unit of cotton = 2 units of wheat. LN curve shows production possibility curve for Country B and is based on the cost ratio of 1 unit of wheat = 1 unit of cotton. MN is a pure economic surplus and can be shared by the two countries through trade. Any rate of exchange between M and N will benefit both countries.

The classical theory has been criticized for being clumsy and dangerous tool of analysis. It does not examine as to what extent the cheapness of production

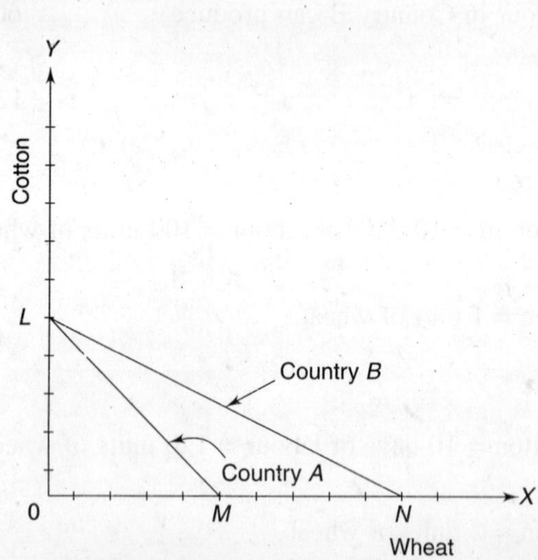

Fig. 5.3 Production-possibility curve under comparative cost difference

in one country is due to low wage, low interest, or other expenses. Besides, it does not consider the complete cost differences in different countries.

Modern Theory of International Trade

The classical theory demonstrates that international trade arises due to differences in comparative costs. However, it does not explain as to why these differences in comparative costs arise. Heckscher and Ohlin attempted to explain the factors which cause differences in the comparative costs of different countries and, in a way, overcome the limitations of classical theory. Their theory is known as Modern Theory of International Trade. Classical and Modern Theories of International Trade do not contradict but supplement each other.

Modern Theory of International Trade was developed on the following assumptions:

(i) Only two factors of production and two nations were considered.

However, later on it was extended to more number of nations without altering its methods or conclusions in anyway. It made the theory more complex.

(ii) Factor of productions are interregionally mobile while internationally immobile.

(iii) The production is subject to the law of constant returns in both the countries.

(iv) Only transportation of goods has been considered, i.e., exports will pay for imports.

(v) There are no cost of transportation, insurance or tariff.

(vi) Factors like endowments, demand conditions and physical conditions are fixed in each country.

Modern Theory of International Trade may be stated as follows:

(i) Immediate cause of interregional or international trade is the difference in relative prices of factor of production in two regions or two nations.

(ii) Differences in factor prices arise due to differences in the factor endowments. The existence of qualitative difference among factors of production (for example, land may be qualitatively different in the two regions and could be easily solved by classifying these factors under different groups for purposes of interregional comparison. If Country A possesses large amount of some factors of production relatively to another Country B, assuming that the difference in the supply of factors are not offset by the difference in the demand conditions, the prices of these factors will be lower in Country A as compared to Country B. Country A will, therefore, possesses a comparative cost advantage in the production of goods which employ more factors relatively abundant in it. Similarly, Country B will posseses a comparative cost advantage in the production of commodities, which employ more factors relatively abundant in it. Thus, both Country A and Country B will specialize in the production and export of commodities, which employ more of their relatively abundant factors and less of their relatively scarce factors.

(iii) If production is subject to increasing return, the international trade can arise even if the factor endowments are similar in both the countries. It will be profitable for both the countries to specialize in the production of some commodities and to obtain others in exchange. However, if factor endowments and the demand conditions are similar in both the countries, there will be no international trade if production is subject to constant return.

Criticism:

(i) The assumption that the demand condition, supply of factors of production and the conditions of production remain unchanged has been criticized This does not hold in the actual world.

(ii) Beside availability of factors of production, the difference in comparative cost may arise due to psychological, social, economic and political conditions, which vary from country to country. These institutions may be favourable for production of certain commodities. For example, system of taxation is of particular importance in this respect.

(iii) A country deficient in capital and technology might develop over a period of time.

TERMS OF TRADE

Terms of trade refers to the prices at which goods or services are exchanged. In international trade, however, terms of trade refers to a country's export exchange rate for imports and it depends upon the relation between the prices of export goods and the prices of import goods.

Factors on which Terms of Trade Depend

Terms of trade of commodities depend upon the demand and supply forces, collectively called reciprocal demand by J.S. Mill.

If India's demand for foreign goods is greater than the demand for India's goods abroad consequently, rate of increase in prices of import will be greater than the rate of increase in prices of export.

Then, terms of trade will deteriorate for India.

On the other hand,

If India's demand for foreign goods is less than the demand for India's goods abroad consequently, Rate of increase in prices of import will be less than the rate of increase in prices of export.

Then, terms of trade will move in favour of India.

If the foreign demand for Indian goods is rising, it results in a greater rise in the price of Indian exports and the terms of trade will move in favour of India. So, the terms of trade will depend upon the elasticity of:

(i) a country's demand for imports,

(ii) foreign demand for its exports in the international market,

(iii) supply of exports, and

(iv) supply of imports.

FREE TRADE VS. PROTECTION

Under free trade, entry and exit of any foreign firm is free in the domestic market of participating countries. Ultimately, all participating firms benefit. It enables a country to buy and consume those goods which it cannot produce or can produce only at a higher cost. However, presence of cheap imported goods affect the domestic producer adversely. Sometimes, interest of future may be sacrificed for those of the present.

To protect the domestic product from international competition, countries impose many restrictions on international trade. Some of them are discussed below.

Tariffs or Custom Duties

A tariff or custom duty on the import of commodities is one of the earliest and the most widely used method of limiting imports. Tariff may be imposed in the following forms:

(i) Uni-linear or single column tariff system — It refers to preferential tariff system under which it may give exclusive trade privileges to nations related to it by political, racial or regional negotiations.

(ii) Specific duty vs. Ad valorem duty — If the tariff is imposed and calculated on the basis of physical units, it is known as specific duty. Whereas if the duty is imposed on the basis of value of goods, it is known as ad valorem duty.

(iii) Custom duty vs. Countervailing duty — If the tariff is imposed on imported goods for the purpose of raising their prices to protect domestic producers from loss it is known as custom duty. However, a countervailing duty will be in addition to the original custom duty and the purpose is to ensure the degree of protection originally intended.

Quantitative Restrictions

Imposing direct limitation upon the physical amounts of certain goods that may be imported during a given period of time. Generally, licensing or quota is used for this type of restriction.

Exchange Restrictions

Under this system, goods are classified according to their importance and to assign priority for their imports accordingly. Exchange control has obvious advantages in restricting trade but it has generally been felt that it leads to distortion in production and trade. Ultimately, it leads to too much of administrative corruption and arbitrariness.

Other Methods

Multiple exchange rates (under which different exchange rates are applied for different types of goods), the so-called sanitary regulations (to prevent the import of goods on the basis of health and welfare), import surcharge (special taxes on dutiable import) and linked purchase regulations (which require a fixed proportionate purchase of domestic articles for every import) are some of the other methods for restricting foreign trade.

Arguments in Favour of and Against Protection

(i) Protection is required for the young and newly started industries, otherwise such industries will never be able to establish themselves. Once they establish themselves, protection may be removed.

(ii) Though protection helps industries in a country, the consumer suffers because he is being denied access to foreign goods at a cheaper rate.

(iii) Curtailment of imports (by imposing duties on foreign goods) implies a decrease in exports too. If all the countries do this, none would gain.

(iv) In countries where the people enjoy high real wages, it is often felt that their standard of living will be undermined if cheap goods are imported from countries where wages are low.

(v) Protection equalizes the cost of production of home and foreign countries. For example, if the internal cost of a colour TV is Rs. 15,000 and that of a similar foreign TV is Rs. 13,000, than to equalize the prices, a duty of Rs. 2000 will be levied on the import.

During 1990s, most of the countries (including India) liberalized their markets. Firms were made free to operate from any liberalized economy depending upon the relative advantage. In fact, advent of information and communication technology (ICT) has made it possible to shift part of the production process, which can be digitally transferred to a place where it can be performed in a cost effective way. Many developed countries like USA and UK are outsourcing their work to developing countries including India. Outsourcing of work was a major issue in the last presidential election of USA.

BALANCE OF PAYMENT

Balance of payment is a systematic record of all economic transactions between its own residents of foreign countries during a given period of time (generally one year). While balance of trade relates only to visible imports and exports, balance of payment is more comprehensive in scope than balance of trade because current account in balance of payment includes invisible trade as shipping, banking, insurance, tourist and traffic along with visible items, which can be counted at port. The balance of payments of a country is kept in standard double entry book keeping under which each international transaction undertaken by residents of a country results in a credit and debit entry of equal size.

Advantages of maintaining balance of payment:

(i) It provides information to the government and other interested organisation regarding the international transaction status of the country.

(ii) It helps the government in taking decisions regarding the monetary and fiscal policy on the one hand, and trade payment questions on the other.

Structure of Balance of Payment

Balance of payment normally consists of two sections: current account and capital account. The current account deals with payments for currently produced goods and services. The capital account, on the other hand, deals with debts and claims. Differences between current account and capital account are explained in Table 5.1.

Table 5.1 Comparison between Current Account and Capital Account

Sl. No.	*Current account*	*Capital account*
1.	It includes interest earned or paid on claims and also on gifts and donations.	It includes payment on claims only.
2.	It directly affects the national income and level of income in the country. For instance, when Indian firms sell their currently produced goods and services in foreign markets and vice versa, producers of these goods and services get income.	It does not have such direct effect on the level of income. It influences volume of assets which a country holds.

Whether balance of payment is favourable or not, depends on the current account as follows:

(i) Balance of payment will be balanced if amount of export done by a country is equal to the import made by the country, i.e., export = import.

(ii) It is adverse if export is less than import.

(iii) It is favourable if export is greater than import.

When there is a deficit in the current account of the balance of payments, the country meets its deficit through:

(i) Drawing on the past accumulated balance of the country, which it may be keeping as a reserve in a foreign country, e.g., India holds in London.

(ii) Drawing from the International Monetary Fund.

(iii) External assistance from other countries by way of loans and grants.

If a country has an adverse balance of payment in any year, it may be corrected by using one or more of the above methods. But if a country runs into adverse balance year after year, it is going to face a serious problem.

DUMPING

Dumping is the sale of a good abroad at a price lower than the selling price of the same good, at the same time, and in the same circumstances at home. Dumping may be classified into two categories: (i) international dumping and (ii) persistent dumping.

(i) International dumping

It means occasional foreign sales below the home price or even below the cost of production with some specific objective. Few such objectives are mentioned below:

(a) In a market, prices are temporarily low because of a recession.

(b) To establish a foothold in a foreign market.

(c) To drive out an existing foreign competition or to force it to join a cartel.

(d) To dispose of occasional domestic surplus, which might result from optimistic production plans or from a decline in demand. The producer may prefer to sell the occasional surpluses in foreign market at comparatively lower prices rather than spoiling the regular domestic market by announcing occasional price cuts.

(e) To dispose of remnants at the end of the season, which are almost unsaleable at home. Sometimes the consignee may reject the goods or it may not be possible for him to keep up his contract. In such a case, it might be less profitable but better to sell the goods in the foreign market for whatever they fetch rather than reshipping them home.

(f) To obtain badly needed foreign exchange. It is this kind of dumping which is very disturbing for the importing countries.

(ii) Persistent dumping

It means continuous sales abroad at prices lower than those charged at home. It may be done due to difference in the demand curves for a particular commodity in different countries. If, for instance, the domestic demand curve is inelastic and the foreign demand curve is highly elastic, it will be profitable for the producer to charge a comparatively lower price and sell larger volume in the foreign market.

DEVALUATION

Since 1949, with the establishment of International Monetary Fund (IMF), the external values of the currencies of the member nations of IMF have been scientifically fixed and deviation from them is not normally permissible. While making the exchange rate stable, the IMF does not want it to absolutely rigid. So a provision has been made in the working of IMF for deliberate reduction in the home currency's external purchasing power. This is known as devaluation.

Devaluation is used to correct a balance of payment deficit; but only as a last resort. It has major repercussions on the domestic economy. For example, holders of foreign currency will then pay a lower price for the domestic goods and the price of imports in the home market will rise. If there is no increase in the production of export goods, they will then earn less foreign exchange which will be a matter of concern for balance of payments. Indian currency has been devalued twice. First, in 1966 and again, in 1991. During both periods, India was facing very high inflation and large government budget deficit which led the government to devalue money.

RATE OF EXCHANGE

The price of a currency in terms of another currency is known as 'Rate of Exchange'. Exchange rates are regularly quoted between all major currencies, but frequently US dollar is used as a standard to express and compare all rates. The exchange rate of fully convertible currencies is determined, like price of any other commodity, by supply and demand conditions in the market in which it is traded, i.e., the foreign exchange market. More fundamentally, such supply and demand conditions are determined by whether the country's basic balance of payment position is in surplus or in deficit.

Alternatively, the exchange rate is determined as a price equating the flow of supply and demand for a currency but as the relative price of two currencies, so that any factor which influences the value of a currency will influence its international exchange rate too. People's expectations about changes in domestic money supplies and their effect also plays a significant role in determining the exchange rate and helps to explain the observed volatility of exchange rates.

INTERNATIONAL ORGANISATIONS

The First World War during 1914 to 1919 and then great crash of 1929 disrupted the economy of the whole world. Even the economically powerful ones were badly affected. In futile attempts to protect them, several countries had resorted to competitive devaluation of their currencies, exchanged preferential tariffs with favoured trading partners, increased their import duties to abnormal heighs and imposed various types of trade restrictions to balance their payments. The chaotic situation undermined the global trading system throughout the 1930s until commencement of the Second World War. The Second World War was the direct result of conflicts and tensions and the absence of cooperation among countries. It was feared that after the cessation of hostilities, countries were going to face large-scale unemployment and surplus labour. The desperate economic condition of both victors and vanquished was likely to create problems for international trade. It was against this background that members of the International Economic Conference, which was held at Bretton Woods in July 1944, decided to create three institutions — International Monetary Fund (IMF), the International Bank for Reconstruction and Development (the IBRD) or World Bank and the General Agreement on Tariffs and Trade (GATT). These institutions are also known as Bretton Woods Institutions.

International Monetary Fund (IMF)

International Monetary Fund started its operation on March 1, 1947. Article 1 of the Fund Agreement states the purpose of the Fund as follows:

(i) To promote international monetary cooperation through a permanent institution, which provides, the machinery for consultation and collaboration on international monetary problems.

(ii) To facilitate the expansion and balanced growth of international trade and thereby contribute to the promotion and maintenance of high levels of employment and real income among member countries.

(iii) To promote exchange stability and to avoid competitive exchange depreciation.

(iv) To provide for multilateral convertibility of currencies and to remove all exchange controls and restrictions.

(v) To help members with funds to correct their balance of payments deficits.

Fund and the par values

According to the provisions of the Fund Charter, every member country should fix the par value of its currency. The par value cannot be changed unless it is necessary to correct a fundamental disequilibrium. A member country can change the par value of its currency by 10% after notifying to the Fund and in case of larger change, the Fund may either lower it or object to it but the IMF is powerless to prevent the change.

Transactions of the Fund

According to the provisions of the Fund, all member countries subscribe quota as Special Drawing Right (SDR) of which 25 per cent has to be kept as dollar or gold with the IMF and 75 per cent in the form of local currency with the country. In any given year, the country can purchase foreign currencies up to 25 per cent of its quota. It can continue to purchase foreign currencies year after year up to 125 per cent of its subscription in form of gold or dollar. Since a country has to purchase foreign currencies by paying its own currency, so the country's total currency held by the IMF can be upto 200 per cent of the total subscription quota.

In order to meet the balance of payment deficits, India has also borrowed from the Fund.

The World Bank

The International Bank for Reconstruction and Development — the IBRD or World Bank, for short — began its operation in June 1946. Like the Fund, the Bank is an international cooperative organization associated with United Nations having the status of a specialized agency. Its aim is to assist the economic development of its member countries and to raise the standard of living of the people.

Purpose of the Bank, as set forth in the Articles of Agreement is as follows:

(i) To assist in the reconstruction and the development of the territories of members by facilitating the investment of capital for productive purposes including the restoration of economies destroyed or disrupted by war (hence the name: Bank of Reconstruction) and the encouragement for the development of productive facilities and resources in less developed countries.

(ii) To promote private investment by means of guarantees or participation in loans and to supplement private investment by its own finances.

(iii) To promote long term balanced growth of international trade and the maintenance of equilibrium in balance of payments by encouraging international investment for development of the productive resources of the members, thereby, assisting in raising productivity, the standard of living and condition of labour within the member countries.

However, the Bank was not able to meet all the capital demand of the developing economies under its format. So, two other affiliated organizations were established. First, International Finance Corporation (IFC), to subscribe equity capital to private companies and second International Development Association (IDA), to supply soft loans for general development purposes. Within the restrictions imposed by its constitution, the Bank has been particularly concerned with the economic development of the developing countries.

General Agreement on Tariff and Trade (GATT)

GATT, now transformed into World Trade Organisation (WTO), became operational in 1948 with the intention of introducing a rule of law in international trade relations. It was based on the concept of nondiscrimination. Each member country must treat others equally without discrimination. It prohibited discriminatory tariffs and prescribed that each country must apply the same rate to the imports from all members without distinction. Successive rounds of GATT took place, which succeeded in reducing tariff levels in the developed countries from the average of 40 per cent in 1948 to less than 4 per cent by the end of eighth round of negotiations, which is popularly known by the name of place where it was held, i.e., Uruguay Round. Besides tariff and trade liberalization, the principal aim of Uruguay Round. was to strengthen the multilateral trading system to face the needs of the future. It was feared that with tariffs descending to insignificant levels, countries might be tempted to use non-tariff measures for the purpose of protection. At the same time, over the period, structure of employment and contribution of various sectors to Gross Domestic Product (GDP) of developed countries had experienced a qualitative change. It was increasing in developed countries including USA. Thus, need of developing a mechanism in international trade in service sector was felt. During the eighth round of negotiations, a new safeguard agreement, the World Trade Organisation (WTO) was developed in succession to the GATT. It is a comprehensive dispute settlement mechanism with a wider ambit covering international trade in both goods and services. The second aspect was related to the strengthening of the existing GATT rules pertaining to anti-dumping actions, subsidies and counter-vailing measures custom valuation methods, technical barriers to trade and other sundry aspects. The WTO became operational on January 1, 1995. Salient features of WTO are as follows.

Agreement on agriculture

It provides a framework for the long-term reform of agricultural trade and domestic policiės over the years to come. It provides for commitments in the area of market access, domestic support and export competition. The tariffs resulting from this transformation, as well as other tariffs on agricultural products are to be reduced on an average by 36 per cent in the case of developed countries and 24 per cent in the case of developing countries. Subsidies given on agriculture was expected to be curtailed to give same playing level to all member countries in the international market.

Agreement on market access

The member nations need to curtail all types of discriminatory practices imposed on foreign goods in the domestic market. They were asked to cut all kinds of tariffs on industrial and farm goods by an average of about 37 per cent. The developed countries like USA and European Union are expected to cut tariffs by one-half.

Agreement on Trade Related Investment Measures (TRIMs)

The Agreement on TRIMs introduction of national treatment and removal of all qualitative restrictions to foreign investments. Some of these restrictions are obligations to use local inputs, for production for exports only to obtain imported inputs, to balance foreign exchange on importing inputs with foreign exchange earnings through export, and not to export more than a specified proportion of the local production.

Agreement on Intellectual Property Rights (TRIPs)

Trade related TRIPs pertain to patents and copyrights. Earlier, there was provision of granting process patents to food, medicines, drugs and chemical products. A particular process was patented and not the final product. So, in many cases, especially in pharmaceutical products with very minor change in the process, same end result was achieved without giving royalty to the inventor. The TRIPs agreement now provides granting product patents in all areas. Protection will continue for 20 years for patents and 50 years for copyrights.

Agreement on General Agreement on Trade in Services (GATS)

For the first time, trade in services like banking, insurance, education, travel, maritime, transportation, mobility of labour, etc., have been brought within the ambit of GATS. GATS provides a multilateral framework, which would govern trade in services under conditions of transparency and progressive liberalization. It spells out certain obligations like grant of most favoured nation (MFN) status to other member nations with respect to trade in services.

The international economic environment is so congenial for Indian engineering professionals as never before. Liberalization, implementation of WTO norms and advent of information and communication technology (ICT) has opened up many new employment opportunities for them. Many multinational corporations (MNCs) have established their base in India to take benefits of India's talented engineering manpower and other resources. Almost 100 international companies have established their R&D centres in India. Many firms from the developed economies are sending low-end and high-end production processes, popularly known as call centres and knowledge Process Outsourcing (KPO), to India.

EXERCISES

A. Objective

1. Following are some of the factors which favour international trade. List them in the order of importance: (For one mark each)

(a) Stage of economic development

(b) Foreign investment

(c) Differences in factor endowment

2. Fill in the blanks: **(For 1/2 mark each)**

(a) The principle of comparative costs states that a country specializes and exports those goods in which it has cost -------- and imports those goods in which it has cost --------.

(b) The basic cause for international trade to take place is difference in --------.

(c) According to classical economists, factors of production are -------- mobile within countries.

[**Ans:** 1. c, a and b; 2. (a) advantage, disadvantage; (b) factor endowment; (c) perfectly]

B. Subjective **(For five or seven marks each)**

1. Discuss some of the differences and similarities between interregional and international trade.
2. Discuss salient features of Classical Theory of International Trade.
3. Discuss Modern Theory of International Trade.
4. What do you mean by dumping? Discuss its effects on local industries.
5. What do you mean by devaluation of money?
6. Discuss the significance of Bretton Wood institutions in global economic environment.
7. How WTO is going to benefit Indian engineers?

References and Suggested Readings

1. Howard S. Ellis and Loyd A. Metzler (Ed). "Readings in the theory of International Trade". The American Economic Association, Geoge Allen and Unwin Ltd., London.
2. Bo Sodersten and Geoffrey Reed. "International Economics". Macmillan Press Ltd., London.
3. Trilok N. Sindhwani, "The Global Business Game: A Strategic Perspective". Macmillan India, New Delhi.
4. Anant K. Sundaram and J. Steward Black, "The International Business Environment". Prentice-Hall of India Private Limited, New Delhi.

6

Public Finance, Economic Governance, Development and Planning

Purpose of this chapter is to acquaint the reader with:

- Concept of Public Finance, Principle of Maximum Social Advantage
- Sources of income of a Government, Tax, Subsidy
- Fiscal Policy, Deficit Financing
- Public Expenditure, Reasons for growth of Public Expenditure
- Economic Governance of a Country: Capitalist, Socialist and Mixed economy
- Concept of Economic Development
- Concept of Planning, Significance of Planning in Economic Development.

One of the main objectives of each country of world is to improve its economic condition. Improvement in economic condition refers to a situation where a country aspires and works in the direction to achieve higher level of output than what it has already achieved. To achieve higher level of economic prosperity, economic resources must be utilized in predecided judicious way. In *Laissez faire* economy, government is not supposed to play any role in economic activity. However, in the present-day world, governments of all the economies are participating, directly or indirectly in the economic activities. Even in the capitalist economies like USA and UK, government policies revolve around economic considerations. Government spends large amount of money in providing social security to its masses. Governments of many of the developed countries like France give huge subsidy to its farmers.

PUBLIC FINANCE

Public finance deals with the financial aspects of government, i.e., central, state and local government. It studies the ways and means through which the government obtains its revenue and spends it.

Subject matter of public finance mainly consists of:

(i) **Public income** refers to various sources of income of a government and the principles of taxations.

(ii) **Public expenditure** consists of the study of the principles of public expenditure and its effects on people from different segments of the society.

(iii) **Public debt** studies the causes and the methods of publics borrowing as well as public debt management.

(iv) **Financial administration** includes the preparation and sanctioning of the budget, auditing, etc.

(v) **Economic stabilization** studies the use of fiscal policies to bring about economic stability in the country.

SOURCES OF INCOME OF A GOVERNMENT

Sources of income of a government can be grouped under two broad categories, i.e., tax revenue and non-tax revenue. Tax revenue includes taxes on income and expenditure, taxes on property and capital transactions and taxes on commodities and services. Non-tax revenue includes currency, coinage and mint along with interest earned on receipts, dividends and profits. Other non-tax revenues include income from general, social and community services and economic services provided by the government. Grants-in-aid, contributions from foreign countries and international organizations are also non-tax revenues of a government.

PRINCIPLE OF MAXIMUM SOCIAL ADVANTAGE

Principle of maximum social advantage refers to a situation where:

(i) Public authorities should spend or distribute resources in such a way that the marginal utility or welfare from all the spending for public is equal.

(ii) Public expenditure should be carried on upto the point where marginal social benefit of the last rupee spent by the government should be equal to marginal sacrifice of the last rupee realized by taxation and fee.

Therefore,

Marginal social benefit to the rupee spent by the government = Marginal sacrifice of the last rupee realized by taxation and fee.

When citizens of a country give tax to the government, they lose money, which they could have spent to derive utility. In that way, they sacrifice utility. Loss of utility per unit currency is more for poor than for the rich. Therefore, the rich should pay higher rate of tax than the poor. Again, people receive utility from the facilities given by the government. Loss of utility when people pay tax needs to be equal to the gain of utility from the facilities provided by the

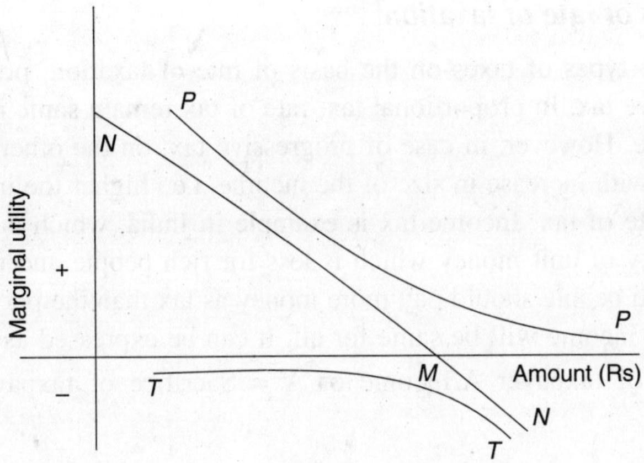

Fig. 6.1

government using money collected through tax. Of course, different sets of people pay tax and use the utilities provided by the government.

However, utility from facilities = Loss of utility by paying taxes

In Fig. 6.1, *PP* curve shows utility derived from the goods and services provided by the government and *TT* curve shows the disutility for citizens when they pay tax to the government. *M* is the amount of money, which should be collected as tax by the government. At *M*, both utility and disutility are equal.

TAX

Tax is compulsory contribution by citizens of a country to the government exchequer. For example, income tax, sales tax, etc. Tax is different from fees paid by citizens of a country on the services provided by government. As discussed in the previous section, the amount of money collected through tax may not be spent by the government on the same group of persons. In fact, tax paid and the services which are provided by the government from the money collected as tax are used by different segments of the society. Generally, tax is paid by rich persons and government facilities as government schools and hospitals are used by the poor. However, fee is paid by the same person who uses the services and the amount of fee is in direct proportion to the volume of services or goods used.

Taxation should be certain, timely and economical to collect. Government spends money on the establishment through which tax is collected. If it is not economical, the state will not be benefited from the collection of taxation.

Types of taxes

Taxes can be classified on the basis of following criteria.

On the basis of rate of taxation

There are two types of taxes on the basis of rate of taxation: proportional tax and progressive tax. In proportional tax, rate of tax remain same irrespective of size of income. However, in case of progressive tax, on the other hand, rate of tax increases with increase in size of the income, i.e., higher the income, higher will be the rate of tax. Income tax is example in India, which is based on the marginal utility of unit money which is less for rich people and more for poor people. So rich people should pay more money as tax than the poor so that ratio of sacrifice to income will be same for all. It can be expressed as follows:

Sacrifice of taxpayer A/Income of A = Sacrifice of taxpayer B/Income of B.

On the basis of burden of tax

There are two types of tax on the basis of burden of tax: direct tax and indirect tax. In case of direct tax, tax is paid by the same person on whom burden of tax falls. As in case of income tax, tax is paid by the same person who has earned income. However, in case of indirect tax, different persons pay the tax and bear its burden. For example, sales tax is imposed on the producer of a product but its burden is shifted to the distributor, the distributor shifts it to the retailer who includes tax paid by him in the price. Ultimately, tax is paid by the customer. Burden of tax or the relative incidence of tax is divided between the producer and the consumer. The relative incidence is determined by the relative price elasticities of demand (e_d) and supply (e_s). If e_d is greater than e_s, the relative burden is less on consumers. If e_d is less than e_s, the relative burden is more on consumers. The concept may be useful for the seller of a commodity in deciding the extent of burden he should transfer to customers.

Value Added Tax (VAT) is a comprehensive form of tax which is imposed on all goods and services (except export and government services). Its special characteristic being that it falls on the value added at each stage from the stage of production to retail shop. VAT is nothing but sales tax at source. Instead of collecting it after five months or so, the state government would collect the same in advance and then allow set-offs to the businessmen. Administratively, it is a simpler way of reaching the value added. It enables a country to have an extended system of commodity taxation and avoids the problems of cascading and escalation of costs, which happens in case of sales tax and excise duty. However, for successful implementation of VAT, there is a need to make requisite changes in the maintenance of records and the organizational set-up besides proper education of public. In spite of opposition in the beginning by powerful trading lobbies, VAT was launched in 2005 in India which is one of the most significant financial reforms of independent India.

On the basis of place of production

Taxes are imposed on the basis of place of production. If it is produced within the geographical territory of a country, excise duty is imposed. If it is produced in foreign country and then imported by a country, government of that country imposes custom duty on the product. Sometimes imposition of custom duty is used by the government of a country to raise price of the imported product within that country.

SUBSIDY

Part of cost of production paid by government to an industry with an objective to keep the price of product of the concerned industry below its cost of production is known as subsidy. It may be given due to any of the following reasons:

(i) To lower the price of a product if it is used by less well-off section of the society. For example, food subsidy ensures that the poor can have square meal a day.

(ii) To promote eco-friendly product. For example, governmert gives subsidy to CNG fuel because it is eco-friendly fuel and government wants the consumers to use it.

(iii) As a counterbalancing measure to the custom duty imposed by an importing country, government of native country may give subsidy.

GOVERNMENT CONTROL: FISCAL POLICY

Any government has two types of tools through which they control macroeconomic environment of the country. They are monetary policy and fiscal policy. Monetary policy has been discussed in the chapter 'Macroeconomics'. Fiscal policy refers to the management of volume of currency in circulation or purchasing power in the hands of public through tax and subsidy. Though tax is a major source of income for the government but sometimes it is used for controlling inflation also. The government imposes high rate of taxation which decreases purchasing power of people. Imposition of tax does not mean that the government does not want people to use a particular commodity. However, imposition of tax or subsidy is to induce people to use or not to use. Subsidy is given on fertilizers to induce farmers to use fertilizers in their farms, which will ultimately increase the farm productivity. Similarly, tax rebate is given to income tax payee on investing money on schemes of Life Insurance Corporation. Taxpayers will invest money to take tax rebate but ultimately, their life will be insured.

DEFICIT FINANCING

The term 'deficit financing' has been defined by the Planning Commission of India as, 'the term to denote the direct addition to gross national expenditure through budget deficit' (First Five-Year Plan). Deficit financing, thus, refers to the ways in which the budgetary gap is financed. The government opts to the method of financing when it is unable to cover its total expenditure from normal sources of revenue, such as taxation, fees, income from government properties and undertakings, proceeds of loans, small savings, superannuation, contributions and other capital receipts and funds at its disposal. Thus, deficit financing, in that case, is undertaken by government by drawing upon its accumulated cash balance or borrowing from the central bank of the country or both.

In underdeveloped countries, where banking habits are not fully developed and where majority of transactions are carried out through common money, deficit financing mainly takes place by borrowing from the central bank. In advanced countries, where banking habits are fully developed, deficit financing takes the form of additional credit creation through the commercial bank. The deficit financing has an expansionary effect on the total money supply in the country. Thus, the government needs to be careful to opt for deficit financing. If deficit financing is carried out for productive activities, it increases effective demand and generates employment. On the contrary, if unproductive activities like war is financed, it creates inflation.

PUBLIC EXPENDITURE

Public expenditure is the expenditure incurred by public authorities — central, state and local governments — either for the satisfaction of collective needs of the citizens or for promoting their economic and social welfare. It should be pushed in all directions and under all heads in such a way that the net social benefit of the society could be maximized.

Reasons for Growth of Public Expenditure

In recent years, there has been phenomenal increase in the public expenditure. Some of the reasons are as follows:

(i) Increase in the activities of the governments: It has enlarged the spectrum of services supplied to the consumer free of cost or at less than the cost of production in order to relieve distress and to utilize unemployed resources and labour. This type of expenditure is also incurred to lift the country out of depression or for lifting poor people above poverty line.

(ii) Industrial development: A large amount of public expenditure in form of tax relief, subsidy, or tax holiday, is given for industrial development of an area.

(iii) Nationalization of industries and trade: In many countries, the government is entrusted with the responsibility of producing quality goods at reasonable prices. Till 1990, public sector was playing a crucial role in industrial sector even in India. However, Industrial Policy 1991 has decreased role of government in industrial development.

(iv) Rising trend of prices: With the increase in the price level, government is compelled to pay more for the production of commodities and services which are under the government sector.

(v) Increase in defence expenditure: The public expenditure is increasing due to increase in defence expenditure in most countries of the world. In recent times, defence cost has accelerated as a result of more sophisticated technology being used for defence purposes.

(vi) Urbanization: Increasing urbanization of population is an important cause of rising public expenditure. Urban population requires larger amount of public expenditure for providing basic amenities than the rural population.

Effects of Public Expenditure on Production

Public expenditure can affect the production of a country in two ways — directly and indirectly. Industries in the public sector make a direct contribution to the Gross National Product (GDP) or national income. Expenditure on railways, irrigation, general administration, post and telegraph, roads, etc. are indirectly productive. They contribute as infrastructure in production. Indirect effects of public expenditure on production can be evaluated by enquiring into its effect upon the following factors:

(i) Effects upon the ability to work, save and invest: Public sector expenditure can increase the ability of people to work, save and invest in many ways. Public expenditure on education, medical services, cost-effective housing facilities, better means of transport and communication, etc., will increase the efficiency and ability of persons to work and save. Again, public expenditure for increasing the salaries and wages of people and supply of essential commodities at cheap rate will increase their purchasing power and ultimately, standard of living, which in turn enhances their efficiency, Hence, their ability to work and save may increase. Likewise, public expenditure incurred for making law and order, which creates confidence in the mind of the people and hence, it encourages them to make investment in productive activities. On the other hand, if a large proportion of public expenditure is wasted on the production of intoxicants and other goods, which are harmful for health and efficiency, than that may have an adverse effects on the ability to work, save and invest.

(ii) Effects on willingness to work, save and invest: A person's willingness to work, save and invest is adversely affected, if he considers that his present savings and investment will not earn sufficient income in future. On the contrary, if a person is confident that his present savings and investment will fetch good dividend to him, his willingness to work, save and invest is enhanced. Hence, the government should spend maximum public expenditure on providing social security measure without directly affecting saving and investment expenditure.

(iii) Effects on diversion of economic resources between uses and localities: Public expenditure on defence, police, judiciary, etc., are required to create peace and security under which better and optimum utilization of existing resources may be possible. But at the same time, it should not be too large as it can create an adverse effect on the production. The public expenditure should also be incurred on construction of infrastructure, which is one of the prerequisites for economic development of an area. Public expenditure in the form of subsidies to manufacturing sector helps in accelerating the production of existing industries as well as in diverting resources to establish new industries.

ECONOMIC GOVERNANCE OF A COUNTRY

All economies of the world have limited resources at their disposal. They are confronted with the problem of what to produce, how to produce and for whom to produce, On the basis of these questions, economic governance can be divided into three. i, Capitalist, ii, Socialist and iii, Mixed economy. Major differences between these three have been discussed in Table 6.1.

Table 6.1 Various Economic Systems

Economic system	*What to produce*	*How to produce*	*For whom to produce*
Capitalist	Price mechanism. Only those commodities for which consumers are willing to pay a price per unit sufficiently high to cover at least the full cost of producing them including profit.	Price mechanism. It shows the demand for and supply of the product and available cost-effective utilization of inputs.	Price mechanism. The economy will produce those commodities that satisfy the wants of those people who have money to pay for the products and services.
Socialist	Planning Committee decides.	Planning Committee decides.	Planning Committee decides.
Mixed	Both price mechanism as well as the Government (may be through Planning Board).	Price mechanism for general products and government for necessary products.	In the name of equity and fairness, governments usually modify the workings of the price mechanism by taking from the rich (through taxation) and redistributing to the poor (through subsidies and welfare payments).

What to Produce

It refers to the choice every economy has to make about goods and services to be produced and what quantity to be produced. Since resources are limited, no economy can produce as much of every good or service as desired by all members of the economy. More of one good or service usually means less of other. Therefore, every economy must choose exactly which goods and services to produce and how much to produce.

How to Produce

It refers to the choice of combination of factors and the particular techniques to use in producing good or service.

For Whom to Produce

It refers to the distribution aspect as to how the total output is to be divided among different consumers. Since resources and, therefore, goods and services are scarce in every economy, no society can satisfy all the wants of its entire population. Thus, a problem of choice arises.

Capitalist Economy

In capitalist economy, the government does not interfere in the economic activities. Adam Smith termed it a situation of *laissez faire*. Price mechanism and market forces decide what has to be produced, how much of it has to be produced and how it has to be distributed in a society. Individuals are free to buy if they have required purchasing power and firms are free to produce if there is demand in the market. Fundamental feature of capitalism is freedom to have private ownership of property, which passes to legal heirs after death of the owner.

Advantages

(i) Incentive for invention and innovation.

(ii) Efficient use of resources.

Disadvantages

(i) Inequalities in distribution of income and wealth.

(ii) Class struggle between owner of resources and labour exists and labour always blame the owners for their plight.

(iii) It is difficult for poor to sustain in the market-driven economy.

Socialist Economy

After industrial revolution of 14th century and beginning of large-scale production, it was increasingly felt by labour that profit of an enterprise is not equally being distributed among different factors of production. Culmination of the feeling of exploitation among working class was one of the main reasons of 'French Revolution' and 'Russian Revolution'. These gave rise to 'Socialist Pattern of Governance of an Economy'. In this system of economy, central or planning committees takes decisions about what to produce, how to produce and how much to produce. Most drastic difference between capitalism and socialism is the ownership of means of production. Countries as Vietnam, China, and Cuba are example of socialist pattern of economy. Once U.S.S.R. was the most powerful socialist state but now, it has been fragmented into many independent states following different forms of economic system.

Advantages

(i) Equitable distribution of income.
(ii) Balanced development of society.
(iii) No class struggle.
(iv) Better allocation of resources.

Disadvantages

(i) Lack of incentive.
(ii) State monopoly.

Mixed economy

Mixed economy is a mixture of both capitalism and socialism. The ownership is partly in the hands of the state and partly in the hands of private enterprise. Large number of economies including India follow mixed form of economic governance. In mixed economy, both price mechanism as well as the government through planning board decide what to produce, how to produce, and how to distribute.

Advantages

(i) Public sector participates in core areas for faster development of the economy and for the benefit of common man. Private sector operates in less important areas.
(ii) State takes care of the poor through social security measures.

Disadvantage

(i) Neither capitalism nor socialism exist. So, it lacks advantage of both capitalism and socialism.

ECONOMIC DEVELOPMENT

Economic Growth and Economic Development: They are, generally, used as synonyms to discuss a situation of rise in national income of a country. However, some economists have drawn a fine line between economic growth and economic development. Economic growth means more output while economic development implies more output as well as a change in the technical and institutional arrangements by which it is produced and distributed. It is an indicator of society's well-being and countries are compared on the basis of state of economic development.

Economic development can be measured in the following ways:

(i) Gross National Product (GNP) : Most common method to measure economic development is in terms of an increase in country's GNP over a period of time. However, its main limitation is its inability to consider the size of population.

(ii) Per capita real income: The second method of measurement of economic development relates to an increase in the per capita real income in the economy over a period of time. However, the national income is not equally distributed across its population. So, an increase in the per capita real income of the economy does not mean that life of the masses has improved. Such a measure also subordinates other questions as structure of society, state of health and education facility, size and composition of population, etc.

(iii) Social and Economic indicators: Some economists have advocated that per capita real income is not able to portray the actual well being of all as the distribution of income is skewed. So, an index made of social and economic indicator will be able to portray real picture. These days, countries are being ranked on the basis of both social and economic indicators. Life expectancy at birth, infant mortality, and percentage of population with access to potable water can be some of the indicators, which may be considered to explain economic development. However, limitation of this method is unanimity among economists about the indicators, which should be taken into consideration.

Countries have been divided into two on the basis of level of economic development as developed economies and developing economies. In general, countries with very high national income, per capita income, less population employed in agriculture, e.g., USA, UK and Germany, etc. are referred as developed economies. However, those countries, which have real per capita incomes less than a quarter of the per capita income of the United States, are regarded as developing economies. These countries have some specific characteristics as lower national income, higher percentage of population dependence on agriculture, low rate of capital formation, etc., for example, most of the countries of Asia and Africa including India have these features. However, rate of economic development in India and China, in recent years, has increased significantally, and they are on the verge of becoming superpower.

In recent decades economists have turned their attention to data that ask people how happy or satisfied they are with their lives. Much of the early research concluded that the role of income in determining well-being was limited, and that only income has partial infinence on individual well-being.

PRINCIPLES OF PLANNING

Earlier *liassez-faire* was in vogue. Economic activities were guided by self-interest alone. The government was not supposed to interfere and involve in the economic activities. Large-scale industrial production and post-First World War, economic environment witnessed class struggle under capitalism, exploitation of labour and centralization of economic power. These circumstances changed economic thinking. Regional variations and miserable situation of labour class sought state intervention. As a result, economic planning is evolved in a systematic and scientific manner. It helps in optimum utilization of resources, which ultimately achieves maximum benefit. Planning is done by individuals, organizations and the economy. Soviet Union pioneered in the field of economic planning and made considerable progress. It has provided a model for developing countries including India. Planning by direction is practised in a socialist economy. A central planning committee directs people what they ought to do or not to do. In a democratic country like India, planning may not be implemented in that way but through inducement. The government gives benefits in the form of tax benefit, tax holiday, subsidy, etc., to induce people to do things, which the government believes beneficial for people.

Objective of economic planning is to set targets for optimum utilization of resources, which a country needs to accomplish to derive maximum benefit for its people. Objectives are directly related to targets. These targets vary significantly between countries and regions. Some of the objectives of planning may be contradictory as choice between more outputs versus more employment avenues. Underdeveloped countries, generally have to choose between these two objectives which have different directions.

PLANNING AND ECONOMIC DEVELOPMENT

All countries, whether developed or developing, strive to boost standard of living of their people and to achieve higher level of economic development. To make economic development sustainable, countries have to take care of exploitation and utilization of natural resources in a balanced way; boosting employment *en bloc*; attaining self-sufficiency and tending the economy to rise steadily towards self-sustaining growth. However, it is only possible in a planned economy. Unplanned economy has numerous defects, as possibility of over or under-production, uneven exploitation of labour and cut-throat competition resulting in economic waste.

A planned economy always consists of a wide scope and is pervading. There is neither possibility of lopsided development nor unbalanced economic growth. For example, a single firm or a group of firms controls such a small fraction of output of a single commodity and therefore, take into account such a small part of the whole industrial activity. They are only concerned about the well-being of a particular firm and at most their employees. However, they may not be aware of or may not like the consequences of their action. Plastics, wine or cigarette industries are some of the examples where the industry does not take care of the consequences of its production or use. The government or a central authority can only visualize the social welfare. In India, the central authority, i.e., Planning Commission takes stock of development after every five years and frame programmes for the use of available resources to achieve planned targets in next five years.

In developing economies, economic planning and government interventions are imperative due to some other reasons also. First, in such countries, a wide gap persists between consumption requirements and subsequent investment. The government is expected to judiciously invite and allow foreign investment. However, after liberalization and globalization, governments of most of the countries have relaxed terms and conditions for foreign investment. In fact, countries adopt several methods to invite foreign investment to fill the gap between demand for and supply of investment.

However, even now planning and government intervention are important to protect interest of the vulnerable group in the society. Free play of market forces may increase the competitiveness among the firms but this may lead to lopsided growth. Proper planning is inevitable to achieve holistic and inclusive growth of the economy.

EXERCISES

A. Objective

1. Fill up the blanks: **(For 1/2 mark each)**

(i) ____________ taxes are imposed on income and wealth and ____________ taxes are imposed on commodities.

(ii) Direct taxes fall heavily on higher incomes and wealth, hence they have ____________ effect on income and wealth distribution of an economy.

(iii) Direct taxes have ____________ scope.

(iv) Vast resources have to be raised in an economy for ____________.

Ans. (i) direct, indirect; (ii) favourable; (iii) limited; (iv) economic development

2. Write True or False: **(For 1/2 mark each)**

(i) Sources of income of government in an economy consist of tax revenue and non-tax revenue.

(ii) In socialist economies, planning is done by inducement.

(iii) Incidence of direct tax can be shifted to others.
(iv) Fiscal policy refers to tax and subsidy.
(v) Through deficit financing, budgetary gap is financed.
(vi) Income tax is an indirect tax.
(vii) Private enterprises flourish under socialist pattern of economy.
(viii) Central Planning Committee decides what to produce under capitalist pattern of economy.

Ans. (i) True; (ii) False; (iii) False; (iv) True;
(v) True; (vi) False (vii) False; (viii) False

B. Subjective

1. Discuss different sources of income of a government.
2. Discuss the principle of maximum social advantage in detail.
3. Discuss the importance of indirect tax in a developing economy.
4. Discuss the role of deficit financing in an economy.
5. Defferentiate between economic growth and economic development.
6. Discuss the importance of economic planning to achieve economic development.
7. How fiscal policy can be used for induced planning? Explain.
8. Differentiate between capitalist economy vs. socialist economy.
9. Is mixed economy is the best system to govern a country? Discuss.

References and Suggested Readings

1. R.A. Musgrave, "The Theory of Public Finance", McGraw Hill, New York.
2. A.R. Prest, "Public Finance in Theory and Practice", Weiden Feld and Nicholson, London.
3. Amitava Bose, Mihir Rakshit and Anup Sinha, "Issues in Economic Theory and Public Policy", Oxford University Press, New Delhi.
4. Yujira Hayami, "Development Economics", Oxford University Press, New Delhi.
5. Gerald M. Meier and James E. Rauch, "Leading Issues in Economic Development", Oxford University Press, New Delhi.
6. Thorvaldur Gylfason, "Principles of Economic Growth", Oxford University Press, New Delhi.
7. I.G. Patel, "Economic Reforms and Global Change". Macmillan India Ltd., New Delhi.
8. Public Interest Research Group, "Swiss TNCs in India". Madhyam Books, New Delhi.

7

Cost Concept and Cost Management

Purpose of this chapter is to acquaint the reader with:

- Types of Cost
- Variance Analysis, Preparation of Cost Sheet
- Cost Improvement

All types of expenses, which are incurred by the producer in the process of production or in other words, in the process of transforming inputs into output are called cost. As engineers, in their professional life, evaluate alternative course of action to select the most cost effective one, they need to understand various types of cost. To understand example of a class of students may be taken. It may be divided on the basis of sex of students, area of residence, preference for meal and in so many other ways but these divisions may not be mutually exclusive. Similarly, cost also may be divided in several ways, but they are not mutually exclusive. Since there are large numbers of determinants of cost, cost may be classified in many ways. Some of them are discussed below.

TYPES OF COST

Total Cost, Average Cost and Marginal Cost

All types of costs, which a firm incurs in course of producing or acquiring a good or a service is called total cost. The total cost is also known as acquisition cost or outlay costs. Examples of total cost is cost of production of car.

Average cost is the cost per unit produced.

Marginal cost is the increase in cost as a result of a unit change in output. In other words, the additional costs incurred when there is a unit change in the existing output of goods and services. They have been further discussed in Figs. 7.1 and 7.2.

Fixed Cost, Variable Cost and Incremental Cost

Fixed cost is that part of the total cost of a firm which does not vary with the variation in output over a range of production. In other words, it remains same over a range of production due to indivisibility of the factor of production. They are also known as overhead cost, period cost, indirect cost or capacity cost. If the production increases, the fixed cost per unit decreases, as the total fixed cost is divided between increasing numbers of units, cost of machine and tools, rent of buildings are some of the examples of fixed cost. If cost of machine is Rs. 10,000 and units produced are 500, then fixed cost per unit will be $= \frac{10000}{500}$ = Rs. 20. If number of units produced increases to 1000, the fixed cost/unit $= \frac{10,000}{1000}$ = Rs 10.

Variable cost is directly proportional to the volume of goods or services produced. It means change in variable cost is directly proportional to the number of units produced. Variable cost increases when volume of production increases and vice versa. As variable cost is directly related to the number of units produced, it is also known as product cost or direct cost. Examples of variable costs are material costs and casual labour costs.

Semi-variable or semi-fixed cost remains constant up to certain level of production but beyond that they change as units of production change. Such changes are not directly proportional to the change in production, e.g., repairs and maintenance of machinery and supervision charges.

Incremental cost may be defined as the difference in total costs resulting from a complemented change in the policy or addition to the costs resulting from a change in the nature or the level of business activity. While taking a decision, it must be taken care that the incremental revenue must exceed the incremental cost (IR > IC).

Short Run Cost and Long Run Cost

To understand short run cost and long run cost, we must first discuss 'short run' and 'long run'. Short run is a period in which the firm can adjust its output according to the change in demand only by changing variable factor of production such as raw material and casual labour but does not have time to change its fixed factors of production such as scale of the plant. However, the firm can adjust its output according to the change in demand by changing both fixed and variable factors of production in long run. So, short run cost function may be stated as an explicit function of the level of output and it is the cost of the fixed inputs.

Total cost (Fig. 7.1) may be expressed as

$$TC = f(q) + a \tag{1}$$

where a = fixed cost, which is independent of the level of output and q is the unit produced.

If $q = 0$, it would mean that the firm is not employing any variable factor of production and hence, absence of variable costs in the short run. In such a case, equation (1) may be written as,

$$TC = 0 + a$$

This would mean that, even at zero output level, the firm has to incur fixed costs. A number of other cost functions may be derived from equation (1) as follows:

$$TC = f(q) + a$$

$$= TVC + TFC$$

Therefore, $TVC = f(q)$

where TVC = Total Variable Cost

$$AC = TC/q = \{f(q) + a\}/q$$

where AC = Average Cost

$$AVC = TVC/q = f(q)/q$$

where AVC = Average Variable Cost

$$AFC = TFC/q = a/q$$

where AFC = Average Fixed Cost

$$MC = dTC/dq$$ (differentiation of TC with respect to q)

where MC = Marginal Cost

AC, AVC and MC are all second-degree curves, which first decline and then increase as output expanded. MC function reaches its minimum before AC function and AVC function. Also, AVC function reaches its minimum before AC function.

Again, MC curve cuts the minimum points of the AVC and AC curves from below which states the equality between AVC, and MC is achieved before and at the lower point than equality between AC and MC.

The AFC function in Fig. 7.2 is a rectangular hyperbola. It spreads over a large number of units as output increases and, therefore, leads to zero

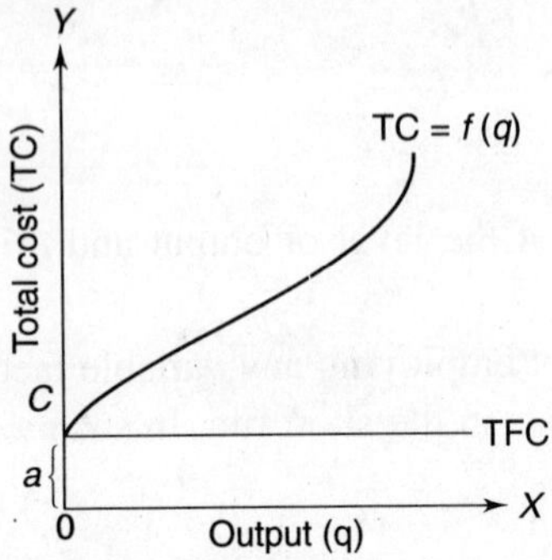

Fig. 7.1

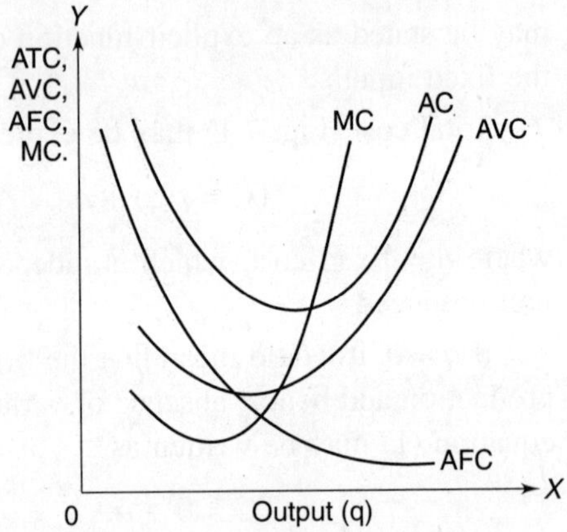

Fig. 7.2

(but it will never be zero in the short run). It proves that the vertical distance between the AC function and the AVC function equals the AFC function and, therefore, decreases as output expands.

The fundamental rule of equilibrium (where the product will be most cost efficient) is MC = MR. It means that the fixed cost (a) generally has no effect upon firm's optimizing decisions during the period of short run. During this time period, the fixed costs must be paid regardless of the level of firm's output and it merely adds a constant term to its profit (π) equation. The fixed cost term (*a*) vanishes upon differentiation, and MC is independent of its level.

But sometimes fixed costs may also enter into optimizing decisions of a firm. The maximum loss that a firm would be ready to bear in the short run must not be greater than this constant (i.e., the fixed cost). The firm will never bear the loss, which may be more than the amount of its fixed cost. The moment loss is more than the fixed cost (i.e., it covers a part of AVC), the firm should discontinue production and accept a loss equal to its fixed cost.

The long run average cost curve and long run total cost curve can be obtained by joining minimum points of short run average costs curves (Fig. 7.3) and short run total cost curves (Fig. 7.4) respectively.

Opportunity Cost

Opportunity cost represents the benefits or revenue foregone by pursuing one course of action rather than the other. This means when the best alternative is adopted, it is obvious that the second-best alternative cannot be implemented and its benefits are foregone. Thus, the benefit of this second-best alternative, which has been sacrificed due to the selection of the best alternative is known as the opportunity cost of the best alternative. This type of cost is imaginary

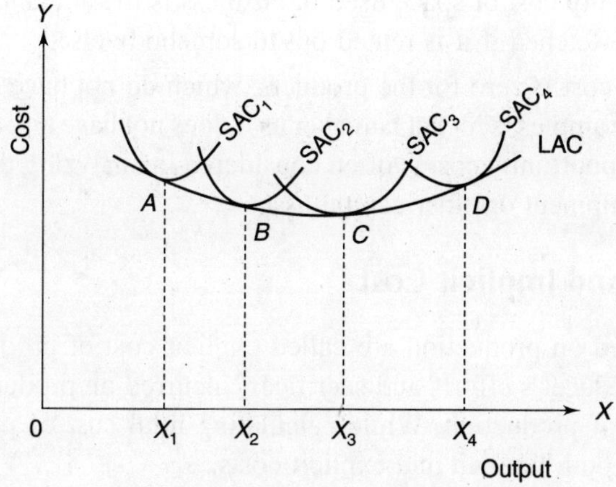

Fig. 7.3

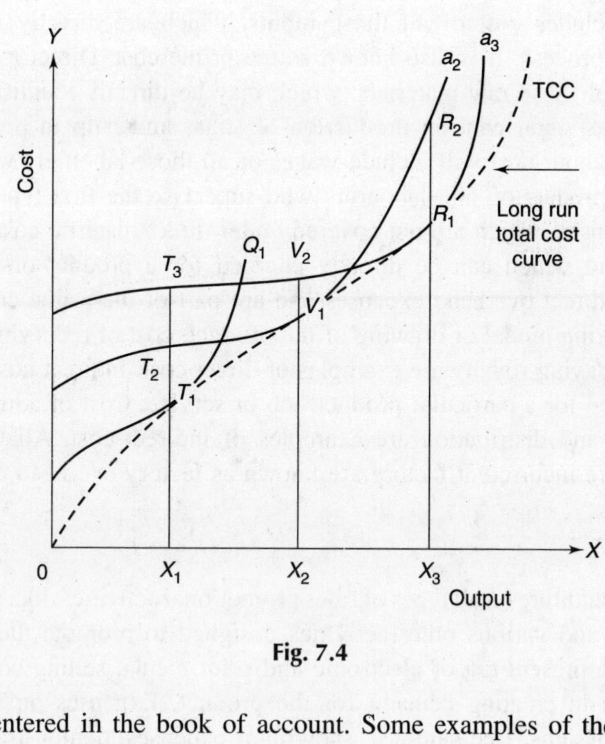

Fig. 7.4

and is not entered in the book of account. Some examples of the opportunity costs are:

(i) Opportunity cost of the funds employed in the firm is the amount of interest, which otherwise could have been earned.

(ii) Opportunity cost of labour in own business is the wage which one would have earned by accepting a job outside.

(iii) Opportunity cost of space used in business is the amount of rent, which could be fetched if it is rented out to somebody else.

Opportunity cost is zero for the products, which do not have any alternative use. One of the examples is rocket launcher as it does not have any alternative use. The concept of opportunity cost is often considered in analyzing the replacement of a piece of equipment or other capital asset.

Explicit Cost and Implicit Cost

Expenses incurred on production are called explicit cost of production. On the other hand, a producer's efforts and sacrifices, incurred on production is known as implicit cost of production. While calculating total cost of production, one should calculate both implicit and explicit costs.

Direct Cost and Indirect Cost

Direct cost includes cost of all those inputs, which are directly involved in production or process. It is also known as the prime cost. Direct material cost includes cost of those raw materials, which may be directly identifiable to the product such as sugar cane in production of sugar and pulp in production of paper. Direct labour cost will include wages of all those labourers who directly participate in production and labourers who supervise the first type of labour. All other expenses, which are not covered under direct material cost and direct labour cost and which can be directly charged for a product or service are known as the direct overhead expenses and are part of the prime cost. Cost of designing, making model or drawing of the product, cost of rectifying defective work, cost of paying royalty are examples of direct cost. Indirect cost cannot be directly charged for a particular product, job or service. Cost of administration, advertisement and distribution are examples of indirect cost. All the indirect costs, which are incurred at factory are known as factory overhead cost.

Selling Cost

It includes expenditure on all types of sales promotional activities, like advertising, sales network and various other activities designed to promote the sales of a product. In the present era of electronic and print media, selling cost plays an important role in creating demand for the product. Expenses on advertising, publicity, neon signs, free samples, showroom expenses, demonstration of the product, are examples of selling cost.

Life Cycle Cost

All types of cost, both recurring and non-recurring that occur from innovation, initiating production for businass to disposing of obsolete or old products are known as life cycle cost. It includes cost of R&D, cost of production, cost of distribution, cost of after-sales service and cost of disposal of obsolete or old product. Earlier, enterprises were interested only up to marketing of the product. However, after liberalization the market has become so competitive that more and more enterprises are taking care of after-sales services and even disposal of the old products as their marketing strategy. Thus, life cycle cost has become fashionable in recent years.

Sunk Cost

All efforts of considering cost from its different perspectives are to minimize it. However, some of the costs may have occurred in the past and has no relevance to estimation of costs for any alternative course of action is known as sunk cost. It is common to all alternatives. Sunk cost might exist in past expenditure that cannot be received or capital that has already been invested and cannot be retrieved. As by any effort, it cannot be altered in future, it is not relevant for engineers.

Standard Cost

At planning level, expected cost in completion of the whole process is calculated by the management. It is known as 'Standard Cost', which is arrived at by adding all the possible expenses. It is different from historical cost, which is calculated from the past cost information. However, when the product is implemented, there may be some deviation between standard cost and actual cost due to time lag between planning and implementation. Management makes every effort to keep actual cost as near as possible to the standard cost and in case of any deviation, management takes corrective measures. At the same time, standard cost must be decided judiciously, which can be achieved operationally. Again, before deciding standard cost, inflation and other macroeconomic variables must be taken into account, which affect the general price level and, ultimately, may lead to increase in price level of the inputs. Looking at the importance of standard cost, it should be calculated strictly on the basis of fixed norms and past experience.

Recurring Cost and Non-recurring Cost

Recurring costs are repetitive in nature and occur in an organization when similar goods or services are produced on a repetitive basis. Along with variable cost, it includes some of the items of fixed cost also. Example is monthly rent payment for office space by an engineering firm. On the other hand, non-recurring costs are non-repetitive and one time cost in nature. Purchase of an office space is an example of non-recurring cost.

VARIANCE ANALYSIS

Any study of deviation between standard cost and actual cost is known as variance analysis. It is carried out to detect any deviation from standard cost, so that management can take corrective measures to control deviation and minimize cost. When the actual cost exceeds the standard cost, the difference is referred to as an unfavorurable variance or red variance. Such variance are normally recorded in red and if does not exceed, it is termed favourable or black variance. Thus, it provides feedback information for management control. However, variance can be used for control and evaluation only if the standard has been calculated accurately and there is possibility of measuring performance accurately. Variance may be calculated for all types of cost as per the requirement of management. Here, three main type of variance have been discussed. They are as follows.

Direct Material Cost Variance

It is the difference between standard cost and actual cost of material. It may be calculated as:

Material cost variance = Standard material cost for actual output – Actual material cost

= Standard price × standard quantity – Actual price × Actual quantity

Example 1

Standard price (SP) = Rs. 100 per kg

Standard quantity (SQ) = 100 kg

Actual price (AP) = Rs. 150 per kg

Actual quantity (AQ) = 120 kg

Solution:

Material Cost Variance = (SP × SQ) – (AP × AQ)

= (100 × 100) – (150 × 120) = 10000 – 18000 = Rs. 8000.

Direct Labour Cost Variance

It is the difference between the standard labour cost for the actual production and the actual labour cost. It may be calculated as:

Labour cost variance (LCV) = Standard labour cost for actual ourput – Actual labour costs

= Standard rate/time unit × Standard time for actual output – Actual rate/time unit × Actual time

= (SR × ST) – (AR × AT)

Example 2

Standard wage rate = Rs. 60/day

Standard time = 6 days

Actual time = 5 days

Actual wage rate = Rs. 100/day

Solution:

Labour cost variance = (SR × ST) – (AR × AT)

(60 × 6) – (5 × 100)

= 360 – 500 = Rs. 140

Direct Overhead Cost Variance

It is the difference between standard overheads absorbed or received in actual output and the actual overheads cost. Standard overhead rate can be calculated either by calculating on the basis of time or on the basis of unit.

Standard overhead rate per hour = Budgeted overhead/Budgeted hours

Standard overhead rate per unit = Budgeted overhead/Budgeted output

Formula for overhead cost variance (if unit rate is considered)

= Standard overheads for actual output – Actual overhead

Example 3

	Budget	*Actual*
Production	15000	12000
Standard hours	7500	7000
Overheads	Rs. 15000	Rs. 18000
Fixed	Rs. 7500	Rs. 7500
Variable	Rs. 7500	Rs. 10500

Calculate overhead cost variance

Solution:

Standard unit rate = Rs. 15000/15000 = Re. 1

Standard hour rate = Rs. 15000/7500 = Rs. 2

If calculated by unit rate, Overhead cost variance = Standard overhead cost for actual production – Actual overhead

= 12000 × 1 – 18000 = Rs. 6000

or, if calculated by standard hourly rate

= Standard hours for actual output × Standard hourly rate – Actual overhead

$= 2 \times 7500/15000 \times 12000 - 18000$

= Rs. 6000.

Disposition of Variance

Once the variance analysis has been made, it is for the management to find out causes for variance and how to dispose of those amounts because variances are unabsorbed cost balance. Most variances are disposed of at the end of the accounting year. However, there is no uniformity of opinion among the experts for proper disposition of these variances. Following alternative methods are used for the purpose:

(i) To adjust all or part of the amount as cost of sales.
(ii) To transfer all or part of the amount as an exceptional profit or loss.
(iii) To distribute all or part of the amount over inventories of materials, work in progress, finished goods and cost of goods sold.

Preparation of Cost Sheet

In accounting, there is a well-defined formal way to enter several costs in cost sheet to find out total cost. Preparation of cost sheet is important because it gives detail of different expenditure included in the total cost, which can be used for further cost analysis. Format of cost sheet is given below.

Table 7.1 Cost Sheet or Cost Structure

Particular	*Cost*	*Description*	*Amount in Rs.*
Direct material			
+ Direct labour			
+ Direct overhead expenses			
	Prime cost		
Factory overheads			
	Factory cost or Work cost		
+ Office and administrative overheads			
	Cost of production		
+ Selling and distributional overheads			
	Total cost		
+ Profit			
	Selling price		

The format of cost sheet or cost structure has been developed on the assumption that production is done in the premises of factory and administrative building may be adjacent (or apart but connected via information and communication technology) to the factory premises. Direct labour cost, direct material cost and direct overhead cost are prime costs. Along with prime cost, cost incurred on machine and other expenses, which can be calculated per unit produced and has incurred within factory, makes factory cost. Factory cost along with expenses incurred on administration such as salary of administrative staff and expenditure on telephone bills make cost of production. Expenses incurred outside premises of factory and administrative office, are added to cost of production to make total cost. Total cost plus profit become selling price.

There are some items, which should not be written in the cost sheet as they are purely financial items and they do not come under cost of production. They are as follows:

(i) Items such as fines and penalties or interest on debentures and profit on sale of fixed assets, damage received through a court of law or interest received on bank deposits should not be written in the cost sheet as they are purely financial charges and income.

(ii) Abnormal gains and losses and appropriation of profit such as charitable donation, income tax or appropriation to sinking funds should not be written in cost sheet.

Example 4

Prepare a cost sheet for the month ended 30th December, 2012 of Kalyan Ltd.

Particular	*Rs.*
Raw material — Existing stock	7,000.00
Purchase	15,000.00
Closing stock	5,000.00
Direct wages	25,000.00
Direct expenses	15,000.00
Factory rent, insurance, lighting, supervision	35,000.00
Cost of plant and machinery	12,000.00
Indirect wages	20,000.00
Advertisement, publicity, free sample	2,000.00
Salesmen travelling expenses	2,000.00
Salary of office staff	10,000.00
Telephone and postage	2,000.00
Audit fee	4,000.00
Profit	10% of total cost

Solution:

Cost Sheet of Kalyan Ltd.

Particular	*Description*	*Amount in Rs.*
Direct wage + Direct raw material + Direct expenses	 Existing stock + purchase – Closing stock	25,000.00 17,000.00 15,000.00
	Prime Cost	**57,000.00**
+ Indirect wage + Cost of plant and machinery + Factory rent, insurance, lighting, supervision		20,000.00 12,000.00 35,000.00
	Factory Cost	**124,000.00**
+ Salary of office staff + Telephone and postage Audit fee		10,000.00 2,000.00 4,000.00
	Cost of production	**140,000.00**
+ Advertisement, publicity, free sample + Salesmen travelling expenses		2,000.00 2,000.00
	Total Cost	**144,000.00**
+ Profit	10% of Total cost	14,400.00
Selling price		158,400.00

Example 5

The accounts of Monalisa Manufacturing Ltd. for the year ended 31st December, 2012 is shown below:

Particular	*Rs.*
Stock of material on 01-01-2012	97500.00
Material purchased	75000.00
Salary of Factory Staff	12000.00
Salary of General Office Staff	14500.00
Bad debts written off	7000.00
Salesmen's salary and commission	11575.00
Depreciation written off of furniture	750.00
Rent, taxes and insurance (factory)	13000.00
Direct wages	54000.00

Contd...

Contd...

General expenses	21000.00
Gas and water (factory)	21000.00
Manager's salary (10% of opening material stock)	9750.00
Depreciation on plant and tools	7500.00
Carriage outwards	3000.00
Direct expenses	12000.00
Rent (office), taxes, insurances	2500.00
Gas, water (office)	450.00
Stock of materials 31.12.2012	15500.00

Profit is 10% of the material cost. Prepare a cost sheet for the year ended on 31.12.2012

Solution:

Cost sheet for the year ended on 31.12.2012

Particular	*Description*	*Amount in Rs.*
Direct raw material	Existing stock of material on 01.01.2012	97500.00
	+ material purchased	+ 75000.00
	– closing stock on 31.12.2004	– 15500.00 = 157000.00
+ Direct wages		54000.00
+ Direct expenses		12000.00
	Prime Cost	223000.00
+ Drawing salary of factory staff	+ 12000.00	
+ Rent, taxes, insurance (factory)	+ 13000.00	
+ Gas and water (factory)	+ 21000.00	
+ Depreciation of plant and tools	+ 7500.00	53500.00
	Factory Cost	276500.00
+ Salary of office staff	+ 14500.00	
+ Rent (office), taxes, insurance	+ 2500.00	
+ Gas and Water (office)	+ 450.00	
+ Depreciation of written off furniture	+ 750.00	
+ General Expenses	+ 21000.00	39200.00
	Cost of Production	315700.00
+ Selling and Distribution Expenses	+ 11575.00	
+ Bad debts	+ 7000.00	
+ Sales man's salary and Commission	+ 11575.00	
+ Carriage outward	+ 3000.00	33150.00
	Total Production	348850.00
+ Profit (10 % of the Material Cost)		15700.00
	Selling Price	364550.00

Example 6

From the following information, calculate the prime cost and work cost.

Particular	*Rs.*
Raw material consumed	1,75,000
Salary paid to employees	1,00,000
Direct expenses	25,000
Factory overheads 20% of prime cost	
Factory scrap sold	7,000
Opening stock of work-in-progress	15,000
Closing stock of work-in-progress	20,000

Solution:

Amount of work cost

Particular		*Rs.*
	Raw material consumed	1,75,000.00
	+ Direct wage	1,00,000.00
	+ Direct expenses	25,000.00
Prime Cost		3,00,000.00
	+ Factory overheads @ 20% of prime cost	60,000.00
	– Factory scrap sold	7,000.00
	Particular	*Rs.*
	+ Opening stock of works-in-progress and	15,000.00
	– Closing stock of work-in-progress	20,000.00
Work Cost of Factory Cost		402000.00

Example 7: At the beginning of the period, the stock of raw material was worth Rs. 25000. Thereafter, 500 tonnes of raw material were purchased at the rate of Rs. 550/tonnes. The closing stock was Rs. 45000. The carriage, freight and other duties paid on purchase amounted to Rs. 6000, 200 and 250 respectively. Find the cost of raw material consumed.

Solution:

Cost of raw material consumed

Particular	*Rs.*
Opening stock of raw material	25,000.00
+ Purchase of raw material (Rs. 500 × Rs. 550)	27,500.00
+ Expenses to purchase (Rs. 6000 + Rs. 200 + Rs. 250)	6,450.00
– Closing stock of raw material	45000.00
Cost of raw material consumed	13950.00

Cost Improvement

Determination of actual cost is very important for accounting purpose. Information about actual cost enables the management to take necessary action for cost improvement which is one of the prerequisites for enhancing competitiveness of the firm to sustain in the market especially in the era of liberalization and opening up of the economy. There are two aspects of cost improvement. They are cost control and cost reduction. Cost control encompasses three stages. First is setting-up the target, i.e., calculating standard cost. It is followed by comparing actual cost with the standard cost and last step is taking required measures to minimize deviation of actual cost from the standard cost. Purpose of cost control measures is to ensure that costs incurred are within the prescribed limit. Cost control is, therefore, a continuous process. However, the scope of cost reduction is much wider. It is a well-knit programme, which incorporates drastic action for cost saving, sometimes even by changing rigid boundaries laid down by the standards or targets. It is a process of achieving reduction in cost through improved design, better tools, new layouts, incentive schemes, etc. However, it must be understood that reduction due to windfall's gain, changes in government policies, etc., are not treated as cost reduction.

Steps for Cost Improvement

Following essential steps are required to be taken for effective cost improvement measure:

(i) While setting standards and norms, scope of cost reduction is to be explored.

(ii) Strict control on actual expenditure may be exercised.

(iii) Reporting and monitoring system should be strengthened.

(iv) Right climate must be provided to all the employees to encourage creativity.

(v) An all-round cost consciousness in the organization needs to be inculcated.

EXERCISES

A. Objective (For 1/2 marks each)

Write true or false for each of the following:

(i) Marginal cost is same for all units for production.

(ii) In short run, a firm can change its inputs only.

(iii) Cost function explains the relationship between the input and the output of a commodity and the cost incurred in its production.

(iv) Variance is the difference between standard cost and actual cost.
(v) One can find opportunity cost in the book of account.
(vi) Short term is a fixed time frame for three years.
(vii) Direct overhead expenses are parts of prime cost.

Ans. (i) False; (ii) False; (iii) True; (iv) True;
(v) False; (vi) False; (vii) True

B. Subjective (Four marks each)

1. Differentiate between
   (i) Average cost and marginal cost
   (ii) Actual cost and opportunity cost
   (iii) Fixed cost and variable cost
   (iv) Short run cost and long run cost
2. Why concept of sunk cost is not relevant for engineers?
3. Discuss opportunity cost and its relevance for engineers.
4. Discuss significance of variance analysis for an enterprise.
5. Discuss disposition of variance.
6. Discuss the process of cost improvement in detail.

C. Numerical Problems (For four marks each)

1. Calculate the material cost variance if
   Standard price = Rs. 17 per kg
   Actual price = Rs. 19 per kg
   Standard quantity = 100 kg.
   Actual quantity used = 95 kg
2. Calculate the labour cost variance if
   Standard wage rate = Rs. 200/day
   Standard days = 400
   Actual days = 380
   Actual wage rate = Rs. 225/day
3. Calculate the overhead cost variance if

	Budgeted	*Actual*
Production	500	400
Standard	100	95
Overheads	Rs. 1000	Rs. 1200
Fixed	Rs. 600	Rs. 600
Variable	Rs. 400	Rs. 600

4. The following information is available from the books for the month ended 31st March, 2014:

Sl. No.	Items	Rs.
1.	Direct material	9,00,000.00
2.	Direct labour	7,50,000.00
3.	Selling and distribution overhead	5,25,000.00
4.	Administrative overhead	4,20,000.00
5.	Factory overhead	4,50,000.00
6.	Profit	6,09,000.00

Number of items produced is 1000. You are required to prepare a cost sheet indicating the prime cost, work cost, cost of production and selling price.

5. From the following information, you are required to prepare cost sheet for the month of March 2014 and also find out selling price per unit, if the margin of profit is Rs 20 on the total cost. Units produced and sold during the month were 10,000.

Cost data for the Month 2008.

Sl. No.	Items	Rs.
1.	Raw material consumed	2,00,000.00
2.	Direct labour charges	4,00,000.00
3.	Direct expenses	50,000.00
4.	Factory overheads	50% of prime cost
5.	Office overheads	20% of work cost
6.	Selling and distribution expenses	Rs. 5 per unit sold

Part III
Topics of Applied Economics

8

Project Planning

Purpose of this chapter is to acquaint the reader with:

- Steps in project planning
- Market survey, elasticity of demand, demand estimation and forecasting
- Decision analysis, budget preparation and input-output analysis
- Managing finance, sources of finance, capital budgeting
- Selection of location, inputs and machine, operation planning, material handling
- Factors which affect price determination
- Profit maximizing output and price determination under monopoly
- Profit maximizing output and price determination under perfect competition

Project planning can be explained with the help of an analogy, e.g., mountaineering. The primary job for mountaineering is to select the right mountain. Then fix the goal. The target has to be commensurate with the resources available—the mission statement. Next, select the right people with right skills, attitude and commitment to stretch to the limit. The right team members can make vital difference between success and failure, or between life and death. Then provide the mountaineers the necessary tools. The project manager must ensure that his people are not asked to trudge the snow with canvas shoes. The mountaineer must know when to withdraw to the base camp and when to mount an assault.

Nowadays, more and more engineers are heading organizations as owner or Managing Directors, an engineer needs to be very efficient in engineering activity but in management too. The biggest failure of any firm has been the inability of its leader to read the business proposal correctly. This chapter focuses on formulating the correct approach in project planning and execution. A project consists of interrelated activities, which need to be executed to complete the entire task. The activities are interrelated and they need to be performed in a logical sequence to maximize the return.

Step 1: Market Survey, Business Risk and Forecasting
Step 2: Planning and Budget Preparation
Step 3: Managing Finance
Step 4: Arranging Inputs
Step 5: Profit Maximization
Step 6: Evaluation and Feedback

STEP 1: MARKET SURVEY AND FORECASTING

Any project planning starts with market survey. Market survey is a commercial survey to assess the feasibility of the business proposal. It provides necessary statistical information to know its demand function to take effective short-run operating decisions and long-run planning decisions. For example, one must know the effect of changing prices on demand to establish or change its price policy. In the long-run planning, good estimates of the sensitivity of demand to both structure of population and changes in income level enable a firm to assess future growth potential and, thus, to establish effective long run programme for expansion.

Sensitivity of demand to its determinants is a crucial factor in business planning. We have already discussed elasticity of demand, i.e., price, cross income and advertisement in the Chapter 2. Here, we will elaborate it a little further.

Elasticity of Demand and Demand Estimation

To be profitable, the volume of goods and services to be produced must be in accordance with the demand for the product. Except the perfectly competitive market, seller in every other market has to know the influence of price on the quantity demanded for the product to maximise return. If the price elasticity of demand for the product is inelastic, he can charge a high price for it. To a monopolist, knowledge of elasticity of demand for his product can be helpful in practising discrimination,[1] thus, exploiting the existence of the prevailing differences in price elasticity in different parts of the market. Elasticity of demand is not the only factor, which the individual producer considers when contemplating a change in price; but certainly, it is one of the very important considerations.

Price Elasticity of Demand—Dividing Marginal Cost by Average Cost

Example 1 Find price elasticity e_d, if the demand function $q = 25 - 4p + p^2$ were q is the demand for commodity at price p.

Solution: Since $q = 25 - 4p + p^2$

$\therefore$ Marginal function $= \dfrac{dq}{dp} = -4 + 2p$

Average function $= q/p = \dfrac{25 - 4p + p^2}{p}$

$$|e_d| = \frac{\text{Marginal function}}{\text{Average function}} = \frac{(-4 + 2p)\,p}{25 - 4p + p^2}$$

The expression gives the elasticity as a function of p. We can, therefore, easily find the point elasticity at any particular price level.

1. Suppose $p = 4$, then $|e_d| = \dfrac{(-4 + 8)4}{25 - 16 + 16} = \dfrac{16}{25} = 0.64$ (Approx.)

   $\therefore$ Demand at $p = 4$ is less than unit elastic.

2. Suppose $p = 5$, then $|e_d| = \dfrac{(-4 + 10)5}{25 - 20 + 25} = 1$

   At $p = 5$, the elasticity of demand is unitary.

3. Suppose $p = 8$, then elasticity is

$$|e_d| = + \frac{(-4 + 16)8}{25 - 32 + 64} = \frac{96}{57} = 1.7 \text{ (Approx.)}$$

   which is greater than 1; so that demand is said to be more than unit elastic at $p = 8$.

Price Elasticity of Demand—Simple Arithmetic Calculations

Example 2 The demand law is given by $q = 10 - p$ near the point $q = 4$ and $p =$ Rs. 6. If the price increases by 5%; determine the per cent decrease in demand and hence an approximation to the elasticity of demand.

Solution: At $p =$ Rs. 6; price increases by 5%, hence increased price

$$= 6 + \frac{6 \times 5}{100} = 6.30$$

$\therefore$ Rise in price = 6.30 – 6.0 = Rs. 0.30.

Corresponding to this increased price, the new demand is

$$q = 10 - 6.30 = 3.30$$

$\therefore$ Decrease in demand = 3.30 – 4 = 0.7

Thus, we have,

Rise in price = 0.30;

$\therefore$ Per cent rise in price $= \left\{+\left(\dfrac{0.30}{6}\right) \times 100\right\} = 5\%$

Fall in demand = 0.70,

$\therefore$ Per cent decrease in demand $= \left\{-\left(\dfrac{0.70}{4}\right) \times 100\right\} = 17.5\%$

$\therefore \quad |e_d| =$ Percentage change in demand/percentage change in price

$$= \left|\frac{17.5\%}{5\%}\right|$$

$$= 3.5$$

Price elasticity is more than unit.

Example 3 The price elasticity of demand for milk is equal to unity (=1) and at the price of Rs. 35 per litre, a milk confectionery shop demands 70 litres milk.If the price become Rs. 40 per litre, how much milk the shopkeeper will purchase if it does not intend to increase its expenditure on milk.

Solution: If new demand is q,

$$e_d = \frac{\text{New demand–old demand}}{\text{New price–old price}} \times \frac{\text{Old price}}{\text{Old demand}}$$

or, $$1 = -\left(\frac{q-70}{40-35} \times \frac{35}{70}\right)$$

or $$-q + 70 = 10$$

or, $$q = 70 - 10 = 60$$

So, the shop will purchase 60 litres of milk.

Example 4 If the $e_d = 1$, five kg of grapes are demanded at Rs. 80 per kg. At what price six kg of grapes will be demanded?

Solution Let new price = p

$$e_d = -\frac{\text{New demand–old demand}}{\text{New price–old price}} \times \frac{\text{Old price}}{\text{Old demand}}$$

or, $$1 = \left(\frac{6-5}{p-80} \times \frac{80}{5}\right)$$

or, $$1 = -\left(\frac{16}{p-80}\right)$$

or, $$p - 80 = -16$$

or, $$p = -16 + 80 = 64$$

So, at price of Rs. 64/kg, six kg of grapes will be demanded.

Price Elasticity of Demand—Use of Calculus

Example 5 If the demand law is $x = \dfrac{20}{p+1}$, find e_d with respect to price at the point where $p = 4$.

Solution: $$|e_d| = -\frac{dx}{dp} \times \frac{p}{x} = -\frac{20}{(p+1)^2} \times \frac{p\,(p+1)}{20}$$

$$= -\frac{p}{p+1}$$

at $$p = 4,\ e_d = -\frac{4}{5}$$

So, at price Rs. 4, elasticity of demand will be 4/5 (less than one).

Cross Elasticity of Demand

Example 6 The price of q_1 increases from Rs. 60 per kg to Rs. 75 per kg. As a result, the demand for q_2 increases from 7 kg to 10 kg. What is the cross elasticity of demand of q_1 for q_2?

Solution: $$dp_1 = 75 - 60 = \text{Rs } 15$$
$$dq_2 = 10 - 7 = 3$$

where dp_1 is change in price of q_1 and dq_2 is change in demand of q_2

$$e_d^* = \frac{dq_2}{dp_1} \cdot \frac{p_1}{q_2} = \frac{3}{15} \times \frac{60}{7} = \frac{12}{7} = +1.7$$

= which is a positive quantity

∴ Commodities q_1 and q_2 are competitive.

Example 7 Following are the demand functions for the commodities q_1 and q_2:

$$q_1 = p_1^{-1.3}\ p_2^{0.7}$$
$$q_2 = p_1^{0.6}\ p_2^{-0.5}$$

Determine whether the commodities q_1 and q_2 are complementary or competitive.

Solution: $$e_d^* = \frac{dq_1}{dp_2} \times \frac{p_2}{q_1} = 0.7\, p_1^{-1.3}\ p_2^{-0.3} \times \frac{p_2}{p_1^{-1.3}\ p_2^{0.7}}$$

= 0.7 which is a positive quantity, therefore, q_1 and q_2 are competitive.

Income Elasticity of Demand

Example 8 When income of a household was Rs. 60,000 per month. It bought 20 litres of milk per month. When income increased to Rs. 75,000 per month, it purchased 24 litres of milk per month. Assuming no change in the price of milk, what is the income elasticity of demand for milk?

Solution: Income elasticity of demand as e_y is measured with the help of following formula:

$$e_y = \frac{dq}{dy} \times \frac{y}{q}$$

where dq = change in demand

dy = change in income

y = original income

q = original demand

$$e_y = \frac{24 - 20}{75000 - 60000} \times \frac{60000}{20}$$

$$= \frac{4}{5}$$

Income elasticity of demand is positive, so it is a normal good and it is less than unity, so, a necessity good.

Example 9 At present, national income in the Indian economy is growing at the rate of 6% and income elasticity of the software sector $e_y = 2.0$. At what rate, a firm for software development can expect to grow?

Solution: Software sector can expect to grow by $e_y \times$ Rate of growth of national income of the Indian economy

$$= 6 \times 2 = 12\%$$

However, it must be considered that relation between demand and income is not always straight. It also depends on suddenness and permanence of a change in rate of growth of national income.

Advertisement Elasticity of Demand

Example 10 A mall owner is taking stock of his expenditure on advertisement. It has increased its expenditure from Rs. 50 thousand to Rs. 75 thousand each on advertisement of X_1 and X_2. Statistics on its pre- and post- advertisement sell is given below:

Commodity	*Pre-Advertisement Sale*	*Post-Advertisement Sale*
X_1	3 lakh	3.12 lakh
X_2	5 lakh	7.70 lakh

Find out their advertisement elasticity and nature of commodities X_1 and X_2.

Solution: $$e_A \text{ for } X_1 = \frac{\text{Change in demand}}{\text{Change in amount of money spent on advertisement}}$$

$$\times \frac{\text{Original amount of money spent on advertisement}}{\text{Original demand}}$$

$$= \frac{312 - 300}{75 - 50} \times \frac{50}{300} = \frac{12}{25} \times \frac{1}{6} = .08$$

$$e_A \text{ for } X_2 = \frac{(770 - 500)}{(75 - 50)} \times \frac{50}{500}$$

$$= 10.8 \times 0.1 = 1.08$$

Advertisement elasticity for commodity X_1 is less than one and for commodity X_2, it is more than one. Commodity X_2 is luxury, may be used by young people, who are more influenced by advertisement whereas X_1 is a necessary commodity.

BUSINESS RISK ANALYSIS

In the globalised environment, movement of firms is quite common. They move all over the world to exploit two types of benefits. First is internal or organisational and the second one is external or environmental benefit. Again, there are two types of internal benefits. They are as follows:

(i) To get the benefits of world wide market imperfections (including matching a rival's move);

(ii) To avail the opportunities that arise along with the life cycle of a firm's product.

Again, firms go abroad to exploit two types of environmental or external befits also. These benefits are:

(i) Responding to the macroeconomic imperatives for globalisation; and

(ii) Exploiting the competitive advantage of nations.

The firm can enter the foreign market in four ways depending on comparative cost advantage: i. Produce domestically and then export; ii. Enter into a contractual agreement to undertake certain part of the production process to other country; iii. Completing the whole production process in foreign country; iv. Doing different part of the production process in different country wherever that is cost-effective. However, venturing in a foreign land involves a lot of risk which may not be absolute but relative. A firm must take a comparative risk analysis before taking decision for a place or a country over the other. Risks are discussed along with cost and benefit under capital budgeting. Following risks must be taken into consideration in a comparative analysis:

1. **Economic Indicators to evaluate Business Risk** - To begin with, information regarding macroeconomic indicators as Gross Domestic Product (GDP), inflation rate, taxing system, unemployment rate and the balance of payment are very important to judge the business environment. Beside these, some microeconomic variables as physical infrastructure, i.e., electricity, roads, etc., should also be considered. Not only availability of the infrastructure as electricity but their quality and time taken in getting such connection has significant bearing on the profitability of a firm. Along with them, availability of raw material, skilled manpower, structure of market, etc., are very crucial which need to be assessed before taking a business initiative.

2. **Financial Indicators to Evaluate Business Risk** - International business operation is affected by conditions financial indicators as status of money and capital market, time taken in getting bank loan, devaluation of local currency. These need to be assessed.
3. **Political Indicators to evaluate Business Risk** - There are political risk involved with a place which influences operation and profitability of a business organisation. Some of macro political risks are external war, internal conflict between two regions or two groups of people, terrorist indulgence, unstable government and law and order. There are some micro political indicators also as official dishonesty, time taken in getting permission.
4. **Social Indicators to evaluate Business Risk** - Societal cohesiveness, acceptance to foreign citizen, law and order situation, institutional framework, etc., affect the performance. Institutional framework is some of the "givens" which makes a framework to operate. On the basis of evaluation of these indicators, the firm can evaluate expected performance in a particular country.
5. **Legal Indicators to Evaluate Business Risk**- Legal framework and the degree with which these are implemented, have important bearing for growth of any international venture.

World Development Indicator 2012, a World Bank initiative has published 'Business environment: enterprise surveys' in which it has ranked all the member countries on the basis of indicators as % of management time in dealing with officials and average number of meetings with tax officials regarding regulations and tax, time required to obtain permits and licenses, Informal payments to public officials (Corruption), Losses due to theft, robbery, vandalism, and arson (Crime), Firms formally registered when operations started (Informality), Firms with female participation in ownership, Firms using banks to finance investment, value lost due to electrical outages (Infrastructure), Internationally recognized quality certification ownership (Innovation), average time to clear direct exports through customs, firms offering formal training. These indicators are considered very crucial to analyse business risk.

FORECASTING

Demand forecasting is an indicator to estimate the amount, which is going to be demanded of a particular product in future. In other words, demand forecast is estimation of future demand for a product under the given market condition. All required inputs to produce that product are scarce and needs to be utilized judiciously. So, all enterprises look for as accurate forecasting as possible for their products. While price elasticity and cross elasticity are useful for pricing policy, income elasticity can be used for forecasting demand for the product in future. It will enable the producer to arrange all the required inputs well in advance and will avoid deficiency or over-stocking in accordance with expected income growth. The enterprise will make necessary modification in advertising and have proper capital planning.

A good forecasting method must have the ability to forecast accurately. It may be judged by observing the predictions made in the past, whether these predictions have been proved accurate or not. The method must be simple and easily understandable. It needs to be cost effective too.

1. Criteria for Selection of Forecasting Method

There are several criteria to select a forecasting method. Some of them are discussed below:

(i) Prefer the forecasting method, which is based on reasoning and logic.
(ii) Persons with appropriate skills should only forecast.
(iii) As the future is uncertain, the forecaster must tell his assumptions on which forecasting has been made.
(iv) Different techniques of forecasting must be taken into account.
(v) Previous year's forecast must be taken into account while forecasting further. It should be examined as to why the previous forecasts were right or wrong.

Evaluating a Forecast

Following considerations must be kept in mind before evaluating a forecast:

(i) It is necessary that every forecast needs to be made for a specified period of time. For example, a forecaster says that the price of the Reliance shares will increase. Then, it can never be proved false as such predictions have not been made for a particular period.
(ii) While evaluating forecasts, one must be careful that the forecast has not been made on changed macroeconomic variables, which may be under consideration initially by the government. For example, a forecast is made on the assumption that in future the government is going to declare some incentives for the industries, but in due course, such measures may not be declared by the government.
(iii) It is a fact that forecasts are made by man not by God. So, it cannot be cent per cent right.
(iv) Further, it is important that business policies of an enterprise must be changed according to the forecasts. Suppose, a forecaster says that price of a particular raw material is going to increase, then inventory policies must be changed accordingly. The raw material must be procured when the price is low.

Criterion for demand forecast

(i) On the basis of time: short term vs. long term
(ii) On the basis of level of forecasting: macro, industry vs. firm
(iii) On the basis of nature of the product: new product vs. established product

(i) On the basis of time

(a) Short-term forecasting: Short-term forecasting covers a period of three months, six months or at most, one year depending on the nature of the product. If the demand fluctuates from one month to another or from year to year, short-term forecasting is advisable.

Purpose of short-term forecasting may be as follows:

- To adopt suitable product policy, so that the problem of overproduction or short supply of raw material, machine, etc. can be avoided.
- To have proper control of inventory.
- To set the sales targets.
- To arrange the financial requirements in advance to meet the demand.

(b) Long-term forecasting: Long-term forecasting covers a period of 5, 10 or 20 years. The period, here, also depends upon the nature of product, but beyond 12 years, the future is assumed as uncertain. But in many industries like ship-building, petroleum refinery, paper, etc., long-term forecasting is needed, as the total cost of equipment is quite high.

Purpose of long-term forecasting may be as follows:

- To plan for the new unit of production or expansion of the existing unit, to meet the demand in future.
- To plan the long-term financial requirements.
- To train the personnel so that manpower requirement can be met in future.

(ii) On the basis of level of forecasting

(a) Macro level forecasting: Macro level forecasting is concerned with business environment prevailing in the economy, which is measured by industrial growth rate, growth rate of national income or public expenditure, trend of saving or investment and population growth rate. Such external data constitute the basic assumptions on which the business must base its forecasts. These macro-economic variables have special significance for a firm's demands such as:

- Increase in Gross National Product (GNP) indicates rising market potential for consumer goods.

- If the rate of saving is going to be high, there will be less demand for consumer goods.
- High population growth implies rise in future demand for all type of goods.
- Forecast about tax, subsidy or government expenditure can also increase or decrease the demand for product accordingly.

(b) Industry level forecasting: It is prepared by different associations like FICCI or Employers' Association. It is prepared to understand growth trend of a particular industry.

(c) Firm level forecasting: It is important from managerial point of view. Forecast may be general or specific depending upon the requirement. The firm may find a general forecast useful, but it usually needs to be broken down into commodity-wise/product-wise forecasts and forecasts by areas of sales. After getting information about demand forecast, a firm plans its course of action like what should be its scale of operation, how to manage capital and other inputs, etc.

(iii) On the basis of nature of the product

(a) It is important to clarify products such as producer goods, consumer durables, or consumer goods and services. Economic analysis indicates distinctive patterns of demand for each of these different categories.

(b) Finally, in every forecast, special factors peculiar to the product and the market, must be taken into account. The nature of the competition in the market, how for the situation is complicated by uncertainty or non-measurable risk and the possibility of error of inaccuracy in the forecast must be seriously considered. Political factors such as economic policies of the ruling party and stable government are also important. Sociological factors are of great importance in some markets, e.g., in the case of women's dresses. Women of both Europe and Middle East countries want to look beautiful but for an exporter, it is very important to take care of cultural difference of both the places. Likewise, the role of psychology, what people think about the future, their own personal prospects and about products and brands, are vital factors for firms and industries.

(c) Forecast of a new product.

Following factors must be considered before making forecast of a new product:

- Treat the demand for a new product as extension of an existing similar old product.
- Treat the new product as a replacement for some existing product.

- Estimate demand by making inquiries from customers.
- Offer the new products for sale in a sample market.
- Survey the customers' reaction via dealers.
- Internet and social networking sites should also be used for getting customer feedback.

Methods used for forecasting

There are various methods for forecasting. Here, only four methods, which are generally employed for forecasting, have been discussed.

(i) Survey of buyers' opinion

This is a direct method for making short-term forecasting, in which the customers are asked what they are thinking to buy in near future, say in coming months or next year.

Advantages

(a) Directly based on users' response.

(b) Requires little time and less money.

Disadvantages

(a) Consumers' buying intentions are irregular.

(b) When consumers have to select between different alternatives, they are unable to foresee their choices.

(c) Buyers may be anxious for purchasing the products but due to certain limitations they may be unable to purchase them.

(ii) Collective opinion or sales person's polling

In this method, forecasting depends upon the salesmen's estimation because salesmen are closely watching customer behaviour. Hence, they can estimate more properly about the products and their future requirement. All the estimates are consolidated to know the total estimate of the sales. This final estimate then goes through severe checking to avoid undue imagination, which is done many times by the salesmen. The revised estimates are then reexamined in the light of factors like expected change in design, change in prices, advertisements, competition and future changes such as purchasing power of local people, employment and population.

Advantages

(a) This method is simple and requires no statistical techniques.

(b) The forecasts are based on the knowledge of salesmen who are directly responsible for sales.

(c) In practice, this method is much useful in the case of new products.

Disadvantages

(a) This method is useful only for short-term forecasting, i.e., at most for one year.

(b) As the forecasting is dependent upon the salesmen's estimation and if sales quotas are fixed for them then they, in general, underestimate the forecast.

(c) As salesmen may not be aware of change in the economic environment, the estimate made by them may not be correct.

(d) As the estimation is an important work, it must not be done on the salesman feedback.

(iii) Delphi method

This technique is based on the judgement of a panel of experts to arrive at a convergent view regarding the forecast. The panel is presented with a series of questions and their replies are treated anonymously. The answers are fed back to the group along with other information. If the decision does not converge, they may be asked to reconsider their answers and to provide a second opinion. The Delphi forecast can also be conducted by post, using an anonymous panel of experts. In another variant, if experts do not have enough knowledge of the subject, they may be asked to weigh their own knowledge on each of the question, and their replies are then multiplied by that weight.

Advantages

(a) This method is simple and requires no statistical techniques.

(b) The forecasts are based on the information provided by experts, so the information, thus, gathered can be considered reliable.

(c) At the time of political elections, this method is being used to forecast winnability of the various candidates.

Disadvantages

(a) This method is useful only for short-term forecasting, i.e., at most for one year.

(b) As the forecasting is dependent upon the experts' estimation, it may be biased.

(iv) Trends through regression method

The trend factor in a time series may be estimated in a number of ways. The most frequently used method is to visually fit a straight line through the observed points in a graph relating the various points in time. Established firms have considerable data on sales. These data are arranged in a chronological order, known as "times series". The trend line is projected by some statistical method, generally, by the regression method. This method involves the following steps:

(a) See if a relationship exists between the demand for a product and certain economic indicators.

(b) Establish the relationship through the method of least squares and derive the regression equation: $Y = a + bX$. Once this regression equation is derived, the value of Y, i.e., demand for a commodity, can be forecast for any value of X.

For example, suppose demand for television (TV) is related to the level of disposable income. So, level of disposal income is independent variable and demand for television is dependent variable. We need to establish the regression equation from which the values of Y for different values of X can be predicted.

(c) In the regression equation, a and b are constants (intercept and gradient respectively) whose value has to be calculated. To calculate the two values, two simultaneous equations are required. All values in time series data for regression equation have been added for equation (i) and all such variables have been multiplied by X to get equation (ii) as given below:

$$\Sigma Y = na + b\Sigma X \qquad \text{(i)}$$

$$\Sigma XY = a\Sigma X + b\Sigma X^2 \qquad \text{(ii)}$$

Suppose we get the values of a and b as 5.36 and 0.66 respectively, from some observed data relating to the sales of TV at different levels of disposable income, then the regression equation will be

$$Y = 5.36 + 0.66X$$

Advantage

Regression analysis is a useful and more precise tool of demand forecasting.

Disadvantages

(i) It is based on past data, thus if the future behaviour of the firm disagrees from the past, it will fail.

(ii) The accuracy of measurement of independent variable determines the degree to which the confidence can be placed in the forecast value of the dependent variable.

Example 11 Suppose a firm is manufacturing automobiles. The sales for the last five years are as follows:

Year	*2008*	*2009*	*2010*	*2011*	*2012*
Sales	110	130	150	160	180

Make a forecast for the year 2016, using the least square method.

Solution:

Year X	*Index X*	*Sales Y*	X^2	*XY*
2008	1	110	1	110
2009	2	130	4	260
2010	3	150	9	450
2011	4	160	16	640
2012	5	180	25	900
$N = 5$	$\Sigma X = 15$	$\Sigma Y = 730$	$\Sigma X^2 = 55$	$\Sigma XY = 2360$

Making two simultaneous equations (i) and (ii) from the equation $Y = a + bx$

$$\Sigma Y = na + b \sum X \quad \text{(i)}$$

$$\Sigma XY = a \sum X + b \sum X^2 \quad \text{(ii)}$$

Now putting values in the simultaneous equations (i) and (ii), we get

$$730 = 5a + 15b \quad \text{(iii)}$$

$$2360 = 15a + 55b \quad \text{(iv)}$$

Solving equations (iii) and (iv), we get

$$\therefore \quad Y = 95 + 17X \quad \text{(v)}$$

Forecasting demand for automobile for the year 2016, if year 2008 is 1 then year 2016 will be 9

$$Y = 95 + 17 \times 9 = 248$$

There will be demand for 248 automobile in 2016.

Example 12 The annual sales of company Excel are as follows:

Year	*2008*	*2009*	*2010*	*2011*	*2012*
Sales in Rs.	45000	56000	78000	46000	75000

By the method of least square, estimate the annual sales for 2015.

Solution:

Year	*Sales in Rs. 1000 (Y)*	*X (index for year)*	X^2	*XY*
2008	45	1	1	45
2009	56	2	4	112
2010	78	3	9	234
2011	46	4	16	184
2012	75	5	25	375
$N = 5$	$\Sigma Y = 300$	$\Sigma X = 15$	$\Sigma X^2 = 55$	$\Sigma XY = 950$

To calculate '*a*' and '*b*', making two simultaneous equations (i) and (ii) from the least square equation as follow:

$$\Sigma Y = na + b \sum X \quad \text{(i)}$$

$$\Sigma XY = a \sum X + b \, \Sigma X^2 \quad \text{(ii)}$$

Putting the values from the above table in equations (i) and (ii), we get

$$300 = 5a + 15b \quad \text{(iii)}$$

$$950 = 15a + 55b \quad \text{(iv)}$$

Solving equations (iii) and (iv), we get $a = 45$ and $b = 5$. So the forecasting for the year 2015 will be

$$Y = 45 + 5\,(8)$$
$$= 45 + 40 = \text{Rs. } 85{,}000$$

The expected sale is far Rs. 85000/-

A real challenge for the forecaster comes when the management plans to take a drastic change in their approach as to change or revise its sales or production all together. During those crucial time, an analyst generally considers following factors:

(i) Trend
(ii) Seasonal variations
(iii) Cyclical fluctuations
(iv) Irregular or random forces

STEP 2: PLANNING AND BUDGET PREPARATION

After evaluating demand forecast, a firm takes decision about its scale of operation, prepares its plan, decides to manage its finances and other inputs.

Decision Analysis

A decision, in general, may be defined as the selection by the decision maker to an act, considered to be best out of available options according to some predesigned standard. The decision-making process involves following important steps:

(i) Finding out various alternative courses of action from which final decision has to be made, known as act.
(ii) Identifying the possible outcomes called the states of nature or events for the problem. The events are beyond the control of the decision maker.
(iii) The pay off function is the combination of acts and events.

Decision Making Environment

Decisions are made under the following three type of environment.

(i) Decision under condition of certainty

Here, we know with complete certainty about the future outcome, and it is easy to analyze the situation and make decision accordingly. It is a hypothetical situation because in real-world, future is never certain.

(ii) Decision under condition of uncertainty

It refers to situations where more than one outcome can result from any single decision. The decision maker lacks sufficient knowledge to assign probabilities to the various state of nature. Situations like launching a new product in the market, drilling a rig for the exploration of oil are some examples. Some of the criteria which are discussed below, may help in taking decision under this kind of situation. They have been discussed with the help of the following example.

Example 13 The research department of a confectionery company has recommended to the marketing department to launch a chocolate with three different tastes. The marketing manager has to decide the type of taste to be launched under the following estimated payoffs for various levels of profit: (Degree of optimism = 0.6)

Type of Taste	*Estimated Levels of Profit*		
	20,000	*10,000*	*2,000*
I	35	20	15
II	45	25	9
III	70	30	5

Solution: The company is going to launch chocolates for the first time. So, it does not have any prior information about the demand. Demand is not under the control of the company but the company is aware that if the demand is going to be 20,000 then the profit will be 35 for the type I of chocolate 45 for type-II and so on. All the values are proportionate to each other, therefore, no unit of measurement has been given. Decision according to different criteria have been discussed as below:

Type of Taste	*Estimated Level of Profit*			*Maximum estimated level of profit for that particular type*	*Minimum estimated level of profit for that particular type*
	20,000	*10,000*	*2,000*		
i	ii	iii	iv	v	vi
I	35	20	15	35	15
II	45	25	9	45	9
III	70	30	5	70	5

Maximax Criterion
Market is very optimistic. So, expected profit is maximum (this maximum is) out of all maximum. From the 'v' column, '70' is maximum which is for the III type. So, according to this criterion Type III will be suggested.
Minimax Criterion
Market is comparatively less optimistic. Here, expected profit is minimum of all maximum. Maximum of each type will be considered (col. v) and minimum out of all maximum will be selected. So, Type I will be suggested
Maximin Criterion
Market is least optimistic. Selection will be done of maximum out of all minimum estimated level of profit, i.e., from the col. vi is 15. So, Type I will be suggested.

Laplace criterion (Criterion of Rationality) Being new product, there is no information about the probability of occurrence. So, equal probability will be given to each expected level of occurrence.				
Type I	$\frac{1}{3} \times 35 + \frac{1}{3} \times 20 + \frac{1}{3} \times 15$	$\frac{70}{3}$	23.3	Out of these three, Type III is suggested as it is maximum
Type II	$\frac{1}{3} \times 45 + \frac{1}{3} \times 25 + \frac{1}{3} \times 9$	$\frac{79}{3}$	26.3	
Type III	$\frac{1}{3} \times 70 + \frac{1}{3} \times 30 + \frac{1}{3} \times 5$	$\frac{105}{3}$	35	
Hurwicz Criterion (Criterion of Realism) Leonid Hurwicz propounded a combination of two criteria. Decision maker's degree of optimism is represented by α. The value of α varies between 0 and 1, where 0 correspond to total pessimism and 1 correspond to total optimism. Here, it is 0.6.				
Type I	$0.6 \times 35 + (1 - 0.6)15$	27		Out of these three, Type III is suggested as it is maximum
Type II	$0.6 \times 45 + (1 - 0.6)9$	30.6		
Type III	$0.6 \times 70 + (1 - 0.6)5$	44		

Savage Criterion (Minimax Regret Criterion)					
Developed by L.J. Savage. The criterion is based on the concept of regret or opportunity loss. Selecting a course of action that minimizes the maximum regret. Regret will be calculated as maximum payoff which could have been earned-profit which has been earned.					
	If the demand is going to be 20,000 then 70 will be maximum estimated level of profit	If the demand is going to be 10,000 then 30 will be maximum estimated level of profit	If the demand is going to be 2,000, then 15 will be maximum estimated level of profit	Maximum level of regret	Type III will be selected as it minimizes the maximum regret
Type I	70 – 35 = 35	30 – 20 = 10	15 – 15 = 0	35	
Type II	70 – 45 = 25	30 – 25 = 5	15 – 9 = 6	25	
Type III	70 – 70 = 0	30 – 30 = 0	15 – 5 = 10	10	

(iii) Decision under conditions of risk

Under condition of risk, the decision maker can take decision from several possible options whose probability of occurrence can be found out objectively from the past data. There are following criterion through which decision may be taken under condition of risk:

(a) Expected Monetary Value (EMV) criterion: Under this criterion, following steps are taken:

- 1st Conditional Monetary Value for each act-event combination is to be listed along with their corresponding probability.
- 2nd to determine Expected Monetary Value, each Conditional Monetary Value is multiplied with corresponding probability.
- 3rd all Expected Monetary Values are calculated column wise.
- 4th expected level of production which correspond to highest expected monetary value will be selected.

Example 14 A baker finds from the past data that the cost of making a bread packet is Rs. 25. The selling price of the bread packet is Rs. 30, if it is sold within a week, and it could be disposed of at Rs. 20 per packet at the end of the week, if remained unsold. Frequency of weekly sales is given below:

Weekly Sales	*10*	*11*	*12*	*13*	*14*	*15*
No. of Weeks	0	10	20	40	30	0

Find out how many packets the baker should make by Expected Monetary Value criterion.

Solution: Cost of producing a packet of bread = Rs. 25

Selling price of the packet of bread = Rs. 30

If unsold, disposal price = Rs. 20

Profit if an item is sold = Rs. 30 – Rs. 25 = Rs. 5

Loss, if an item is unsold Rs 25 – Rs. 20 = Rs. 5

To calculate probability, total number of weeks may be considered one and number of week for each event will be calculated.

Table 8.1 Conditional Profit

Sales	*Probabilities*	*Production*			
		11	*12*	*13*	*14*
11	0.10	Rs. 55	55 – 5 = Rs. 50	55 – 10 = Rs. 45	55 – 15 = Rs. 40
12	0.20	Rs. 55	Rs. 60	60 – 5 = Rs. 55	60 – 10 = Rs. 50
13	0.40	Rs. 55	Rs. 60	Rs. 65	65 – 5 = Rs. 60
14	0.30	Rs. 55	Rs. 60	Rs. 65	Rs. 70

Table 8.2 Expected Profit

Sales	*Probabilities*	*Expected profit (in Rs.) from making*			
		11	*12*	*13*	*14*
11	0.10	55 × .1 = 5.5	50 × .1 = 5.0	45 × 0.1 = 4.5	40 × 0.1 = 4.0
12	0.20	55 × .2 = 11.0	60 × .2 = 12.0	55 × 0.2 = 11.0	50 × 0.2 = 10.0
13	0.40	55 × .4 = 22.0	60 × .4 = 24.0	65 × 0.4 = 26.0	60 × 0.4 = 24.0
14	0.30	55 × .3 = 16.5	60 × .3 = 18.0	65 × 0.3 = 19.5	70 × 0.3 = 21.0
Total		55.0	59.0	61.0	59.0

Hence, optimum number of packets of bread to be produced = 13

(b) Expected Opportunity Loss (EOL) criterion: An alternative approach to maximizing expected monetary value (EMV) is to minimize expected opportunity loss (EOL). Under this criterion, following steps are taken:

1. The Conditional Profit table for each act-event combination with the corresponding event probability are listed.
2. For each event, the Conditional Opportunity Loss (COL) is calculated by subtracting the payoff from a maximum payoff for that event, which could have been earned.
3. To determine the Expected Opportunity Loss (EOL) values for each act, COL is multiplied with corresponding probability and all of them are summed up column wise.
4. Lastly, the act, which corresponds to the minimum EOL value, is selected.

Table 8.3 Conditional Profit

Sales	*Probabilities*	*Production*			
		11	*12*	*13*	*14*
11	0.10	Rs. 55	Rs. 55 – 5 = 50	Rs. 55 – 10 = 45	Rs. 55 – 15 = 40
12	0.20	Rs. 55	Rs. 60	Rs. 60 – 5 = 55	Rs. 60 – 10 = 50
13	0.40	Rs. 55	Rs. 60	Rs. 65	Rs. 65 – 5 = 60
14	0.30	Rs. 55	Rs. 60	Rs. 65	Rs. 70

From the above table, conditional loss table will be made.

Table 8.4 Conditional Opportunity Loss

Sales	*Probabilities*	*Possible Production Action (Alternative)*			
		11	*12*	*13*	*14*
11	0.10	55 – 55 = 0	55 – 50 = 5	55 – 45 = 10	55 – 40 = 15
12	0.20	60 – 55 = 5	60 – 60 = 0	60 – 55 = 5	60 – 50 = 10

13	0.40	65 – 55 = 10	65 – 60 = 5	65 – 65 = 0	65 – 60 = 5
14	0.30	70 – 55 = 15	70 – 60 = 10	70 – 65 = 5	70 – 70 = 0

Table 8.5 Expected Opportunity Loss

Sales	*Probabilities*	*Possible Production*			
		11	*12*	*13*	*14*
11	0.10	0 × .10 = 0	5 × .1 = .5	10 × .1 = 1	15 × .1 = 1.5
12	0.20	5 × .20 = 1.0	0 × .2 = 0	5 × .2 = 1	10 × .2 = 2
13	0.40	10 × .4 = 4	5 × .4 = 2	0 × .4 = 0	5 × .4 = 2
14	0.30	15 × .3 = 4.5	10 × .3 = 3	5 × .3 = 1.5	0 × .3 = 0
Σ		9.5	5.5	3.5	5.5

The optimum stock position is 13 which will minimize the expected opportunity loss. Thus, the optimum number of items to be produced = 13.

Decision Tree

In any decision-making process, the combination of all the possible actions and potential events can be depicted graphically through decision tree method. This method is effective for demonstration and presentation. All possible options are shown as branches. A decision node is shown by a square and the state of nature (chance) node by circle.

Steps in decision tree analysis are:

(i) Identify the decision points and the alternative courses of action at each point systematically.

(ii) At each decision point, assess the risk (probability) associated with the different possible outcomes and the related payoff values.

(iii) Commencing from the final stage of decision points compute the expected payoff values under different courses of action.

(iv) Choose the course of action, which yields the best payoff from each of the decisions.

(v) Proceed backward to the next stage of decision points and again compute the expected payoff values under different course of action, considering only the selected strategies under that step of decision tree.

(vi) Finally, identify the strategies to be adopted from start to end under different possible outcomes for the situation a whole.

Example 15 A student has scored good marks in the examination of class XII. So, he can get admission in any of the stream as law, medical or engineering. Probability of getting admission in law is 0.8. If passed successfully, he will get a job of Rs. 85,000/month. Probability of getting admission in engineering stream is 0.6. If passed successfully, he will get a job of Rs. 100,000/month.

Probability of getting admission in medical stream is 0.4. If passed successfully, he will get a job of Rs. 150,000/month. Which option should he take?

Solution:

Expected Monetary Value (EMV) of node A = 0.8 × 85,000 + 0.2 × 0 = Rs. 68000

Expected Monetary Value (EMV) of node B = 0.4 × 1,50,000 + 0.6 × 0 = Rs. 60,000

Expected Monetary Value (EMV) of node C = 0.6 × 1,00,000 + 0.4 × 0 = Rs. 60.000

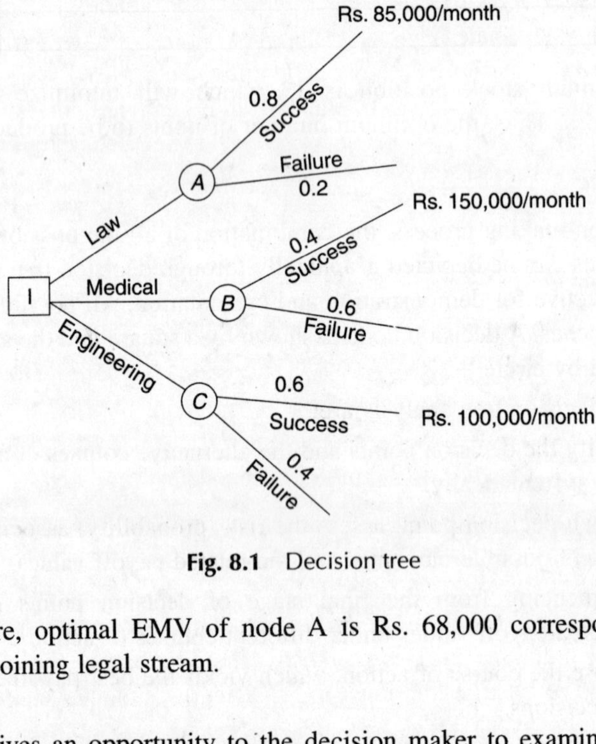

Fig. 8.1 Decision tree

Therefore, optimal EMV of node A is Rs. 68,000 corresponding to the decision of joining legal stream.

Advantage

(i) It gives an opportunity to the decision maker to examine all possible outcomes, positive or negative.

(ii) It can be successfully applied to various situations.

Disadvantage

(i) It becomes highly complicated when independent alternative and dependent variables are presented in the problem.

(ii) Ordinarily, it does not take into account the changing worth of money with the passage of time.

(iii) It analyses the problem in terms of expected values and thus, yields an 'average' valued solution.

(iv) At times, there is inconsistency in assigning probabilities for different events.

Budget Preparation

Optimum profit can only be extracted from any business venture, if it is properly planned from beginning to end. Budget is a tool of management for planning future activities including estimate of sales, expenditure, production, etc., for a business enterprise. It is carried out to assess the possible future line of action for a definite period of time and to indicate the expected business result. It should be prepared by taking the help of previous statistical data.

Since planning is looking ahead, anticipating problems and finding their solutions, budget may be used as a means for planning, coordinating and controlling. It coordinates among different segments of organization so as to operate at the most efficient level and yield maximum profit. Systematic appraisal of results is made to ensure that planned and actual remain same. Remedial actions are taken, if there is any deviation. Plans are regularly compared with actual results regarding expenses and performances through budget.

Purpose of a budget

(i) To make a programme of systematic development.

(ii) To decide basis for the expenditure of funds.

(iii) To provide basis for checking of working of the concern by monitoring their efficiency and economy.

(iv) To keep a check over expenditure in various departments.

(v) To make periodical evaluation of management policies.

(vi) To provide basis for examining the achievements of the organisation.

Essentials of a budget

(i) Information about future activities—Information about the proposed future activities, both in the short run and the long run of the business should be clearly laid down to facilitate the budget preparation.

(ii) Clearly defined business policies—To prepare a good budget, it is essential to have clearly laid down business policies. After knowing them, budget is prepared considering their effects on each department.

(iii) Cost information—While preparing budget, information regarding all types of costs are essential. Budget can only be prepared after analyzing several types of cost and other policies as margin of profit etc.

(iv) Allocating authority and responsibility—Effective implementation of the budget is only possible when authority and responsibility are properly allocated among personnel.

STEP 3: MANAGING FINANCE

No business dream can be made true unless the entrepreneur is able to arrange required finance for investment which may be defined as the acquisition of durable productive facilities in expectation of gain in future. It consists of physical capital like plant, equipment, machinery, etc. as well as non-physical capital like training of personnel, etc. The management does not only require sufficient finance but also need to spend it very judiciously. So, making wise investment decision is a key task of the management.

Fixed Capital and Working Capital

Fixed capital is the capital in the form of building, machinery, etc. whose life is more than one year. Working capital represents net investment in short run assets. It is usually defined as current assets minus current liabilities. The major elements of current assets are stocks, trade debtors and cash (in hand and at bank). The major element of current liabilities is trade creditors.

The size of capital depends on the nature of the firm and expected change in demand of capital, which is likely to take place over time. Some of the reasons for change in demand may be:

(i) change in interest rate,
(ii) change in market demand,
(iii) change in season,
(iv) change in the state of the economy, and
(v) change in production methods.

Sources of Finance

In order to start any business activity, there must be adequate finance for purchasing fixed assets (building, machinery, etc.), raw material and to meet other expenses till the money comes back (including profit) after sale.

So, before starting any business activity one must assess the financial requirement and the sources of financing them. There are two sources of finance, internal and external which may be examined.

Internal sources of finance

(i) Retained equity earning—It implies retaining the earnings of the shareholders for internal reinvestment. Every rupee retained means it has not been distributed to the existing shareholders. In such circumstances, the management should protect the interest of the shareholders.
(ii) Depreciating provisions—Depreciation is a measure of internally generated funds. It refers to the maintenance of a capital stock to replace the existing machinery when it becomes uneconomical to use.

(iii) Deferred taxation—As there may be some time lag between earning and payment of taxation, the amount may be available for use before payment.

(iv) Personal funds or inherited funds—There must be some personal or inherited funds, which are very important for earning the confidence of external financiers.

External sources of finance

(i) Permanent or long-term sources of finance

It includes:

(a) Saving—Personal saving, which may be available for business purpose.

(b) Loans—Money, which is borrowed for business purpose.

(c) Shares—Funds that are collected through issuing of shares.

(d) Debentures—It is a certificate of indebtedness issued by the corporation. A fixed rate of interest is paid on debentures and the amount is repayable after the stated number of years. These are generally unsecured bonds, which have no claims on any specific asset of the company but are backed by the earning power and general credit of the company as viewed by the investor. For this reason, only companies with a very good profit record and a high financial standing can hope to sell unsecured bonds or debentures.

(e) Corporate bonds—Corporate bonds are of two types. First is unsecured bonds that are debentures in which the corporation has no responsibility. Second is secured bonds in which some form of claim on the assets of the corporation is tied. If the corporation fails to pay interest to the investor or does not return the money back after the predecided number of years, the corporation has to pay some fine. Mortgage bonds are examples of secured bonds.

(f) Public deposits—Public may be asked to deposit their money directly with the company for a fixed short/long period ranging from half year to seven years.

(g) Including more partners—Capital may be raised by adding more partners in the business.

(ii) Medium source of finance

(a) Bank loan—Medium terms loans are easily available from commercial and other banks on reasonable interest rate.

(b) Hire purchase—The hirer needs to purchase machinery (goods) and payments may be made in a number of periodical instalments. At the end of the period when all the instalments have been paid, the possession of the goods passes to the hirer.

(c) Sale and lease back—To generate funds, a company may sell some of its property to an investment company with a right to lease back at an agreed rent.

(d) Equipment leasing— Many types of fixed assets such as land, equipment and machinery can be obtained on lease for a number of years.

(e) Profit flow back—The whole profit is not distributed to shareholders or owners as dividends, rather a portion of it is retained in the business and used to finance expansion and growth of the concern.

(iii) Short-term sources of finance

(a) Credit facilities—Credit is a good source of short-term finance.

(b) Trade credit—Financial assistance may come from some other firms with whom the firm may have business dealings. This type of financial assistance is known as trade credit.

(iv) Specialist institutions

Industrial financial corporations—Finances can be borrowed from an insurance company, state financial corporations and industrial development corporations.

Capital Budgeting

Capital is an important input for any enterprise. So, the management budgets its capital judiciously to earn maximum profit. Capital budgeting refers to the process of planning capital projects, raising funds for it and efficiently allocating resources to those capital projects whose returns are expected to extend beyond one year (the choice of one year is arbitrary, but one year is adopted because it is a convenient cut-off for distinguishing between various expenditure). The term 'capital budget' is used interchangeably with capital expenditure decisions, capital expenditure management, long-term investment decisions and management of fixed assets, etc. Capital budgeting may be categorized in the following ways:

(i) Cost reduction—Investments in training, machinery or other capital assets that reduce the cost of producing output.

(ii) Output expansion—Investments that accommodate increased output in response to actual or expected increase in demand.

(iii) Expansion by developing new products and/or markets—Expenditures for the development and production of new products and/or the development of new markets by adding sales or by opening new outlets.

(iv) Government regulation—Expenditures incurred follows rules laid down by government for safety, environmental and other rules.

Capital budgeting requires information on production costs, advertising, availability of funds, sales and, therefore, generally involves all areas of management. Furthermore, because of its critical long run significance, the capital budgeting process usually is reviewed on a continuous basis by the top management of the firm. It generally confronts with three types of questions, which are discussed as follows.

(i) How much money will be required for expenditure in near future, i.e., demand for capital?

The starting point for capital budget is a survey to know anticipated requirement for capital in a firm. Future needs of the firm can be assessed only after considering surveys of explicit capital requirement for one year or at the most two years because capital requirement in the distant future is very difficult to visualize. Since the objective of capital expenditure is to increase the profits, the amount of money required for such expenditure is determined by expected profitability. Therefore, demand for capital is measured on the basis of rate of return, which the management expects to earn by making different amounts of investment over varying time spans as within a month, in three months, next six months, and so on.

(ii) How much money will be available for investment, i.e., supply of capital?

Analysis of supply of capital is also an important aspect to be considered for capital budgeting. It involves the question like: how much finances should be realized internally and how much reliance should be and can be placed on external sources of finance. Regarding internal sources of finance also, the company needs to forecast its ability to generate finance. What share of earning should be distributed as dividend and how much should be retained for reinvestment in the long run projects. These decisions depend on various factors such as shareholder's acceptance for keeping their earnings for reinvestment or what percentage of earning should be held back for contingencies and growth. External sources depend on the state of the capital market, the company's reputation, financial soundness and an outlook of the person behind the company.

(iii) How should the available money be allocated to the various competing projects, i.e., capital rationing?

Capital rationing is basically an allocation aspect of financing. Based on its demand and supply estimates, the firm decides the total amount of investment and its allocation among alternative proposals of investment. This aspect, therefore, deals with the final selection of projects or activities.

The process of making capital budgeting decision consists of six phases, viz., planning, evaluation, selection, implementation, control and audit. Planning involves identification, preliminary analysis and initial screening of investment opportunities to make formal investment proposals. Evaluation involves making cash-flow projections for proposals. Formal capital budgeting procedures are applied to accept or reject proposals in the selection phase. At the implementation stage, funds are obtained for necessary assets to be acquired. During the control phase, the results of active projects are analyzed to detect and explain variations between actual and expected performances. Auditing is carried out to evaluate the performance of accepted projects.

STEP 4: ASSEMBLING ALL INPUTS

Selection of Site

It is very important for a firm to select a suitable site. It plays a crucial role in success or failure of a project. Therefore, it should be based upon a careful consideration of all factors that are essentially needed in efficient running of the particular project.

Selection of location for a firm can be done in two stages.

(i) General location of a firm—Following factors are important in this respect:

(a) Availability of inputs like raw material, efficient and cheap labour.

(b) Proximity to market.

(c) Availability of infrastructure like road, power and transport facility.

(d) Suitable geographical condition, if required for specific industry.

(e) Availability of capital.

(f) Business and commercial facilities.

(g) Existence of related industries.

(ii) Selection of particular site— Following factors are important in this respect:

(a) Availability of cheap land.

(b) Comparative cost of bricks, sand, cement, lime, steel and other materials required for construction.

(c) Facilities for the upkeeping and general maintenance.

(d) Cheap possibilities for disposing of trade waste.

Input and Machine

The list of inputs required with their amount as well as place from where to procure these raw materials should be made in advance after considering scale of production. Following factors are important in this respect:

(a) Nature of demand of the product in the market.

(b) Whether the demand is regular or seasonal, it is fixed or fluctuating.

(c) Quantity of power, water, land and raw materials available.

(d) Types of business organization and its investment capacity.

Subcontracting Consideration

As the technology is changing very fast, it is always not profitable to produce everything in the same organization, because specialized machines, plants, and skilled workers for each component may not be cost effective or afforded by a single concern. The decision about a particular item, whether to purchase or to manufacture is taken by planning department after making a thorough study of the relative merits and demerits. The system of subcontract leads to the growth of ancillary industries around the main concern. Advent of information and communication technology (ICT) has made it possible to shift part of the production process to a far-off place also. Criteria to 'make' or 'buy' have been further discussed in the chapter on "Engineering Economics".

Operation Planning

Operation planning involves the following steps:

(i) Dividing the project into distinct activities
(ii) Estimating time requirement for each activity
(iii) Estimating precedence relationships among the activities
(iv) Constructing the network

Best method of manufacturing is selected out of available alternative so that, wastage of material, labour, machine and time can be eliminated/minimized.

Material Handling

The material handling problem must be studied before initiation of production. Material handling devices should be selected after consideration of the following factors:

(i) Type of product
(ii) Size and shape of product
(iii) Method of manufacture
(iv) Production rate of the plant
(v) Availability of space
(vi) Power availability

STEP 5: EXECUTION

Internally, the execution or implementation phase determines the start to finish times of each and every activity. These can be summarized in the form of a time chart. All activities can be classified as critical and non-critical. For non-critical activity, the amount of slack time must be shown on the same time chart. It will be useful at the time of adjusting non-critical activities for resource allocation.

However, external execution or implementation is governed by price and different forms of market, in which the firm is operating.

Price

Market price of a commodity is the price that prevails in the market at any time, which is subject to change. The market price of a commodity at a certain time is determined by the interaction of forces of demand and supply. No buyer will be prepared to pay anything more than the marginal utility of the product to him. He would rather like to pay less. On the other hand, no seller will be prepared to accept anything less than the cost of production of commodity to him. He would like to charge as high a price as possible. Marginal utility and marginal cost of production are two limits. The price fluctuates between them. It is fixed at a point where both of them, marginal cost and marginal utility are equal. Competition between buyers raises the price and competition between sellers lowers the price. Normal price is the price, which is likely to prevail in the long run, if sufficient time is allowed for adjustment between demand and supply. Normal price is neither abnormally high nor abnormally low. It is more or less a constant price, and the market price fluctuates above and below it. The governing factor for the normal price is the cost of production or supply of a commodity. It, therefore, tends to be equal to its marginal cost of production.

Price determination for a product or service is crucial because it effects the earnings of the concern. At the same time, it is also a difficult task because prices are determined by considering large number of complex and interdependent factors. Following are some of the main factors which affect price:

(i) Cost factor—The price must cover the average cost and earn a reasonable margin of profit.

(ii) Nature of market—Composition of market and nature of prospective buyers of the product is very important in determining price of a product. So, it will be useful to know which section of the society is going to use the product. Will it be used by rich or poor, male or female, child, young or old people. The idea is to know all this to assess the relative utility of the product to the consumers to determine the value, which the prospective buyer will place upon the article and ultimately, the price is fixed in this light.

(iii) Competitor's price—Number of competitors and each competitor's price for similar items should be kept in mind.

(iv) Channel of distribution—Longer is the chain of distribution, higher is the margin added to cost in fixing the prices. Ultimately, the customer gets the good at higher prices. That is why, many of the big companies have ventured these days, in retail business. It curtails the margin for longer chain of distribution and customer gets goods at lower prices.

(v) Warranty and after-sales services—These also have a bearing on the pricing of goods because cost of after-sales services are also included in the price.

(vi) Margin for rebate/concession—A proper adjustment should also be made for regular or irregular rebates, concessions, cuts or other reduction in prices allowed to consumers to attract them.

(vii) Government policy—If government perceives that a particular product is used by masses and rise in its price will adversely affect that section, than the government gives subsidy which makes price low. On the contrary, some tax may be imposed to contract demand as for cigeratte. Import duties may be imposed on some foreign good to protect domestic producers.

(viii) Buying habit of the costumer—The prices depend upon the buying habits of the customer, whether they are price conscious or quality conscious.

(ix) Nature of sales—Whether the demand for product is seasonal (like ice cream, water coolers, desert coolers, etc.) or throughout the year, it is an important factor for taking decision about the price.

(x) Demand and supply—Demand and supply are two forces pulling in opposite directions. They are balanced (known as equilibrium) at the market price where demand equals supply. At any price, higher than the equilibrium price, the seller will find some of the articles left unsold. At a price, lower than the equilibrium price, demand will exceed the supply and there will be shortage of the commodity. The market price is only a short-term equilibrium price and fluctuates on the influence of demand and supply.

(xi) Public utility items—Water, electricity, city passenger transport service, and supply of cooking gas are a few examples of public utility items. The broad aspects of price policy of these items is to promote demand, to ensure maximum utilization of the total available capacity.

(xii) Price discrimination[1]—There are some markets where the demand is elastic because of the availability of the substitute, and some others where the demand is inelastic because no other alternative is available.

Revenue of Firm

Equilibrium is achieved at a point where marginal cost is equal to marginal revenue. Marginal cost has already been discussed, here we will discuss marginal revenue.

If any demand function is represented by $p = f(q)$, total revenue is the product of quantity of product demanded (q) and price per unit of output.

$$\text{TR} = p \times q$$

or, $$\text{TR} = q \times f(q) \qquad \{\text{since } p = f(q)\},$$

Marginal revenue represents the change in TR for every additional unit of output (q) therefore, $\text{MR} = \frac{d(\text{TR})}{dq}$ (differentiation of TR with respect to q)

$$\text{AR} = \frac{\text{TR}}{q} = p \quad \text{(where } p \text{ is price)}$$

Relations between revenue curves has been shown in Table 8.6.

Table 8.6 Revenue Relationship

Quantity Demanded	*Average Revenue (AR)*	*Total Revenue (TR)*	*Marginal Revenue (MR)*
1	9	9	9
2	8	16	7
3	7	21	5
4	6	24	3
5	5	25	1
6	4	24	−1
7	3	21	−3
8	2	16	−5
9	1	9	−7

Relationship between elasticity of demand and total revenue has been shown in Table 8.7.

Table 8.7 Elasticity of Demand and Total Revenue

Change in Price	*Price Elasticity Greater than Unit ($e_d > 1$)*	*Unit Elasticity ($e_d = 1$)*	*Price Elasticity Less than Unit ($e_d < 1$)*
Price rises	TR falls	TR unchanged	TR rises
Price falls	TR rises	TR unchanged	TR falls

Profit Maximizing Output and Price Determination under Monopoly and Perfect Competition

At perfect competition, the price is determined by market (or industry). It will have equilibrium price at that point where total demand for a commodity is equal to its total supply. We have observed that industry demand is the sum total of all the quantities demanded by consumers at a given price. Similarly, aggregate supply is sum total of all quantity supplied by producers at a given price. As both demand and supply are functions of prices, we have, $D = f(p) = D(p)$

$S = f(p) = S(p)$

At equilibrium, $D(p) = S(p)$

or, $D(p) - S(p) = 0$

At any other price, there will be either excess demand or excess supply.

Diagrammatically, the equilibrium price and output of the industry is shown in Fig. 8.2.

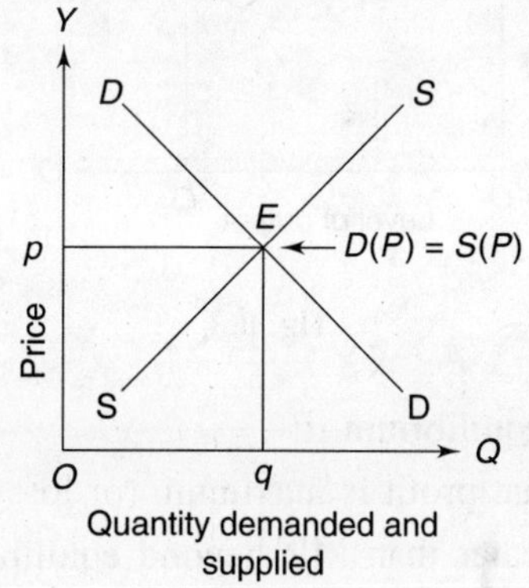

Fig. 8.2

In Fig. 8.2 equilibrium price is *op* and output is *oq*.

Example 16 Given the demand function and supply function as

$$D = 500 - 100p$$

$$S = 50 + 50p$$

Find out the equilibrium price and output level of the firm.

Solution: At equilibrium, $D = S$

$$500 - 100p = 50 + 50p$$

or, $150p = 450$

or, $p = 3$

So, equilibrium output will be

$$D = 500 - 300 = 200 \text{ units.}$$

Short-run equilibrium of the firm

We have seen that an individual firm under the condition of perfect competition cannot influence the market price. The demand curve of the firm is always horizontal (perfectly elastic). So, the price is given and at that price, the producer has to supply product. Hence, in the short run, a firm may earn profits or incur losses too. The firm will stay in the market even if it incurs loss till the point the price covers the variable cost.

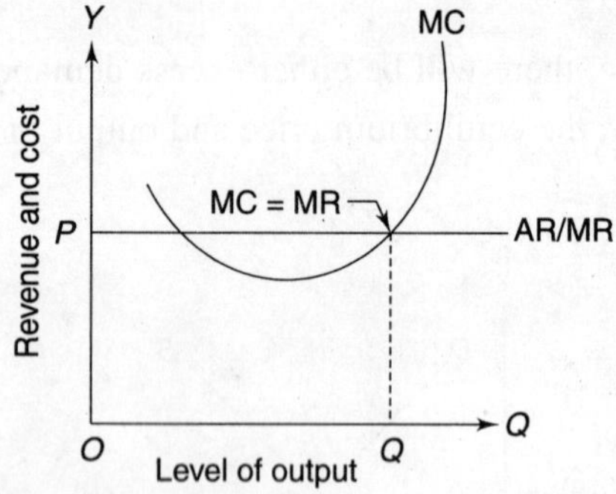

Fig. 8.3

The firm will be at equilibrium if:

(i) MC = MR, so that profit is maximum (or loss is minimum).

(ii) MC must be greater than MR beyond equilibrium, so that there is no possibility of increasing equilibrium profits.

(iii) Price must be greater than or equal to average variable cost (AVC). Thus, in the case of loss, the total loss does not exceed fixed cost.

Long-run equilibrium of the firm

Long run is a planning period, so there is no possibility of loss in the long run. In perfect competition, there is also no possibility of above normal profits in the long run due to free entry and exit of firms. The condition of equilibrium are:

(i) MC = MR so, that profit is maximum.

(ii) MC must be greater than MR beyond equilibrium so that there is no possibility of increasing profit.

(iii) Price must be greater than or equal to average total cost (ATC), so that there is no loss.

(iv) The equilibrium is at the lowest point of AC, that means there is no excess capacity.

$$P = \text{MC}$$

Hence, the only decision left at the firm's discretion is the determination of output at the given price so that its profit is maximized.

So, $\pi = \text{TR} - \text{TC}$

where π = Profit of an enterprise

TR = Total revenue

TC = Total cost

For maximization of π, necessary condition is

$$\frac{d\pi}{dq} = \frac{d(\text{TR})}{dq} - \frac{d(\text{TC})}{dq} = 0$$

or MR = MC

As at the price

AR = MR

$\therefore$ P = AR = MR = MC.

Sufficient condition is

$$\frac{d^2\pi}{dq^2} = \frac{d^2(\text{TR})}{dq^2} \frac{-d^2(\text{TC})}{dq^2} < 0$$

Example 17 Given the demand function and total cost function of the perfect competitive firm as

$$p = 32 - q$$

and $$\text{TC} = q^2 + 8q + 4$$

What level of output will maximize total profit? What are the corresponding values of price (p), profit (π) and total revenue (TR)?

Solution: For profit maximization, the following two conditions must be satisfied:

(i) $$\frac{d\pi}{dx} = \frac{d(\text{TR})}{dx} - \frac{d(\text{TC})}{dx} = 0 \text{ or MR = MC}$$

(ii) $$\frac{d^2\pi}{dx^2} = \frac{d^2(\text{TR})}{dx^2} - \frac{d^2(\text{TC})}{dx^2} < 0$$

$$\pi = \text{TR} - \text{TC}$$

where, π = profit, TR = total revenue, TC = Total cost

and $$\text{TR} = p \cdot q$$

$$= (32 - q)q$$

$$= 32q - q^2$$

Also $$\text{MR} = \frac{d(\text{TR})}{dq} = 32 - 2q$$

Similarly, $\quad \text{TC} = q^2 + 8q + 4$

Also $\quad \text{MC} = \dfrac{d(\text{TC})}{dq} = 2q + 8$

At equilibrium, MR – MC = 0

or, $\quad 32 - 2q - 2q - 8 = 0$

$$q = 6$$

For second order condition

$$\frac{d^2\pi}{dq^2} = \frac{d^2(\text{TR})}{dq^2} - \frac{d^2(\text{TC})}{dq^2} < 0$$

Putting $q = 6$ in demand function, we have

$$p = 32 - 6$$
$$= 26$$

Putting $q = 6$ in total revenue equation, we get

$$\text{TR} = 32 \times 6 - 6^2$$
$$= 192 - 36$$
$$= 156$$
$$p = 26 \text{ and TR} = 156$$
$$\text{TC} = 88$$

$\therefore \quad \pi = \text{TR} - \text{TC} = 68$ Ans.

Monopoly

Short-run equilibrium

Under monopoly firm and industry are same. So, no firm will sell its product at loss even during short run. However, a monopolist can decide either price or quantity and not both. The equilibrium conditions are:

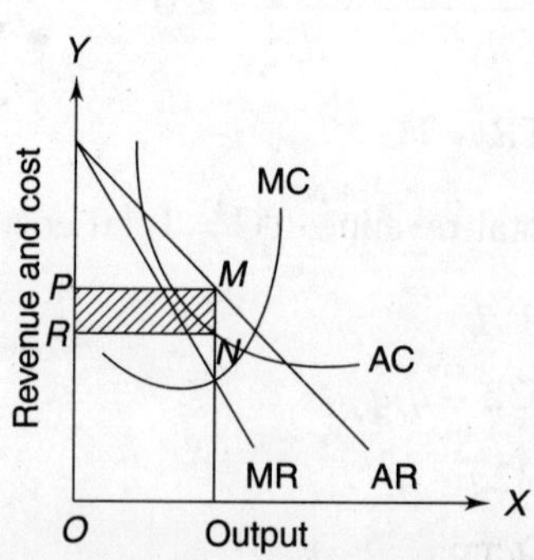

Fig. 8.4

1. MC = MR
2. MC must be greater than MR beyond equilibrium.

Long-run equilibrium

The equilibrium conditions are:

(i) Price must be greater than or equal to ATC.
(ii) MC = MR
(iii) MC must be greater than MR beyond equilibrium.
(iv) As the slope of the MR curve is double of the AR curve, monopolist earns supernormal profit which is equal to the shaded area PMNR in the Fig. 8.4.

Example 18 Consider a monopolist who faces a linear demand function, $p = 80 - 6q$, and also has a linear total cost function, TC = 50 + 20q. What will be the equilibrium level of output, price and profit? Also prove the second order condition for profit maximization.

Solution: Given: $p = 80 - 6q$ (i)

$$\text{TC} = 50 + 20q \qquad \text{(ii)}$$

We may calculate TR functions as TR = pq

Put the value of p from the given demand function, we get

$$\text{TR} = 80q - 6q^2 \qquad \text{(iii)}$$

$$= 50 + 20q \qquad \text{(iv)}$$

$$\pi = \text{TR} - \text{TC}$$

$$= 80q - 6q^2 - 50 - 20q \qquad \text{(v)}$$

For profit maximization,

$$\frac{d\pi}{dq} = 80 - 12q - 20 = 0$$

or, $12q = 60$

or, $q = 60/12 = 5$

Putting $q = 5$ in (i), we get

$$p = 80 - 6 \times 5 = 80 - 30 = 50$$

Similarly, putting $q = 5$ in eqn. (v), we get

$$\pi = 400 - 150 - 50 - 100 = 100$$

$\therefore$ $p = 50$

and $\pi = 100$

The second order condition for profit maximization is $d^2\pi/dx^2 < 0$

Here, $d^2\pi/dx^2 = -12 < 0$ proved.

STEP 6: EVALUATION AND FEEDBACK

Evaluation and feedback from the users are very important for improving efficiency of any organization. For internal evaluation, an organization uses the arrow diagram and time chart for continuous monitoring and progress reporting. In this phase, the network is updated on the variations in the planned or existing schedule. Feedback from the customer is also taken by organizations for its improvement and growth.

Notes

1. Price discrimination is charging two different prices in the different markets. To maximize total revenue, higher prices are charged in market where price elasticity of demand is less than unit and lower prices are charged in market where price elasticity of demand is more than unit.

EXERCISES

A. Objective (For 1/2 mark each)

Write 'True' or 'False' for each of the following:

(i) In perfectly competitive market, a firm will be in equilibrium where MC = MR.

(ii) In monopoly, AR > MR at the point of equilibrium.

(iii) In monopoly, there is no supply curve.

(iv) While deciding price, nature of customer is not taken care of.

Ans. (i) True; (ii) True; (iii) False; (iv) False;

B. Subjective (For 7 marks each)

(i) Elucidate demand forecasting for new products.

(ii) Examine the relative merits and demerits of different forecasting methods.

(iii) Discuss the various steps to be taken under Delphi method.

(iv) Discuss Total Revenue, Average Revenue and Marginal Revenue curve and their relationship.

(v) Discuss price determination under Monopoly.

(vi) Discuss price determination under Perfect Competition.

C. Numerical Problems

1. Elasticity of demand

(i) The price of a commodity is reduced from Rs. 10 to Rs. 9 and this reduction in price resulted an increase in demand from 100 to 115. Calculate price elasticity of demand. **[Ans:** $e_d = 1.5$]

(ii) The demand for two commodities are given by:

$$q_1 = P_1^{-1.2} P_2^{0.5}$$

and

$$q_2 = P_1^{0.3} P_2^{0.8}$$

Find out whether the two commodities are competitive or complimentary.

[**Ans:** Competitive]

2. Demand forecasting

(i) The annual sales of ABC Co. are as follows:

Year	*2007*	*2008*	*2009*	*2010*	*2011*	*2012*
Sales (Rs. crores)	40	50	55	60	58	67

On the basis of linear regression equation, estimate the sales for the years 2018 and 2019. [**Ans:** $a = 38.62$; $b = 4.68$; 2018 = 94.78; 2019 = 99.46]

3. Decision analysis

(i) The estimated sales of proposed three types of biscuit are given below:

Type of Biscuit	*Estimated level of sale (units)*		
	Rs. 25,000	*15,000*	*7,000*
Elaichi	60	35	3
Butter	45	30	5
Plain	35	30	10

Determine which alternative should the company choose, if they adopt the

(a) Maximin criterion
(b) Maximax criterion
(c) Hurwicz criterion (the degree of optimism being 0.70)
(d) Laplace criterion
(e) Minimax regret criterion

Ans: (a) Plain (b) Elaichi (c) Elaichi
(d) Elaichi (e) Elaichi

(ii) A newspaper boy gets newspapers from the local office at the rate of Rs. 3 each and sells from his shop at Rs. 5.50 each. However, he has to tell the office in advance as to how many copies he will buy. The office takes back those copies at ₹1 each copy which he is not able to sell. Determine from EMV criterion, how many copies should he take everyday. The daily demand has the following probability distribution:

No. of newspaper sold	*≤ 50*	*51*	*52*	*53*	*54*	*55*	*≥ 56*
Probabilities	0	15	20	10	35	20	0

Ans: 54 copies of newspaper

(iii) Zenex company is currently working with a process, which after paying for material, labour, etc. brings a profit of Rs. 64,000. The following alternatives are made available to the company:

(a) The company can conduct research (R_1) which is expected to cost Rs. 40,000 having 80% chances of success. If it proves success, the company gets a gross income of Rs. 78,000.

(b) The company can conduct research (R_2), which is expected to cost Rs. 44,000 having a probability of 75% success. If it proves success, the gross income will be Rs. 83,000

(c) The company can pay Rs. 35,000 as royalty for a new process, which will bring a gross income of Rs. 62,000.

(d) The company continues with the ongoing process.

Because of limited resources, it is assumed that only one of the two types of research can be carried out at a time. Use decision tree analysis to locate the optimal strategy for the company.

[**Ans:** d. Continue with on going process]

4. Profit maximizing price and output determination

(i) Given the demand function as $q = 45 - 3p$.

(a) Derive the Total Revenue, Average Revenue and Marginal Revenue function.

Hint: $\text{TR} = qp, \text{AR} = \frac{\text{TR}}{q}, \text{MR} = \frac{d\text{TR}}{dq}$

Now put $p = 1$ and calculate MR, AR and TR

$p = 2$ and so on

(b) Calculate the elasticity of demand for decrease in price from Rs. 12 to Rs. 10.

Hint: put $p = 12$ and calculate q

$p = 10$ and calculate q

Now find out e_d [**Ans:** $e_d = -4$]

(ii) Given demand and the total cost function of a perfectly competitive firm as

$$p = 32 - q$$

$$\text{and} \quad \text{TC} = q^2 + 8q + 4$$

Find the level of output, which maximizes total profit (π). What arc corresponding values of p.

[**Ans:** Level of output which maximises profit = 6 unit price = Rs. 26]

(iii) If the demand function is

$$p = 20 - 4q \text{ and}$$

the total cost function is TC = $8q - q^2$

Find out equilibrium price and quantity.

(**Ans:** Quantity = 2; price = Rs. 12)

(iv) Given the demand function $p = 90 - q$ and cost function TC = $10 + 2q + 3q^2$. Calculate profit maximizing output of a monopolist firm. What would be the impact of a tax of Rs. 8 per unit of output on price and profit respectively.

Hint: Add $8q$ to the cost equation (TC) for tax

[**Ans:** Before imposition of tax p = Rs. 79 and profit = Rs. 474

After imposition of tax p = Rs. 80 and profit (π) = Rs. 390]

(v) A sitar manufacturer can sell q sitars per week at p rupees each, where $5q = 375 - 3p$. The cost of production is $(500 + 13q + \frac{q^2}{5})$ rupees. How many sitars should be manufactured for maximum profit? What is the profit?

Quantity = 30 where the profit will be maximum

Profit = Rs. 1180/-

References and Suggested Readings

1. Alpha C. Chiang, "Fundamental Methods of Mathematical Economics," McGraw-Hills International Editions.
2. RGD Allen, "Mathematical Analysis for Economics," AITBS Publishers & Distributers.
3. R.R. Barthwal, "Industrial Economics," New Age International Publishers.

9

Accountancy

Purpose of this chapter is to acquaint the reader with:

- Meaning of Accountancy and its Significance for Engineers
- Types of Accountancy
- Cost Centres and Costing Method
- Double Entry System: Single and Double Entry Systems
- Joint Venture Account and Consignment Account
- Balance Sheet

ACCOUNTANCY

In a scientific experiment, required data are systematically recorded during the course of experiment after fitting apparatus in the right sequence. On the basis of these data, result is estimated and suitable corrective measures are taken, if required. In the same fashion, all financial data of a business organisation are recorded, summarized and analyzed in accountancy to understand financial position and to improve the current and future financial performance of the business. So, accountancy is an art of recording, classifying and analyzing financial data in a scientific manner. It is rightly regarded as language of business, which may be used for logical analysis of financial status in decision making and policy formulation at the level of the firm. So, some of the functions performed in accountancy are as follows:

(i) All financial transactions are recorded.

(ii) These transactions are sorted, classified and analyzed.

(iii) Separate and combined effects of each transaction are discussed.

(iv) Assets and liability of the firm and ultimately balance sheet of the firm are made.

(v) Balance sheet may be used as source of information about inventory position.

(vi) Availability of cash with the firm may be known.

(vii) Loss or profit of the firm may be calculated.

Significance of Accountancy for Engineers

Engineers have to compare alternatives on the basis of economic aspect besides technical aspect, for adopting right investment criteria. Even after selecting it, the most suitable course of action, the management would like to know the result of the financial investment. Accounting data provides them such information. Thus, engineers need to have proper understanding of such data to be able to analyze, compare and contrast different courses of action to use them in decision making and cost controlling.

Types of Accountancy

There are different types of accountancy, namely, financial accountancy, cost accountancy, management accountancy, social accountancy, legal accountancy and government accountancy. In fact, accountancy may be applied to any field of study whose financial performance is to be monitored and analyzed for improvement. It is one of the reasons to consider environmental accountancy so seriously these days. However, only financial accountancy, cost accountancy and management accountancy have been discussed here, as they are relevant for engineering economic analysis.

Cost accountancy deals with a system of measuring the cost incurred during the process of performing an activity. In Economics, production is referred as transformation of a set of input into a set of output. Cost accountancy deals with assigning monetary value to all inputs. While direct cost is directly assigned to variable factors of production, indirect costs are first pooled together and then appropriated to the fixed factors of production in equitable manner. However, as it merely deals with cost, management continuously looks for more information for internal and external use. Financial accountancy is mainly concerned with financial statement, which may be used by external users such as investors, banks, government and financial analysts. It is mainly concerned with balance sheet and other profit or loss statement of a firm from which financial status of the firm can be known. It gives end result to the user but does not tell anything regarding the financial process as the firm may not like to tell the whole world through which the firm is undergoing. Financial accounts are prepared in accordance with the generally accepted accounting principles so that comparisons may be made about performance of a firm at two points of time or between two or more firms at the same point of time. During 1950s, emphasis of accounting shifted towards management use, which led to emergence of a new branch of accountancy, i.e., management accountancy. While cost accountancy discusses merely about cost, management accountancy provides more information to the management for taking decision. So, management accountancy may be referred as a combination of cost accountancy and financial accountancy, which uses techniques of both accountancy as per requirement of management. All these three systems of accountancy have been compared and contrasted in Table 9.1.

Table 9.1 Comparison and Contrast between Three Systems of Accountancy

Sl. No.	*Particulars*	*Financial Accountancy*	*Cost Accountancy*	*Management Accountancy*
1.	User	External as share-holders, bank.	Internal	Internal
2.	Format	Fixed, which facilitates the inter-firm comparison.	Not fixed, made according to the requirement.	Not fixed, made according to the requirement.
3.	Time schedule	Fixed, generally one year.	Not fixed.	Not fixed.
4.	Information	Past	Present	Future

All these systems of accountancy are concerned with systematic recording analyzing and presenting the financial data taken from same source, i.e., book of account. However, purpose of collecting and interpreting data in all these three types of accounting are different. There is a fixed format in case of financial accountancy. However, there is neither fixed time schedule nor fixed format in management and cost accountancy. According to the requirement, it is developed. While financial and cost accountancy give data about past and present, management accountancy is always concerned with quality of information for future management activities such as decision making, planning and control.

COST CENTRES

For the sake of better cost supervision, an organization may divide the whole process into few 'cost centres'. These cost centres may be a person or a location, which may be at the lower level of administration and simply accumulates information about incurred cost. The manager concerned does not have any control over sales revenue, profit or investment. Simply, he has to ascertain cost, which may be used for the purpose of cost control. Cost centre may be of two types: personal cost centre and impersonal cost centre. If a cost centre consists of a person or a group of persons, as a personnel department, it is called personal cost centre and if it consists of a certain sequences of production operations or services, it is called impersonal cost centres. Some of the examples of impersonal cost centre are maintenance department, assembly department, etc.

Costing Methods

For cost calculation of any production activity, each unit which contributes in production must be assigned cost. Different methods are used for this purpose.

Here, two methods, which are based on actual cost, have been discussed. They are job costing and process costing.

(i) Job costing: This method of costing is suitable for a firm, which produces a specific number of products or services. Each job is of comparatively short duration and it is performed as per the customer requirement. Each work is taken as separate costing unit for the purpose of cost ascertainment and control. This method may be used by the firms, which are engaged in civil engineering work as construction of roads, bridges, flyovers, buildings, etc. Firms engaged in software development can also practise this type of costing. In case of firm, which produces work in batches such as manufacturing unit or exporting firms, batch is the unit of accounting.

(ii) Process costing: Through production process, a set of inputs are transformed into a set of outputs. The whole process of such transformation can be broken into a sequence of short duration jobs where output of previous process becomes input of existing process and so on and so forth. Each process may be regarded as cost centre and a separate account is opened for them. The output passing through the process may also be recorded. Total output for a period divided by unit processed during the period gives the cost per unit in this process. The method of cost calculation is convenient for large manufacturing units.

BOOKKEEPING

To express financial status of any business enterprise, systematic record of all the business transactions is required. Bookkeeping deals with the processes of scientific recording of all the business transactions expressed in terms of money. Basis of accounting is information regarding transactions. However, all such information regarding transactions must be supported by documentary evidence. They are known as source documents. Cash memo, cheques, debit and credit notes, invoices or bills are some of the source documents. In other words, bookkeeping is a subset of accountancy, which is only concerned with recording and classifying business transactions. The following two systems of bookkeeping may be used:

(i) Single Entry System

(ii) Double Entry System

Single Entry System

Single entry system of bookkeeping is a traditional system of bookkeeping. Under this system, importance is given to personal accounts. Here, for all debtors and creditors, personal ledgers are maintained and for all cash receipts and payments, cash account is maintained. Sometimes purchase and sales books are also prepared. It is cost, time and labour saving system. Generally, it is used by small traders due to ease of writing accounts, or due to lack of knowledge of scientific system of bookkeeping.

Double Entry System

Double entry system of bookkeeping is logical and scientific method of bookkeeping. In double entry system of bookkeeping, each and every transaction is noted twice, one in the debit side and other at credit side, even if the transaction may or may not involve cash. For example, if *M* sells goods worth Rs. 1000 to *N* and *N* does not immediately pay for them, the transaction has taken place twice for the purpose of accounting. In this case, the sale will be recorded in books of *M* immediately after the sale and other transactions when he actually receives payment for the same. This would mean that two transactions have taken place, i.e., one when the goods were sold and the other when money was received. Similarly, in *N*'s book also, two transactions will be recorded, i.e., one at the time of receipt of goods and other, when he paid money.

Table 9.2 Comparison between Single Entry System and Double Entry System of Bookkeeping

Particulars	*Single Entry System*	*Double Entry System*
Accounts, which are considered	Under this system, only personal accounts are operated.	All three, personal, real and nominal accounts are operated.
Transactions, which are recorded	For some transactions, two accounts are affected whereas for some other transactions only one account is affected.	Both aspects of each transaction, i.e., debit and credit are entered separately.
Test of mathematical accuracy	It is an incomplete method of bookkeeping. Neither trial balance can be made, nor mathematical accuracy of any financial information can be calculated.	This system is a complete method of bookkeeping. Trial balance can be made from double entry system of bookeeping.
Financial status	As transactions are made on the basis of memory in this system, it cannot provide true picture of financial status.	True picture regarding financial status can be provided in this system.
Concern for adjustment	Not specific care is given for adjustment.	Care and concern is given for adjustment.
Appropriateness	It is best suited for small enterprises, non-governmental organizations, small educational institutions and personal organizations, which are controlled directly.	It is suited to all type of organizations.
Legal acceptability	Documents of accounts prepared by this method are not accepted in the court of law.	Documents of accounts prepared by this method are accepted in the court of law.

Rules of Debit and Credit in Double Entry System of Bookkeeping

Accounts are broadly divided into two classes, i.e., Personal Account and Impersonal Account. Personal Account refers to accounts of a particular person. Transaction of everything else except persons comes under Impersonal Accounts. All impersonal accounts are again subdivided into Real Accounts and Nominal Accounts. Things, which have physical existence are called tangible goods. The accounts of tangible goods are called real accounts. Accounts of income, expenses, gains and losses are called nominal accounts.

Examples of some of the transactions are:

(i) Sudhir purchased goods worth Rs. 10,000 on credit from Mukesh.

As a result of this transaction, Sudhir received benefit in form of good's from Mukesh, who gave the goods. The transaction would effect good's account and Mukesh's account. Here good's account shall be debited and Mukesh's account will be credited.

(ii) Yash purchased goods valued Rs. 5000 from Jatin on cash.

The nature of this transaction is different from the nature of transaction discussed above. Yash did receive the benefit, i.e., goods but he has also paid for them. Hence, it is immaterial to record as from whom he purchased them. Here, good's account shall be debited and cash account will be credited.

Table 9.3 Rules of Debit and Credit

Kind of Account	*Account to be Debited*	*Account to be Credited*
Personal account	Account of person who receives something	Account of person who gives some thing
Real account	Account of thing which comes in	Account of thing which goes out
Nominal account	Account of expense or loss	Account of income or gain

RULES OF JOURNAL

All transactions are recorded in the journal in a chronological order, i.e., date-wise. Format of journal is columnar, which are five in numbers. The third column is meant for writing the page number of the ledger, on which the debit or credit entry has been posted. Since posting to ledger takes place after jounalising, ledger folios are written after some time, when the corresponding ledger entry has been made. The amount of debit entry is entered in the fourth column and amount of credit entry in the fifth column.

Specimen of journal

Date	Particular	L.F.	Amount (Debit) Rs.	Amount (Credit) Rs.
(i)	(ii)	(iii)	(iv)	(v)

Example 1 Journalise the transactions given below in the books of Mohan Sehgal and post to ledger.

2010	Detail	Amount in Rs
February 1	Mohan Sehgal started business with a capital of	3,00,000
February 2	He purchased a laptop	24,540
February 3	He bought goods on credit from Messers Kalash Agencies	1,000
February 3	He purchased postage stamps worth	50
February 5	He sold goods for cash	270
February 7	He sold goods on credit to Messers Asha Stores	7,500
February 9	Goods were found defective and were returned to Messers Kalash Agencies.	1,000
February 11	Cash was paid to Messers Kalash Agencies	800
February 12	He deposited in bank	1,00,000
February 13	He received cash from Messers Asha Stores	6,500
February 15	Paid insurance premium by cheque	32,500
February 28	Paid rent for February	12,000
February 28	Paid salary of clerk	75,000
February 28	Paid electric bill	3,500

Solution:

Journal

Date 2010	Particular	L. F.	Dr. Amount Rs.	Cr. Amount Rs.
February 1	Cash A/c Dr. To capital A/c (Being capital brought in by proprietor)	1 2	3,00,000	 3,00,000
February 2	Laptop A/c Dr. To cash A/c (Being purchased a laptop)	3 1	24540	 24540
February 3	Goods A/c Dr. To Kalash Agencies A/c (Being purchased from Kalash Agencies on credit)	3 4	1,000	 1,000
February 3	Postage A/c Dr. To cash A/c (Being purchased postage stamp for cash)	5 1	50	 50

Contd...

Contd...

February 5	Cash A/c Dr. To goods A/c (Being goods sold for cash)	1 3	270	 270
February 7	Asha Stores A/c Dr. To goods A/c (Being goods sold on credit to Asha Stores)	6 3	7500	 7500
February 9	Kalash Agencies A/c Dr. To goods A/c (Being defective goods returned to Kalash Agencies)	4 3	1000	 1000
February 11	Kalash Agencies A/c Dr. To cash A/c (Being defective goods returned to Kalash Agencies)	4 3	800	 800
February 12	Bank A/c Dr. To cash A/c (Being the purchase of stationery)	7 1	1,00,000	 1,00,000
February 13	Cash A/c Dr. To Asha Stores A/c (Being cash received from Asha Stores)	1 6	6500	 6500
February 15	Insurance premium A/c Dr. To cash A/c (Being paid insurance)	8 7	32500	 32500
February 28	Rent A/c Dr. To cash A/c (Being paid rent)	8 1	12000	 12000
February 28	Salaries A/c Dr. To cash A/c (Being paid salaries)	8 1	75000	 75000
February 28	Electricity A/c Dr. To cash A/c (Being paid electric bill)	8 1	3500	 3500
	Grand Total	Rs.	5,64,660	5,64,660

LEDGER

Ledger is the principal book of accounts. It has already been stated that a journal is kept only to facilitate the passing of entries in the ledger. Every entry made in the journal must be posted into the ledger. The ledger is a book of accounts and in respect of every journal entry, one ledger account has to be debited and another ledger account has to be credited. As it has been discussed in the format given below, each page (or account) is divided into two sides — the right-hand side or credit side and left-hand side or debit side. Each side has columns of varying sizes for (i) Date, (ii) Particulars, (iii) Journal folio no. and (iv) Amount.

Ledger Format

Debit				*Credit*			
Date	Particular	Journal Folio (JF)	Amount in Rs.	Date	Particular	Journal Folio (JF)	Amount in Rs.
I	II	III	IV	V	VI	VII	VIII

The making of entries in the ledger from the journal (or books of original entries) is known as posting. Entries recorded in the journal (or other books of original entry) is the basis of entries in the ledger and if any mistake creeps up in the process of journalizing, it would automatically be passed on into the ledger. Thus, great care should be exercised in journalizing.

Balancing Ledger Accounts

At the end of every month (or any other fixed period), all the accounts in a ledger are balanced. The process has been discussed below:

(i) The first step is to total up the two sides of the account concerned on a rough piece of paper.

(ii) Generally, the total of one side would be more than that of the other.

(iii) The difference is then entered in the amount column of the lighter side.

(iv) The total of the two sides will now be the same, which is now drawn, taking care that the two totals appear against each other or in the same line. It should be noted that a single line is drawn across the amount column before writing the total.

(v) After totals have been written, a double line is drawn across the amount column.

(vi) Next, the balance is brought down on the opposite side of the account. "To Balance c/d" is written on the debit side before balancing; and it will be brought down on the credit side, and "By Balance b/d" will be written in the particular column on the credit side, and vice versa.

Example 2 Transactions are posted from Journal to Ledger.

Cash A/c

Debit				*Credit*			
Date 2010	Particulars	J.F.	Amount Rs.	Date	Particulars	J.F.	Amount Rs.
Feb 1	To Capital A/c	1	300000	Feb 2	By Laptop A/c	1	24540
Feb 5	To Goods A/c	2	270	Feb 3	By Postage A/c	1	50
Feb 13	To Asha Store A/c	2	6500	Feb 12	By Kalash Agencies A/c	2	800

Contd...

				Feb 12	By Bank A/c	2	100000
				Feb 28	By Rent	2	12000
				Feb 28	By Salaries	2	75000
				Feb 28	By Salaries	2	3500
					By Balance b/d		90880
Total			306770				306770
March 1	To Balance c/d		90880				

Ledger
Capital A/c

Debit				Credit			
Date 2010	Particulars	J.F.	Amount Rs.	Date	Particulars	J.F.	Amount Rs.
				Feb 1	By Cash A/c	1	300000
	To Balance c/d		300000				
Total			300000				300000
March 1					By Balance b/d		300000

Ledger
Leptop A/c

Debit				Credit			
Date 2010	Particulars	J.F.	Amount Rs.	Date	Particulars	J.F.	Amount Rs.
Feb 2	To Cash A/c	1	24540				
					By Balance b/d		24540
Total			24540				24540
March 1	To Balance c/d		24540				

Ledger
Goods A/c

Debit				Credit			
Date 2010	Particulars	J.F.	Amount Rs.	Data	Particulars	J.F.	Amount Rs.
Feb 3	To Kalash Agencies A/c	1	1000	Feb 5	By Cash A/c	2	270
Feb 5	To Goods A/c	2	270	Feb 7	To Asha Stores A/c	2	7500
Feb 13	To Asha Stores A/c	2	6500	Feb 9	By Kalash Agencies A/c	2	1000
	To Balance c/d		1000				
Total			8770				8770
March 1					By Balance b/d		1000

Ledger
Postage A/c

Debit				*Credit*			
Date	Particulars	J.F.	Amount Rs.	Date	Particulars	J.F.	Amount Rs.
Feb 3	To Cash A/c	1	50				
					By Balance b/d	To Balance	50
Total			50				50
March 1	To Balance c/d		50				

Ledger
Asha Stores A/c

Debit				*Credit*			
Date	Particulars	J.F.	Amount Rs.	Date	Particulars	J.F.	Amount Rs.
Feb 7	To Goods A/c	1	7500	Feb 13	By Cash A/c	2	6500
					By Balance b/d		1000
Total			7500				7500
March 1	To Balance c/d		1000				

Ledger
Kalash Agencies

Debit				*Credit*			
Date	Particulars	J.F.	Amount Rs.	Date	Particulars	J.F.	Amount Rs.
Feb 9	To Goods A/c	1	1000	Feb 3	By Goods A/c	1	10000
Feb 11	To Cash A/c	2	800				
					By Balance b/d		800
Total			1800				1800
March 1	To Balance c/d		800				

Ledger
Bank A/c

Debit				*Credit*			
Date	Particulars	J.F.	Amount Rs.	Data	Particulars	J.F.	Amount Rs.
Feb 12	To Cash A/c	2	1,00,000	Feb 15	By Insurance Premium A/c	2	32500
					By Balance b/d		67500
Total			1,00,000				1,00,000
March 1	To Balance c/d		67500				

Ledger
Insurance Premium A/c

Debit				*Credit*			
Date	Particulars	J.F.	Amount Rs.	Date	Particulars	J.F.	Amount Rs.
Feb 15	To Bank A/c	2	32500				
					By Balance b/d		32500
Total			32500				32500
March 1	To Balance c/d		32500				

Ledger
Rent A/c

Debit				*Credit*			
Date	Particulars	J.F.	Amount Rs.	Date	Particulars	J.F.	Amount Rs.
Feb 28	To Cash A/c	3	12000				
					By Balance b/d		12000
Total			12000				12000
March 1	To Balance c/d		12000				

Ledger
Salaries A/c

Debit				*Credit*			
Date	Particulars	J.F.	Amount Rs.	Date	Particulars	J.F.	Amount Rs.
Feb 28	To Cash A/c	3	75000				
					By Balance b/d		75000
Total			75000				75000
March 1	To Balance c/d		75000				

Ledger
Electricity A/c

Debit				*Credit*			
Date	Particulars	J.F.	Amount Rs.	Date	Particulars	J.F.	Amount Rs.
Feb 28	To Cash A/c	3	3500				
					By Balance b/d		3500
Total			3500				3500
March 1	To Balance c/d		3500				

(Transactions from 1st to 10th have been entered in Journal-1, 11th to 19th have been entered in Journal-2 and 21st onward have been entered in Journal-3.)

Total of coloumn of debit and credit are equal in journal but is not equal in case of ledger

JOINT VENTURE ACCOUNT

Joint ventures are made for specific and limited purposes and are separate from their usual activities. Parties in venture are called co-ventures. There is no specific act to govern joint ventures. The profit or loss is ascertained at the end of specific venture (if the venture continues for a short period of time) or on interim basis annually (if venture continues for a long period of time). Co-ventures can maintain the accounts for joint venture in the manner that suits them in a particular situation. They can either have separate sets of book or the account can be maintained even in one of the co-venturer's book also. Plant, machinery and other fixed assets when used in ventures are first charged to venture account at cost. On completion of the venture such assets are revalued and shown as revenue of the venture. Thus, accounting approach for measurement of venture's profit is totally different.

CONSIGNMENT ACCOUNT

If the consignor sends goods for sale to the consignee and the consignee sells them on behalf of and at the risk of the consignor, the consignee maintains consignment account which he periodically, sends to the consignor. Whether they have earned profit or incurred loss in any transaction, there are some rules for making entries, which are as follows:

(i) Enter cost of goods and other expenses incurred or to be incurred on the left-hand side or debit side.

(ii) Put down the cost proceeds also as the cost of goods remaining unsold on the right-hand side or credit side.

(iii) The difference between the total of the two sides will reveal profit or loss.

Credit > Debit = Profit

Debit > Credit = Loss

BALANCE SHEET

A balance sheet is a financial statement, which shows financial status of a business entity at a given time. Financial status includes assets, liabilities and capital at a specified date. It is commonly, prepared annually. However, it is prepared in between also as per the requirement.

A balance sheet is divided in two parts. The left side carries description of capital and liabilities and the right side carries description of assets and properties. 'To' and 'By' are not written on it. There is fixed order to enter property and liabilities in a balance sheet. Generally, following are two methods to make entries:

(i) In order of permanence: Entries are made on the basis of their permanence. Most permanent entries are made first. Less permanent entries are made after that so on and so forth. This kind of balance sheet is made by public limited companies.

(ii) In order of liquidity: Entries are made in the balance sheet on the basis of liquidity as from liquid to permanent liabilities. By this method, balance sheet is made in other forms of organizations except public limited companies.

Aims of Balance Sheet

It gives information about

(i) Ratio in which a firm keeps its money between cash in hand, cash in bank and other forms of properties and securities.

(ii) the firm's contingent liabilities.

(iii) availability of capital with the firm in the beginning of the year. And what is the current position after adding and subtracting net profit or loss.

(iv) how much money the firm has to give to other persons, firms and organizations and how much money they have to receive.

(v) the financial status of the firm. Financial comparison of a company at two points of time or between two or more companies can be made on the basis of balance sheet.

Format of Balance Sheet

Balance Sheet of __________ as at __________

Capital and Liabilities	*Amount Rs*	*Assets and Properties*	*Amount Rs*
Bills Payable		Cash in hand	
Bank Overdraft		Cash at Bank	
Creditors		Bills Receivable	
Loan		Investment	
Capital		Debtors	
Add Net Profit		Stock (closing)	
Less Net Loss		Furniture and fitting	
Less Drawings		Plant and machinery	
		Land and building	
		Goodwill	
Total		Total	

Terminology of accountancy:

1. Capital: It is cash, goods and other assets like building and equipment.
2. Capital formation: Addition to the reproducible wealth of a country that is retained for use in further production.
3. Consignment: It is the goods dispatched to agents for selling on behalf of the firm.
4. Commission: It is remuneration to a person (or agent) by the firm, for his services to the firm.
5. Creditor: Creditor gets money from others.
6. Current assets: These include items, which can be converted into cash within a short period of time, say one year or less.
7. Debtor: He pays money to others.
8. Discount: It is the deduction allowed to the buyer on the list price.
9. Drawings: It is the withdrawal of money by the owner for his personal use.
10. Liabilities: These are debts owned by a firm to other persons. These may be loans, overdraft bills payable, etc.
11. Liquid assets: These can be readily converted into money.
12. Other assets: These are assets like patents and copyrights.
13. Turnover: It is total sales of an enterprise.

EXERCISES

A. Objective

State whether the following statements are 'True' or 'False':

(i) Payment made by cheque is supposed to be very safe.

(ii) The amount with which a businessmen starts business is called wealth.

(iii) Journal is systematic record of all borrowings.

(iv) Every transaction affects two accounts at the same time.

(v) Big business can run without the help of bookkeeping.

(vi) Net profit or loss can be checked by bookkeeping.

(vii) Cost accounting does not help in price fixation.

(viii) Main purpose of cost accounting is to maximize profit.

Ans. (i) False; (ii) False; (iii) False; (iv) True;
(v) False; (vi) False; (vii) False; (viii) True

B Subjective

1. Who are the users of accounting information? Why do they need accounting information?
2. Describe the importance and significance of bookkeeping to an engineer and a businessman.
3. What do you understand by bookkeeping?
4. Distinguish between bookkeeping and accountancy. Explain the objectives and advantages of bookkeeping.
5. What is meant by Double Entry System of bookkeeping? How it is an improvement over Single Entry System of bookkeeping? Illustrate your answer with suitable examples.
6. Discuss significance of balance sheet.

C Numerical Problems

1. Journalise the following transactions and post them to ledger accounts:

2011	*Particulars*	*Amount in Rs.*
Jan 1	Ram deposited the amount in bank	30,000.00
Jan 5	Bought goods for cash	3,000.00
Jan 6	Cash sales	2,000.00
Jan 7	Sold goods to Hari on credit	3,000.00
Jan 8	Purchased goods from Karim on credit	2,000.00
Jan 10	Paid wages to workman	20000.00
Jan 15	Received from Hari and allowed him discount	1,000.00 20.00
Jan 20	Paid Karim And was allowed discount	1,980.00 20.00
Jan 31	Paid rent	20,000.00

2. Journalise the following transactions and post them to ledger accounts:

2010	*Particulars*	*Amount in Rs.*
Jan 1	Ram deposited the amount in bank	2,00,000.00
Jan 5	Bought goods on credit	2,500.00
Jan 6	Cash sales	2,000.00
Jan 7	Sold goods to Kapil on cash	1,000.00
Jan 8	Purchased goods from Karim on credit	2,000.00
Jan 10	Paid Ram And was allowed a discount	600.00 40.00

Contd...

Contd...

Jan 15	Received from Manoj And allowed him discount	2,000.00 30.00
Jan 20	Drew from bank	1,000.00
Jan 25	Drew for personal use	6000.00
Jan 31	Received interest in cash from Karim	500.00
Jan31	Paid rent in cash	30,000.00

3. Journalise the following transactions and post them to ledger account:

2010	*Particulars*	*Amount in Rs.*
Jan 4	Paid cash for trade expenses	6,000.00
Jan 5	Bought goods on credit cash	2,500.00
Jan 6	Sold goods to Ram Narain	2,000.00
Jan 6	Cash sales	2,000.00
Jan 7	Cash sales	1,000.00
Jan 7	Sold goods to Kapil on cash	1,000.00
Jan 8	Purchased goods from Karim on credit	2,000.00
Jan 10	Sold goods to Haque	1,600.00
Jan 10	Paid Ram And was allowed a discount	600.00 40.00
Jan 15	Paid cash for stationery	500.00
Jan 15	Received from Manoj And allowed him discount	2,000.00 30.00
Jan 20	Paid cash for miscellaneous expenses	1150.00
Jan 20	Drew from bank	1,000.00
Jan 25	Purchased goods from Ahuja	600.00
Jan 25	Drew for personal use	60,000.00
Jan 30	Received interest in cash from Karim	1500.00
Jan 31	Paid rent in Cash	10,000.00
Jan 31	Ram deposited the amount in bank	1,000.00
Jan 31	Received interest in cash from Karim	550.00
Jan 31	Paid Rent in cash	20,000.00

4. Journalise the following transactions and post them to ledger.

2002		*Rs.*
Jan 1	Started business with cash	1,00,000.00
Jan 2	Deposited into bank	40,000.00
Jan 5	Purchased goods on credit from Ram	4000.00

Contd...

Contd...

Jan 6	Cash paid to Mohan	5,000.00
Jan 10	Cash sales	1000.00
Jan 15	Sold goods to Mohan for credit	2000.00
Jan 20	Received cash from Ram	6000.00
Jan 25	Purchased goods for cash	2000.00
Jan 30	Withdrew cash from bank	1000.00
Jan 31	Paid rent	25,000.00
Jan 31	Paid salaries	20,000.00

10

Introduction to Engineering Economic Analysis

Purpose of this chapter is to acquaint the reader with:

- Simple and Complex Engineering Economic Problems
- Types of Simple Engineering Economic Problem: Elementary Problems and Advance Problems
- Simple Decision-Making Problems: selection of location, selection of raw material, design selection for an operation
- Make or Buy Decision: Break-Even Analysis, Profit-Volume Ratio

Economics is a subject about making choices under conditions of scarcity. Choices have to be made because the resources are limited, while the competing uses for them are unlimited. Engineers also have to take appropriate decisions in their professional pursuit among various alternatives. Each decision involves its own cost and benefit. To evaluate them, an engineer may use economic tools.

There are two types of engineering economic problems faced by engineers, which may be discussed as follows:

Simple Engineering Economic Problems

These problems mainly deal with economic aspect such as:

(i) Which equipment should be selected for a new assembly line?

(ii) Shall a particular component of the engine be made or purchased?

(iii) Which material should be used for making roof, sides and structural support for a new building?

(iv) Which machine should be purchased—a low cost which requires three operators and a more expensive one which requires only two operators?

Complex Engineering Economic Problems

Besides economic aspect, Complex Engineering Economic Problems have environmental, political or social elements also:

(i) Which technology should be adopted? The price of the technology will have economic considerations. Its impact on employment may have social impact. It may have impact on environment also.

(ii) If an MNC wants to start its production unit either in India or China, then availability of resources will come under economic consideration and considerations such as law and order will come under political considerations.

Economic tools are used to solve simple and economic aspects of Engineering Economic Problem. It focuses on cost and revenue of a firm, preferences of a customer at micro level and economic environment such as tax or subsidy, bank rate at macro level. Again, engineering economic problems may require elementary or advance techniques to solve. However, an engineering economic analysis involves following steps (Sullivan et al. p. 8):

(i) Development of feasible alternatives
(ii) Development of cash flow for each alternative
(iii) Analysis and comparison of alternatives
(iv) Performance monitoring and evaluation of results

Engineering Economic Analysis (EEA) is taught separately as one semester course at an advanced level of B.E. or M.E. engineering courses. However, some elementary engineering economic problems have been discussed here to develop interest of engineering students in application of economics in the problems they are going to face in their professional life.

ELEMENTARY ENGINEERING ECONOMIC PROBLEM

To carry out day-to-day business activities, many of the decisions can be taken by using elementary engineering economic analysis. Generally, these problems are targeted to minimize the cost or maximization of profit. Through selection of nearby location, cheaper raw material, reduced machine or process time and enhanced durability of the product, developing network, cost of a product may be reduced. Reduced cost ultimately leads to enhanced profit. Some elementary engineering economic problems are discussed below:

Simple decision-making problem

Some economic problems involve simple decision making which must take following factors into account:

(i) Nature of the demand for the product, i.e., it is regular, seasonal or only one time.

(ii) Is it a necessity or a luxury,

(iii) Quantity demanded.

Example 1 The college shop has put several products on sale. They are as follows:

(i) Compiled previous year's question papers

(ii) Bottle of soft drink

(iii) Packet of salt

Explain how many of these goods you will purchase during sale?

Solution

(i) Even if the compiled previous year's question papers are on sale, only one copy of it will be required.

(ii) Certainly there will demand for at least double number of bottles of soft drink because students can have two bottles at the price of one. It may be more than double also because even those students may purchase who might not purchase at the initial price.

(iii) Salt consumption by an individual is necessary but at the same time, very small amount is required. So, hardly sale will have any effect on the demand.

These may be calculated through price elasticity of demand also.

Example 2 A bakery shop sells pancake. The product is perishable and any remaining unsold after one week in the store is disposed of. The bakery will deliver the pancakes to the store, arrange them in the display space, and remove as well as dispose of any old pancakes. The price charged by the bakery depends on the size of the total weekly order.

Weekly Order	*Price per Packet in Rs.*
Less than 1000 cakes	10.00
1000-1499	9.00
1500-1999	8.00
2000 or more	7.00

The shopkeeper estimates the quantity that can be sold per week, at various selling prices, as follows:

Selling Price	*Quantity Sold per Week*
12.00	300 packets
11.00	600 packets
10.00	1200 packets
9.00	1700 packets
8.00	2300 packets

How many packets should be purchased per week? At which of the five prices listed above should they be sold?

Solution

Quantity Sold per Week	*Selling Price per Packet*	*Income in Rs.*	*Purchasing Price per Packet*	*Cost in Rs.*	*Profit in Rs.*
300 packets	12.00	3600.00	10.00	3000.00	600.00
600	11.00	6600.00	10.00	6000.00	600.00
1200	10.00	12000.00	9.00	10800.00	1200.00
1700	9.00	15300.00	8.00	13600.00	1700.00
2300	7.00	16100.00	6.50	14950.00	1150.00

Buy 1700 packets of pancakes @ Rs. 8.00 each.

Selection of Location

Though Information and Communication Technology (ICT) has enhanced reach of producer both for procurement of inputs and selling of his product, selection of appropriate location is very significant for survival, sustainability and profit maximization.

Example 3 Suppose you have been assigned the responsibility of selecting site for a flyover in a busy area downtown, in which many of the houses will be dislocated. List three criteria, which you will consider for selecting the location.

Solution

(i) The site that will better serve the future demand for travel measured by an index of vehicle per day, lower accident rate and time lost due to congestion.

(ii) Decayed residential or industrial area.

(iii) Least time lost for travellers due to construction.

Selection of Raw Material

Cost of raw material makes a significant share in the total cost. So, decision about sourcing of raw material of right quality and of sufficient quantity is very important for decision makers.

Example 4 Which type of raw material should be selected for construction of the following:

(i) Rural house

(ii) Highway

(iii) An invitation card for launching of a new model of *X* brand of car

(iv) Thread, which is going to be used by a medical surgeon

(v) Bottle of new international brand of perfume

Solution

(i) Rural house must be made of locally available resource for being cost effective.

(ii) At highway, those materials need to be used which enhance speed of vehicle and durability of roads. As regular repair of roads creats diseconomies for transporters.

(iii) It should be made of eco-friendly papers because cost is not the main consideration here. The card will be sent to rich people who may be impressed by the eco-sensitivity of the company.

(iv) It needs to be made up of soluble polymers.

(v) Use of perfume has a psychological effect on the person who is using it. So it needs to be elegant looking.

Example 5 A farmer must decide what combination of seed, water, fertilizer, and pest control will be most profitable for the coming agricultural season. Out of the four plans which he has:

Plan	*Cost/acre in Rs.*	*Income/acre in Rs.*
A	600	800
B	1500	1900
C	1800	2250
D	2100	2500

Which plan should the farmer adopt?

Solution

Plan	*Income-Cost*	*Profit in Rs.*
A	800 – 600	Rs. 200
B	1900 – 1500	Rs. 400
C	2250 – 1800	Rs. 450
D	2500 – 2100	Rs. 400

Plan C yields maximum profit. So, it should be adopted.

Example 6 1000 quintals of marble is required for flooring in a building located in North Delhi. The contractor has two options. The cost details for both are as under.

Sl. No.	*Particular*	*Nearby Shop*	*Outside Shop (from Rajasthan)*
1.	Distance	4 km	100 km
2.	Transportation cost	Rs.700/km./quintal	Rs. 700/km./quintal
3.	Material cost	Rs. 8150/quintal	Rs. 5200/quintal

The quality of marble is same from either the sources. Which options will be proved more profitable? What will be the economic advantage?

Solution

Sl. No.	*Detail*	*Nearby shop*	*Outside shop (From Rajasthan)*
a.	Total Material Cost = Material Cost/quintal × Total Material required	8150 × 1000 = 81,50,000	5200 × 1000 = 52,00,000
b.	Total Transportation Cost = Transportation Cost/km./quintal × Distance × Total Amount Transported	4 × 700 × 1000 = 28,00,000	100 × 700 × 1000 = 700,00,000
Total Cost = Total Material Cost + Total Transportation Cost		8150000 + 2800000 = Rs. 1,09,50,000	5200000 + 70000000 = Rs. 7,52,00,000

So, the first option is economical.

Economic Advantage = 75200000 – 10950000 = Rs 64250000/-

Example 7 An almirah making firm has two options. Either it can use galvanized iron or aluminium as raw material. Both the materials provide equal services. Aluminium sheet costs Rs. 90/m^2 and galvanized iron sheet costs Rs. 70/m^2. Sheet of 60 m^2 size is required. The cost of finishing and bending of galvanized iron almirah is Rs. 5000 while for aluminium, it is Rs. 6050. If aluminium is used as raw material, it is joined by rivets, which costs Rs. 1250 per almirah. While for galvanized iron, it is Rs. 1700 as spot welding is used. The transportation cost for each extra kilogram of weight is Rs. 850. An almirah made by galvanized iron weighs 2 kg heavier than that made from aluminium. Find the better option and calculate economic advantage if all other costs incurred are same.

Solution

Sl. No.	*Detail*	*Aluminum*	*Galvanized Iron*
a.	Cost of sheet/m^2	Rs. 90	Rs. 70
b.	Cost of required sheet = cost of aluminum sheet × total size of sheet required	90 × 60 = Rs. 5400	70 × 60 = Rs. 4200
c.	Cost of making Almirah = finishing and bending + Rivets/spot welding	6050 + 1250 = Rs. 7300	5000 + 1700 = Rs. 6700
d.	Additional Transportation Cost = Additional Transportation Cost/kg + Additional weight	– –	850 × 2 = Rs. 1700
	Total Cost = b + c + d =	Rs. 12,700	Rs. 12,600

So, galvanized iron is more economical

Economic Advantage/Almirah = 12700 – 12600 = Rs. 100

Example 8 In the design of pipes for transportation of crude oil to the underground storage site for distribution, the designer is considering two options, either PVC pipes or reinforced concrete pipes. Because of remote location of oilfields, pipes have to be brought from a distance of 1000 km.

Particular	PVC	Concrete
Quantity required	200 m	200 m
Cost per metre length	Rs. 800	Rs.950
Transportation cost	Rs. 7/kg/50 km	Rs.10/kg/50 km
Weight/metre	7 kg	10 kg

What material should be considered? What is the economic advantage of the selection?

Solution

Sl. No.	Detail	PVC	Concrete
a.	Weight = Weight/meter × Quantity required	7 × 200 = 1400 kg.	10 × 200 = 2000 kg.
b.	Cost of transportation to oil field = Transportation Cost/metre/50km × Distance	7 × 1000/50 = Rs. 140	10 × 1000/50 = Rs. 200
c.	Cost of pipe = Cost/metre × Quantity required	800 × 200 = Rs. 160000	950 × 200 = Rs. 190000
d.	Cost of transporting the pipe = b × weight	140 × 1400 = Rs. 196000	200 × 2000 = Rs. 400000
	Total = c + d =	Rs. 3,56,000	Rs. 5,90,000

Installing PVC pipeline is advisable.

Economic Advantage = 590000 – 356000 = Rs. 2,34,000/-

Example 9 Compare two alternatives for removal of hardness of water. One is lime soda process, in which lime [$Ca(OH)_2$] and soda [Na_2CO_3] are used. Other is zeolite process in which Natrolite [$Na_2O.Al_2O_3.4SO_2.2H_2O$] is used. Price of lime is Rs. 755 per kg and soda is Rs. 390 per kg. Amount which is used to purify 100 litre of water is 5 kg of lime and 3 kg of soda. In the other process, price of zeolite is Rs. 890 per kg and 6 kg of zeolite is used to remove hardness of the same sample of water. The additional cost in setting up of apparatus for lime soda process is Rs. 6000 and for zeolite process Rs. 3900. Which process is economical? What is the economic advantage?

Solution

Sl. No.	Lime Soda process	Zeolite process
a.	Cost of lime/kg = Rs. 755	Cost of zeolite/kg = Rs. 890
b.	Amount of lime used = 5 kg/100 litre of water.	Amount of zeolite used = 6 kg/100 litre of water.
	Total cost on lime = 755 × 5 = Rs. 3775	Total cost on zeolite = 890 × 6 = Rs. 5340
c.	Cost of Soda/kg = Rs. 390	–
d.	Amount of soda used = 3 kg/100 litre of water.	–
e.	Total cost on Soda = 390 × 3 = Rs. 1170	–
f.	Additional cost of setting up of apparatus = Rs. 6000	Additional cost of setting up of apparatus = Rs. 3900
g.	Total Cost = 3775 + 1170 + 6000 = Rs. 10,945	Total Cost = 5340 + 3900 = Rs. 9240

∴ 2nd method is economical.

Economic advantage = 10945 – 9240

= Rs.1705

Design Selection for a Machine

Example 10 Two alternative designs are under consideration for a machine. Either design will serve the purpose and will involve the same material and manufacturing cost except for the lathe and grinder operation.

Design A will require 20 hours of the lathe time and 8.5 hours of grinder time/100 units. Design B will require 16 hours of lathe time and 12 hours of grinder time/100 units. The operating cost of the lathe including labour is Rs. 1100/ hour. The operating cost of the grinder including labour is Rs. 950/hour. Which design should be adopted if 10,000 units are required annually? What is the economic advantage of the best alternative?

Solution Operating cost of lathe time including labour = Rs. 1100/hour

Operating cost of grinder including labour = Rs. 950/hour

	Design A	*Design B*
No. of hours of lathe time/100 units	20 hours	16 hours
No. of hours of grinder time/100 units	8.5 hours	12 hours
Cost/100 units = lathe time/100 unit × cost of operating lathe + Grinder time/100 units × cost of operating grinder	20 × 1100 + 8.5 × 950 = Rs. 30075	16 × 1100 + 12 × 950 = Rs. 29,000
Total Cost/10000	30075 × 100 = Rs. 30,07,500	29,000 × 100 = Rs. 29,00,000

As total cost of design B is less than the design A, decision for design B will be adopted.

Economic advantage of design B over design A per 10,000 units

= 30,07,500 – 29,00,000 = Rs. 1,07,500

Example 11 In the design of a cold-storage, the specifications call for a maximum heat transfer through the walls of 35,000 joules/hr/metre^2 at 35°C temperature difference between the inside surface and the outside surface of the insulation. Two insulating materials being considered are as follows:

Insulation Material	*Cost/cubic metre*	*Conductivity J/hr/m^{2}at°C*
Rock wool	Rs. 855	135
Foamed insulation	Rs. 1250	115

The basic equation for the heat conduction through a wall is $Q = \{K\,(\Delta T)\}/L$

where Q = Heat transfer in J/hr/m^2 of wall

K = Conductivity in J/hr/m^2°C

ΔT = Difference in temperature between the two surfaces in °C

L = Thickness of insulating material in metres

Which insulation material should be selected?

Solution Two steps are required to solve the problem. First, the required thickness of each material must be calculated. Then, since the problem is of providing a fixed output (heat transfer through the wall limited to a fixed maximum amount), the criteria is to minimize the input (cost).

Sl. No.	*Detail*	*Rock Wool*	*Foamed Insulation*
a.	Q = {K(ΔT)} /L or, L =	35000 = {135(35)}/L = 0.135m	35000 = {115(35)}/L = 0.115m
b.	Cost of Insulation/sq. metre of wall: Unit cost = Cost/m^3 × Insulation thickness in metres	855 × 0.135 = Rs. 115.43	1250 × 0.115 = Rs. 143.75

As cost of Rock Wool is less than Foamed Insulation.

Rock Wool should be opted.

$$\text{Economic advantage} = 143.75 - 115.43 = \text{Rs. } 28.32$$

Selection of Production Process

Example 12 For construction purpose, a concrete aggregate mix is required which should contain at least 34% sand by volume. Following options are available:

	Sand	*Coarse*	*Rate*
First source	30%	70%	Rs.12.50 per cubic metre
Second source	42%	58%	Rs. 15.25 per cubic metre

Determine the least cost per cubic metre of blended aggregates.

Solution The least cost of blended aggregates will result from maximum use of the lower cost material. The higher cost material will be used to increase the proportion of sand up to the minimum level (34%) specified.

Let x = portion of blended aggregates from Rs. 12.50/m^2 source.

$1 - x$ = portion of blended aggregates from Rs.15.25/m^2 source.

Sand balance

or, $$x\,(0.30) + (1 - x)\,(0.42) = 0.34$$

or, $$0.30\,x + 0.42 - 0.42x = 0.34$$

or, $$x = \frac{0.34 - 0.42}{0.30 - 0.42} = \frac{-0.8}{-1.2} = 0.66$$

Thus, the blended aggregate will contain:

66% of Rs. 12.50/m^3 material

34% of Rs. 15.25/m^{3}material

The least cost per cubic metre of blended aggregate:

$$= 0.66 \times 12.50 + 0.34 \times 15.25 = \text{Rs. } 13.44/\text{m}^3$$

Example 13 A special type of screw is manufactured at a unit cost of Rs. 2.75 for material and Rs. 4.50 for direct labour. Other cost is 1.5 times direct labour cost. The order calls for three million pieces. Half-way through the order, a new method of manufacture can be put into effect, which will reduce the unit cost of Rs. 2.00 for material and Rs. 3.75 for direct labour, but it will require Rs. 1,00,000 for additional machine. Which process should be taken up?

Solution Our problem only concerns the second half of the order, as there is only one alternative for the first 1.5 million pieces.

	Continue with the Present Method	*Change the Manufacturing Method*
Material Cost	= 15,00,000 × 2.75 = Rs. 41,25,000	= 15,00,000 × 2.00 = Rs. 30,00,000
Direct Labour Cost	= 15,00,000 × 4.50 = Rs. 67,50,000	= 15,00,000 × 3.75 = Rs. 56,25,000
Other Costs	= 1.5 × Direct Labour Cost = 1.5 × 67,50,000 = Rs. 1,01,25,000	= 1.5 × Direct Labour Cost = 1.5 × 56,25,000 = Rs. 84,37,500
Cost of Additional Machine	------	Rs. 1,00,000
Cost of remaining 15,00,000 pieces	= 41,25,000 + 67,50,000 + 1,01,25,000 = Rs. 2,10,00,000	= 30,00,000 + 56,25,000 + 84,37,500 = Rs. 1,70,62,500

To continue with the same method is economical.

Economic advantage = 2,10,00,000 – 1,70,62,500
= Rs. 39,37,500.

Example 14 A contractor is to dig a channel for industrial purpose. He can complete this work in two ways. Either he can dig it manually or with less number of labour and a machine. If the first option is opted, labour is required for 120 days @ Rs. 180/day. For the second option, semi-skilled labour is required for 30 days @ Rs. 390 day and a rented machine costing Rs. 550 per day including cost of oil. Which option should be adopted? What will be the economic advantage?

Solution

Sl. No.	*Particular*	*First Option*	*Second Option*
1.	Labour Cost	= 180 × 120 = Rs. 21600	= 390 × 30 = Rs. 11700
2.	Cost of Machine	—	= 550 × 30 = Rs. 16500
Total Cost		Rs. 21600	Rs. 28200

First method should be adopted.

Economic advantage = 28200 – 21600 = Rs. 6600

Example 15 In a city, water samples need to be tested. There are two methods available.

Particular	*Method X*	*Method Y*
Cost of chemical which is used in test	Rs. 5.00/test	Rs. 7.50/test
Cost of testing machine	Rs. 47500	38750
Cost of labour	Rs. 200/day	Rs. 200/day
Number of samples tested in a day	300	400

Which method should be adopted, if 12,000 samples are to be tested?

Solution

S. No.	*Detail*	*Method X*	*Method Y*
a.	No. of days	12000/300 = 40 days	12000/400 = 30 days
b.	Cost of chemical	5.00 × 12,000 = Rs. 60,000	7.30 × 12,000 = Rs. 87600
c.	Cost of labour	200 × 40 = Rs. 8000	200 × 30 = Rs. 6000
d.	Cost of machine	Rs. 47500	Rs. 38750
	Total = b + c + d	Rs. 115500	Rs. 132350

Method *y* should be adopted.

Economic Advantage = 132350 – 115500 = Rs. 16850

MAKE-OR-BUY DECISION

Make-or-Buy is an important decision for any enterprise for cost reduction or product improvement. Any particular input or segment in the production process which can be made or completed within the enterprise or can be purchased from the market. It has important bearing on the total cost. Advantage and disadvantage of possible alternatives should be evaluated and most cost-effective choice should be made. However, the decisions are not static and may change due to acquisition of a new machine by the enterprise for some other work, but which can be used for the work in question also. Adoption of new technology or change in the relative price of input and the price at which it is available in the market, may also change the decision. So, the decision should be reconsidered after a gap of 1 to 3 years.

Criteria to 'Make'

1. The finished product can be made cheaper by the firm than by other suppliers.
2. If the firm has unused capacity and the product can be made cheaper by the firm than the outside suppliers.

3. The product is manufactured by limited number of other firms, which are unable to meet the demand.
4. The product is important for the firm and requires strict quality control, which may not be maintained by other firms.

Criteria to 'Buy'

1. Huge investment is required.
2. Requirement of very small quantity, temporary or seasonal.
3. Patent or other legal barriers prevent the company from making the product.
4. Company can use resources for some other profitable activity.

Analysis of 'Make' or 'Buy' Decision

There are two type of analysis[1]:

(i) Simple Cost Analysis : It involves comparison of total cost of make-or buy options available before the enterprise.

Example 16 An enterprise has to take decision about a component in its production process.

S. No.	*Particular*	*Make*	*Buy*
a.	Selling price/unit		Rs.700
b.	Direct labour cost	Rs.200/unit	
c.	Direct material cost	Rs. 300/unit	
d.	Direct overhead cost	Rs. 100/unit	
e.	Fixed cost	10,000	

Demand over the next year is estimated at 600 units. Would it be profitable for the company to make?

Solution Variable cost/unit = Direct labour cost/unit + Direct material cost/unit + Direct overhead cost/unit

= (200 + 300 + 100)/unit = Rs. 600/unit

Total variable cost – Rs. 600 × Rs. 600 = Rs. 3,60,000

Fixed cost = Rs. 10,000

Total cost = Fixed cost + Total variable cost = 10,000 + 36,00,00

= Rs. 3,70,000

Purchase cost = Rs. 600 × Rs. 700 = Rs. 4,20,000

It is advisable to make the component

(ii) Cost-Volume-Profit (CVP) Analysis

In Engineering Economics, it is a technique for taking elementary decisions in the short run and based on the assumption of linearity of cost and revenue curve. In the real world analysis, costs and revenue are non linear and the analysis is more complicated, but the explanation given by linear CVP remains same and thus, useful.

π = TR – TC (already discussed in the chapter-Project Planning) ...(equ. i)

where, π = Profit; TR = Total Revenue; S = Sale; TC = Total Cost

It can be further decomposed as

TR = P × Q (where, P = Price/unit; Q = Quantity) ...(equ. ii)

or, [(P – VC/until) + VC/unit] × Q (where, VC = Variable Cost)

or, [MS + VC/unit] × Q (where, MS = Margin of safety/unit)

or, MSXQ + VC/unit XQ ...(equ. iii)

Again,

TC = TFC + TVC

(where, TFC = Total fixed Cost; TVC = Total variable cost) ...(equ. iv)

TVC = VC/unit × Q ...(equ. v)

Now, substituting TR equation (*i*) with equation iii.

or, π = MSXQ + VC/unitXQ – (TFC + VC/unit XQ)

(where, TFC = Total Fixed Cost)

= MSXQ – TFC

= C – TFC (Contribution = MSXQ)

Contribution = Margin of safety/unit × Quantity

Profit = Contribution – Total Fixed Cost

Profit-volume ratio (P/V ratio) establishes a relationship between changes in contribution to changes in sales. This ratio is also known as marginal-income ratio and contribution to sales ratio.

Therefore,

$$\text{Profit-volume ratio (P/V ratio)} = \frac{\text{Contribution}}{\text{Sales}} \times 100$$

It is the rate at which the profit increases with the increase in volume. Any increase in contribution will mean an increase in the profit because fixed costs are assumed to remain constant over the sales. The P/V ratio will remain constant at different levels of production because variable costs as a proportion to sales remain constant.

The contribution is the difference between the sales and the veriable costs. The margin of safety (MS) is the sales over and above the break-even sales. The formula to compute these values is:

Contribution = Sales – Variable costs

Contribution/unit = Selling price/unit – Variable cost/unit

Margin of safety = Actual sales – Break-even sales

The company will earn profit beyond production 1165 units

$$\text{P/V ratio} = \frac{\text{Sales} - \text{Variable cost}}{\text{Sales}} \times 100$$

$$\text{Margin of safety (MS)} = \frac{\text{Profit}}{\text{P/V ratio}}$$

Example 17 Consider the following data of a company for the year 2014:

Sales = Rs. 1,00,000

Fixed cost = Rs. 40,000

Variable cost = Rs. 45,000

Find the following:

(i) Contribution (ii) Profit (iii) P/V ratio (iv) BEP (v) MS

Solution

(i) Contribution = Sales – Variable costs

= Rs. 1,00,000 – Rs. 45,000

= Rs. 55,000

(ii) Profit = Contribution – Fixed cost

= Rs. 55,000 – Rs. 40,000

= Rs. 15,000

(iii) $$\text{P/V ratio} = \frac{\text{Contribution}}{\text{Sales}} \times 100$$

$$\frac{55000}{100000} \times 100 = 55\%$$

(iv) $$\text{BEP} = \text{Fixed cost/P/V ratio} = \frac{40{,}000}{55} \times 100 = \text{Rs. } 72{,}727.27$$

(v) $$\text{MS} = \text{Profit/P/V ratio} = \frac{15000}{55} \times 100 = \text{Rs. } 27{,}272.73.$$

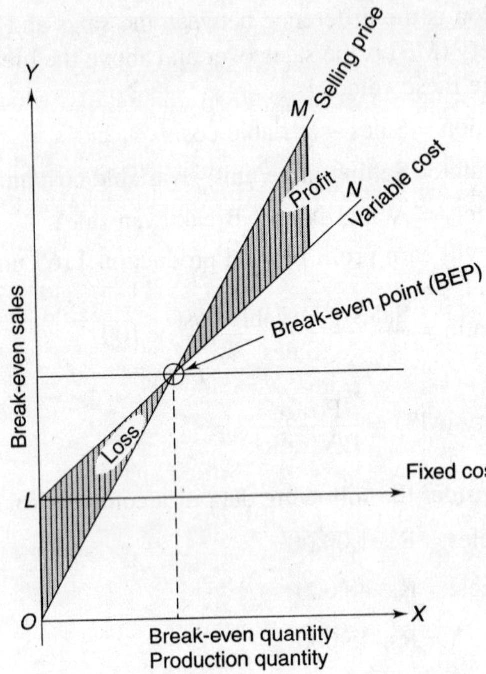

Fig. 10.1 Break-Even Analysis

Break-Even Analysis

Break-Even Analysis is a very useful technique for supply side analysis.

The main objective of break-even analysis is to find the cut-off production volume from where a firm will make profit.

Let

$$P = \text{selling price per unit}$$

$$VC = \text{variable cost per unit}$$

$$FC = \text{fixed cost}$$

$$X = \text{volume of production}$$

The total sales revenue (TR) of the firm is given by the following formula:

$$TR = P \times X$$

The total cost of the firm for a given production volume is given as

$$TC = \text{Total variable cost} + \text{Fixed cost}$$

$$= VC/\text{unit} \times X + FC$$

The linear plots of the above two equations TR and TC are shown in Fig. 10.1. The intersection point of the total revenue line OM and the total cost line LN is called the break-even point. The corresponding volume of production on the X-axis is known as the beeak-even sales quantity. At the intersection point, the total cost is equal to the total revenue. This point is also called the no-loss or no-gain situation. For any production quantity, which is less than the break-even quantity, the total cost is more than the total revenue. Hence, the firm will be making loss. For any production quantity, which is more than the break-even quantity, the total revenue will be more than the total cost.

The formula to find the break-even point and break-even sales quantity:

$$\text{Break-Even Point} = \frac{\text{Fixed cost}}{\text{Selling price/unit} - \text{Variable cost/unit}}$$

$$= \frac{FC}{P/\text{unit} - VC/\text{unit}}$$

$$\text{Break-Even Sales} = \frac{\text{Fixed cost}}{\text{Selling price/unit} - \text{Variable cost/unit}} \times \text{Selling price/unit}$$

$$= \frac{FC}{P - VC} \times P$$

$$\text{BEP} = \frac{\text{Fixed cost}}{\text{P/V ratio}}$$

$$= \frac{\text{Sales} - \text{Variable cost}}{\text{Sales}}$$

Example 18 A computer hardware company purchases computer screen at a cost of Rs. 4500 each. In case the company makes it, the fixed and variable cost would be Rs. 40,00,000 and Rs. 2000/screen respectively. Should the manufacturer make or buy the screen, if the annual demand is of 1500 computers?

Solution

Selling price = Rs. 4500/unit

Fixed cost = Rs. 40,00,000

Variable cost = Rs. 2000/unit

$$\text{BEP} = \frac{4000000}{4500 - 2000} = \text{Rs. } 1600$$

As demand is of 1500 computers, it is advisable to purchase from the market.

Example 19 A company is producing tyres. Cost of machine is Rs. 26,10,000. Cost of labour and raw material is @ Rs. 860/tyre and Rs. 1400/tyre respectively. Manufacturer sells @ Rs. 4500/tyre. What will be the break-even point for the company?

Solution

Fixed cost = 26,10,000

Variable cost/unit = Labour cost/tyre + raw material cost/tyre

= 860 + 1400

= Rs. 2260/tyre

Selling price/unit = Rs. 4500/tyre

$$\text{Break-Even Point (BEP)} = \frac{2610000}{4500 - 2260} = \frac{2610000}{2240} = 1165.18$$

Interest Formulas and Their Applications

In the previous section, cost or benefit has been discussed in length, where two or more alternatives were available and out of them, better one was to be selected. The money received or spent was immediate and at one point of time. The money, received or spent on alternatives were calculated separately to obtain result of all the alternatives to compare each one to select the least costly or most beneficial alternative, but in this section, those problems are being discussed where either the cost or monetary benefit, will take place over a period of time. There is time value of money which depends on demand for and supply of money as well as overall banking policy. Time value of money is calculated through interest rate formula. As you know, the interest rate can be calculated by simple interest rate (SIR) formula as well as compound interest rate (CIR) formula. However, in actual practice, interests are generally, calculated by CIR. Before understanding how interest formula is used for making investment decision, it is very important to know that in how many ways the formula can be used. It has been discussed below:

SINGLE-PAYMENT COMPOUND AMOUNT

Here, the future amount (F) is calculated of a present amount (P) made at an interest rate (r) for t number of years which is compounded annually.

Example 20 A person deposits a sum of Rs. 1,00,000 at the interest of 9% compounded annually for 10 years. What amount he will get after 10 years.

Solution

So, a deposit of Rs. 1,00,000/- at the rate of 9 per cent annually will become Rs. 2,36,736.37 after 10 years.

By substituting general terms in place of numerical values in the below table.

Table 10.1

At the end of	*Principal Amount*	*Interest*	*Total Amount*
0 year	1,00,000	–	Rs. 1,00,000
1st year	1,00,000	= 1,00,000 × 9/100 = 9000	Rs. 1,09,000
2nd year	1,09,000	= 1,09,000 × 9/100 = 9810	Rs. 1,18,810
3rd year	1,18,810	= 1,18,810 × 9/100 = 10692.9	Rs. 1,29,502.9
4th year	1,29,502.9	= 1,29,502.9 × 9/100 = 11655.26	Rs. 1,41,158.16
5th year	1,41,158.16	= 1,41,158.16 × 9/100 = 12704.23	Rs. 1,53,862.39
6th year	1,53,862.39	= 1,53,862.39 × 9/100 = 13847.62	Rs. 1,67,710.01
7th year	1,67,710.01	= 1,67,710.01 × 9/100 = 15093.90	Rs. 1,82,803.91
8th year	1,82,803.91	= 1,82,803.91 × 9/100 = 16452.35	Rs. 1,99,256.26
9th year	1,99,256.26	= 1,99,256.26 × 9/100 = Rs. 17,933.06	Rs. 2,17,189.33
10th year	2,17,189.33	= 2,17,189.33 × 9/100 = 19547.04	Rs. 2,36,736.37

Note: figures have been rounded up to two decimal points

Table 10.2

At the end of	*Principal Amount (P)*	*Interest (r)*	*Final Amount (F)*
0 year	P	–	P
1st year	P	Pr%	$P+Pr = P(1+r\%)^1$
2nd year	$P(1+r\%)$	$P(1+r\%)r\%$	$P(1+r\%)(1+r\%) = P(1+r\%)^2$
3rd year	$P(1+r\%)^2$	$P(1+r\%)^2.r\%$	$P(1+r\%)^2(1+r\%) = P(1+r\%)^3$
4th year	$P(1+r\%)^3$	$P(1+r\%)^3.r\%$	$P(1+r\%)^3(1+r\%) = P(1+r\%)^4$
5th year	$P(1+r\%)^4$	$P(1+r\%)^4.r\%$	$P(1+r\%)^4(1+r\%) = P(1+r\%)^5$
6th year	$P(1+r\%)^5$	$P(1+r\%)^5.r\%$	$P(1+r\%)^5(1+r\%) = P(1+r\%)^6$
7th year	$P(1+r\%)^6$	$P(1+r\%)^6.r\%$	$P(1+r\%)^6(1+r\%) = P(1+r\%)^7$
8th year	$P(1+r\%)^7$	$P(1+r\%)^7.r\%$	$P(1+r\%)^7(1+r\%) = P(1+r\%)^8$
9th year	$P(1+r\%)^8$	$P(1+r\%)^8.r\%$	$P(1+r\%)^8(1+r\%) = P(1+r\%)^9$
10th year	$P(1+r\%)^9$	$P(1+r\%)^9.r\%$	$P(1+r\%)^9(1+r\%) = P(1+r\%)^{10}$
Nth year	$P(1+r\%)^{t-1}$	$P(1+r\%)^{t-1}.r\%$	$P(1+r\%)^{t-1}(1+r\%) = P(1+r\%)^t = F$

Thus, single-payment compound amount can be calculated as

$$F = A + A(1 + r\%) + A(1 + r\%)^2 + \ldots + A(1 + r\%)^{t-2} + A(1 + r\%)^{t-1} \quad \text{...(i)}$$

If equation (i) is multiplied by $(1 + r)$

$$F(1 + r\%) = A(1 + r\%) + A(1 + r\%)^2 + ... + A(1 + r\%)^{t-1} + A(1 + r\%)^t \quad ...(ii)$$

Subtracting equation (i) from equation (ii) gives

$$\text{or,} \quad F(1 + r\%) - F = A(1 + r\%)^t - A$$
$$= A\left[(1 + r\%)^t - 1\right]$$

$$\text{or,} \quad F = A\left[\frac{(1 + r\%)^t - 1}{r\%}\right] = \text{Equal Payment Series Compound Amount} \quad ...(iii)$$

$$\text{and } A = F\left[\frac{r\%}{(1 + r\%)^t - 1}\right] = \text{Equal Payment Series Sinking Fund} \quad ...(iv)$$

$$\text{or,} \quad A = P(1 + r\%)^t\left[\frac{r\%}{(1 + r\%)^t - 1}\right]$$

$$= P\left[\frac{(1 + r\%)^t\, r\%}{(1 + r\%)^t - 1}\right] = \text{Equal Payment Series Capital Recovery} \quad ...(v)$$

In the Table 10.3, coloumn 5 Formula, factor for calculating the unknown factor by alternative method is given. (F/P, $r\%$,t) is known as single-payment compound amount factor.

In the cash flow diagram, all the deposits/disbursements are shown below the line and all receipts/income are shown above the line. The cash flow diagram for all interest formulas is also given in the Table 10.1, coloumn 6. Below is the cash flow diagram of example 20:

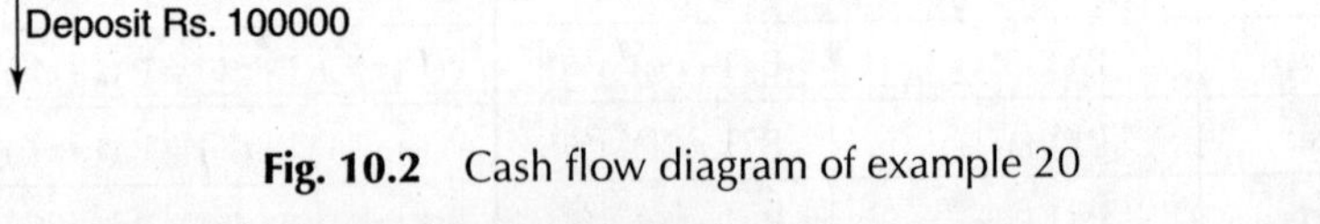

Fig. 10.2 Cash flow diagram of example 20

Uniform Gradient Series Annual Equivalent Amount

Here, the cash flow series is not of constant amount A but increases uniformly by an amount G. It can be divided into two components. (As Fig. D has been shown into two Fig. E and Fig. F in Table 10.3.

$$P = P_1 + P_2$$

where, $\quad P_1 = A\ (P/A,\ r\%,\ t)$

Which has to be calculated for given A. It has already been discussed.

Table 10.3

	Factor	Find	Given	Formula	Cash Flow Diagram ⟶
Single payment	Compound amount	F	P	$F = P(1 + r\%)^t = P(F/P, r\%, t)^*$	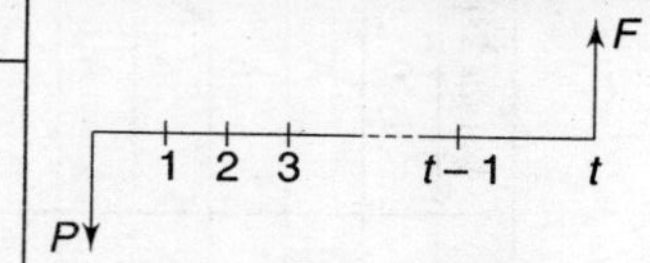 Fig. A
	Present-Worth	P	F	$P = \dfrac{F}{(1 + r\%)^t} = F(P/F, r\%, t)^*$	
Equal payment series	Compound Amount	F	A	$F = A\left[\dfrac{(1 + r\%)^t - 1}{r\%}\right] = A(F/A, r\%, t)^*$	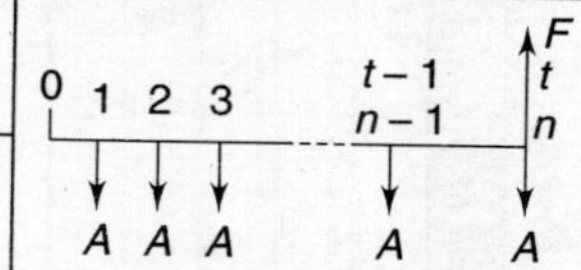 Fig. B
	Sinking Fund	A	F	$A = F\left[\dfrac{r\%}{(1 + r\%)^t - 1}\right] = F(A/F, r\%, t)^*$	
	Present-Worth	P	A	$P = A\left[\dfrac{(1 + r\%)^t - 1}{r\%\ (1 + r\%)^t}\right] = A(P/A, r\%, t)^*$	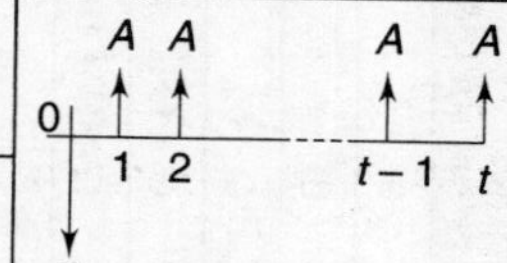 Fig. C
	Capital-Recovery	A	P	$A = P\left[\dfrac{r\%(1 + r\%)^t}{(1 + r\%)^t - 1}\right] = P(A/P, r\%, t)^*$	
Uniform Gradient Series Annual Equivalent		A	G	$A = A_1 \pm G\ \dfrac{(1 + r\%)^t - r\% t - 1}{r\%(1 + r\%)^t - 1)^t - 1}$ $= A_1 + G(A/G, r\%, t)^*$	 Fig. D
		F or P	A		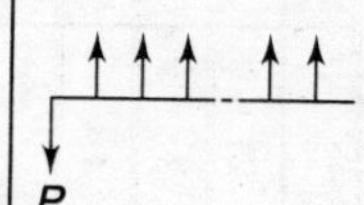 Fig. E 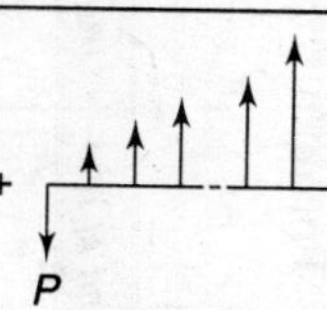 Fig. F

Note: * = are factors of corresponding type of interest formula

Equal Payment Series Present Worth Amount

$$P_2 = G\,(P/G, r\%, t)$$

Formula for P_2 (refer Fig. F) has to be derived.

Table 10.4

End of Year	*Gradient Series*	*Set of series which is equivalent to Gradient Series*	*Annual Series*
0	0	0	0
1	0	0	A
2	G	G	A
3	2G	G + G	A
4	3G	G + G + G	A
–	–	–	–
t–1	(t–2)	G + G + G + ... + G + G + G	A
t	(t–1)	G + G + G + ... + G + G + G	A

The arithmetic gradient series may be thought of as a series of individual cash flows:

Therefore, the value of F will be sum of cash flows = $F^1 + F^2 + F^3 + ... + F^{(t-2)} + F^{(t-1)}$

As equation (iii) of equal payment series compound amount

$$F = G\left[\frac{(1 + r\%)^{t-1} - 1}{r\%}\right] + G\left[\frac{(1 + r\%)^{t-2} - 1}{r\%}\right] + ...$$

$$G\left[\frac{(1 + r\%)^{2} - 1}{r\%}\right] + G\left[\frac{(1 + r\%)^{1} - 1}{r\%}\right]$$

$$= \frac{G}{r\%}\,[(1 + r\%)^{t-1} + (1 + r\%)^{t-2} + ... + (1 + r) - (t - 1)]$$

$$= \frac{G}{r\%}\,[(1 + r\%)^{t-1} + (1 + r\%)^{t-2} ... + (1 + r\%)^2 + (1 + r\%) +] - \frac{nG}{r\%}$$

The bracketed terms constitute the equal-payment series compound amount factor for n years.

$$\therefore \quad F = \frac{G}{r\%}\left[\frac{(1 + r\%)^{n} - 1}{r\%}\right] - \frac{nG}{r\%} \quad ...(vi)$$

As equal payment series sinking fund

$$A = F\left[\frac{r\%}{(1 + r\%)^{t} - 1}\right]$$

Substituting for F from equation (vi)

$$= \frac{G}{r\%}\left[\frac{(1 + r\%)^{t} - 1}{r\%}\right]\left[\frac{r\%}{(1 + r\%)^{t} - 1}\right] - \frac{G}{r\%}\left[\frac{r\%}{(1 + r\%)^{t} - 1}\right]$$

$$= \frac{G}{r\%} - t.\frac{G}{\cancel{r\%}}\left[\frac{\cancel{r\%}}{(1 + r\%)^t - 1}\right]$$

$$= G\left[\frac{1}{r\%} - \frac{t}{(1 + r\%)^t - 1}\right] \quad \text{...(vii)}$$

$$= G\left[\frac{(1 + r\%)^t - 1 - tr\%}{r\% \, (1 + r\%)^t - 1}\right] \quad \text{...(given in summary table)}$$

Nominal and Effective Interest Rate

When interest rate is charged per year, it is called nominal interest rate. In this book nominal interest rate (r) has been used unless referred. Effective interest rate is charged more than once in a year.

Table 10.5

Effective Interest rate	*Frequency within a year*	*What to do*
Quarterly	Four	Divide the rate of interest (r) by four and multiply the time (t) by four
Monthly	Twelve	Divide the rate of interest (r) by 12 and multiply the time (t) by 12
Daily	365	Divide the rate of interest (r) by 365 and multiply the time (t) by 365

Example 21 A company's management foresee that it will require Rs. 10,00,000 at the end of 10th year for modernisation. How much it should deposit now to get the required amount after 10 year. The rate of interest (r) is 9%.

Solution

Given: F = Rs. 10,00,000

t = 10 years

r = 9%

P = ?

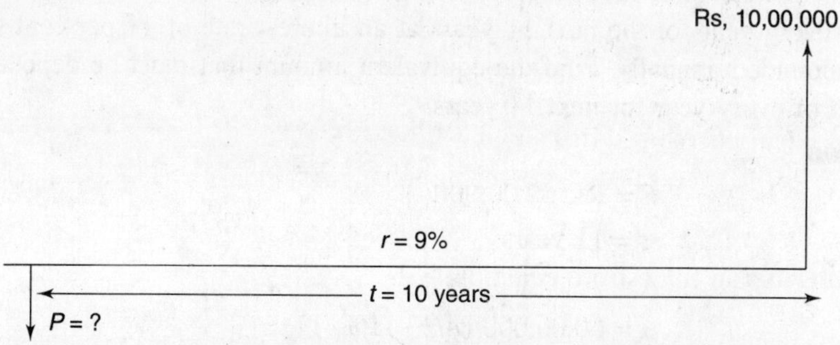

Fig. 10.3 Cash flow diagram of single payment present worth

$$P = F\ (P/F, 9, 10) = 10{,}00{,}000 \times 0.4224$$
$$= \text{Rs. } 422400$$

The company should deposit Rs. 422400.

Example 22 What amount of money saved today will yield Rs. 40,000 in third year and Rs. 55,000 after five year at the 12% rate of interest compounded annually.

Given: F_1 = Rs. 40,000

$t = 3$ yrs.

$r = 12\%$, and

F_2 = Rs. 55,000

$t = 5$ yrs.

$r = 12\%$

And then, $P = ?$

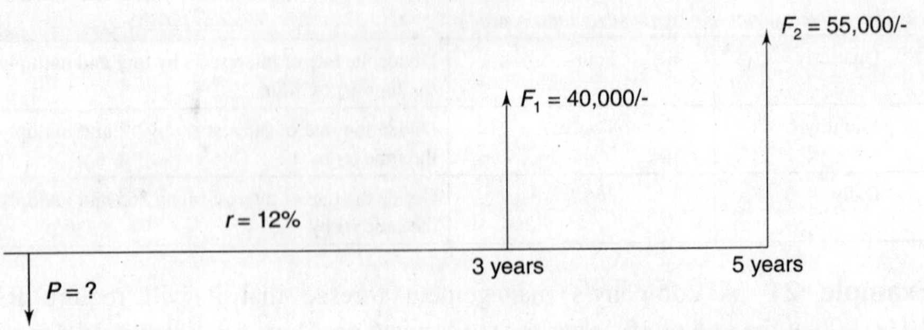

Fig. 10.4 Cash flow diagram of double-payment present worth amount

$$P = F.\ (P/F, r, i) = 40000\ (P/F, 12, 3) + 55000\ (P/F, 12, 5)$$
$$= 40000 \times 0.7118 + 55000 \times 0.5674 = \text{Rs. } 59679$$

The company should deposit Rs. 59679 now.

Example 23 A company has to replace a machine in the production line after 11 years at the cost of Rs. 60,00,000/-. It plans to deposit an equal amount at the end of every year for the next 11 years at an interest rate of 11 per cent which is compounded annually. Find the equivalent amount that must be deposited at the end of every year for next 11 years.

Solution

F = Rs. 60,00,000/-

$t = 11$ years

$A = ?$

$$A = 60{,}00{,}000\ (A/F, 11\%, 11)$$
$$= 60{,}00{,}000 \times 0.0511$$
$$= \text{Rs. } 306600$$

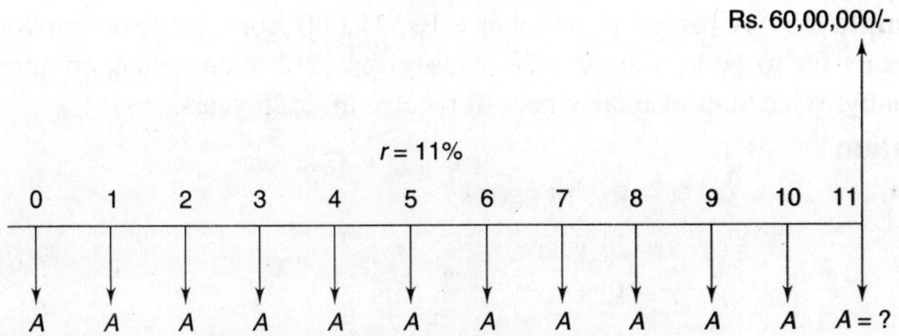

Fig. 10.5 The cash flow diagram of equal-payment series sinking fund amount

The company should deposit eleven instalments of Rs. 3,06,600 to get an amount of Rs. 60,00,000 at the end of eleven years.

Example 24 A household has purchased a house worth 36 lakh by taking its 80% as loan at the rate of interest (r) 11%. It has to be repaid in 15 equal instalments. Calculate the annual instalment amount which the household has to pay to the bank.

Solution

Given: P = 80% of 36 lakh

$r = 11\%$

$t = 15$

$A = ?$

To get P,

$= 80/100 \times 36 =$ Rs. 2880000

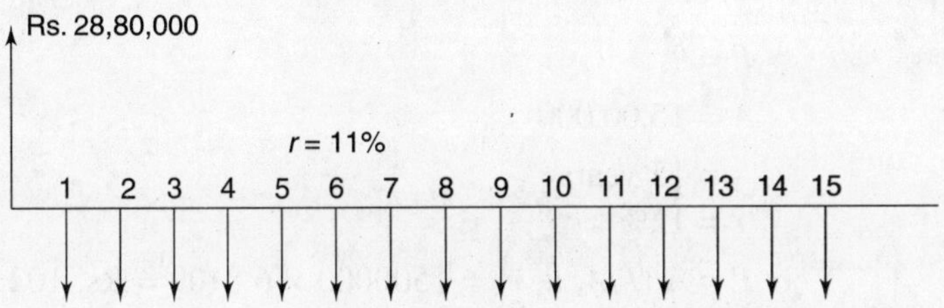

Fig. 10.6 The cash flow diagram of equal-payment series capital recovery amount

To find amount of 15 equal instalment which the person should deposit every year

$$A = P\,(A/P,\ 11,\ 15)$$

$$= 28{,}80{,}000 \times 0.1391 = \text{Rs. } 4{,}00{,}608$$

The company will have to deposit equal instalment of Rs. 4,00,608/year.

Example 25 A person plans to save Rs. 15,000 from the next year for next 25 years for to build a house. The bank gives 12% interest rate, compounded annually. What sum of money he will receive after 25 years.

Solution

$$A = \text{Rs. } 15{,}000$$
$$t = 25 \text{ years}$$
$$r = 12\%$$
$$F = ?$$
$$F = A\ (F/A, r, n)$$
$$= 15000 \times 133.33 = \text{Rs. } 19{,}99{,}950$$

He will receive Rs. 19,99,950 to build the house.

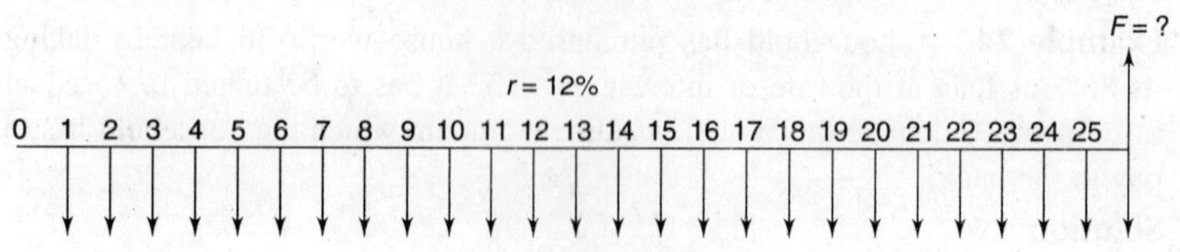

Fig. 10.7 Cash flow diagram of equal-payment series compound amount

Example 26 A company wants to deposit money to create an R&D reserve from which it can get Rs. 15,00,000 every year for next 15 years for R&D. The reserve will grow at the rate of 12 per cent annually. Find out the single payment which should be made now.

Solution

$$P = ?$$
$$A = 15{,}00{,}000$$
$$t = 15 \text{ years}$$
$$r = 12\%$$
$$P = A\ (P/A, n, r) = 1500000 \times 6.8109 = \text{Rs. } 102{,}16{,}350$$

The company should deposit Rs. 102,16,350/-

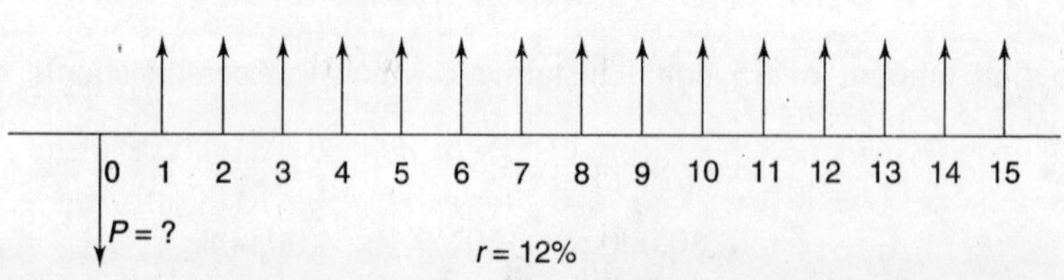

Fig. 10.8 Cash flow diagram of equal-payment series present worth amount

Example 27 A company is planning to expand his business after ten years. To meet the expansion expenditure, at the end of first year, the company is planning to deposit Rs. 10,00,000 in the reserve and from the next year it will increase the amount to be deposited by Rs. 10000 from the previous deposit for the next 9 years with an interest rate of 12%. Calculate the total amount which the company will have for expansion at the end of ten years.

Solution

Here, A_1 = Rs. 10,00,000

G = Rs. 10,000

$r = 12\%$

$t = 10$ years

$A = ?, F = ?$

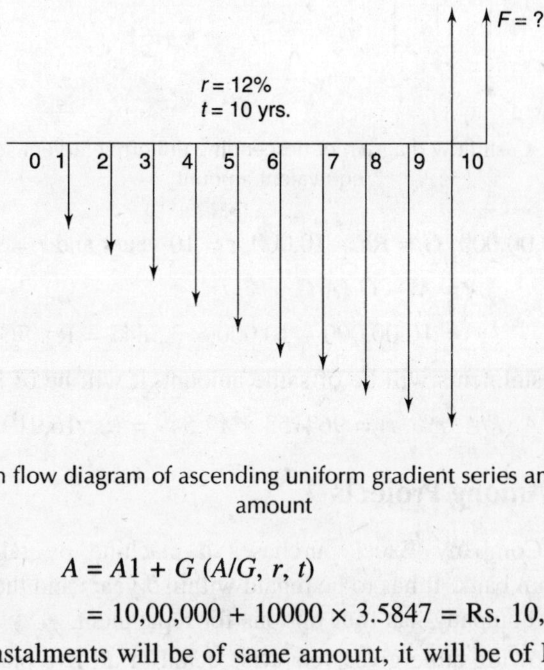

Fig. 10.9 Cash flow diagram of ascending uniform gradient series annual equivalent amount

$A = A1 + G\ (A/G, r, t)$

= 10,00,000 + 10000 × 3.5847 = Rs. 10,35,847

So, if all instalments will be of same amount, it will be of Rs. 1035847

$F = A \times (F/A, r\%, t)$

= 1035847 × 17.549 = Rs. 1,81,78,079

The company will get an amount of Rs. 1,81,78,079

Example 28 A company is planning to expand his business after ten years. At the end of first year the company will like to deposit 10,00,000 in the reserve and from the next year, it will deposit after subtracting 10,000 for the previous year deposit for next 9 years with an interest rate of 12%. Calculate the total amount which the company will have for expansion after 10 years.

Solution

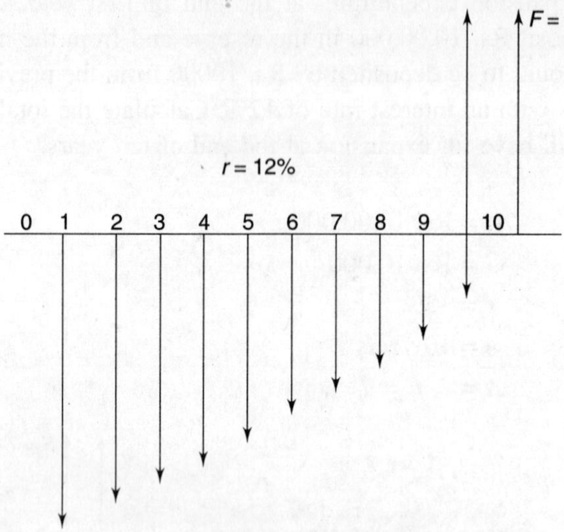

Fig. 10.10 Cash flow diagram of descending uniform gradient series annual equivalent amount

A_1 = Rs. 10,00,000, G = Rs. – 10,000, t = 10 years and r = 12% per annum

$$A = A_1 - G\ (A/G, r\%, t)$$

$$= 10{,}00{,}000 - 10{,}000 \times 3.5847 = \text{Rs. } 964153$$

So, if all instalments will be of same amount, it will be of Rs. 964153/-

$$F = A\ (F/A, r\%, t) = 964153 \times 17.549 = \text{Rs. } 16{,}919{,}921$$

Equivalence Among Projects

Example 29 Company Excel purchases a machine by taking a loan of Rs. 5,00,000 from bank. It has to be repaid within 5 years and the rate of interest is 8%. Now the company has four options for repayment.

Solution Following table gives year wise detail of all five plans:

Table 10.6

At the end of	*Money received (+)*	*Plan 1-Money Paid (–)*	*Plan 2 Money paid (–)*	*Plan 3 Money paid (–)*	*Plan 4 Money paid (–)*
		Each year pay Rs.1,00,000 + interest up to that point of time	Up to end of four years, pay only interest up to that point and pay principal amount at the end of five years	Do not pay anything in between. Pay all principal amount and interest at the end of fifth years	Pay equal amount at the end of all five years

Contd...

0 year	Rs. 5,00,000/-				
1st year		= 1,00,000 + 8/100*5,00,000 = 100000 + 40000 = Rs. 1,40,000	= 8/100*5,00,000 = Rs. 40,000	Nil	125228.2
2nd year		= 1,00,000 + 8/100*4,00,000 = 100000 + 32000 = Rs. 132000	= 8/100*5,00,000 = Rs. 40,000	Nil	125228.2
3rd year		= 1,00,000 + 8/100*3,00,000 = 100,000 + 24000 = Rs. 124000	= 8/100*5,00,000 = Rs. 40,000	Nil	125228.2
4th year		1,00,000 + 8/100*2,00,000 = 100,000 + 24000 = Rs. 116000	= 8/100*5,00,000 = Rs. 40,000	Nil	125228.2
5th year		1,00,000 + 8/100*1,00,000 = 100,000 + 8000 = Rs. 108000/-	= 8/100*5,00,000 + 5,00000 = Rs. 40,000 + 500000 = Rs. 540000	684275.6	125228.2
Total Amount Paid		Rs. 6,20,000/-	Rs. 7,00,000/-	Rs. 6,84,275.6/-	Rs. 626141.00

Detail of Plan 3

At the end of	*Principal*	*Interest*	*Total Amount*	*Amount Paid*
1st Year	500000	40000	540000	–
2nd Year	540000	43200	543200	–
3rd Year	543200	43456	586656	–
4th Year	586656	46932.48	633588.5	–
5th Year	633588.5	50687.08	684275.6	684275.6

Detail of Plan 4

At the end of	*Principal*	*Interest*	*Total Amount*	*Principal Paid*	*Amount Paid*
1st Year	500000	40000	540000	85228.23	125228.2
2nd Year	414771.77	33181.74	447953.5	92046.49	125228.2
3rd Year	322725.282	25818.02	348543.3	99410.21	125228.2
4th Year	223315.074	17865.21	241180.3	107363	125228.2
5th Year	115952.05	9276.164	125228.2	115952.1	125228.2
		126141.1			

Present worth of Rs. 5 lakh = future worth of Rs. 6,20,000 after 5 years = Plan 1

Or, Present worth of Rs. 5 lakh = future worth of Rs. 7,00,000 after 5 years = Plan 2

Or, Present worth of Rs. 5 lakh = future worth of Rs. 6,84,275.6 after 5 years = Plan 3

Or, Present worth of Rs. 5 lakh = future worth of Rs. 626141 after 5 years = Plan 4

Therefore,

Future worth after 5 years of Rs. 6,20,000 = Rs. 7,00,000 = Rs. 6,84,275.6 = Rs. 6,26,141.00

Since all four plans repay a present sum of Rs. 5,00,000 in five years @ interest of 12%, they all are equal.

Out of four opinions which one is the best can be decided by following three methods:

1. Present worth method
2. Future worth method
3. Annual equivalent method,

These methods have been discussed in detail in the next chapter.

Note

1. There is one more method, i.e., Economic Analysis method which considers 'Purchase Model' and 'Manufacturing model' of Inventory of Analysis.

EXERCISES

A. Objective **(For 1/2 marks each)**

(i) College management has decided to save money. List two items, which the college can use to save money.

(ii) College management of DTU has decided to spend more money on R&D. From which account the college should divert money for this purpose.

(iii) List two measures, which the college should take to encourage students to conserve electricity.

(iv) An automobile manufactuer is considering to locate automobile assembly plant either in the Delhi or neighbouring states. List two points which he should consider.

(v) Identify possible objective for establishing special economic zone in India.

Ans: (i) Uneconomical use of electricity, uneconomical use of college transport;

(ii) R&D is part and parcel of education;

(iii) Put fine for uneconomical use, give prizes to those who try to conserve electricity;

(iv) Tax structure of the state, number of clients, which the firm will attract at the location;

(v) Attract investors in India.

B. Subjective (For seven marks each)

1. Discuss with example 'Simple Problem' and 'Complex Problem'.
2. Discuss Break-Even Analysis in detail.
3. Why a firm should opt to 'Buy'?
4. Why a firm should opt to 'Make'?
5. Discuss applications of interest formula in engineering economics?

C. Numerical Questions

1. A contractor has the following options for doors and windows for a hospital building.

   For doors and door frames, he has the following option:

S. No.	*Particular*	*Weight*	*Material & making cost*
A.	Doors:		
1.	Wooden doors	825 kg	Rs. 13000
2.	Plywood doors	700 kg	Rs. 11500
B.	Door frames:		
1.	Steel frames	50 kg	Rs. 4500
2.	Aluminium frame	32 kg	Rs. 2500

   Considering all combinations, the contractor has four options. Transportation cost is 13/kg. in each case. Which combination of door frame he should adapt and what is the economic advantage?

   [**Hint:** Find out cost of A1B1, A1B2, A2B1 and B2A2]

   [**Ans:** Contractor should made plywood door with aluminium frame.

   Economic Advantage = Rs. 2234]

2. A contractor requires 2000 metric tonnes of hard steel to construct an over-bridge on a railway crossing. He contacted the local agents and also a factory, which is about 300 km from the site producing steel. The

cost coated by the local agents is Rs. 25,000 per metric tonnes and that by the factory is Rs. 22,000 per metric tonnes. The transportation cost is Rs. 800/100 km/metric tonnes which will be charged by the factory. Which course should be specified considering the economic advantage? What is that advantage?

[**Ans:** Purchasing from factory; Economic Advantage = Rs. 12,00,000]

3. Amar Company Limited has the following details:

   Fixed cost = Rs. 40,00,000

   Varibale cost per unit = Rs. 300

   Selling price per unit = Rs. 500

   Find the break-even point. [**Ans:** 20000]

4. Consider the following data of a company for the year 2010-11

   Sales = Rs. 80,000

   Fixed cost = Rs. 15,000

   Variable cost = 35,000

   Find the following:

   (i) Contribution (ii) Profit (iii) P/V ratio (iv) BEP (v) MS

   [**Ans:** Contribution = Rs. 45000
   Profit = Rs. 30,000
   P/V ratio = 56.25%
   BEP = Rs. 26666.67
   MS = Rs. 53333.33]

5. Consider the following data of a company for the year 2011-12

   Sales = Rs. 2,40,000

   Fixed cost = Rs. 50,000

   Variable cost = Rs. 75,000

   Find the following:

   (i) Contribution (ii) Profit (iii) P/V ratio (iv) BEP
   (v) Margin of safety

   [**Ans:** Contribution = Rs. 1,65,000
   Profit = Rs. 115,000
   P/V ratio = 206.25%
   BEP = Rs. 24242.24
   Margin of Safety = Rs. 55757.57]

6. Ahuja Company Ltd. has the following details:

   Fixed cost = Rs. 60,00,000

   Variable cost per unit = Rs. 250

Selling price per unit = Rs. 350

Find the break-even point. [**Ans:** 60,000]

7. If a person deposits Rs. 15,000 now. How much he will receive at the end of 10 years if the rate of interest is 12% compounded annually? [**Ans:** Rs. 4650]
8. If a company expects that it will require Rs. 10,00,000 after nine year for expansion. How much it should deposit to get the required amount if rate of interest is 11% compounded annually? [**Ans:** Rs. 390900]
9. If a company requires Rs. 12 lakh at the end of 5th year for its expansion programme. What should be the size of equal amount which should be deposited every year which will give the required amount at the end of 5th year. Rate of interest is 10% which is compounded annually? [**Ans:** Rs. 196,560]
10. A person saves Rs. 51,000 annually for next twelve years. How much money he will get at the end of twelfth year. If the money is compounded annually at 12%. [**Ans:** Rs. 1230783]
11. A person is planning for his retired life. He has 15 years of service and he has planned to save every year Rs. 40,000. If it is compounded at the rate of 12% annually, how much he will get at the time of retirement. [**Ans:** Rs. 1,491,200]
12. A grandparent is planning to gift his newly born grandchild a bike which will cost approximately Rs. 5 lakh when he will be 18 years of age and a foreign trip which will cost approximately Rs. 11 lakh when he will be 25 years of age. How much money the grandparent should deposit which will be compounded annually @10%. [**Ans:** Rs. 191480]
13. How much a firm should deposit to get Rs. 10 lakh after 15 years and Rs. 18 lakh after 21 years. Rate of interest is 11%, which is compounded annually. [**Ans:** Rs. 410,060]
14. A person is depositing Rs. 12,000/- and from the next year, he has planned to deposit 500 less of the previous year amount for five year. What final amount he will get at the end of sixth year if the rate of interest is 11% compounded annually. [**Ans:** Rs. 86261.20]
15. Consider following cash flow diagram. Calculate the total amount at the end of the 15th year at the interest rate of 11%, compounded annually.

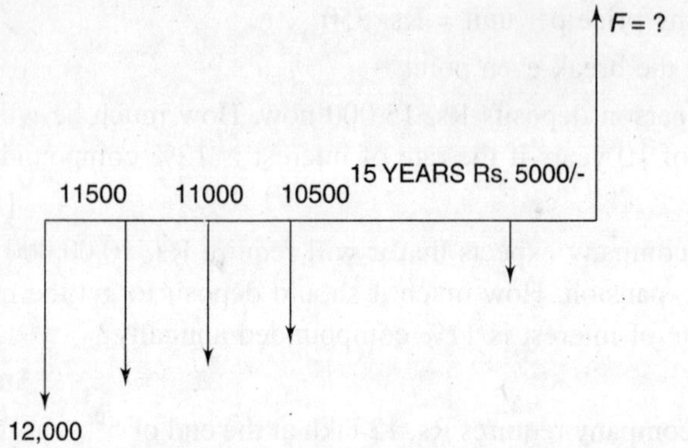

[Ans: Rs. 324654.53]

16. A company deposits Rs. 50,000 for five years at the rate of interest 12% which is compounded quarterly. How much the company will get after 5 years?

[Ans: Rs. 90300]

17. Determine the present worth, P of the cash flow diagram.

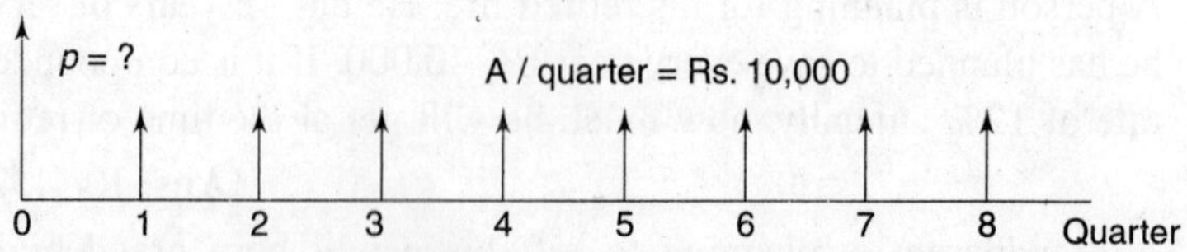

The interest rate is 12%/ year. Interest rate is compounded quarterly.

[Ans: Rs. 203888]

18. Consider the following cash flow diagram. Find the present worth using an interest rate of 12%, compounded annually.

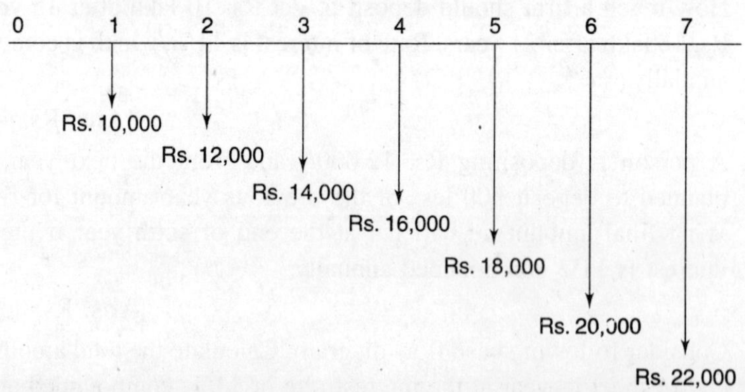

[Ans: Rs. 68927.07]

References and Suggested Readings

1. Sullivan William G., James A. Bontadelli, Elin M. Wicks and E. Paul DeGarmo, "Engineering Economy", Pearson Education' Asia, Eleventh Edition.
2. John F. Marshall and Vipul K. Bansal, "Financial Engineering", Prentice-Hall of India Private Limited, New Delhi.
3. O.P. Khanna, "Industrial Engineering and Management", Dhanpat Rai Publications (P) Ltd., Delhi.
4. Donald G. Newnan, Jerome P. Lavelle, Teg G. Eschenbash, "Engineering Economic Analysis", Engineering Press, Austin, Texas.

11

Further Analysis on Engineering Economics

Purpose of the chapter is to acquaint the reader with:

- Evaluating Projects
  - Present Worth Method
  - Future Worth Method
  - Annual Equivalent Method
  - Rate of Return Method
- Replacement Analysis

As we have already discussed that objective of Engineering Economics is as follow.

Table 11.1

Condition	*Objective*
Fixed input	Maximize output
Minimize input	Fixed output
Neither input nor output is fixed	Maximize (output - input)

To achieve it, a firm has to select the best out of various alternatives available. In this chapter, method of selecting best financial alternative out of all, has been discussed.

EVALUATING PROJECTS

Engineering proposals are made to convert plans with precise specifications and feasible economic criteria into products, structures, or systems through construction and/ or productions. These products, structures or systems have utility as they have the capacity to satisfy human need.

It has already been discussed under 'Production' in chapter 2 that a set of inputs are transformed in a set of output and in chapter 8 on, 'Project Planning' that transformation of right set of inputs in right proportion should undergo in right sequence of process to get optimum output. So, at all levels of production, engineering economics problem may arise. There may be more than one option to perform a particular process and an engineer is supposed to select most cost effective process out of all available. Thus, engineering students are advised to understand the concept of comparing proposals well and proceed logically through correct cash flow diagram to solve engineering economic problems. Discussing all type of engineering problems is beyond scope of the book. Here, three methods for comparing proposals have been discussed.

Present Worth Method of Comparison

Each project has different cash flow and to compare mutually exclusive alternatives, in the last section of the previous chapter we have discussed that cash flows can be manipulated in variety of ways. One of the easiest ways to compare them is to discount future worth of all to present time, i.e., point zero by assuming interest rate (r) over given number of years (t).

$$\begin{aligned} PW\,(r\%) &= F_0/(1 + r)^0 + F_1/(1 + r)^1 + F_2/(1 + r)^2 \\ &\quad + F_3/(1 + r)^3 + \ldots + F_t\,(i + r)^t \\ &= (P/F,\, r\%,\, t) \end{aligned}$$

where,

$r\%$ = interest rate per compounding period

t = number of years

Future Worth Method of Comparison

In the Future Worth Method of comparison, present values of different cash flows is discounted to future value at the rate of interest r and time t. Ultimately, the maximum future worth of net revenue or with the minimum future worth of net cost is selected.

$$\begin{aligned} FW\,(r\%) &= P_0\,(1 + r)^0 + P_1\,(1 + r)^1 + P_2\,(1 + r)^2 \\ &\quad + P_3\,(1 + r)^3 + \ldots + F_t\,(i + r)^t \\ &= (F/P,\, r\%,\, t) \end{aligned}$$

where, r = interest rate per compounding period

t = number of years

Annual Equivalent Method of Comparison

In this method, cost or benefit of all the alternatives are discounted to annual equivalent (A) amount with given r rate of interest and t time and then, they are compared. The alternative with maximum revenue or minimum in terms of cost is selected.

Example 1 Prime Manufacturing is planning to expand its production operation. It has identified three machines which are technologically equicapable to serve the purpose. The initial outlay and annual revenues with each of the machines are given below:

	Initial Outlay (Rs.)	*Annual revenue*	*Life (in years)*
Machine I	Rs. 5,45,000	Rs. 2,50,000	15
Machine II	Rs. 6,14,000	Rs. 3,30,000	12
Machine III	Rs. 6,00,900	Rs. 3,50,000	10

If the rate of interest is 12%, which machine the company should opt for? Find out the result by all three methods.

Solution:

Present Worth Method

Machine I

$$\text{Initial outlay} = P = \text{Rs. } 5{,}45{,}000$$
$$\text{Annual revenue} = A = \text{Rs. } 2{,}50{,}000$$
$$\text{Life} = T = 15 \text{ years}$$
$$PW\,(12\%) = -545000 + 250000 \times (P/A,\ 12\%,\ 15)$$
$$= -545000 + 250000 \times 6.811 = \text{Rs. } 1157750$$

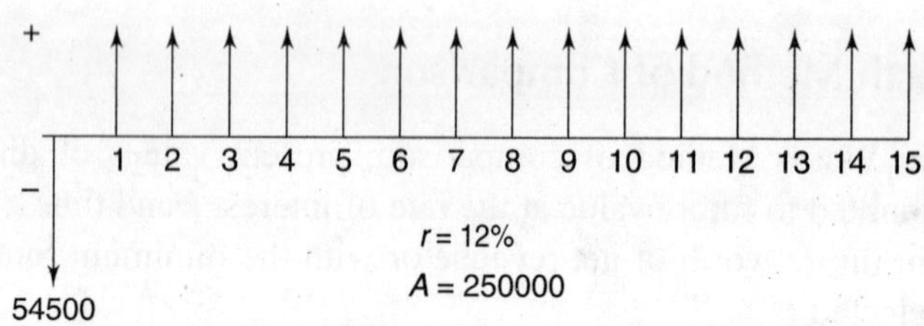

Fig. 11.1.a The cash flow diagram for machine 1

Machine II

$$\text{Initial outlay} = P = \text{Rs. } 6{,}14{,}000$$
$$\text{Annual revenue} = A = \text{Rs. } 330000$$
$$\text{Life} = T = 12 \text{ years}$$
$$PW\,(12\%) = -614000 + 330000 \times (P/A,\ 12\%,\ 12)$$
$$= -614000 + 330000 \times 6.194$$
$$= \text{Rs. } 1430020$$

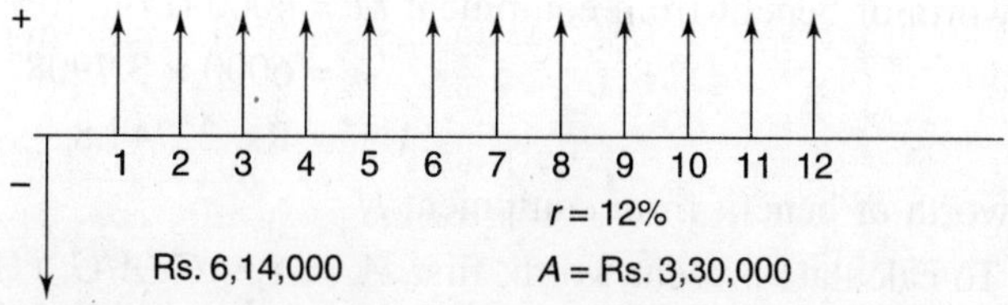

Fig. 11.1.b The cash flow diagram for machine II

Machine III

Initial outlay = P = Rs. 6,00,900

Annual revenue = A = Rs. 350000

Life = T = 10 years

$$PW\ (12\%) = -6{,}14{,}000 + 3{,}50{,}000 \times (P/A,\ 12\%,\ 10)$$
$$= -6{,}14{,}000 + 3{,}50{,}000 \times 5.650$$
$$= \text{Rs. } 13{,}63{,}500$$

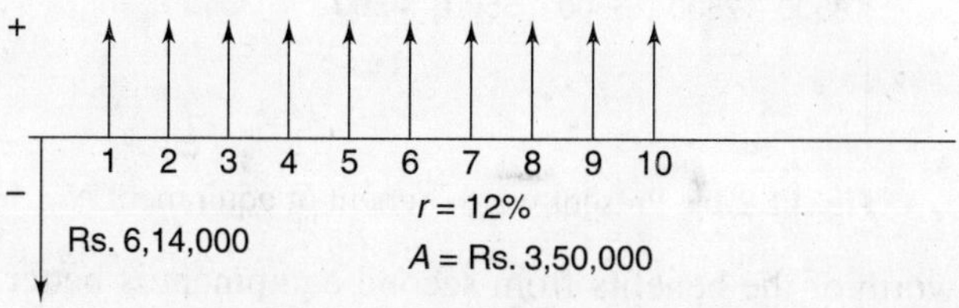

Fig. 11.1.c The cash flow diagram for machine III

So, second machine will be most beneficial by the Present Worth Method.

Example 2 Excel, has two options for equipment. Cost of both the options is Rs. 23500/- and useful lives for five years and no salvage value. Equipment M will fetch benefit of Rs. 6000 annually. Equipment N will fetch benefit of Rs. 8500 in the first year but will decline Rs. 1000 annually as Rs. 7500 in the second year, Rs. 6500 in the third year, Rs. 5500 in the fourth year and Rs. 4500 in the last year. With interest at 10% which device the firm should purchase.

Solution: Period during which both equipment give good service and the price is same. So, with same cost, the firm will like to maximise present worth of benefits.

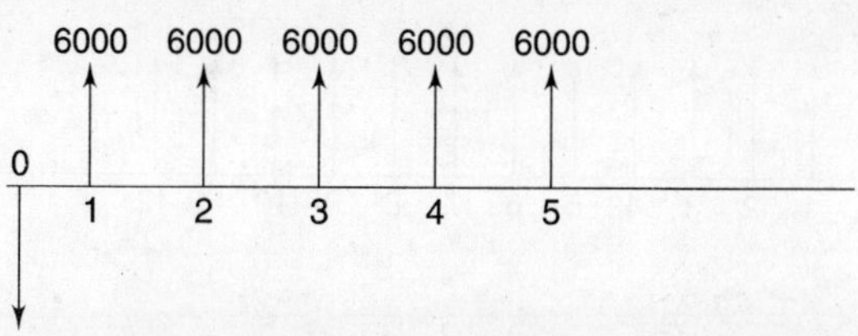

Fig. 11.2.a Present worth benefit of equipment M

Present worth of benefit from equipment $M = 6000\ (P/A, 10\%, 5)$

$= 6000 \times 3.7908$

$= \text{Rs. } 22744.8$

Present worth of benefit from equipment N

To calculate present worth, first, $A = A_1 - G\ (A/G, r\%, t)$

$= 8500 - 1000\ (A/G, 10\%, 5)$

$= 8500 - 1000 \times 1.8101$

$-8500 - 1810.1 = \text{Rs. } 6689.9$

Present worth of benefit from equipment $N = 6689.9\ (P/A, 10\%, 5)$

$= 6689.9 \times 3.7908$

$= \text{Rs. } 25360.073$

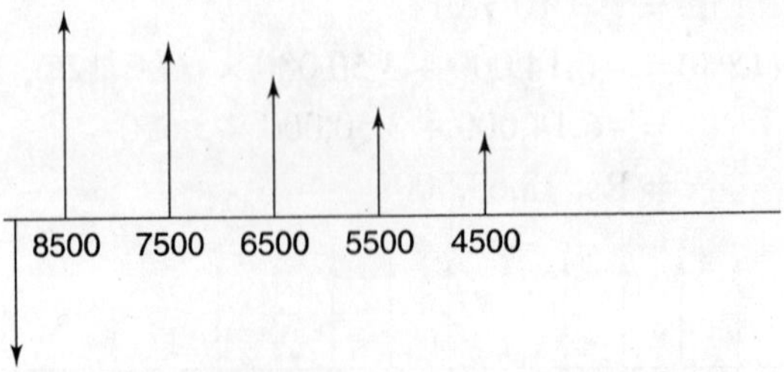

Fig. 11.2.b Present worth benefit of equipment N

Present worth of the benefits from second equipment is better than the first one so the firm should opt for the equipment N.

Example 3 A company invests in one of the two mutually exclusive alternatives. The life of both alternatives is 12 years with the following investment annual returns and salvage value.

	Alternatives	
	A	B
Investment	8,30,000	7,45,000
Annual Equal Return	3,10,000	2,70,000
Salvage value	1,50,000	2,10,000

Determine the best alternative based on the annual equivalent method by assuming = 10%.

Solution

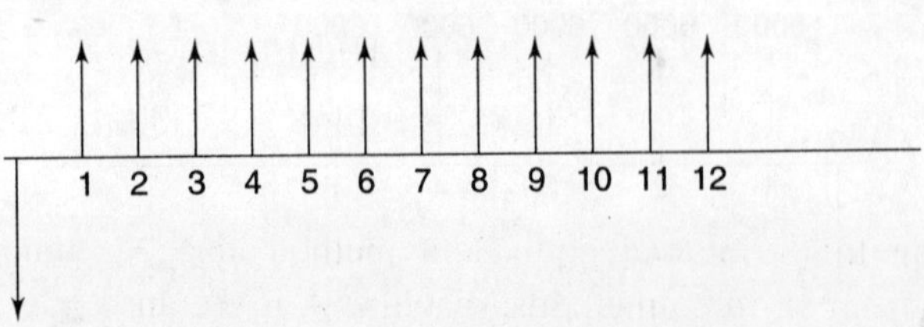

Fig. 11.3 Cash flow of proposals

Alternative A

Initial Investment, P = Rs. 8,30,000

Annual equal return, A = 3,10,000

Salvage Value (Rs.) F = Rs. 1,50,000

PW of Machine A (10%) = – 8,30,000 + 3,10,000 (P/A, 12, 10) + 1,50,000 (P/F, 12, 10)

= – 8,30,000 + 3,10,000 × 6.8137 + 1,50,000 × 0.3186

= Rs. 13,30,037

PW of Machine B (10%) = – 745000 + 270000 (P/A, 12, 10) + 210000 (P/F, 12, 10)

= – 745000 + 270000 × 6.8137 + 210000 × 0.3186

= Rs. 1161605

So, according to the present worth method, Machine A should be opted.

Future Worth Method

FW of Machine A (10%) = – 83000 (F/P, 12, 10) + 310000 (F/A, 12, 10) + 150000

= – 830000 × 3.138 + 310000 × 21.384 + 150000

= Rs. 4174500

FW of Machine B (10%) = – 745000 (F/P, 12, 10) + 270000 (F/A, 12, 10) + 210000

= – 745000 × 3.138 + 270000 × 21.384 + 210000

= Rs. 3645870

According to the future worth method also Machine A should be selected.

Annual Equivalent Method

AE of Machine A (10%) = – 830000 (A/P, 12, 10) + 310000 + 150000 (A/F, 12,10)

= – 830000 × 0.1468 + 310000 + 150000 × 0.0468

= Rs. 195176

AE of Machine B (10%) = – 745000 (A/P, 12, 10) + 270000 + 210000 (A/F, 12, 10)

= – 745000 × 0.1468 + 270000 + 210000 × 0.0468

= 170462

According to the annual equivalent method also Machine A should be selected. So, from all three methods, machine A is the answer.

Rate of Return Method

In the previous chapter, we discussed four plans to repay Rs, 5,00,000 in five years with interest of 8% per annum. The total interest paid to the lender varied depending on loan repayment plan. However, in all the plans, amount of loan was Rs. 5,00,000 and rate on interest was 8%. The cash flow of all the plans was such that at the end of five years there was nothing left unpaid. So, 8% will be defined as 'internal rate of return'. If rate of return is not known, it can be calculated. However, there is no convenient direct method to calculate, it can be found out by trial and error method.

To calculate the rate of return for an investment, all the possible consequences of the investment are converted into cash flow. Then the cash flow is resolved for the unknown value of r^*

$$\text{As, } PW \text{ of benefits-} PW \text{ of cost} = 0$$

$$\text{Or, } PW \text{ of benefits} = PW \text{ of cost}$$

$$\text{Or, } PW \text{ of benefits}/PW \text{ of cost} = 1$$

Example 4 A Rs. 87500 investment brings an annual return of 2500 for next five years. Calculate the rate of return on the investment?

Solution: Using, PW of benefits/PW of cost = 1

$$\text{Or, } 25000 \times (P/A, r^*, 5) = 87500$$

$$\text{Or, } (P/A, r^*, 5) = 87500/25000$$

$$= 3.5$$

From a compound interest rate table, find value of the interest rate of (P/A, r^*, 5) which is equal to 3.5 for r^* = 12, the value is 3.605 and for 15, the value is 3.352. As no tabulated value of r gives this value on either side of desired value 3.5, interpolation will be done to find the value of r for which the sign of the present worth function charges from positive to negative.

Because we have both a positive and a negative.

∴ The answer r^* can be determined by using the similar triangle dashed in Fig. 11.4.

$$\frac{\text{line } BA}{\text{line } BC} = \frac{\text{line } dA}{\text{line } de}$$

where BA, for example is the line segment: $B - A = 15\% - 12\%$

Thus,

or,
$$\frac{15\% - 12\%}{3.605 - (-3.352)} = \frac{r\% - 12\%}{3.605 - 0}$$

or,
$$r^*\% = 12\% + \left(\frac{3.605 - 0}{3.605 + 3.352}\right) \times 3\%$$

$$= 12\% + \frac{10.815}{6.957}$$

$$= 12\% + 1.55\% = 13.55\%$$

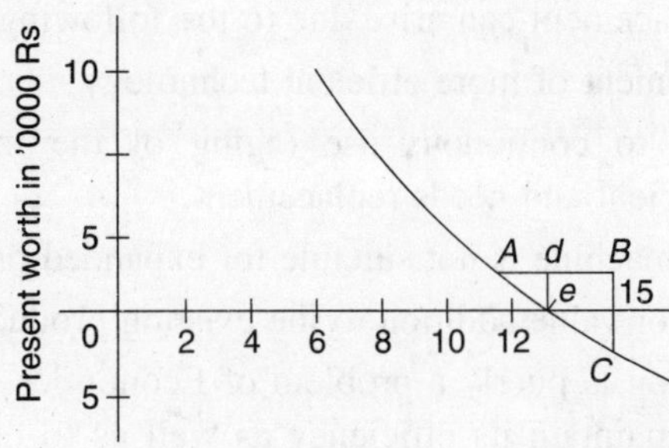

Fig. 11.4 Net present worth vs. Interest rate r

Example 5 A bond was purchased by an investor at Rs. 950. The bond is going to yield Rs. 40 at the end of every six months and Rs. 1000 at the end of nine years. What will be the rate of return for the investor?

Solution: As Rs. 40 is biannual interest payment. So $t = 18$

As, Investment = Return

or, $$950 = 40\,(P/A, r, t) + 1000\,(P/F, r, t)$$

By trial and error, r will be found out,

take $r = 5$

$$= 40 \times 11.690 + 1000 \times .4155 = 883.1$$

Benefit is low than the cost, so try lower rate of interest, take $r = 4$

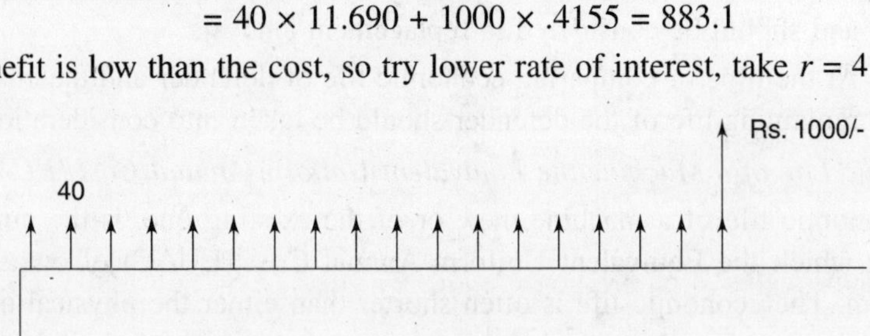

Fig. 11.5 Cash flow diagram of bond whose interest is added biannually

$$= 40 \times 12.659 + 1000 \times .4936 = 999.96$$

So, interest rate is between 4% and 5%. To be more precise, it will interpolated

$$r^* = 4\% + 1\% \left[\frac{(999.96 - 950.00)}{999.96 - 883.1}\right]$$

$$= 4\% + 1\% \times 0.42752 = 4.43\%$$

REPLACEMENT DECISION

In a production process several machines, tools and equipment are used. Any organisation needs to, off and on, replace part to maintain its efficiency and to optimise profit. The need of replacement can arise due to the following reasons:

i. Due to development of more efficient technology
ii. Normally, due to continuous use (aging of the machine) machine becomes inefficient and needs replacement.
iii. If the existing machine is not suitable for expanded production.
iv. It can happen for value addition to the existing product.

Replacement decision is purely a problem of Economics. It is very critical for an organisation to maintain its efficiency as well as to optimise its profit. To achieve the dual objective, the management has to decide whether it should replace the defender by challenger now, or shall keep for one or more additional year? The defender is the existing asset which is considered for replacement. The challenger is the asset which is proposed to be purchased as a replacement of the existing one. Following points must be considered while making decision about replacement:

i. The management needs to be careful for not discussing sunk cost[1] in the replacement analysis.
ii. Market value of the existing asset should be considered. It is always better to take the outsider's view point on the market value.
iii. There may be income tax implications on sale or depreciation of property and should be considered in replacement analysis.
iv. At the time of comparing economic life of defender and the challenger, remaining life of the defender should be taken into consideration.

Economic Life of a Machine/the Equivalent Uniform Annual Cost (EUAC)

The economic life of a machine, new or of the existing one, is the number of years at which the Equivalent Uniform Annual Cost (EUAC) of ownership is minimum. The economic life is often shorter than either the physical or useful life of the asset due to increasing operating and maintenance cost in the later years of asset ownership.[2] The challenger asset selected to replace the defender is one which has the lowest minimum cost life of all the competing mutually exclusive challengers. The defender should be kept as long as its marginal cost is less than the minimum Equivalent Uniform Annual Cost of the challenger over its own economic life.

Example 6 The cost of a machine is Rs. 22,000 and has no salvage value after it is installed. First one year repair and maintenance cost will be covered under warranty but in the second year, the maintenance cost will be Rs. 600. Also, operating cost of the machinery is Rs. 1400 in the first year and thereafter, it will increase with an arithmetic gradient of Rs. 350 in successive years. If interest is 9 per cent, compute the useful life of the machinery that results in minimum of its Equivalent Uniform Annual Cost (EUAC).

Solution

Table 11.2 Calculation of EUAC for the Machine

Number of years	*EUAC of capital Recovery Cost*	*EUAC of Maintenance and Repair Cost*	*EUAC of Operating Cost*	*EUAC total*
(t)	Rs. 22000(A/P, 9%, t)	600 (A/P, 9%, t)	1400 + 350(A/G, 9%,t)	(ii + iii + iv)
(i)	(ii)	(iii)	(iv)	(v)
1	23980	0	1400	25380
2	12507	286.8	1567.3	14361.1
3	8692.2	565.8	1730.05	10988.05
4	6641.8	835.8	1887.55	9365.15
5	5511	1096.8	2039.8	8647.6
6	4758.6	1350	2187.5	8296.1
7	4226.2	1616.4	2329.95	8172.55
8	3828	1859.4	2467.85	8155.25
9	3522.2	2094.6	2600.85	8217.65
10	3278	2322.6	2729.3	8329.9
11	3082.2	2544	2852.85	8479.05
12	2919.4	2757.6	2971.85	8648.85
13	2783	2964	3086.3	8833.3
14	2668.6	3163.8	3196.55	9028.95
15	2569.6	3356.4	3302.25	9228.25

The total EUAC data have been plotted in figure and from both table 11.2 and diagram- 11.6, total EUAC is lowest in the eighth year which is Rs. 8155.25.

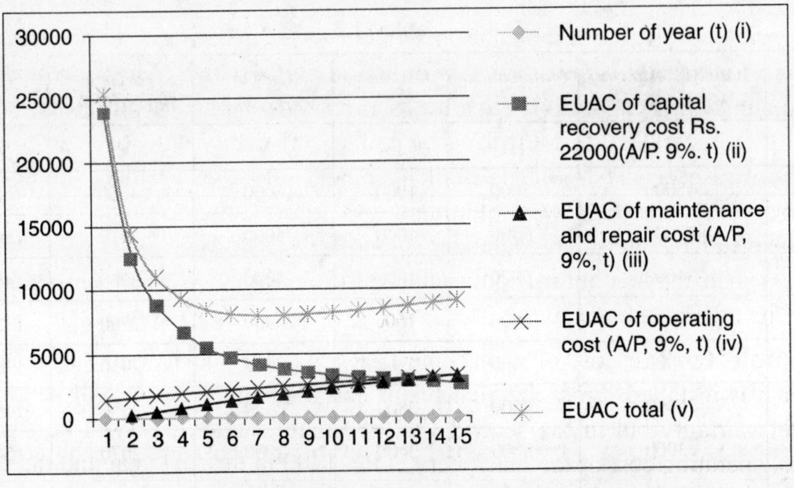

Fig. 11.6 EUAC of various costs of the machine

Marginal Cost[3] Data

Contrary to EUAC data which can be applied for any number of consecutive years, marginal cost data is the yearly cost for keeping the asset functional. So, for calculation of yearly marginal cost, year-to-year values under the following headings need to be known over its economic life:

(a) The capital recovery cost (loss in market value and lost interest for a year)

(b) Yearly operating and maintenance cost

(c) Yearly taxes and insurance, and

(d) Any other expenses occurred during that year.

Example 7 A new machine has the following cost.

Investment cost	*Market value*	*Annual Operation and Maintenance cost*	*Annual Insurance cost*	*Useful life*	*Interest rate*
Rs. 45000	Market value decreases by 5000 in the first year and after that, decreases by a gradient of Rs.1000 till the amount of decrease becomes Rs. 2000. Beyond that the market value decreases by an constant amount of Rs. 2000.	Rs. 5000 in the first year and thereafter increases by Rs. 500 every year	Rs. 1000 year for the first three years and thereafter, increases by Rs. 600 every year	8 years	9%

Solution

From the problem itself annual cost for operation and maintenance, insurance as well as-to-year market value of the machine for its whole useful life can be calculated, which are required to calculate the marginal cost.

Table 11.3

Year	*Initial Investment/ Market Value*	*Maintenance*	*Insurance*	*Loss in Market Value*	*Forgone interest@9%*	*Total*
I	II	III	IV	V	VI	VII
1	45000	5000	1000	6000	4050	16050
2	39000	5500	1000	5000	3510	15010
3	34000	6000	1000	4000	3060	14060
4	30000	6500	1600	3000	2700	13800
5	27000	7000	2200	2000	2430	13630
6	25000	7500	2800	2000	2250	14550
7	23000	8000	3400	2000	2070	15470
8	21000	8500	4000	2000	1890	16390

Now, marginal cost, i.e., year-to-year cost can be calculated for 8 year useful life of the machine. In the table.given above marginal cost is lowest in the fifth year.

Example 8 A ten-year-old equipment is being considered for replacement. It can be sold for Rs. 5000 now, and it is believed this same salvage value can also be obtained in future years. The current maintenance cost is Rs. 1000 per year and is expected to increase by Rs. 200 per year in future years. If the equipment is retained in service, compute the economic life that results in a minimum EUAC, based on 09% interest.

Solution Here,

The salvage value = Rs. 5000 and it is not expected to decline furher.

The annual cost of this investment capital = 5000*(0.09) = Rs. 450

The maintenance cost = Rs. 1000 + Rs. 200G

Table 11.4 A Year-by-Year Computation of EUAC

Year (t)	*Age of Equipment in years*	*EUAC of invested capital*	*EUAC of maintenance = 1000 + 200 (A/G, 09%, t)*	*Total*
1	10	450	= 1000 + 200 × 3.798 = 1759.6	2219.6
2	11	450	= 1000 + 200 × 4.151 = 1830.2	2291.2
3	12	450	= 1000 + 200 × 4.491 = 1898.2	2360.2
4	13	450	= 1000 + 200 × 4.818 = 1963.6	2426.6
5	14	450	= 1000 + 200 × 5.133 = 2026.6	2490.6

From table and graph, it can be seen that annual cost of continuing operation is increasing. So, the economic life at the minimum EUAC is one year.

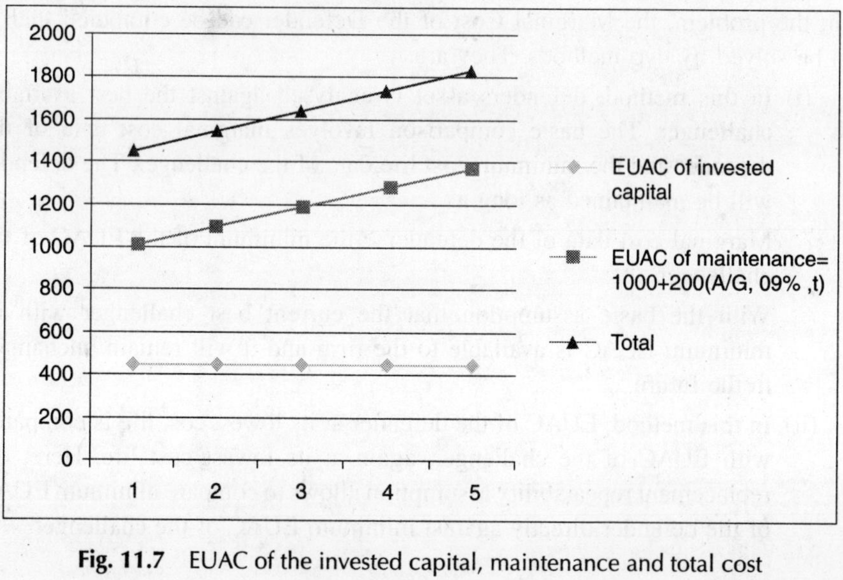

Fig. 11.7 EUAC of the invested capital, maintenance and total cost

Example 9 A 3-year-old machine, whose current market value is Rs.12,000, is being analyzed to determine its economic life in a replacement analysis. Compute its economic life using a 12% interest rate. Salvage value and maintenance estimates are given in the Table 11.5.

Solution

Table 11.5 EUAC of Capital Recovery, Maintenance and Total Cost

Years of remaining life (t)	*Estimated salvage value (S) end of year t P = Rs.12000*	*Estimated maintenance cost for year*	*EUAC of capital recovery (P-S)*(A/P,12%,t) + Si*	*EUAC of maintenance 100(A/G, 12%,t)*	*Total EUAC*
0	12000	0	0	0	0
1	11000	0	12100	0	12100
2	10000	100	1576.2	48	1624.2
3	9000	200	1202.1	94	1296.1
4	8000	300	1115.5	138	1253.5
5	7000	400	963.8	181	1144.8
6	6000	500	829.6	222	1051.6
7	5000	600	705.4	262	967.4←
8	5000	700	687.4	300	987.4
9	5000	800	673.6	337	1010.6
10	5000	900	662.7	376	1038.7

A minimum EUAC of 967.4 is computed at year 7 for the existing machine.

REPLACEMENT ANALYSIS TECHNIQUES

If in the problem, the Marginal Cost of the Defender can be computed than it can be solved by two methods. They are:

(i) In this method, defenders asset is analysed against the best available challenger. The basic comparison involves marginal cost data of the defender and the minimum cost life data of the challenger. The defender will be maintained as long as

Marginal cost data of the defender ≥ the minimum of the EUAC of the challenger

With the basic assumption that the current best challenger with its minimum EUAC is available to the firm and it will remain unchanged in the future.

(ii) In this method, EUAC of the defender at its lowest cost life is compared with EUAC of the challenger, again at its lowest cost life. Here, the replacement repeatability assumption allows to compare minimum EUAC of the defender directly against minimum EUAC of the challenger.

(iii) But if the Marginal Cost of the Defender cannot be computed than EUAC of the defender over its remaining useful life is compared with the EUAC of the challenger at its minimum cost life. However, in making the basic comparison an often complicating factors deciding what first cost to assign to the challenger and the defender assets.

Example 10 Two years ago, a machine was purchased at a cost of Rs. 4,00,000 to be useful for ten years. Its salvage value at the end of its life is Rs. 60,000. The annual maintenance cost is Rs. 60,000. The market value of the present machine is Rs. 3,20,000. Now a new machine to cater to the need of the present machine is available at Rs. 3,80,000 to be useful for eight years. Its annual maintenance cost is Rs. 45,000. The salvage value of the new machine is Rs. 40,000. Using an interest rate of 11%, find whether it is worth replacing the present machine with the new machine?

Solution The case of defender

Purchase price = Rs. 4,00,000 two years ago

Present value = Rs. 3,20,000

Annual maintenance cost = Rs. 60,000

Salvage Value (SV) = Rs. 60,000

Remaining life = 8 years

Interest rate = 11%

The annual equivalent cost = AE (11%) = (P-SV) (A/P, 11%, 8) + SV × r + A

= 320000 – 60000 (0.1943) + 60000 × 11% + 60000 = Rs. 374942

The case of challenger

Purchase price (P) = Rs. 3,80,000

Salvage Value (SV) = Rs. 40000

Annual maintenance cost = Rs. 40000

Life = 8 years

Interest rate = 11%

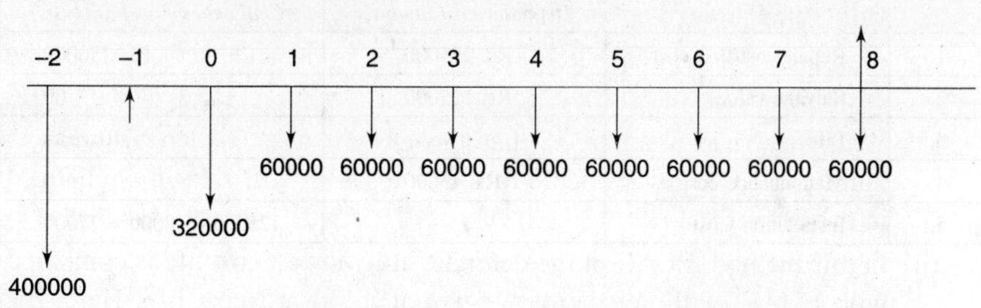

Fig. 11.8.a Cash flow diagram of the defender

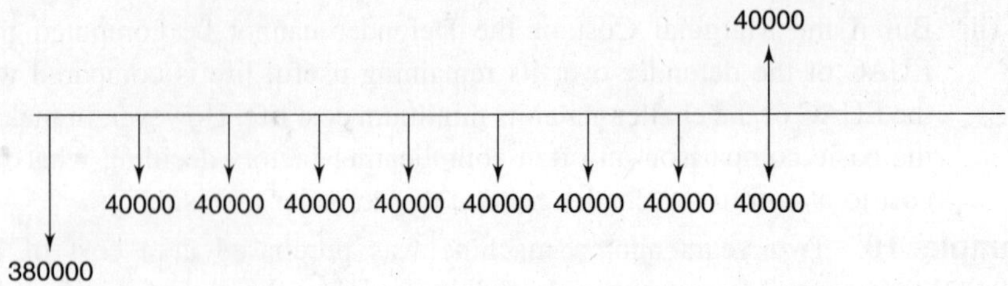

Fig. 11.8.b Cash flow diagram of the challenger

Annual equivalent cost of the challenger = AE (11%) = (P-SV) (A/P, 11%, 8) + SV × r + A

$$= (380000 - 400000) \times .1943 + 40000 \times .11 + 40000$$

$$= \text{Rs. } 40514$$

The annual equivalent cost of the defender is less than the cost of the challenger. So, the firm should continue with the existing machine.

Example 11 A furnace in a manufacturing firm Excel must either be repaired or replaced. Repair cost would be Rs. 2,75,000 and would make the furnace fit for an additional six years of service. If it is replaced, it is estimated that its net salvage value would be Rs. 1,25,000 at the time of retirement from service. The new designed nano-coated furnace would cost Rs. 7,50,000 and would meet the foreseeable requirements of the next ten years but would have no salvage value. It is estimated that the annual maintenance cost of the repaired furnace would exceed that of the nano-coated furnace by Rs. 45,000. If the old furnace is replaced by a new one, the scrape value of the old furnace would exceed the replacement cost by Rs. 48,000. Assume rate of interest as 10%. The management should opt for the repair or replacement?

Solution

Table 11.6 Comparative Cost Analysis

Sl. No.	*Item*	*Alternative-1*	*Alternative-2*
		Defender cost analysis	*Challenger's cost analysis*
1.	Repair cost/first cost	Rs. 275000	Rs. 750000
2.	Salvage value	Rs. 125000	00
3.	Life	6 years	10 years
4.	Maintenance cost	Rs. 45000	0
5.	Installation Cost		125000 – 48000 = 77000

Analysis of Alterative-I

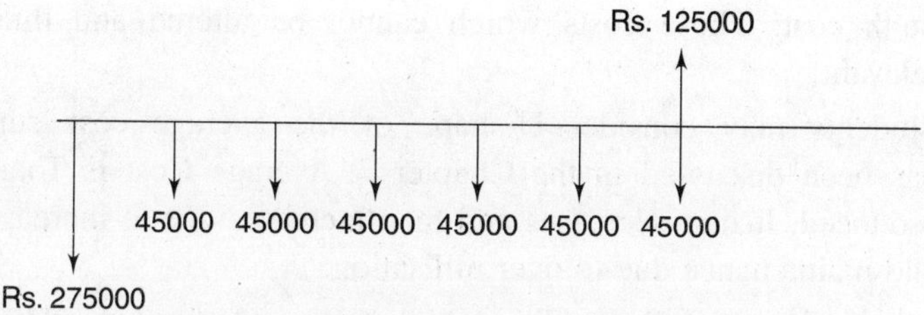

Fig. 11.9.a Cash flow diagram of Alternative I

$$AE\ (10\%) = (\text{P-SV})\ (A/P,\ 10\%,\ 6) + \text{SV} \times r + A$$

$$= (275000 - 125000) \times .2296 + 125000 \times .1 + 45000 = \text{Rs. } 91940$$

Analysis of Alternative II

Annual Equivalent cost of alternative 2 = $AE\ (10\%) = (\text{P-SV})\ (A/P,\ 10\%,10)$ = (750000 – 77000) × .1627 = Rs. 109497.1

Annual equivalent cost of alternative 1 is less than alternative 11. Therefore, the firm should repair rather replace the existing furnace.

After-Tax Replacement Analysis

After-tax analysis, very often changes the results of before-tax analysis and it gives real picture as imposition of tax is inevitable. There is wide variety of taxes that are imposed. The after tax analysis must consider the effect of ordinary taxes as well as gains and losses due to asset disposal in calculating the after-tax costs. The after-tax marginal cost of ownership will involve foregone gains or loss, forgone interest, annual loss in after-tax value, and annual operating/ maintenance cost and insurance.

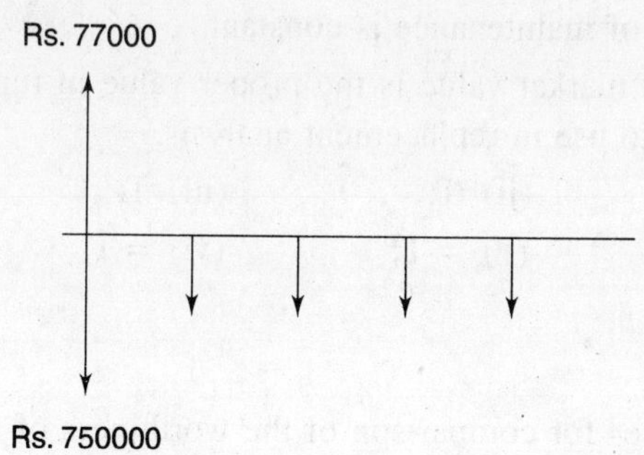

Fig. 11.9.b Cash Flow diagram of Alternative II

Note

1. Sunk cost: Those costs which cannot be altered and thus, are not relevant.
2. Students may consider U-shape of the average cost curve which has been discussed in the Chapter 7. Average Cost is Total cost/unit produced. It first decreases and then increases due to increase in repair and maintenance due to over utilisation.
3. Marginal cost is the additional cost in producing an additional unit. $MC = \frac{d(TC)}{dx}$, i.e., differentiation of total cost with respect to unit produced.
4. This is opportunity cost.

EXERCISES

A. Objective

1. Write 'True' or 'False' **(For 1/2 marks each)**

(i) The capital recovery cost is not considered for replacement analysis.

(ii) Data is needed for the defender and challenger as well as the assumption made regarding the required period of service and future innovation of challengers.

(iii) The replacement decision is a function of both the defender and the challenger.

(iv) The book-value of an equipment is the action of past or sunk cost and it should not be included in the analysis.

(v) The EUAC of installed cost will decline as the service life increases. The EUAC of maintenance is constant.

(vi) The present market value is the proper value in rupees of the defender equipment to use in replacement analysis.

Ans: (i) F; (ii) T; (iii) T;
(iv) = T; (v) = T; (vi) = T

B. Subjective

1. Discuss bases for comparison of the worthiness of a project.
2. Discuss present worth method of comparison.
3. Discuss future worth method of comparison.
4. Discuss reasons for replacement.

C. Numerical Problems

(i) A manufacturing company is planning to buy a robot for its forging unit. It has identified two different companies for the supply of the robot. The detail of the cost and incremental revenue of using robot are summarized as following table:

	Brand	
	Gen X	*Bullet Y*
Initial cost (Rs.)	7,00,000	5,00,000
Annual incremental revenue (Rs)	2,00,000	1,40, 000
Life (years)	8 yrs	10 yrs
Life-end salvage value	60,000	80,000

The minimum attractive return for the company is 12%. Suggest the best brand of robot to the company based on the present worth method.

[**Ans:** Gen X]

(ii) A machine was purchased two years ago for Rs. 75,000. Its annual revenue is Rs. 35,000. Its present worth Rs. 72,000 and remaining life is six years. At the end of working life, the salvage value is Rs. 17,000. Now the company is offering an improved machine whose cost is 75,000. Its annual revenue is Rs. 42,000 and life is six years. The company is willing to take the old machine at Rs. 40,000, if it is replaced by the new one. The salvage value of the new machine is Rs. 30,000. Assume an interest rate of 11% compounded annually. Whether the company should retain or replace the machine.

[**Ans:** Company should replace the previous machine with new machine.]

(iii) A manufacturer is offered two machines *X* and *Y*. Life of both the machine is eight years. *X* is priced at Rs. 22,000 and annual maintenance cost is estimated at Rs. 2500. Salvage value is 2000 at the eight years. Price of Machine *Y* is Rs. 18,000 and the annual maintenance cost in the first year is 1500 and that it increases by Rs. 200 every year. Salvage value for machine *Y* is negligible. Assume the rate of interest as 12% compounded annually. Whether the manufacturer should opt for machine *X* or *Y*. [**Ans:** Machine *Y* is economical]

(iv) Three years back, a machine was purchased at a cost of Rs. 7,00,000 to be useful for twelve years. Its salvage value at the end of its estimated life is Rs. 2,00,000. Its annual maintenance cost is Rs. 85,000. The market value of the machine is Rs. 5,00,000. A new machine to cater the need of existing machine is available at Rs. 6,50,000 to be useful for nine years. Its annual maintenance cost is Rs. 60,000. The salvage value of the new machine Rs. 1,00,000. Using an interest rate of 09%

compounded annually, find whether it is worth replacing the present machine with the new one.

[**Ans:** Existing machine is better. It should be continued]

References and Suggested Readings

1. Donald G. Newnan, Jerome P. Lavelle and Ted G. Eschenbach, "Engineering Economic Analysis" Engineering Press, Austin, Texas.
2. G.J. Thuesan and W.J. Fabrycky, "Engineering Economy", Prentice-Hall of India, New Delhi.
3. R. Panneerselvam, "Engineering Economy" Prentice-Hall of India, New Delhi.

Part IV
Interest Factors for Discrete Compounding

Table A.1 $\frac{1}{2}$ % INTEREST FACTORS FOR DISCRETE COMPOUNDING

t	*Single Payment*		*Equal Payment Series*				*Uniform gradient-series factor*
	Compound-amount factor	*Present-worth factor*	*Compound-amount factor*	*Sinking-fund factor*	*Present-worth factor*	*Capital-recovery factor*	
	To find F Given P F/P, r, t	*To find P Given F P/F, r, t*	*To find F Given A F/A, r, t*	*To find A Given F A/F, r, t*	*To find P Given A P/A, r, t*	*To find A Given P A/P, r, t*	*To find A Given G A/G, r, t*
1	1.005	0.9950	1.000	1.0000	0.9950	1.0050	0.0000
2	1.010	0.9901	2.005	0.4988	1.9851	0.5038	0.4988
3	1.015	0.9852	3.015	0.3317	2.9703	0.3367	0.9967
4	1.020	0.9803	4.030	0.2481	3.9505	0.2531	1.4938
5	1.025	0.9754	5.050	0.1980	4.9259	0.2030	1.9900
6	1.030	0.9705	6.076	0.1646	5.8964	0.1696	1.9900
7	1.036	0.9657	7.106	0.1407	6.8621	0.1457	2.9801
8	1.041	0.9609	8.141	0.1228	7.8230	0.1278	3.4738
9	1.046	0.9561	9.182	0.1089	8.7791	0.1139	3.9666
10	1.051	0.9514	10.228	0.0978	9.7304	0.1028	4.4589
11	1.056	0.9466	11.279	0.0887	10.6770	0.0937	4.9501
12	1.062	0.9419	12.336	0.0811	11.6189	0.0861	5.4406
13	1.067	0.9372	13.397	0.0747	12.5562	0.0797	5.9302
14	1.072	0.9326	14.464	0.0691	13.4887	0.0741	6.4190
15	1.078	0.9279	15.537	0.0644	14.4166	0.0694	6.9068
16	1.83	0.9233	16.614	0.0602	15.3399	0.0652	7.3940
17	1.088	0.9187	17.697	0.0565	16.2586	0.0615	7.8803
18	1.094	0.9141	18.786	0.0532	17.1728	0.0582	8.3668
19	1.099	0.9096	19.880	0.0503	18.0824	0.0553	8.8504
20	1.105	0.9051	20.979	0.0477	18.9874	0.0527	9.3343
21	1.110	0.9006	22.084	0.0453	19.8880	0.0503	9.8173
22	1.116	0.8961	23.194	0.0431	20.7841	0.0481	10.2883
23	1.122	0.8916	24.310	0.0411	21.6757	0.0461	10.7806
24	1.127	0.8872	25.432	0.0393	22.5629	0.0443	11.2611
25	1.133	0.8828	26.559	0.0377	23.4456	0.0427	11.7407
26	1.138	0.8784	27.692	0.0361	24.3240	0.0411	12.2196
27	1.144	0.8740	28.830	0.0347	25.1980	0.0397	12.0976
28	1.150	0.8697	29.975	0.0334	26.0677	0.0384	13.1747
29	1.156	0.8653	31.124	0.0321	26.9330	0.0371	13.6610

Contd...

t	*Single Payment*		*Equal Payment Series*				*Uniform gradient-series factor*
	Compound-amount factor	*Present-worth factor*	*Compound-amount factor*	*Sinking-fund factor*	*Present-worth factor*	*Capital-recovery factor*	
	To find F Given P F/P, r, t	*To find P Given F P/F, r, t*	*To find F Given A F/A, r, t*	*To find A Given F A/F, r, t*	*To find P Given A P/A, r, t*	*To find A Given P A/P, r, t*	*To find A Given G A/G, r, t*
30	1.161	0.8610	32.280	0.0310	27.7941	0.0360	14.1266
31	1.167	0.8568	33.441	0.0299	28.6508	0.0349	14.6012
32	1.173	0.8525	34.609	0.0289	29.5033	0.0339	15.0760
33	1.179	0.8483	35.782	0.0280	30.3515	0.0330	15.5480
34	1.185	0.8440	36.961	0.0271	31.1956	0.0321	16.0203
35	1.191	0.8398	38.145	0.0262	32.0312	0.0312	16.4916
40	1.221	0.8191	44.159	0.0227	36.1722	0.0277	18.8356
45	1.252	0.7990	50.324	0.0199	40.2072	0.0249	21.1596
50	1.283	0.7793	56.645	0.0177	44.1428	0.0227	23.4624
55	1.316	0.7601	63.126	0.0159	47.9815	0.0209	25.7447
60	1.349	0.7414	69.770	0.0143	51.7256	0.0193	28.0064
65	1.383	0.7231	76.582	0.0131	55.3775	0.0181	30.2476
70	1.418	0.7053	83.566	0.0120	58.9394	0.0181	32.4680
75	1.454	0.6879	90.727	0.0110	62.4137	0.0160	34.6676
80	1.490	0.6710	98.068	0.0102	56.8023	0.0152	36.8474
85	1.528	0.6545	105.594	0.0095	69.1075	0.0145	39.0066
90	1.567	0.6384	113.311	0.088	72.3313	0.0138	411451
95	1.606	0.6226	121.222	0.0083	75.4757	0.0133	43.2633
100	1.647	0.6073	129.334	0.0077	78.5427	0.0127	45.3613

Table A.2 $\frac{3}{4}$ % INTEREST FACTORS FOR DISCRETE COMPOUNDING

t	*Single Payment*		*Equal Payment Series*				*Uniform gradient-series factor*
	Compound-amount factor	*Present-worth factor*	*Compound amount factor*	*Sinking-fund factor*	*Present-worth factor*	*Capital-recovery factor*	
	To find F Given P F/P, r, t	*To find P Given F P/F, r, t*	*To find F Given A F/A, r, t*	*To find A Given F A/F, r, t*	*To find P Given A P/A, r, t*	*To find A Given P A/P, r, t*	*To find A Given G A/G, r, t*
1	1.008	0.9926	1.000	1.0000	0.9926	1.0075	0.0000
2	1.015	0.9852	2.008	0.4981	1.9777	0.5056	0.4981
3	1.023	0.9778	3.023	0.3309	2.9556	0.3384	0.9950
4	1.030	0.9706	4.045	0.2472	3.9261	0.2547	1.4907
5	1.038	0.9633	5.076	0.1970	4.8894	0.2045	1.9851
6	1.046	0.9562	6.114	0.1636	5.8456	0.1711	2.4782
7	1.054	0.9491	7.159	0.1397	6.7946	0.1472	2.9701
8	1.062	0.9420	8.213	0.1218	7.7366	0.1293	3.4608
9	1.070	0.9350	9.275	0.1078	8.6716	0.1153	3.9502
10	1.078	0.9280	10.344	0.0967	9.5996	0.1042	4.4384
11	1.086	0.9211	11.422	0.0876	10.5207	0.0951	4.9253
12	1.094	0.9142	12.502	0.0800	11.4349	0.0875	5.110
13	1.102	0.9074	13.601	0.0735	12.3424	0.0810	5.8954
14	1.110	0.9007	14.703	0.0680	13.2430	0.0755	6.3786
15	1.119	0.8940	15.814	0.0632	14.1370	0.0707	6.8606
16	1.127	0.8873	16.932	0.0591	15.0243	0.0666	7.3413
17	1.135	0.8807	18.059	0.0554	15.9050	0.0629	7.82207
18	1.144	0.8742	19.195	0.0521	16.7792	0.0596	8.2989
19	1.153	0.8677	20.339	0.0492	17.6468	0.0567	8.7759
20	1.161	0.8612	21.491	0.0465	18.5080	0.0540	9.2517
21	1.170	0.8548	22.652	0.0442	19.3628	0.0517	0.0517
22	1.179	0.8484	23.822	0.0420	20.2112	0.0495	10.1994
23	1.188	0.8421	25.001	0.0400	21.0533	0.0475	10.6714
24	1.196	0.8358	26.188	0.0382	21.8892	0.0457	11.1422
25	1.205	0.8296	27.385	0.0365	22.7188	0.0440	11.6117

Contd...

t	Single Payment		Equal Payment Series				Uniform gradient-series factor
	Compound-amount factor	Present-worth factor	Compound amount factor	Sinking-fund factor	Present-worth factor	Capital-recovery factor	
	To find F Given P F/P, r, t	To find P Given F P/F, r, t	To find F Given A F/A, r, t	To find A Given F A/F, r, t	To find P Given A P/A, r, t	To find A Given P A/P, r, t	To find A Given G A/G, r, t
26	1.214	0.8234	28.590	0.0350	23.5422	0.0425	12.0800
27	1.224	0.8173	29.805	0.0336	24.3595	0.0411	12.5470
28	1.233	0.8112	31.028	0.0322	25.17.07	0.0397	13.0128
29	1.242	0.8052	32.261	0.0310	25.9759	0.0385	13.4774
30	1.251	0.7992	33.503	0.0299	26.7751	0.0374	13.9407
31	1.261	0.7932	34.754	0.0288	27.5683	0.0363	14.4028
32	1.270	0.7873	36.015	0.0278	28.3557	0.0353	14.8636
33	1.280	0.7815	37.285	0.0268	29.1371	0.0343	15.3232
34	1.289	0.7757	38.565	0.0259	29.9128	0.0334	15.7816
35	1.299	0.7699	39.854	0.0251	30.6827	0.0326	16.2387
40	1.348	0.7417	46.446	0.0215	34.4469	0.0290	18.5058
45	1.400	0.7145	53.290	0.0188	38.0732	0.0290	20.7421
50	1.453	0.6883	60.394	0.0166	41.5665	0.0241	22.9476
55	1.508	0.6630	67.769	0.0148	44.9316	0.0223	25.1223
60	1.566	0.6387	75.424	0.0133	48.1734	0.0208	27.2665
65	1.625	0.6153	83.371	0.0120	51.2963	0.0195	29.3801
70	1.687	0.5927	91.620	0.0109	54.3046	0.0184	31.4634
75	1.751	0.5710	100.183	0.0100	57.2027	0.0175	33.5163
80	1.818	0.5501	109.073	0.0092	59.9945	0.0167	35.5391
85	1.887	0.5299	118.300	0.0085	62.6838	0.0160	37.5318
90	1.959	0.5105	127.879	0.0078	65.2746	0.0153	39.4946
95	2.034	0.4917	137.823	0.0073	67.7704	0.0148	41.4277
100	2.111	0.4737	148.145	0.0068	70.1746	0.0143	43.3311

Table A.3 1% INTEREST FACTORS FOR DISCRETE COMPOUNDING

t	*Single Payment*		*Equal Payment Series*				*Uniform gradient-series factor*
	Compound-amount factor	*Present-worth factor*	*Compound amount factor*	*Sinking-fund factor*	*Present-worth factor*	*Capital-recovery factor*	
	To find F Given P F/P, r, t	*To find P Given F P/F, r, t*	*To find F Given A F/A, r, t*	*To find A Given F A/F, r, t*	*To find P Given A P/A, r, t*	*To find A Given P A/P, r, t*	*To find A Given G A/G, r, t*
1	1.010	0.9901	1.000	1.0000	0.9901	1.0100	0.0000
2	1.020	0.9803	2.010	0.4975	1.9704	0.5075	0.4975
3	1.030	0.9706	3.030	0.3300	2.9410	0.3400	0.9934
4	1.041	0.9610	4.060	0.2463	3.9020	0.2563	1.4876
5	1.051	0.9515	5.101	0.1960	4.8534	0.2060	1.9801
6	1.062	0.9421	6.152	0.1626	5.7955	0.1726	2.4710
7	1.072	0.9327	7.214	0.1386	6.7282	0.1486	2.9602
8	1.083	0.9235	8.286	0.1207	7.6517	0.1307	3.4478
9	1.094	0.9143	9.369	0.1068	8.5660	0.1168	3.9337
10	1.105	0.9053	10.462	0.0956	9.4713	0.1056	4.4179
11	1.116	0.8963	11.567	0.0865	10.3676	0.0965	4.9005
12	1.127	0.8875	12.683	0.0789	11.2551	0.0889	5.3815
13	1.138	0.8787	13.809	0.0784	12.1338	0.0824	5.8607
14	1.149	0.8700	14.947	0.0669	13.0037	0.0769	6.3384
15	1.161	0.8614	16.097	0.0621	13.8651	0.0721	6.8143
16	1.173	0.8528	17.258	0.0580	14.7179	0.0680	7.2887
17	1.184	0.8444	18.430	0.0543	15.5623	0.0643	7.7613
18	1.196	0.8360	19.615	0.0510	16.3983	0.0610	8.2323
19	1.208	0.8277	20.811	0.0481	17.2260	0.0581	8.7017
20	1.220	0.8196	22.019	0.0454	18.0456	0.0554	9.1694
21	1.220	0.8114	23.239	0.0430	18.8570	0.0530	9.1694
22	1.245	0.8034	24.472	0.0409	19.6604	0.0509	10.0998
23	1.257	0.7955	25.716	0.0389	20.4558	0.0489	10.5626
24	1.270	0.7876	25.973	0.0371	21.2434	0.0471	11.0237
25	1.282	0.7798	28.243	0.0354	22.0232	0.0454	11.4831

Contd...

t	*Single Payment*		*Equal Payment Series*				*Uniform gradient-series factor*
	Compound-amount factor	*Present-worth factor*	*Compound amount factor*	*Sinking-fund factor*	*Present-worth factor*	*Capital-recovery factor*	
	To find F Given P F/P, r, t	*To find P Given F P/F, r, t*	*To find F Given A F/A, r, t*	*To find A Given F A/F, r, t*	*To find P Given A P/A, r, t*	*To find A Given P A/P, r, t*	*To find A Given G A/G, r, t*
26	1.295	0.7721	29.526	0.0339	22.7952	0.0439	11.9409
27	1.309	0.7644	30.821	0.0325	23.5596	0.0425	12.3971
28	1.321	0.7568	32.129	0.0311	24.3165	0.0411	12.8516
29	1.335	0.7494	33.450	0.0299	25.0658	0.0399	13.3045
30	1.348	0.7419	34.785	0.0288	25.8077	0.0388	13.7557
31	1.361	0.7346	36.133	0.0277	26.5423	0.0377	14.2052
32	1.375	0.7273	37.494	0.0267	27.2696	0.0367	14.6532
33	1.389	0.7201	38.869	0.0257	27.9897	0.0357	15.0995
34	1.403	0.7130	40.258	0.0248	28.7027	0.0348	15.5441
35	1.417	0.7059	41.660	0.0240	29.4086	0.0340	15.9871
40	1.489	0.6717	48.886	0.0205	32.8347	0.0305	18.1776
45	1.565	0.6391	56.481	0.0177	36.0945	0.0277	20.3273
50	1.645	0.6080	64.463	0.0155	39.1961	0.0255	22.4363
55	1.729	0.5785	72.852	0.0137	42.1472	0.0237	24.5049
60	1.817	0.5505	81.670	0.0123	44.9550	0.0223	26.5333
65	1.909	0.5237	90.937	0.0110	47.6266	0.0210	28.5217
70	2.007	0.4983	100.676	0.0099	50.1685	0.0199	30.4703
75	2.109	0.4741	110.913	0.0090	52.5871	0.0190	32.3793
80	2.217	0.4511	121.672	0.0082	54.8882	0.0182	34.2492
85	2.330	0.4292	132.979	0.0075	57.0777	0.0175	36.0801
90	2.449	0.4084	144.863	0.0069	59.1609	0.0169	37.8725
95	2.575	0.3886	157.354	0.0064	61.1430	0.0164	39.6265
100	2.705	0.3697	170.481	0.0059	63.0289	0.0159	41.3426

Table A.4 $1\frac{1}{4}$ % INTEREST FACTORS FOR DISCRETE COMPOUNDING

t	Single Payment		Equal Payment Series				Uniform gradient-series factor
	Compound-amount factor	Present-worth factor	Compound amount factor	Sinking-fund factor	Present-worth factor	Capital-recovery factor	
	To find F Given P F/P, r, t	To find P Given F P/F, r, t	To find F Given A F/A, r, t	To find A Given F A/F, r, t	To find P Given A P/A, r, t	To find A Given P A/P, r, t	To find A Given G A/G, r, t
1	1.013	0.9877	1.000	1.0000	0.9877	1.0126	0.0000
2	1.25	0.9755	2.013	0.4970	1.9631	0.5095	0.4932
3	1.038	0.9635	3.038	0.3293	2.9265	0.3418	0.9895
4	1.051	0.9516	4.076	0.2454	3.8780	0.2579	1.4830
5	1.064	0.9398	5.127	0.1951	4.8177	0.2076	1.9729
6	1.077	0.9282	6.191	0.1616	5.7459	0.1741	2.4618
7	1.091	0.9168	7.268	0.1376	6.6627	0.1501	2.9491
8	1.105	0.9055	8.359	0.1197	7.5680	0.1322	3.4330
9	1.118	0.8943	9.463	0.1057	8.4623	0.1182	3.9158
10	1.132	0.8832	10.582	0.0946	9.3454	0.1071	4.3960
11	1.147	0.8723	11.714	0.0854	10.2177	0.0979	4.8744
12	1.161	0.8616	12.860	0.0778	11.0792	0.0903	5.3506
13	1.175	0.8509	14.021	0.0714	11.9300	0.0839	5.8248
14	1.190	0.8404	15.196	0.0659	12.7704	0.0784	6.2968
15	1.205	0.8300	16.386	0.0611	13.6004	0.0736	6.7669
16	1.220	0.8198	17.591	0.0569	14.4201	0.0694	7.2350
17	1.235	0.8097	18.811	0.0532	15.2298	0.0657	7.7009
18	1.251	0.7997	20.046	0.0499	16.0293	0.0624	8.1645
19	1.266	0.7898	21.296	0.0470	16.8191	0.0595	8.6264
20	1.282	0.7801	22.563	0.0444	17.5991	0.0569	9.0861
21	1.298	0.7704	23.845	0.0420	18.3695	0.0545	9.5439
22	1.314	0.7609	25.143	0.0398	19.1303	0.0523	9.9993
23	1.331	0.7515	26.457	0.0378	19.8818	0.0503	10.4528
24	1.347	0.7423	27.788	0.0360	20.6240	0.0485	10.9044
25	1.364	0.7331	29.135	0.0344	21.3570	0.0469	11.3539

Contd...

t	*Single Payment*		*Equal Payment Series*				*Uniform gradient-series factor*
	Compound-amount factor	*Present-worth factor*	*Compound amount factor*	*Sinking-fund factor*	*Present-worth factor*	*Capital-recovery factor*	
	To find F Given P F/P, r, t	*To find P Given F P/F, r, t*	*To find F Given A F/A, r, t*	*To find A Given F A/F, r, t*	*To find P Given A P/A, r, t*	*To find A Given P A/P, r, t*	*To find A Given G A/G, r, t*
26	1.381	0.7240	30.499	0.0328	22.0810	0.0453	11.8012
27	1.399	0.7151	31.880	0.0314	22.7960	0.0439	12.2465
28	1.416	0.7063	33.279	0.0301	23.5022	0.0426	12.6898
29	1.434	0.6976	34.695	0.0289	24.1998	0.0414	13.1311
30	1.452	0.6889	36.128	0.0277	24.8886	0.0402	13.5703
31	1.470	0.6804	37.580	0.0267	25.5690	0.0392	14.0074
32	1.488	0.6720	39.050	0.0257	26.2410	0.0382	14.4425
33	1.507	0.6637	40.538	0.0247	26.9047	0.0372	14.8756
34	1.526	0.6555	42.045	0.0238	27.5601	0.0363	15.3066
35	1.545	0.6475	43.570	0.0230	28.2075	0.0355	15.7357
40	1.644	0.6085	51.489	0.0195	31.3266	0.0320	17.8503
45	1.749	0.5718	59.915	0.0167	34.2578	0.0292	19.9144
50	1.861	0.5374	68.880	0.0146	37.0125	0.0271	21.9284
55	1.980	0.5050	78.421	0.0128	39.6013	0.0253	23.8925
60	2.107	0.4746	88.573	0.0113	42.0342	0.0238	25.8072
65	2.242	0.4460	99.375	0.0101	44.3206	0.0226	27.6730
70	2.386	0.4192	110.870	0.0091	46.3206	0.0226	29.4902
75	2.539	0.3939	123.101	0.0082	48.4886	0.0207	31.2594
80	2.702	0.3702	136.116	0.0074	50.3862	0.0199	32.9812
85	2.875	0.3479	149.965	0.0067	52.1696	0.0192	34.6560
90	3.059	0.3270	164.701	0.0061	53.8456	0.0186	36.2844
95	3.255	0.3073	180.382	0.0056	55.4207	0.0181	37.8671
100	3.463	0.2888	197.067	0.0051	56.9009	0.0176	39.4048

Table A.5 1 1/2 % INTEREST FACTORS FOR DISCRETE COMPOUNDING

t	*Single Payment*		*Equal Payment Series*				*Uniform gradient-series factor*
	Compound-amount factor	*Present-worth factor*	*Compound amount factor*	*Sinking-fund factor*	*Present-worth factor*	*Capital-recovery factor*	
	To find F Given P F/P, r, t	*To find P Given F P/F, r, t*	*To find F Given A F/A, r, t*	*To find A Given F A/F, r, t*	*To find P Given A P/A, r, t*	*To find A Given P A/P, r, t*	*To find A Given G A/G, r, t*
1	1.015	0.9852	1.000	1.0000	0.9852	1.0150	0.0000
2	1.030	0.9707	2.015	0.4963	1.9559	0.5113	0.4963
3	1.046	0.9563	3.045	0.3284	2.9122	0.3434	0.9901
4	1.061	0.9422	4.091	0.2455	3.8544	0.2595	1.4814
5	1.77	0.9283	5.152	0.1941	4.7827	0.2091	1.9702
6	1.093	0.9146	6.230	0.1605	5.6972	0.1755	2.4566
7	1.110	0.9010	7.323	0.1366	6.5982	0.1516	2.9405
8	1.127	0.8877	8.433	0.1186	7.4859	0.1336	3.4219
9	1.143	0.8746	9.559	0.1046	8.3605	0.1196	3.9008
10	1.161	0.8617	10.703	0.0934	9.2222	0.1084	4.3772
11	1.178	0.8489	11.863	0.0843	10.0711	0.9993	4.8512
12	1.196	0.8364	13.041	0.0767	10.9075	0.0917	5.3227
13	1.214	0.8240	14.234	0.0703	11.7315	0.0853	5.7917
14	1.232	0.8119	15.450	0.0647	12.5434	0.0747	6.2582
15	1.250	0.7999	16.682	0.0600	13.3432	0.0750	6.7224
16	1.269	0.7880	17.932	0.0558	14.1313	0.0708	7.1819
17	1.288	0.7767	19.201	0.0521	14.9077	0.0671	7.6431
18	1.307	0.7649	20.489	0.0488	15.6726	0.0638	8.0997
19	1.327	0.7536	21.797	0.0459	16.4262	0.0609	8.5539
20	1.347	0.7425	23.124	0.0433	17.1686	0.0583	9.0057
21	1.367	0.7315	24.471	0.0409	17.9001	0.0559	94.550
22	1.388	0.7202	25.838	0.0387	18.6208	0.0537	9.9018
23	1.408	0.7100	27.225	0.0367	19.3309	0.0517	10.3482
24	1.430	0.6996	28.634	0.0349	20.0304	0.0499	10.7881
25	1.451	0.6892	30.063	0.0333	20.7196	0.0483	11.2276

Contd...

t	*Single Payment*		*Equal Payment Series*				*Uniform gradient-series factor*
	Compound-amount factor	*Present-worth factor*	*Compound amount factor*	*Sinking-fund factor*	*Present-worth factor*	*Capital-recovery factor*	
	To find F Given P F/P, r, t	*To find P Given F P/F, r, t*	*To find F Given A F/A, r, t*	*To find A Given F A/F, r, t*	*To find P Given A P/A, r, t*	*To find A Given P A/P, r, t*	*To find A Given G A/G, r, t*
26	1:473	0.6790	31.514	0.0317	21.3986	0.0467	11.6646
27	1.495	0.6690	32.987	0.0303	22.0676	0.0453	12.0992
28	1.517	0.6591	34.481	0.0290	22.7267	0.0440	12.5334
29	1.540	0.6494	35.999	0.0278	23.3761	0.0428	12.9610
30	1.563	0.6398	37.539	0.0266	24.0158	0.0416	13.3883
31	1.563	0.6303	39.102	0.0256	24.6462	0.0406	13.8111
32	1.610	0.6210	40.688	0.0246	25.2671	0.0396	14.2366
33	1.634	0.6118	42.299	0.0237	25.8790	0.0387	14.6555
34	1.659	0.6028	43.933	0.0228	26.4817	0.0378	15.0711
35	1.684	0.5939	45.592	0.0219	27.0756	0.0369	15.4882
40	1.814	0.5513	54.268	0.0184	29.9159	0.0334	15.4882
45	1.954	0.5117	63.614	0.0157	32.5523	0.0307	19.5074
50	2.105	0.4750	73.683	0.0136	34.9997	0.0286	21.4277
55	2.268	0.4409	84.530	0.0118	37.2715	0.0268	23.2894
60	2.443	0.4093	96.215	0.0104	39.3803	0.0254	25.0910
65	2.632	0.3799	108.803	0.0092	41.3378	0.0242	26.8392
70	2.835	0.3527	122.364	0.0082	43.1549	0.0232	28.5290
75	3.055	0.3274	136.973	0.0073	44.8416	0.0223	30.1611
80	3.291	0.3039	152.711	0.0066	46.4073	0.0216	31.7421
85	3.545	0.2821	169.665	0.0059	47.8607	0.0209	33.2628
90	3.819	0.2619	187.930	0.0053	49.2099	0.0203	34.7398
95	4.114	0.2431	207.606	0.0048	50.4622	0.0198	36.1008
100	4.432	0.2256	228.803	0.0044	51.6247	0.0194	37.5286

Table A.6 2 % INTEREST FACTORS FOR DISCRETE COMPOUNDING

t	*Single Payment*		*Equal Payment Series*				*Uniform gradient-series factor*
	Compound-amount factor	*Present-worth factor*	*Compound amount factor*	*Sinking-fund factor*	*Present-worth factor*	*Capital-recovery factor*	
	To find F Given P F/P, r, t	*To find P Given F P/F, r, t*	*To find F Given A F/A, r, t*	*To find A Given F A/F, r, t*	*To find P Given A P/A, r, t*	*To find A Given P A/P, r, t*	*To find A Given G A/G, r, t*
1	1.020	0.9804	1.000	1.0000	0.9804	1.0200	0.0000
2	1.040	0.9612	2.020	0.4951	1.9416	0.5151	0.4951
3	1.061	0.9423	3.060	0.3268	2.8839	0.3468	0.9868
4	1.081	0.9239	4.122	0.2426	3.8077	0.2626	1.4753
5	1.104	0.9057	5.204	0.1922	4.7135	0.2122	1.9604
6	1.126	0.8880	6.308	0.1585	5.6014	0.1785	2.4423
7	1.149	0.8706	7.434	0.1345	6.4720	0.1545	2.9208
8	1.172	0.8535	8.583	0.1165	7.3255	0.1365	3.3961
9	1.195	0.8368	9.755	0.1025	8.1622	0.1225	3.8621
10	1.219	0.8204	10.950	0.0913	8.9826	0.1113	4.3367
11	1.243	0.8043	12.169	0.0822	9.7869	0.1022	4.8021
12	1.268	0.7885	13.412	0.0746	10.5754	0.0946	5.2643
13	1.294	0.7730	14.680	0.0681	11.3484	0.0881	5.7231
14	1.319	0.7579	15.974	0.0626	12.1063	0.0826	6.1786
15	1.346	0.7430	17.293	0.0578	12.8493	0.0778	6.6309
16	1.373	0.7285	18.639	0.0537	13.5777	0.0737	7.0799
17	1.400	0.7142	20.012	0.0500	14.2919	0.0700	7.5256
18	1.428	0.7002	21.412	0.0467	14.9920	0.0667	7.9681
19	1.457	0.6864	22.841	0.0438	15.6785	0.0638	8.4073
20	1.486	0.6730	24.297	0.0412	16.3514	0.0612	8.8433
21	1.516	0.6598	25.783	0.0388	17.0112	0.0588	9.2760
22	1.546	0.6468	27.299	0.0366	17.6581	0.0566	9.7055
23	1.577	0.6342	28.845	0.0347	18.2922	0.0547	10.1317
24	1.608	0.6217	30.422	0.0329	18.9139	0.0529	10.5547
25	1.641	0.6095	32.030	0.0312	19.5235	0.0512	10.9745

Contd...

t	*Single Payment*		*Equal Payment Series*				*Uniform gradient-series factor*
	Compound-amount factor	*Present-worth factor*	*Compound amount factor*	*Sinking-fund factor*	*Present-worth factor*	*Capital-recovery factor*	
	To find F Given P F/P, r, t	*To find P Given F P/F, r, t*	*To find F Given A F/A, r, t*	*To find A Given F A/F, r, t*	*To find P Given A P/A, r, t*	*To find A Given P A/P, r, t*	*To find A Given G A/G, r, t*
26	1.673	0.5976	33.671	0.0297	20.1210	0.0497	11.3910
27	1.707	0.5859	35.344	0.0283	20.7069	0.0483	11.8043
28	1.741	0.5744	37.051	0.0270	21.2813	0.0470	12.2145
29	1.776	0.5631	38.792	0.0258	21.8444	0.0458	12.6214
30	1.811	0.5521	40.568	0.0247	22.3965	0.0447	13.0251
31	1.848	0.5413	42.379	0.0236	22.9377	0.0436	13.4257
32	1.885	0.5306	44.227	0.0226	23.4683	0.0426	13.8230
33	1.922	0.5202	46.112	0.0217	23.9886	0.0417	14.2172
34	1.961	0.5100	48.034	0.0208	24.4986	0.0408	14.6083
35	2.000	0.5000	49.994	0.0200	24.9986	0.0400	14.9961
40	2.208	0.4529	60.402	0.0166	27.3555	0.0366	16.8885
45	2.438	0.4102	71.893	0.0139	29.4902	0.0339	18.7034
50	2.692	0.3715	84.579	0.0118	31.4236	0.0318	20.4420
55	2.972	0.3365	98.587	0.0102	33.1748	0.0302	22.1057
60	3.281	0.3048	114.052	0.0088	34.7609	0.0288	23.6961
65	3.623	0.2761	131.126	0.0076	36.1975	0.0276	25.2147
70	4.000	0.2500	149.978	0.0067	37.4986	0.0267	26.6632
75	4.416	0.2265	170.792	0.0059	38.6771	0.0259	26.6632
80	4.875	0.2051	193.772	0.0052	39.7445	0.0259	28.0434
85	5.383	0.1858	219.144	0.0046	40.7113	0.0246	30.6064
90	5.943	0.1683	247.157	0.0041	41.5869	0.0241	31.7929
95	6.562	0.1524	278.085	0.0036	42.3800	0.0236	32.9189
100	7.245	0.1380	312.232	0.0032	43.0984	0.0232	33.9863

Table A.7 3% INTEREST FACTORS FOR DISCRETE COMPOUNDING

t	*Single Payment*		*Equal Payment Series*				*Uniform gradient-series factor*
	Compound-amount factor	*Present-worth factor*	*Compound-amount factor*	*Sinking-fund factor*	*Present-worth factor*	*Capital-recovery factor*	
	To find F Given P F/P, r, t	*To find P Given F P/F, r, t*	*To find F Given A F/A, r, t*	*To find A Given F A/F, r, t*	*To find P Given A P/A, r, t*	*To find A Given P A/P, r, t*	*To find A Given G A/G, r, t*
1	1.030	0.9709	1.000	1.0000	0.9709	1.0300	0.0000
2	1.061	0.9426	2.030	0.4926	1.9135	0.5226	0.4926
3	1.093	0.9152	3.091	0.3225	2.9286	0.3535	0.9803
4	1.126	0.8885	4.184	0.2390	3.7171	0.2690	1.4631
5	1.159	0.8626	5.309	0.1884	4.5797	0.2184	1.9409
6	1.194	0.375	6.468	0.1546	5.4172	0.1846	2.4138
7	1.230	0.8131	7.662	0.1305	6.2303	0.1605	2.8819
8	1.267	0.7894	8.892	0.1125	7.0197	0.1425	3.3450
9	1.305	0.7664	10.159	0.0984	7.7861	0.1284	3.8032
10	1.344	0.7441	11.464	0.0872	8.5302	0.1172	4.2565
11	1.384	0.7224	12.808	0.0781	9.2526	0.1081	4.7049
12	1.426	0.7014	14.192	0.0705	9.9540	0.1005	5.1485
13	1.469	0.6810	15.618	0.0640	10.6350	0.0940	5.1485
14	1.513	0.6611	17.086	0.0585	11.2961	0.0885	6.0211
15	1.558	0.6419	18.599	0.0538	11.9379	0.0838	6.4501
16	1.605	0.6232	20.157	0.0496	12.5611	0.0796	6.8742
17	1.653	0.6050	21.762	0.0460	13.1661	0.0760	7.2936
18	1.702	0.5874	23.414	0.0427	13.7535	0.0727	7.7081
19	1.754	0.5703	25.117	0.0398	14.3238	0.0698	8.1179
20	1.806	0.5537	26.870	0.0372	14.8775	0.0672	8.5229
21	1.860	0.5376	28.676	0.0349	15.4150	0.0649	8.9231
22	1.916	0.5219	30.537	0.0328	15.9369	0.0628	9.3186
23	1.974	0.5067	32.453	0.0308	16.4436	0.0608	9.7094
24	2.033	0.4919	34.426	0.0291	16.9356	0.0591	10.0954
25	2.094	0.4776	36.459	0.0274	17.4132	0.0574	10.4768

Contd...

t	*Single Payment*		*Equal Payment Series*				*Uniform gradient-series factor*
	Compound-amount factor	*Present-worth factor*	*Compound-amount factor*	*Sinking-fund factor*	*Present-worth factor*	*Capital-recovery factor*	
	To find F Given P F/P, r, t	*To find P Given F P/F, r, t*	*To find F Given A F/A, r, t*	*To find A Given F A/F, r, t*	*To find P Given A P/A, r, t*	*To find A Given P A/P, r, t*	*To find A Given G A/G, r, t*
26	2.157	0.4637	38.553	0.0259	17.8769	0.0559	10.8535
27	2.221	0.4502	40.710	0.0246	18.3270	0.0546	11.2256
28	2.288	0.4371	42.931	0.0233	18.7641	0.0533	11.5930
29	2.357	0.4244	45.219	0.022`	19.1885	0.0521	11.9558
30	2.427	0.4120	47.575	0.0210	19.6005	0.0510	12.3141
31	2.500	0.4000	50.003	0.0200	20.0004	0.0500	12.6678
32	2.575	0.3883	52.503	0.0191	20.3888	0.0491	13.0169
33	2.652	0.3770	55.078	0.0182	20.7658	0.0482	13.3616
34	2.732	0.3661	57.730	0.0173	21.1318	0.0473	13.7018
35	2.814	0.3554	60.462	0.0165	21.4872	0.0465	14.0375
40	3.262	0.3066	75.401	0.0133	23.1148	0.0433	15.6502
45	3.782	0.2644	92.720	0.0108	24.5187	0.0408	17.1556
50	4.384	0.2281	112.797	0.0089	25.7298	0.0389	18.5575
55	5.082	0.1968	136.072	0.0074	26.7744	0.0374	19.8600
60	5.892	0.1697	163.053	0.0061	27.6756	0.0361	21.0674
65	6.830	0.1464	194.333	0.0052	28.4529	0.0352	22.1841
70	7.918	0.1263	230.594	0.0043	29.1234	0.0343	23.2145
75	9.179	0.1090	272.631	0.0037	29.7018	0.0337	24.1634
80	10.641	0.0940	321.363	0.0031	30.2008	0.0331	25.0354
85	12.336	0.0811	377.857	0.0027	30.6312	0.0327	25.8349
90	14.300	0.0699	443.349	0.0023	31.0024	0.0323	26.5667
95	16.578	0.0603	519.272	0.0019	31.3227	0.0319	27.2351
100	19.219	0.0520	607.288	0.0017	31.5989	0.0317	27.8445

TABLE A.8 4% INTEREST FACTORS FOR DISCRETE COMPOUNDING

t	*Single Payment*		*Equal Payment series*				*Uniform gradient-series factor*
	Compound-amount factor	*Present-worth factor*	*Compound-amount factor*	*Sinking-fund factor*	*Present-worth factor*	*Capital-recovery factor*	
	To find F given P F/P, r, t	*To find P Given F P/F, r, t*	*To find F Given A F/A, r, t*	*To find A Given F A/F, r, t*	*To find P Given A P/A, r, t*	*To find A Given P A/P, r, t*	*To find A Given G A/G, r, t*
1	1.040	0.9615	1.000	1.0000	0.9615	1.0400	0.0000
2	1.082	0.9246	2.040	0.4902	1.8861	0.5302	0.4902
3	1.125	0.8890	3.122	0.3204	2.7751	0.3604	0.9739
4	1.170	0.8548	4.246	0.2355	3.6299	0.2755	1.4510
5	1.217	0.8219	5.416	0.1846	4.4518	0.2246	1.9216
6	1.265	0.7903	6.633	0.1508	5.2421	0.1908	2.3857
7	1.316	0.7599	7.898	0.1266	6.0021	0.1666	2.8433
8	1.369	0.7307	9.214	0.1085	6.7328	0.1485	3.2944
9	1.423	0.7026	10.583	0.0945	7.4353	0.1345	3.7391
10	1.480	0.6756	12.006	0.0833	8.1109	0.1233	4.1773
11	1.539	0.6496	13.486	0.0742	8.7605	0.1142	4.6090
12	1.601	0.6246	15.026	0.0666	9.3851	0.1066	5.0344
13	1.5665	0.6006	16.627	0.0602	9.9857	10.1002	5.4533
14	1.732	0.5775	18.292	0.0547	10.5631	0.0947	5.8659
15	1.801	0.5553	20.024	0.0500	11.1184	0.0900	6.2721
16	1.873	0.5339	21.825	0.0458	11.6523	0.0858	6.6720
17	1.948	0.5134	23.698	0.0422	12.1657	0.0822	7.0656
18	2.026	0.4936	25.645	0.0390	12.6593	0.0790	7.4530
19	2.107	0.4747	27.671	0.0361	13.1339	0.0761	7.8342
20	2.191	0.4564	29.778	0.336	13.5903	0.0736	8.2091
21	2.279	0.4388	31.969	0.0313	14.0292	0.0713	8.5780
22	2.370	0.4220	34.248	0.0292	14.4511	0.0692	8.9407
23	2.465	0.4057	36.618	0.0273	14.8569	0.0673	9.2973
24	2.563	0.3901	39.083	0.0256	15.2470	0.0656	9.6479
25	2.666	0.3751	41.646	0.0240	15.6221	0.0640	9.9925

Contd...

t	*Single Payment*		*Equal Payment series*				*Uniform gradient-series factor*
	Compound-amount factor	*Present-worth factor*	*Compound-amount factor*	*Sinking-fund factor*	*Present-worth factor*	*Capital-recovery factor*	
	To find F given P F/P, r, t	*To find P Given F P/F, r, t*	*To find F Given A F/A, r, t*	*To find A Given F A/F, r, t*	*To find P Given A P/A, r, t*	*To find A Given P A/P, r, t*	*To find A Given G A/G, r, t*
26	2.772	0.3607	44.312	0.0226	15.9828	0.0626	10.3312
27	2.883	0.3468	47.084	0.0212	16.3296	0.0612	10.6640
28	2.999	0.3335	49.968	0.0200	16.6631	0.0600	10.9909
29	3.119	0.3207	52.966	0.0189	16.9837	0.0589	11.3121
30	3.243	0.3083	56.085	0.0178	17.2920	0.0578	11.6274
31	3.373	0.29965	59.328	0.0169	17.5885	0.0569	11.9371
32	3.508	0.2851	62.701	0.0160	17.8736	0.0580	12.2411
33	3.648	0.2741	66.210	0.0151	18.1477	0.0551	12.5396
34	3.794	0.2636	69.858	0.0143	18.4112	0.0543	12.8325
35	3.946	0.2534	73.652	0.0136	18.6646	0.0536	13.1199
40	4.801	0.2083	95.026	0.0105	19.7928	0.0505	14.4765
45	5.841	0.1712	121.029	0.00083	20.7200	0.0483	15.7047
50	7.107	0.1407	152.667	0.0066	21.4822	0.0466	16.8123
55	8.646	0.1157	191.159	0.0052	22.1086	0.0452	17.8070
60	10.520	0.0951	237.991	0.0042	22.6235	0.0442	18.6972
65	12.799	0.0781	294.968	0.0034	23.0467	0.0434	19.4909
70	15.572	0.0642	364.290	0.0028	23.3945	0.0428	20.1961
75	18.945	0.0528	448.631	0.0022	23.6804	0.0422	20.8206
80	23.050	0.0434	551.245	0.0018	23.9154	0.0418	21.3719
85	28.044	0.0357	676.090	0.0015	24.1085	0.0415	21.8569
90	34.119	0.0293	817.983	0.0012	24.2673	0.0412	22.2826
95	41.511	0.0241	1012.785	0.0010	24.3978	0.0410	22.6550
100	50.505	0.0198	1237.624	0.0008	24.5050	0.0408	22.9800

Table A.9 5% INTEREST FACTOR FOR DISCRETE COMPOUNDING

t	*Single Payment*		*Equal Payment Series*				*Uniform gradient-series factor*
	Compound-amount factor	*Present-worth factor*	*Compound-amount factor*	*Sinking-fund factor*	*Present-worth factor*	*Capital-recovery factor*	
	To find F Given P F/P, r, t	*To find P Given F P/F, r, t*	*To find F Given A F/A, r, t*	*To find A Given F A/F, r, t*	*To find P Given A P/A, r, t*	*To find A Given P A/P, r, t*	*To find A Given G A/G, r, t*
1	1.050	0.9524	1.000	1.0000	0.9524	10500	0.0000
2	1.103	0.9070	2.050	0.4878	1.8594	0.5378	0.4878
3	1.158	0.8638	3.153	0.3172	2.7233	0.3672	0.9675
4	1.216	0.8227	4.310	0.2320	3.5460	0.2020	1.4391
5	1.276	0.7835	5.526	0.1810	4.3295	0.2310	1.905
6	1.340	0.7462	6.802	0.1470	5.0757	0.1970	2.3579
7	1.407	0.7107	8.142	0.1228	5.7864	0.1728	2.8052
8	1.477	0.6768	9.549	0.1047	6.4632	0.1547	3.2445
9	1.551	0.6446	11.027	0.0907	7.1078	0.1407	3.6758
10	1.629	0.6139	12.587	0.0795	7.7217	0.1295	4.0991
11	1.710	0.5847	14.207	0.0704	8.3064	0.1204	4.5145
12	1.796	0.5568	15.917	0.0628	8.8633	0.1128	4.9219
13	1.886	0.5303	17.713	0.0565	9.3936	0.1065	5.3215
14	1.980	0.5051	19.599	0.0510	9.8987	1.1010	5.7133
15	2.079	0.4810	21.579	0.0464	10.3797	0.0964	6.0973
16	2.183	0.4581	23.658	0.0423	10.8378	0.0923	6.4736
17	2.292	0.4363	25.840	0.0387	11.2741	0.0887	6.8423
18	2.407	0.4155	28.132	0.0356	11.6896	0.0856	7.2034
19	2.527	0.3957	30.539	0.0328	12.0853	0.0828	7.5569
20	2.653	0.3769	33.066	0.0303	12.4622	0.0803	7.9030
21	2.786	0.3590	35.719	0.0280	12.8212	0.0780	8.2416
22	2.925	0.3419	38.505	0.0260	13.1630	0.0760	8.5730
23	3.072	0.3256	41.430	0.0241	13.4886	0.0741	8.8971
24	3.225	0.3101	44.502	0.0225	13.7987	0.0725	9.2140
25	3.386	0.2953	47.727	0.0210	14.0940	0.0710	9.5238

Contd...

t	*Single Payment*		*Equal Payment Series*				*Uniform gradient-series factor*
	Compound-amount factor	*Present-worth factor*	*Compound-amount factor*	*Sinking-fund factor*	*Present-worth factor*	*Capital-recovery factor*	
	To find F Given P F/P, r, t	*To find P Given F P/F, r, t*	*To find F Given A F/A, r, t*	*To find A Given F A/F, r, t*	*To find P Given A P/A, r, t*	*To find A Given P A/P, r, t*	*To find A Given G A/G, r, t*
26	3.556	0.2813	51.113	0.0196	14.3752	0.0696	9.8266
27	3.733	0.2679	54.669	0.0183	14.6430	0.0683	10.1224
28	3.920	0.2551	58.403	0.0171	14.8981	0.0671	10.4114
29	4.116	0.2430	62.323	0.0161	15.1411	0.0661	10.6936
30	4.322	0.2314	66.439	0.0151	15.3725	0.0651	10.9691
31	4.538	0.2204	70.761	0.0141	15.5928	0.0641	11.2381
32	4.765	0.2099	75.299	0.0133	15.80267	0.0633	11.5005
33	5.003	0.1999	80.064	0.0125	16.0026	0.0625	11.7566
34	5.253	0.1904	85.067	0.0118	16.1929	0.0618	12.0083
35	5.516	0.1813	90.320	0.0111	16.3742	0.0611	12.2498
40	7.040	0.1421	120.800	0.0083	17.1591	0.0583	13.3775
45	8.985	0.113	159.700	0.0063	17.7741	0.0563	14.3644
50	11.467	0.0872	209.348	0.0048	18.2559	0.0548	15.2233
55	14.636	0.0683	272.713	0.0037	18.6335	0.0537	15.9665
60	18.679	0.0535	353.584	0.0028	18.9293	0.0528	16.6062
65	23.840	0.0420	456.798	0.0022	19.1611	0.0522	17.1541
70	30.426	0.0329	588.529	0.0017	19.3427	0.0517	17.6212
75	38.833	0.0258	756.654	0.0013	19.4850	0.0513	18.01780
80	49.561	0.0202	971.229	0.0010	19.5965	0.0510	18.3520
85	63.254	0.0158	1245.087	0.0008	19.6838	0.0508	18.6340
90	80.730	0.0124	1594.607	0.0006	19.7523	0.0506	18.8712
95	103.035	0.0097	2040.694	0.0005	19.8059	0.0505	19.0689
100	131.501	0.0076	2610.025	0.0004	19.8479	0.0504	19.2337

TABLE A.10 6% INTEREST FACTORS FOR DISCRETE COMPOUNDING

t	*Single Payment*		*Equal Payment Series*				*Uniform gradient-series factor*
	Compound-amount factor	*Present-worth factor*	*Compound-amount factor*	*Sinking-fund factor*	*Present-worth factor*	*Capital-recovery factor*	
	To find F Given P F/P, r, t	*To find P Given F P/F, r, t*	*To find F Given A F/A, r, t*	*To find A Given F A/F, r, t*	*To find P Given A P/A, r, t*	*To find A Given P A/P, r, t*	*To find A Given G A/G, r, t*
1	1.060	0.9434	1.000	1.0000	0.9434	1.0600	0.0000
2	1.124	0.8900	2.060	0.4854	1.8334	0.5454	0.4854
3	1.191	0.8396	3.184	0.3141	2.6730	0.3741	0.9612
4	1.262	0.7921	4.075	0.2286	3.4651	0.2886	1.4272
5	1.338	0.7473	5.637	0.1774	4.2124	0.2374	1.8836
6	1.419	0.7050	6.975	0.1434	4.9173	0.2034	2.3304
7	1.504	0.6651	8.394	0.1191	5.5824	0.1791	2.7676
8	1.594	0.6274	9.897	0.1010	6.2098	0.1610	3.1952
9	1.689	0.5919	11.491	0.0870	6.8017	0.1470	3.6133
10	1.791	0.5584	13.181	0.0759	7.3601	0.1359	4.0220
11	1.898	0.5268	14.972	0.0668	7.8869	0.1268	4.4213
12	2.012	0.4970	16.870	0.0593	8.3839	0.1193	4.8113
13	2.133	0.4688	18.882	0.0530	8.8527	0.1130	5.1920
14	2.261	0.4423	21.015	0.0476	9.2950	0.1076	5.5635
15	2.397	0.4173	23.276	0.0430	9.7123	0.1030	5.9260
16	2.540	0.3937	25.673	0.0390	10.1059	0.0990	6.2794
17	2.693	0.3714	28.213	0.0355	10.4773	0.0955	6.6240
18	2.854	0.3504	30.906	0.0324	10.8276	0.0924	6.9597
19	3.026	0.3305	33.760	0.0296	11.1581	0.0896	7.2867
20	3.207	0.3118	36.786	0.0272	11.4699	0.0872	7.6052
21	3.400	0.2942	39.993	0.0250	11.7641	0.0850	7.9151
22	3.604	0.2775	43.392	0.0231	12.0416	0.0831	8.2166
23	3.820	0.2618	46.996	0.0213	12.3034	0.0813	8.5099
24	4.049	0.2470	50.816	0.0197	12.5504	0.0797	8.7951
25	4.292	0.2330	54.865	0.0182	12.7834	0.0782	9.0722

Contd...

t	*Single Payment*		*Equal Payment Series*				*Uniform gradient-series factor*
	Compound-amount factor	*Present-worth factor*	*Compound-amount factor*	*Sinking-fund factor*	*Present-worth factor*	*Capital-recovery factor*	
	To find F Given P F/P, r, t	*To find P Given F P/F, r, t*	*To find F Given A F/A, r, t*	*To find A Given F A/F, r, t*	*To find P Given A P/A, r, t*	*To find A Given P A/P, r, t*	*To find A Given G A/G, r, t*
26	4.549	0.2198	59.156	0.0169	13.0032	0.0769	9.3415
27	4.822	0.2074	63.706	0.0157	13.2105	0.0757	9.6030
28	5.112	0.1956	68.528	0.0146	13.4062	0.0746	9.8568
29	5.418	0.1846	73.640	0.0136	13.5907	0.0736	10.1032
30	5.744	0.1741	79.058	0.0127	13.7648	0.0727	10.3422
31	6.088	0.1643	84.802	0.0118	13.9291	0.0718	10.5740
32	6.453	0.1550	90.890	0.0110	14.0841	0.0710	10.7988
33	6.841	0.1462	97.343	0.0103	14.2302	0.0703	11.0166
34	7.251	0.1379	104.184	0.0096	14.3682	0.0696	11.2276
35	7.686	0.1301	111.435	0.0090	14.4983	0.0690	11.4319
40	10.286	0.0972	154.762	0.0065	15.0463	0.0665	12.3590
45	13.765	0.0727	212.744	0.0047	15.4558	0.0647	13.1413
50	18.420	0.0543	290.336	0.0035	15.7619	0.0635	13.7964
55	24.650	0.0406	394.172	0.0025	15.9906	0.0625	14.3411
60	32.988	0.0303	533.128	0.0019	16.1614	0.0619	14.7910
65	44.145	0.0227	719.083	0.0014	16.2891	0.0614	15.1601
70	59.076	0.0169	967.932	0.0010	16.3846	0.0610	15.4614
75	79.057	0.0127	1300.949	0.0008	16.4559	0.0608	15.7058
80	105.796	0.0095	1746.600	0.0006	16.5091	0.0606	15.9033
85	141.579	0.0071	2342.982	0.0004	16.5490	0.0604	16.0620
90	189.465	0.0053	3141.075	0.0003	16.5787	0.0603	16.1891
95	253.546	0.0040	4209.104	0.0002	16.6009	0.0602	16.2905
100	339.302	0.0030	5638.368	0.0002	16.6176	0.0602	16.3711

Table A.11 7% INTEREST FACTORS FOR DISCRETE COMPOUNDING

t	*Single Payment*		*Equal Payment Series*				*Uniform gradient-series factor*
	Compound-amount factor	*Present-worth factor*	*Compound-amount factor*	*Sinking-fund factor*	*Present-worth factor*	*Capital-recovery factor*	
	To find F Given P F/P, r, t	*To find P Given F P/F, r, t*	*To find F Given A F/A, r, t*	*To find A Given F A/F, r, t*	*To find P Given A P/A, r, t*	*To find A Given P A/P, r, t*	*To find A Given G A/G, r, t*
1	1.070	0.9346	1.000	1.000	0.9346	1.0700	0.0000
2	1.145	0.8734	2.070	0.4831	1.8080	0.5531	0.4831
3	1.225	0.8163	3.215	0.3111	2.6243	0.3811	0.9549
4	1.311	0.7629	4.440	0.2252	3.3872	0.2952	1.4155
5	1.403	0.7130	5.751	0.1739	4.1002	0.2439	1.8650
6	1.501	0.6664	7.153	0.1398	4.7665	0.2098	2.3032
7	1.606	0.6228	8.654	0.1156	5.3893	0.1856	2.7304
8	1.718	0.5820	10.260	0.0975	5.9713	0.1675	3.1466
9	1.838	0.5439	11.978	0.0835	6.5152	0.1535	3.5517
10	1.967	0.5084	13.816	0.0724	7.0236	0.1424	3.9461
11	2.105	0.4751	15.784	0.0634	7.4987	0.1334	4.3296
12	2.252	0.4440	17.888	0.0559	7.9427	0.1259	4.7025
13	2.410	0.4150	20.141	0.0497	8.3577	0.1197	5.0649
14	2.579	0.3878	22.550	0.0444	8.7455	0.1144	5.4167
15	3.759	0.3625	25.129	0.0398	9.1079	0.1098	5.7583
16	2.952	0.3387	27.888	0.0359	9.4467	0.1059	6.0897
17	3.159	0.3166	30.840	0.0324	9.7632	0.1024	6.4110
18	3.380	0.2959	33.999	0.0294	10.0591	0.0994	6.7335
19	3.617	0.2765	37.379	0.0268	10.3356	0.0968	7.0242
20	3.870	0.2584	40.996	0.0244	10.5940	0.0944	7.3163
21	4.141	0.2415	44.865	0.0223	10.8355	0.0923	7.5990
22	4.430	0.2257	49.006	0.0204	11.0613	0.0904	7.8725
23	4.741	0.2110	53.436	0.0187	11.2722	0.0887	8.1369
24	5.072	0.1972	58.177	0.0172	11.4693	0.0872	8.3923
25	5.427	0.1843	63.249	0.0158	11.6536	0.0858	8.6391

Contd...

t	*Single Payment*		*Equal Payment Series*				*Uniform gradient-series factor*
	Compound-amount factor	*Present-worth factor*	*Compound-amount factor*	*Sinking-fund factor*	*Present-worth factor*	*Capital-recovery factor*	
	To find F Given P F/P, r, t	*To find P Given F P/F, r, t*	*To find F Given A F/A, r, t*	*To find A Given F A/F, r, t*	*To find P Given A P/A, r, t*	*To find A Given P A/P, r, t*	*To find A Given G A/G, r, t*
26	5.807	0.1722	68.676	0.0146	11.8258	0.0846	8.8773
27	6.214	0.1609	74.484	0.0134	11.9867	0.0834	9.1072
28	6.649	0.1504	80.698	0.0124	12.1371	0.0824	9.3290
29	7.114	0.1406	87.347	0.0115	12.2777	0.0815	9.5427
30	7.612	0.1314	94.461	0.0106	12.4091	0.0806	9.7487
31	8.145	0.1228	102.073	0.0098	12.5318	0.0798	9.9471
32	8.715	0.1148	110.218	0.0091	12.6466	0.0791	10.1381
33	9.325	0.1072	118.933	0.0084	12.7538	0.0784	10.3219
34	9.978	0.1002	128.259	0.0078	12.8540	0.0778	10.4987
35	10.677	0.0937	138.237	0.0072	12.9477	0.0772	10.6667
40	14.974	0.0668	199.635	0.0050	13.3317	0.0750	11.4234
45	21.002	0.0476	285.749	0.0035	13.6055	0.0735	12.0300
50	29.457	0.0340	406.529	0.0025	13.8008	0.0725	12.5287
55	41.315	0.0242	575.929	0.0017	13.9399	0.0717	12.9210
60	57.946	0.0173	813.520	0.0012	14.0392	0.0712	13.2321
65	81.273	0.0123	1146.755	0.0009	14.1099	0.0709	13.4700
70	113.989	0.0088	1614.134	0.0006	14.1604	0.0706	13.0002
75	159.876	0.0063	2269.657	0.0005	14.1964	0.0705	13.8137
80	224.234	0.0045	3189.063	0.0003	14.2220	0.0703	13.9274
85	314.500	0.0032	4478.576	0.0002	14.2403	0.0702	14.0148
90	441.103	0.0023	6287.185	0.0002	14.2533	0.0702	14.0812
95	618.670	0.0016	8823.854	0.0001	14.2626	0.0701	14.1310
100	867.716	0.0012	12381.662	0.0001	14.2693	0.0701	14.1703

TABLE A.12 8% INTEREST FACTORS FOR DISCRETE COMPOUNDING

t	*Single Payment*		*Equal Payment Series*				*Uniform gradient-series factor*
	Compound-amount factor	*Present-worth factor*	*Compound-amount factor*	*Sinking-fund factor*	*Present-worth factor*	*Capital-recovery factor*	
	To find F Given P F/P, r, t	*To find P Given F P/F, r, t*	*To find F Given A F/A, r, t*	*To find A Given F A/F, r, t*	*To find P Given A P/A, r, t*	*To find A Given P A/P, r, t*	*To find A Given G A/G, r, t*
1	1.080	0.9259	1.000	1.0000	0.9259	1.0800	0.0000
2	1.166	0.8573	2.080	0.4808	1.7833	0.5608	0.4808
3	1.260	0.7938	3.246	0.3080	2.5771	0.3880	0.9488
4	1.360	0.7350	4.506	0.2219	3.3121	0.3019	1.4040
5	1.469	0.6806	5.867	0.1705	3.9927	0.2505	1.8465
6	1.587	0.6302	7.336	0.1363	4.6229	0.2163	2.2764
7	1.714	0.5835	8.923	0.1121	5.2064	0.1921	2.6937
8	1.851	0.5403	10.637	0.0940	6.7466	0.1740	3.0985
9	1.999	0.5003	12.488	0.0801	6.2469	0.1601	3.4910
10	2.159	0.4632	14.487	0.0690	6.7101	0.1490	3.8713
11	2.332	0.4289	16.645	0.0601	7.1390	0.1401	4.2395
12	2.518	0.3971	18.977	0.0527	7.5361	0.1327	4.5958
13	2.720	0.3677	21.495	0.0465	7.9038	0.1265	4.9402
14	2.937	0.3405	24.215	0.0413	8.2442	0.1213	5.2731
15	3.172	0.3153	27.152	0.0368	8.5595	0.1168	5.5945
16	3.426	0.2919	30.324	0.0330	8.8514	0.0998	7.2940
17	3.700	0.2703	33.750	0.0296	9.1216	0.0980	7.5412
18	3.996	0.2503	37.450	0.0267	9.3719	0.0964	7.7786
19	4.316	0.2317	41.446	0.0241	9.6036	0.0950	8.0066
20	4.661	0.2146	45.762	0.0219	9.8182	0.0937	8.2254
21	5.034	0.1987	50.423	0.0198	10.0168	0.0925	8.4352
22	5.437	0.1840	55.457	0.0180	10.2008	0.0915	8.6363
23	5.871	0.1703	60893	0.0164	10.3711	0.0905	8.8289
24	6.341	0.1577	66.765	0.0150	10.5288	0.0896	9.0133
25	6.848	0.1460	73.106	0.0137	10.6748	0.0888	9.1897

Contd...

t	*Single Payment*		*Equal Payment Series*				*Uniform gradient-series factor*
	Compound-amount factor	*Present-worth factor*	*Compound-amount factor*	*Sinking-fund factor*	*Present-worth factor*	*Capital-recovery factor*	
	To find F Given P F/P, r, t	*To find P Given F P/F, r, t*	*To find F Given A F/A, r, t*	*To find A Given F A/F, r, t*	*To find P Given A P/A, r, t*	*To find A Given P A/P, r, t*	*To find A Given G A/G, r, t*
26	7.396	0.1352	79.954	0.0125	10.8100	0.0925	8.4352
27	7.988	0.1252	87.351	0.0115	10.9352	0.0915	8.6363
28	8.6627	0.1159	95.339	0.0105	11.0511	0.0905	8.8289
29	9.317	0.1073	103.966	0.0096	11.1584	0.0896	9.0133
30	10.063	0.994	113.283	0.0088	11.2578	0.0888	9.1897
31	10.868	0.0920	123.346	0.0081	11.3498	0.0881	9.3584
32	11.737	0.0852	134.214	0.0075	11.4350	0.0875	9.5197
33	12.676	0.0789	145.951	0.0069	11.5139	0.0869	9.6737
34	13.690	0.0731	158.627	0.0063	11.5869	0.0863	9.8208
35	14.785	0.0676	172.317	0.0058	11.6546	0.0858	9.9611
40	21.725	0.0460	259.057	0.0039	11.9246	0.0839	10.5699
45	31.920	0.0313	386.506	0.0026	12.1084	0.0826	11.0447
50	46.902	0.0213	573.770	0.0018	12.2335	0.0818	11.4107
55	68.914	0.0145	848.923	0.0012	12.3186	0.0812	116902
60	101.257	0.0099	1253.213	0.0008	12.3766	0.0808	119015
65	148.780	0.0067	1847.248	0.0006	12.4160	0.0806	12.0602
70	218.606	0.0046	2720.080	0.0004	12.4428	0.0804	12.1783
75	321.205	0.0031	4002.557	0.0003	12.4611	0.0803	12.2658
80	471.955	0.0021	5886.935	0.0002	12.4735	0.0802	12.3301
85	693.456	0.0015	8655.706	0.0001	12.4820	0.0801	12.3773
90	1018.915	0.0010	12723.939	0.0001	12.4877	0.0801	12.4116
95	1497.121	0.0007	18701.507	0.0001	12.4917	0.0801	12.4365
100	2199.761	0.0005	27484.516	0.0001	12.4943	0.0800	12.4545

TABLE A. 13 9% INTEREST FACTORS FOR DISCRETE COMPOUNDING

t	*Single Payment*		*Equal Payment Series*				*Uniform gradient-series factor*
	Compound-amount factor	*Present-worth factor*	*Compound-amount factor*	*Sinking-fund factor*	*Present-worth factor*	*Capital-recovery factor*	
	To find F Given P F/P, r, t	*To find P Given F P/F, r, t*	*To find F Given A F/A, r, t*	*To find A Given F A/F, r, t*	*To find P Given A P/A, r, t*	*To find A Given P A/P, r, t*	*To find A Given G A/G, r, t*
1	1.090	0.9174	1.000	1.0000	0.9174	1.0900	0.0000
2	1.188	0.8417	2.090	0.4785	1.7591	0.5685	0./4785
3	1.295	0.7722	3.278	0.3051	2.5313	0.3951	0.9426
4	1.412	0.7084	4.573	0.2187	3.2397	0.3087	1.3925
5	1.539	0.6499	5.985	0.1671	3.8897	0.2571	1.8282
6	1.677	0.5963	7.523	0.1329	4.4859	0.2229	2.2498
7	1.828	0.5470	9.200	0.1087	5.0330	0.1987	2.6574
8	1.993	0.5019	11.028	0.0907	5.5348	0.1807	3.0512
9	2.172	0.4604	13.021	0.0768	5.9953	0.1668	3.4312
10	2.367	0.4224	15.193	0.0658	6.4177	0.1558	3.7978
11	2.580	0.3875	17.560	0.0570	6.8052	0.1470	4.1510
12	2.813	0.3555	20.141	0.0497	7.1607	0.1397	4.4910
13	3.066	0.3262	22.953	0.0436	7.4869	0.1336	4.8182
14	3.342	0.2993	26.019	0.0384	7.7862	0.1284	5.1326
15	3.642	0.2745	29.361	0.0341	8.0607	0.1241	5.4346
16	3.970	0.2519	33.003	0.0303	8.3126	0.1203	5.7245
17	4.328	0.2311	36.974	0.0271	8.5436	0.1171	6.0024
18	4.717	0.2120	41.301	0.0242	8.7556	0.1142	6.2687
19	5.142	0.1945	46.018	0.0217	8.9501	0.1117	6.5236
20	5.604	0.1784	51.160	0.0196	9.1286	0.1096	6.7675
21	6.109	0.1637	56.765	0.0176	9.2923	0.1076	7.0006
22	6.659	0.1502	62.873	0.0159	9.4424	0.1059	7.2232
23	7.258	0.1378	69.532	0.0144	9.5802	0.1044	7.4358
24	7.911	0.1264	76.790	0.0130	9.7066	0.1030	7.6384
25	8.623	0.1160	84.701	0.0118	9.8226	0.1018	7.8316

Contd...

t	*Single Payment*		*Equal Payment Series*				*Uniform gradient-series factor*
	Compound-amount factor	*Present-worth factor*	*Compound-amount factor*	*Sinking-fund factor*	*Present-worth factor*	*Capital-recovery factor*	
	To find F Given P F/P, r, t	*To find P Given F P/F, r, t*	*To find F Given A F/A, r, t*	*To find A Given F A/F, r, t*	*To find P Given A P/A, r, t*	*To find A Given P A/P, r, t*	*To find A Given G A/G, r, t*
26	9.399	0.1064	93.324	0.0107	9.9290	0.1007	8.0156
27	10.245	0.0976	102.723	0.0097	10.0266	0.0997	8.1906
28	11.167	0.0896	112.968	0.0089	10.1161	0.0989	8.3572
29	12.172	0.0822	124.135	0.0081	10.1983	0.0981	8.5154
30	13.268	0.0754	136.308	0.0073	10.2737	0.0973	8.6657
31	14.462	0.0692	149.575	0.0067	10.3428	0.0967	8.8083
32	15.763	0.0634	164.037	0.0061	10.4063	0.0961	8.9436
33	17.182	0.0582	179.800	0.0056	10.4645	0.0956	9.0718
34	18.728	0.0534	196.982	0.0051	10.5178	0.0951	9.1933
35	20.414	0.0490	215.711	0.0046	10.5668	0.0946	9.3083
40	31.409	0.0318	337.882	0.0030	10.7574	0.0930	9.7957
45	48.327	0.0207	525.859	0.0019	10.8812	0.0919	10.1603
50	74.358	0.0135	815.084	0.0012	10.9617	0.0912	10.4295
55	114.408	0.0088	1260.092	0.0008	11.0140	0.0908	10.6261
60	176.031	0.0057	1944.792	0.0005	11.0480	0.0905	10.7683
65	270.846	0.0037	2998.288	0.0003	11.0701	0.0903	10.8702
70	416.730	0.0024	4619.223	0.0002	11.0845	0.0902	10.9427
75	641.191	0.0016	7113.232	0.0002	11.0938	0.0902	10.9940
80	986.552	0.0010	10950.574	0.0001	11.0999	0.0901	11.0299
85	1517.932	0.0007	16854.800	0.0001	11.1038	0.0901	11.0551
90	2335.527	0.0004	25939.184	0.0001	11.1064	0.0900	11.0728
95	3593.497	0.0003	39916.635	0.0000	11.1080	0.0900	11.0847
100	5529.041	0.0002	61422.675	0.0000	11.1091	0.0900	11.0930

TABLE A.14 10% INTEREST FACTORS FOR DISCRETE COMPOUNDING

t	*Single Payment*		*Equal Payment Series*				*Uniform gradient-series factor*
	Compound-amount factor	*Present-worth factor*	*Compound-amount factor*	*Sinking-fund factor*	*Present-worth factor*	*Capital-recovery factor*	
	To find F Given P F/P, r, t	*To find P Given F P/F, r, t*	*To find A Given A F/A, r, t*	*To find A Given F A/F, r, t*	*To find P Given A P/A, r, t*	*to find A Given P A/P, r, t*	*To find A Given G A/G, r, t*
1	1.100	0.9091	1.000	1.0000	0.9091	1.1000	0.0000
2	1.210	0.8265	2.100	0.4762	1.7355	0.5762	0.4762
3	1.331	0.7513	3.310	0.3021	2.4869	0.4021	0.9366
4	1.464	0.6830	4.641	0.2155	3.1699	0.3155	1.3812
5	1.611	0.6209	6.105	0.1638	3.7908	0.2638	1.8101
6	1.772	0.5645	7.716	0.1296	4.3553	0.2296	2.2236
7	1.949	0.5132	9.487	0.1054	4.8684	0.2054	2.6216
8	2.144	0.4665	11.436	0.0875	5.3349	0.1875	3.0045
9	2.358	0.4241	13.579	0.0737	5.7590	0.1737	3.3724
10	2.594	0.3856	15.937	0.0628	6.1446	0.1628	3.7255
11	2.583	0.3505	18.531	0.0540	6.4951	0.1540	4.0641
12	3.138	0.3186	21.384	0.0468	6.8137	0.1468	4.3884
13	3.452	0.2897	24.523	0.0408	7.1034	0.1408	4.6988
14	3.798	0.2633	27.975	0.0358	7.3667	0.1358	4.9955
15	4.177	0.2394	31.772	0.0315	7.6061	0.1315	5.2789
16	4.595	0.2176	35.950	0.0278	7.8237	0.1278	5.5493
17	5.054	0.1979	40.545	0.0247	8.0216	0.1247	5.8071
18	5.560	0.1799	45.599	0.0219	8.2014	0.1219	6.0526
19	6.116	0.1635	51.159	0.0196	8.3649	0.1196	6.2861
20	6.728	0.1487	57.275	0.0175	8.5136	0.1175	6.5081
21	7.400	0.1351	64.003	0.0156	8.6487	0.1156	6.7189
22	8.140	0.1229	71.403	0.0140	8.7716	0.1140	6.9189
23	8.954	0.1117	79.543	0.0126	8.8832	0.1126	7.1085
24	9.850	0.1015	88.497	0.0113	8.9848	0.1113	7.2881
25	10.835	0.0923	98.347	0.0102	9.0771	0.1102	7.4580

Contd...

t	*Single Payment*		*Equal Payment Series*				*Uniform gradient-series factor*
	Compound-amount factor	*Present-worth factor*	*Compound-amount factor*	*Sinking-fund factor*	*Present-worth factor*	*Capital-recovery factor*	
	To find F Given P F/P, r, t	*To find P Given F P/F, r, t*	*To find A Given A F/A, r, t*	*To find A Given F A/F, r, t*	*To find P Given A P/A, r, t*	*to find A Given P A/P, r, t*	*To find A Given G A/G, r, t*
26	11.918	0.0839	109.182	0.0092	9.1610	0.1092	7.6187
27	13.110	0.0763	121.100	0.0083	9.2372	0.1083	7.7704
28	14.421	0.0694	134.210	0.0075	9.3066	0.1075	7.9137
29	15.863	0.0630	148.631	0.0067	9.3696	0.1067	8.0489
30	17.449	0.0573	164.494	0.0061	9.4269	0.1061	8.1762
31	19.194	0.0521	181.943	0.0055	9.4790	0.1055	8.2962
32	21.114	0.0474	201.138	0.0050	9.5264	0.1050	8.4091
33	23.225	0.0431	222.252	0.0045	9.5694	0.1045	8.5152
34	25.548	0.0392	245.477	0.0041	9.6086	0.1041	8.6149
35	28.102	0.0356	271.024	0.0037	9.6442	0.1037	8.7086
40	45.259	0.0221	442.593	0.0023	9.7791	0.1023	9.0962
45	72.890	0.0137	718.905	0.0014	9.8628	0.1014	9.3741
50	117.391	0.0085	1163.909	0.0009	9.9148	0.1009	9.5704
55	189.059	0.0053	1880.591	0.0005	9.9471	0.1005	9.7075
60	304.482	0.0033	3034.816	0.0003	9.9672	0.1003	9.8023
65	490.371	0.0020	4893.707	0.0002	9.9796	0.1002	9.8672
70	789.747	0.0013	7887.470	0.0001	9.9873	0.1001	9.9113
75	1271.895	0.0008	12708.954	0.0001	9.9921	0.1001	9.9410
80	2048.400	0.0005	20474.002	0.0001	9.9951	0.1001	9.9609
85	3298.969	0.0003	32979.690	0.0000	9.9970	0.1000	9.9742
90	5313.023	0.0002	53210.226	0.0000	9.9981	0.1000	9.9831
95	8556.676	0.0001	85556.760	0.0000	9.9988	0.1000	9.9889
100	13780.612	0.0001	137796.123	0.0000	9.9993	0.1000	9.9928

TABLE A.15 11% INTEREST FACTORS FOR DISCRETE COMPOUNDING

t	*Single payment*		*Equal Payment Series*				*Uniform gradient-series factor*
	Compound-amount factor	*Present-worth factor*	*Compound-amount factor*	*Sinking-fund factor*	*Present-worth factor*	*Capital-recovery factor*	
	To find F Given P F/P, r, t	*To find P Given F P/F, r, t*	*To find F Given A F/A, r, t*	*To find A Given F A/F, r, t*	*To find P Given A P/A, r, t*	*To find A Given P A/P, r, t*	*To find A Given G A/G, r, t*
1	1.110	0.9009	1.000	1.000	0.9009	1.1100	0.0000
2	1.232	0.8116	2.110	0.4739	1.7125	0.5839	0.4739
3	1.368	0.7312	3.342	0.2992	2.4437	0.4092	0.9306
4	1.518	0.6587	4.710	0.2123	3.1024	0.3223	1.3700
5	1.685	0.5935	6.228	0.1606	3.6959	0.2706	1.7923
6	1.870	0.5346	7.913	0.1264	4.2305	0.2364	2.1976
7	2.076	0.4817	9.783	0.1022	4.7122	0.2122	2.5863
8	2.305	0.4339	11.859	0.0843	5.1461	0.1943	2.9585
9	2.558	0.3909	14.164	0.0706	5.5370	0.1806	3.3144
10	2.839	0.3522	16.722	0.0598	5.8892	0.1698	3.6544
11	3.152	0.3173	19.561	0.0511	6.2065	0.1611	3.9788
12	3.498	0.2858	22.713	0.0440	6.4924	0.1540	4.2879
13	3.883	0.2575	26.212	0.0382	6.7499	0.1482	4.5822
14	4.310	0.2320	30.095	0.0332	6.9819	0.1432	4.8619
15	4.785	0.2090	34.405	0.0291	7.1909	0.1391	5.1275
16	5.311	0.1883	39.190	0.0255	7.3972	0.1355	5.3794
17	5.895	0.1698	44.501	0.0225	7.5488	0.1325	5.6180
18	6.544	0.1528	50.396	0.0198	7.7016	0.1298	5.8439
19	7.263	0.1377	56.939	0.0176	7.8393	0.1276	6.0574
20	8.062	0.1240	64.203	0.0156	7.9633	0.1256	6.2590
21	8.949	0.1117	72.265	0.0138	8.0751	0.1238	6.4491
22	9.934	0.1007	81.214	0.0123	8.1757	0.1223	6.6283
23	11.026	0.0907	91.148	0.0110	8.2664	0.1210	6.7969
24	12.239	0.0817	102.174	0.0098	8.3481	0.1198	6.9555
25	13.585	0.0736	114.413	0.0087	8.4217	0.1187	7.1045

Contd...

t	*Single payment*		*Equal Payment Series*				*Uniform gradient-series factor*
	Compound-amount factor	*Present-worth factor*	*Compound-amount factor*	*Sinking-fund factor*	*Present-worth factor*	*Capital-recovery factor*	
	To find F Given P F/P, r, t	*To find P Given F P/F, r, t*	*To find F Given A F/A, r, t*	*To find A Given F A/F, r, t*	*To find P Given A P/A, r, t*	*To find A Given P A/P, r, t*	*To find A Given G A/G, r, t*
26	15.080	0.0663	127.999	0.0078	8.4881	0.1178	7.2443
27	16.739	0.0597	143.079	0.0070	8.5478	0.1170	7.3754
28	18.580	0.0638	159.517	0.0063	8.6016	0.1163	7.4982
29	20.624	0.0485	178.397	0.0056	8.6501	0.1156	7.6131
30	22.892	0.0437	199.021	0.0050	8.6938	0.1150	7.7206
31	25.410	0.0394	221.913	0.0045	8.7331	0.1145	7.8210
32	28.206	0.0355	247.324	0.0040	8.7686	0.1140	7.9147
33	31.308	0.0319	275.529	0.0036	8.8005	0.1136	8.0021
34	34.752	0.0288	306.837	0.0033	8.8293	0.1133	8.0836
35	38.575	0.0259	341.590	0.0029	8.8552	0.1129	8.7594
40	65.001	0.0154	581.827	0.0017	8.9211	0.1117	8.4759
45	109.530	0.0091	986.639	0.0010	9.0079	0.1110	8.6763
50	184.565	0.0054	1668.771	0.0006	9.0417	0.1106	8.8185

TABLE A.16 12% INTEREST FACTORS FOR DISCRETE COMPOUNDING

t	*Single payment*		*Equal Payment Series*				*Uniform gradient-series factor*
	Compound-amount factor	*Present-worth factor*	*Compound-amount factor*	*Sinking-fund factor*	*Present-worth factor*	*Capital-recovery factor*	
	To find F Given P F/P, r, t	*To find P Given F P/F, r, t*	*To find F Given A F/A, r, t*	*To find A Given F A/F, r, t*	*To find P Given A P/A, r, t*	*To find A Given P A/P, r, t*	*To find A Given G A/G, r, t*
1	1.120	0.8929	1.000	1.0000	0.8929	1.1200	0.0000
2	1.254	0.7972	2.120	0.4717	1.6901	0.5917	0.4717
3	1.405	0.7118	3.374	0.2964	2.4018	0.4164	0.9246
4	1.574	0.6355	4.779	0.2092	3.0374	0.3292	1.3589
5	1.762	0.5674	6.353	0.1574	3.6048	0.2774	1.7748
6	1.974	0.50166	8.115	0.1232	4.1114	0.2432	2.1721
7	2.211	0.4524	10.089	0.0991	4.5638	0.2191	2.5515
8	2.476	0.4039	12.300	0.0813	4.9676	0.2013	2.9132
9	2.773	0.3606	14.776	0.0677	5.3283	0.1877	3.2574
10	3.106	0.3220	17.549	0.0670	5.6502	0.1770	3.5847
11	3.479	0.2875	20.655	0.0484	5.9377	0.1684	3.8953
12	3.896	0.2567	24.133	0.0414	6.1944	0.1614	4.1891
13	4.364	0.2292	28.029	0.0357	6.42366	0.1557	4.4683
14	4.887	0.2046	32.393	0.0309	6.6282	0.15.9	4.7317
15	5.474	0.1827	37.280	0.0268	6.8109	0.1468	4.9803
16	6.130	0.1631	42.753	0.0234	6.9740	0.1434	5.2147
17	6.866	0.1457	48.884	0.0206	7.1196	0.1405	5.4353
18	7.690	0.1300	55.750	0.0179	7.2497	0.1379	5.6427
19	8.613	0.1161	63.440	0.0158	7.3608	0.1368	5.8375
20	9.646	0.1037	72.050	0.0139	7.4695	0.1339	6.0202
21	10.804	0.0926	81.699	0.0123	7.5620	0.1323	6.1913
22	12.100	0.0827	92.503	0.0108	7.6447	0.1308	6.3514
23	13.552	0.0738	104.603	0.0096	7.7184	0.1296	6.5010
24	15.179	0.0659	118.155	0.0085	7.7843	0.1285	6.6407
25	17.000	0.0588	133.334	0.0075	7.8431	0.1275	6.7708

Contd...

t	*Single payment*		*Equal Payment Series*				*Uniform gradient-series factor*
	Compound-amount factor	*Present-worth factor*	*Compound-amount factor*	*Sinking-fund factor*	*Present-worth factor*	*Capital-recovery factor*	
	To find F Given P F/P, r, t	*To find P Given F P/F, r, t*	*To find F Given A F/A, r, t*	*To find A Given F A/F, r, t*	*To find P Given A P/A, r, t*	*To find A Given P A/P, r, t*	*To find A Given G A/G, r, t*
26	19.040	0.0525	150.334	0.0067	7.8957	0.1267	6.8921
27	21.325	0.0469	169.374	0.0059	7.9426	0.1259	7.0049
28	23.884	0.0419	190.699	0.0053	7.9844	0.1253	7.1098
29	26.750	0.0374	214.583	0.0047	8.0218	0.1247	7.2071
30	29.960	0.0334	241.333	0.0042	8.0552	0.1242	7.2974
31	33.555	0.0298	271.293	0.0037	8.0850	0.1237	7.3811
32	37.582	0.0266	304.848	0.0033	8.1116	0.1233	7.4586
33	42.092	0.0238	342.429	0.0029	8.1354	0.1229	7.5303
34	47.143	0.0212	384.521	0.0026	8.1566	0.1226	7.5965
35	52.800	0.0189	431.664	0.0023	8.1755	0.1223	7.6677
40	93.051	0.0108	767.091	0.0013	8.2438	0.1213	7.8988
45	163.988	0.0061	1358.230	0.0007	8.2825	0.1207	8.0572
50	289.002	0.0035	2400.018	0.0004	8.3045	0.1204	8.1597

TABLE A.17 13% INTEREST FACTORS FOR DISCRETE COMPOUNDING

t	*Single payment*		*Equal Payment Series*				*Uniform gradient-series factor*
	Compound-amount factor	*Present-worth factor*	*Compound-amount factor*	*Sinking-fund factor*	*Present-worth factor*	*Capital-recovery factor*	
	To find F Given P F/P, r, t	*To find P Given F P/F, r, t*	*To find F Given A F/A, r, t*	*To find A Given F A/F, r, t*	*To find P Given A P/A, r, t*	*To find A Given P A/P, r, t*	*To find A Given G A/G, r, t*
1	1.130	0.8850	1.000	1.0000	0.8850	1.1300	0.0000
2	1.277	0.7831	2.130	0.4695	1.6681	0.5995	0.4695
3	1.443	0.6931	3.407	0.2935	2.3612	0.4235	0.9187
4	1.630	0.6133	4.850	0.2062	2.9745	0.3362	1.3479
5	1.842	0.5428	6.480	0.1543	3.5172	0.2843	1.7571
6	2.082	0.4803	8.323	0.1202	3.9975	0.2502	2.1468
7	2.353	0.4251	10.406	0.0961	4.4226	0.2261	2.5171
8	2.658	0.3762	12.757	0.0784	4.7988	0.2084	2.8685
9	3.004	0.3329	15.416	0.0649	5.1317	0.1949	3.2014
10	3.395	0.2946	18.420	0.0543	5.4262	0.1843	3.5162
11	3.836	0.2607	21.814	0.0458	5.6869	0.1758	3.8134
12	4.335	0.2307	25.650	0.0390	5.9176	0.1690	4.0936
13	4.898	0.2042	29.985	0.0334	6.1218	0.1634	4.3673
14	5.535	0.1807	34.883	0.0287	6.3025	0.1587	4.6050
15	6.254	0.1599	40.417	0.0247	6.4624	0.1547	4.8375
16	7.067	0.1415	46.672	0.0214	6.6039	0.1514	5.0552
17	7.986	0.1252	53.739	0.0186	6.7291	0.1486	5.2589
18	9.024	0.1108	61.725	0.0162	6.8399	0.1462	5.4491
19	10.197	0.0981	70.749	0.0141	6.9380	0.1441	5.6266
20	11.523	0.0868	80.947	0.0124	7.0248	0.1424	5.7917
21	13.021	0.0768	92.470	0.0108	7.1016	0.1408	5.9454
22	14.714	0.0680	105.491	0.0095	7.1695	0.1395	6.0881
23	16.627	0.0601	120.205	0.0083	7.2297	0.1383	6.2206
24	18.788	0.0532	136.831	0.0073	7.2829	0.1373	6.3431
25	21.231	0.0471	155.620	0.0064	7.3300	0.1364	6.4566

Contd...

t	*Single payment*		*Equal Payment Series*				*Uniform gradient-series factor*
	Compound-amount factor	*Present-worth factor*	*Compound-amount factor*	*Sinking-fund factor*	*Present-worth factor*	*Capital-recovery factor*	
	To find F Given P F/P, r, t	*To find P Given F P/F, r, t*	*To find F Given A F/A, r, t*	*To find A Given F A/F, r, t*	*To find P Given A P/A, r, t*	*To find A Given P A/P, r, t*	*To find A Given G A/G, r, t*
26	23.991	0.0417	176.850	0.0057	7.3717	0.1357	6.5614
27	27.109	0.0369	200.841	0.0050	7.4086	0.1350	6.6582
28	30.633	0.0326	227.950	0.0044	7.4412	0.1344	6.7474
29	34.616	0.0289	258.583	0.0039	7.4701	0.1339	6.8296
30	39.116	0.0256	293.199	0.0034	7.4957	0.1334	6.9052
31	44.201	0.226	332.315	0.0030	7.5183	0.1330	6.9747
32	49.947	0.0200	376.516	0.0027	7.5383	0.1327	7.0385
33	56.440	0.0177	426.463	0.0023	7.5560	0.1323	7.0971
34	63.777	0.0157	482.903	0.0021	7.5717	0.1321	7.1507
35	72.069	0.0139	546.681	0.0018	7.5856	0.1318	7.1998
40	132.782	0.0075	1013.704	0.0010	7.6344	0.1310	7.3888
45	244.641	0.0041	1874.165	0.0005	7.6609	0.1305	7.5078
50	450.736	0.0022	3459.507	0.0003	7.6752	0.1303	7.5811

TABLE A. 18 14% INTEREST FACTORS FOR DISCRETE COMPOUNDING

t	*Single Payment*		*Equal Payment Series*				*Uniform gradient-series factor*
	Compound-amount factor	*Present-worth factor*	*Compound-amount factor*	*Sinking-fund factor*	*Present-worth factor*	*Capital-recovery factor*	
	To find F Given P F/P, r, t	*To find P Given F P/F, r, t*	*To find F Given A F/A, r, t*	*To find A Given F A/F, r, t*	*To find P Given A P/A, r, t*	*To find A Given P A/P, r, t*	*To find A Given G A/G, r, t*
1	1.140	0.8772	1.000	1.000	0.8772	1.1400	0.0000
2	1.300	0.7695	2.140	0.4673	1.6467	0.6073	0.4673
3	1.482	0.6750	3.440	0.2907	2.3216	0.4307	0.9129
4	1.689	0.5921	4.921	0.2032	2.9137	0.3432	1.3370
5	1.925	0.5194	6.610	0.1513	3.4331	0.2913	1.7399
6	2.195	0.4556	8.536	0.1172	3.8887	0.2572	2.1218
7	2.502	0.3996	10.730	0.0932	4.2883	0.2332	2.4832
8	2.853	0.3506	13.233	0.0756	4.6389	0.2156	2.8246
9	3.252	0.3075	16.085	0.0622	4.9464	0.2022	3.1463
10	3.707	0.2697	19.337	0.0517	5.2161	0.1917	3.4490
11	4.226	0.2366	23.045	0.0434	5.4527	0.1834	3.7333
12	4.818	0.2076	27.271	0.0367	5.6603	0.1767	3.9998
13	5.492	0.1821	32.089	0.0312	5.8424	0.1712	4.2491
14	6.261	0.1597	37.581	0.0266	6.0021	0.1666	4.4819
15	7.138	0.1401	43.842	0.0228	6.1422	0.1628	4.6990
16	8.317	0.1229	50.980	0.0196	6.2651	0.1596	4.9011
17	9.276	0.1078	59.118	0.0169	6.3729	0.1569	5.0888
18	10.575	0.0946	68.394	0.0146	6.4674	0.1546	5.2630
19	12.056	0.0829	78.969	0.0127	6.5504	0.1527	5.4243
20	13.743	0.0728	91.025	0.0110	6.6231	0.1510	5.5734
21	15.668	0.0638	104.768	0.0095	6.6870	0.1495	5.7111
22	17.861	0.0560	120.436	0.0083	6.7429	0.1483	5.8381
23	20.362	0.0491	138.297	0.0072	6.7921	0.1472	5.9549
24	23.212	0.0431	158.659	0.0063	6.8351	0.1463	6.0624
25	26.462	0.0378	181.871	0.0055	6.8729	0.1455	6.1610

Contd...

t	*Single Payment*		*Equal Payment Series*				*Uniform gradient-series factor*
	Compound-amount factor	*Present-worth factor*	*Compound-amount factor*	*Sinking-fund factor*	*Present-worth factor*	*Capital-recovery factor*	
	To find F Given P F/P, r, t	*To find P Given F P/F, r, t*	*To find F Given A F/A, r, t*	*To find A Given F A/F, r, t*	*To find P Given A P/A, r, t*	*To find A Given P A/P, r, t*	*To find A Given G A/G, r, t*
26	30.167	0.0331	208.333	0.0048	6.9061	0.1448	6.2514
27	34.390	0.0291	238.499	0.0042	6.9352	0.1442	6.3342
28	39.204	0.0255	272.889	0.0037	6.9607	0.1437	6.4100
29	44.693	0.0224	312.094	0.0032	6.9830	0.1432	6.4791
30	50.950	0.0196	356.787	0.0028	7.0027	0.1428	6.5423
31	58.083	0.0172	407.737	0.0025	7.0199	0.1425	6.5998
32	66.215	0.0151	465.820	0.0021	7.0350	0.1421	6.6522
33	75.485	0.0132	532.035	0.0019	7.0482	0.1419	6.6998
34	86.053	0.0116	607.520	0.0016	7.0599	0.1416	6.7431
35	98.100	0.0102	693.573	0.0014	7.0700	0.1414	6.7824
40	188.884	0.0053	1342.025	0.0007	7.1050	0.1407	6.9300
45	363.679	0.0027	2590.565	0.0004	7.1232	0.1404	7.0188
50	700.233	0.0014	4994.521	0.0002	7.1327	0.1402	7.0714

TABLE A.19 15% INTEREST FACTORS FOR DISCRETE COMPOUNDING

t	*Single Payment*		*Equal Payment Series*				*Uniform gradient-series factor*
	Compound-amount factor	*Present-worth factor*	*Compound-amount factor*	*Sinking-fund factor*	*Present-worth factor*	*Capital-recovery factor*	
	To find F Given P F/P, r, t	*To find P Given F P/F, r, t*	*To find F Given A F/A, r, t*	*To find A Given F A/F, r, t*	*To find P Given A P/A, r, t*	*To find A Given P A/P, r, t*	*To find A Given G A/G, r, t*
1	1.150	0.8696	1.000	1.0000	0.8696	1.1500	0.0000
2	1.323	0.7562	2.150	0.4651	1.6257	0.6151	0.4651
3	1.521	0.6575	3.473	0.2880	2.2832	0.4380	0.9071
4	1.749	0.5718	4.993	0.2003	2.8550	0.3503	1.3263
5	2.011	0.4972	6.742	0.1483	3.3522	0.2983	1.7228
6	2.313	0.4323	8.754	0.1142	3.7845	0.2642	2.0972
7	2.660	0.3759	11.067	0.0904	4.1604	0.2404	2.4499
8	3.059	0.3269	13.727	0.0729	4.4873	0.2229	2.7813
9	3.518	0.2843	16.786	0.0596	4.7716	0.2096	3.0922
10	4.046	0.1229	20.304	0.0493	5.0188	0.1993	0.3832
11	4.652	0.2150	24.349	0.0411	5.2337	0.1911	3.6550
12	5.350	0.1869	29.002	0.0345	5.4206	0.1845	3.9082
13	6.153	0.1625	34.352	0.0291	5.5832	0.1791	4.1438
14	7.076	0.1413	40.505	0.0247	5.7245	0.1747	4.3624
15	8.137	0.1229	47.580	0.0210	5.8474	0.1710	4.5650
16	9.358	0.1069	55.717	0.0180	5.9542	0.1680	4.7523
17	10.761	0.0929	65.075	0.0154	6.0472	0.1654	4.9251
18	12.375	0.0808	75.836	0.0132	6.1280	0.1632	5.0843
19	14.232	0.0703	88.212	0.0113	6.1982	0.1613	5.2307
20	16.367	0.0611	102.444	0.0098	6.2593	0.1598	5.3651
21	18.822	0.0531	118.810	0.0084	6.3125	0.1584	5.4883
22	21.645	0.0462	137.632	0.0073	6.3587	0.1573	5.6010
23	24.891	0.0402	159.276	0.0063	6.3988	0.1563	5.7040
24	28.625	0.0349	184.168	0.0054	6.4338	0.1554	5.7979
25	32.919	0.0304	212.793	0.0047	6.4642	0.1547	5.8834

Contd...

t	*Single Payment*		*Equal Payment Series*				*Uniform gradient-series factor*
	Compound-amount factor	*Present-worth factor*	*Compound-amount factor*	*Sinking-fund factor*	*Present-worth factor*	*Capital-recovery factor*	
	To find F Given P F/P, r, t	*To find P Given F P/F, r, t*	*To find F Given A F/A, r, t*	*To find A Given F A/F, r, t*	*To find P Given A P/A, r, t*	*To find A Given P A/P, r, t*	*To find A Given G A/G, r, t*
26	37.857	0.0264	245.712	0.0041	6.4906	0.1541	5.9612
27	43.535	0.0230	283.569	0.0035	6.5135	0.1535	6.0319
28	50.066	0.0200	327.104	0.0031	6.5335	0.1531	6.0960
29	57.575	0.0174	377.170	0.0027	6.5509	0.1527	6.1541
30	66.212	0.0151	434.745	0.0023	6.5660	0.1523	6.2066
31	76.144	0.0131	500.957	0.0020	6.5791	0.1520	6.2541
32	87.565	0.0114	577.100	0.0017	6.5905	0.1517	6.2970
33	100.700	0:0099	664.666	0.0015	6.6005	0.1515	6.3357
34	115.805	0.0086	765.365	0.0013	6.6091	0.1513	6.3705
35	133.176	0.0075	881.170	0.0011	6.6166	0.1511	6.4019
40	267.864	0.0037	1779.090	0.0006	6.6418	0.1506	6.5168
45	538.769	0.0019	3585.128	0.0003	6.6543	0.1503	6.5830
50	1083.657	0.0009	7217.716	0.0002	6.6605	0.1501	6.6205

TABLE A. 20 16% INTEREST FACTORS FOR DISCRETE COMPOUNDING

t	*Single Payment*		*Equal Payment Series*				*Uniform gradient-series factor*
	Compound-amount factor	*Present-worth factor*	*Compound-amount factor*	*Sinking-fund factor*	*Present-worth factor*	*Capital-recovery factor*	
	To find F Given P F/P, r, t	*To find P Given F P/F, r, t*	*To find F Given A F/A, r, t*	*To find A Given F A/F, r, t*	*To find P Given A P/A r, t*	*To find A Given P A/P, r, t*	*To find A Given G A/G, r, t*
1	1.160	0.8621	1.000	1.0000	0.8621	1.1600	0.0000
2	1.346	0.7432	2.160	0.4630	1.6052	0.6230	0.4630
3	1.561	0.6407	3.506	0.2853	2.2459	0.4453	0.9014
4	1.811	0.5523	5.066	0.1974	2.7982	0.3574	1.3156
5	2.100	0.4761	6.877	0.1454	3.2743	0.3054	1.7060
6	2.436	0.4104	8.977	0.1114	3.6847	0.2714	2.0729
7	2.836	0.3538	11.414	0.0876	4.0386	0.2476	2.4170
8	3.278	0.3050	14.240	0.0702	4.3436	0.2302	2.7388
9	3.803	0.2630	17.519	0.571	4.6065	0.2171	3.0391
10	4.411	0.2267	21.321	0.0469	4.8332	0.2069	3.3187
11	5.117	0.1954	25.733	0.0389	5.0286	0.1989	3.5783
12	5.936	0.1685	30.850	0.0324	5.1971	0.1924	3.8189
13	6.886	0.1452	36.786	0.0272	5.3423	0.1872	4.0413
14	7.988	0.1252	43.672	0.0229	5.4675	0.1829	4.2464
15	9.268	0.1079	51.660	0.0194	5.5755	0.1794	4.4352
16	10.748	0.0930	60.925	0.0164	5.6685	0.1764	4.6086
17	12.468	0.0802	71.673	0.0140	5.7487	0.1740	4.7676
18	14.463	0.0691	84.141	0.0119	5.8178	0.1719	4.9130
19	16.777	0.0596	98.603	0.0101	5.8775	0.1701	5.0457
20	19.461	0.0514	115.380	0.0087	5.9288	0.1687	5.1666
21	22.574	0.0443	134.841	0.0074	5.9731	0.1674	5.2766
22	26.186	0.0382	157.415	0.0064	6.0113	0.1664	5.3765
23	30.376	0.0329	183.601	0.0054	6.0442	0.1654	5.4671
24	35.236	0.0284	213.978	0.0047	6.0726	0.1647	5.5490
25	40.874	0.0245	249.214	0.0040	6.0971	0.1640	5.6230

Contd...

t	*Single Payment*		*Equal Payment Series*				*Uniform gradient-series factor*
	Compound-amount factor	*Present-worth factor*	*Compound-amount factor*	*Sinking-fund factor*	*Present-worth factor*	*Capital-recovery factor*	
	To find F Given P F/P, r, t	*To find P Given F P/F, r, t*	*To find F Given A F/A, r, t*	*To find A Given F A/F, r, t*	*To find P Given A P/A r, t*	*To find A Given P A/P, r, t*	*To find A Given G A/G, r, t*
26	47.414	0.0211	290.088	0.0034	6.1182	0.1634	5.6898
27	55.000	0.0182	337.502	0.0030	6.1364	0.1630	5.7500
28	63.800	0.0157	392.503	0.0025	6.1520	0.1625	5.8041
29	74.009	0.0135	456.303	0.0022	6.1656	0.1622	5.8528
30	85.850	0.0116	530.312	0.0019	6.1772	0.1619	5.8964
31	99.586	0.0100	616.162	0.0016	6.1872	0.1616	5.9356
32	115.520	0.0087	715.747	0.0014	6.1959	0.1614	5.9706
33	134.003	0.0075	831.267	0.0012	6.2034	0.1612	6.0019
34	155.443	0.0064	965.270	0.0010	6.2098	0.1610	6.0299
35	180.314	0.0055	120.713	0.0009	6.2153	0.1609	6.0548
40	378.721	0.0026	2360.757	0.0004	6.2335	0.1604	6.1441
45	795.444	0.0013	4965.274	0.0002	6.2421	0.1602	6.1934
50	1670.704	0.0006	10435.649	0.0001	6.2463	0.1601	6.2201

TABLE A.21 17% INTEREST FACTORS FOR DISCRETE COMPOUNDIN

t	*Single Payment*		*Equal payment Series*				*Uniform gradient-series factor*
	Compound-amount factor	*Present-worth factor*	*Compound-amount factor*	*Sinking fund factor*	*Present -worth factor*	*Capital-recovery factor*	
	To find F Given P F/P, r, t	*To find P Given F P/F, r, t*	*To find F Given A F/A, r, t*	*To find A Given F A/F, r, t*	*To find P Given A P/A, r, t*	*To find A Given P A/P, r, t*	*To find A Given G A/G, r, t*
1	1.170	0.8547	1.000	1.0000	0.8547	1.1700	0.0000
2	1.369	0.7305	2.170	0.4608	1.5852	0.6308	0.4608
3	1.602	0.6244	3.539	0.2826	2.2096	0.4526	0.8958
4	1.874	0.5337	5.141	0.1945	2.7432	0.3645	1.3051
5	2.192	0.4561	7.014	0.1426	3.1993	0.3126	1.6893
6	2.565	0.3898	9.207	0.1086	3.5892	0.2786	2.0489
7	3.001	0.3332	11.772	0.0849	3.9224	0.2549	2.3845
8	3.511	0.2848	14.773	0.0677	4.2072	0.2377	2.6969
9	4.108	0.2434	18.285	0.0547	4.4506	0.2247	2.9870
10	4.807	0.2080	22.393	0.0447	4.6586	0.2147	3.2555
11	5.624	0.1778	27.200	0.0368	4.8364	0.2068	3.5035
12	6.580	0.1520	32.824	0.0305	4.9884	0.2005	3.7318
13	7.699	0.1299	39.404	0.0254	5.1183	0.1954	3.9417
14	9.007	0.1110	47.103	0.0212	5.2293	0.1912	4.1340
15	10.539	0.0949	56.110	0.0178	5.3242	0.1878	4.3098
16	12.330	0.0811	66.649	0.0150	5.4053	0.1850	4.4702
17	14.426	0.0693	78.979	0.0127	5.4746	0.1827	4.6162
18	16.679	0.0592	93.406	0.0107	5.5339	0.1807	4.7488
19	19.748	0.0506	110.285	0.0091	5.5845	0.1791	4.8689
20	23.106	0.0433	130.033	0.0077	5.6278	0.1777	4.9776
21	27.034	0.0370	153.139	0.0065	5.6648	0.1765	0.0757
22	31.629	0.0316	180.172	0.0056	5.6964	0.1756	5.1641
23	37.006	0.0270	211.801	0.0047	5.7234	0.1747	5.2436
24	43.297	0.0231	248.808	0.0040	5.7465	0.1740	5.3149
25	50.658	0.0197	292.105	0.0034	5.7662	0.1734	5.3789

Contd...

t	*Single Payment*		*Equal payment Series*				*Uniform gradient-series factor*
	Compound-amount factor	*Present-worth factor*	*Compound-amount factor*	*Sinking fund factor*	*Present -worth factor*	*Capital-recovery factor*	
	To find F Given P F/P, r, t	*To find P Given F P/F, r, t*	*To find F Given A F/A, r, t*	*To find A Given F A/F, r, t*	*To find P Given A P/A, r, t*	*To find A Given P A/P, r, t*	*To find A Given G A/G, r, t*
26	59.270	0.0169	342.763	0.0029	5.7831	0.1729	5.4362
27	69.345	0.0144	402.032	0.0025	5.7975	0.1725	5.4873
28	81.134	0.0123	471.378	0.0021	5.8099	0.1721	5.5329
29	94.927	0.0105	552.512	0.0018	5.8204	0.1718	5.5736
30	111.065	0.0090	647.439	0.0015	5.8294	0.1715	5.6098
31	129.946	0.0077	758.504	0.0013	5.8371	0.1713	5.6419
32	152.036	0.0066	888.449	0.0011	5.8437	0.1711	5.6705
33	177.883	0.0056	1040.486	0.0010	5.8493	0.1710	5.6958
34	208.123	0.0048	1218.368	0.0008	5.8541	0.1708	5.7182
35	243.503	0.0041	1426.491	0.0007	5.8582	0.1707	5.7380
40	533.869	0.0019	3134.522	0.0003	5.8713	0.1703	5.8073
45	1170.479	0.0009	6879.291	0.0001	5.8773	0.1701	5.8439
50	2566.215	0.0004	15089.502	0.0001	5.8801	0.1701	5.8629

TABLE A.22 18% INTEREST FACTORS FOR DISCRETE COMPOUNDING

t	*Single Payment*		*Equal Payment Series*				*Uniform gradient-series factor*
	Compound-amount factor	*Present-worth factor*	*Compound-amount factor*	*Sinking-fund factor*	*Present-worth factor*	*Capital-recovery factor*	
	To find F Given P F/P, r, t	*To find P Given F P/F, r, t*	*To find F Given A F/A, r, t*	*To find A Given F A/F, r, t*	*To find P Given A P/A, r, t*	*To find A Given P A/P, r, t*	*To find A Given G A/G, r, t*
1	1.180	0.8475	1.000	1.0000	0.8475	1.1800	0.0000
2	1.392	0.7182	2.180	0.4587	1.5656	0.6387	0.4587
3	1.643	0.6086	3.572	0.2799	2.1743	0.4599	0.8902
4	1.939	0.5158	5.215	0.1917	2.6901	0.317	1.2947
5	2.288	0.4371	7.154	0.1398	3.1272	0.3198	1.6728
6	2.700	0.3704	9.442	0.1059	3.4976	0.2859	2.0252
7	3.185	0.3139	12.142	0.0824	3.8115	0.2624	2.3526
8	3.759	0.2660	15.327	0.0652	4.0776	0.2452	2.6558
9	4.435	0.2255	19.086	0.0524	4.3030	0.2324	2.9358
10	5.234	0.1911	23.521	0.0425	4.4941	0.2225	3.1936
11	6.176	0.1619	28.755	0.0348	4.6560	0.2148	3.4303
12	7.288	0.1372	34.931	0.0286	4.7932	0.2086	3.6470
13	8.599	0.1163	42.219	0.0237	4.9095	0.2037	3.8449
14	10.147	0.0985	50.818	0.0197	5.0081	0.1997	4.0250
15	11.974	0.0835	60.965	0.0164	5.0916	0.1964	4.1887
16	14.129	0.0708	72.939	0.0137	5.1624	0.1937	4.3369
17	16.672	0.0600	87.068	0.0115	5.2223	0.1915	4.4708
18	19.673	0.0508	103.740	0.0096	5.2732	0.1896	4.5916
19	23.214	0.0431	123.414	0.0081	5.3162	0.1881	4.7003
20	27.393	0.0365	146.628	0.0068	5.3527	0.1868	4.7978
21	32.324	0.0309	174.021	0.0057	5.3837	0.1857	4.8851
22	38.142	0.0262	206.345	0.0048	5.4099	0.1848	4.9632
23	45.008	0.0222	244.487	0.0041	5.4321	0.1841	5.0329
24	53.109	0.0188	289.494	0.0035	5.4509	0.1835	5.0950
25	62.669	0.0160	342.603	0.0029	5.4669	0.1829	5.1502

Contd...

t	Single Payment		Equal Payment Series				Uniform gradient-series factor
	Compound-amount factor	Present-worth factor	Compound-amount factor	Sinking-fund factor	Present-worth factor	Capital-recovery factor	
	To find F Given P F/P, r, t	To find P Given F P/F, r, t	To find F Given A F/A, r, t	To find A Given F A/F, r, t	To find P Given A P/A, r, t	To find A Given P A/P, r, t	To find A Given G A/G, r, t
26	73.949	0.0135	405.272	0.0025	5.4804	0.1825	5.1991
27	87.260	0.0115	479.221	0.0021	5.4919	0.1821	5.2425
28	102.967	0.0097	566.481	0.0018	5.5016	0.1818	5.2810
29	121.501	0.0082	669.447	0.0015	5.5098	0.1815	5.3149
30	143.371	0.0070	790.948	0.0013	5.5168	0.1813	5.3448
31	169.177	0.0059	934.319	0.0011	5.5227	0.1811	5.3712
32	199.629	0.0050	1103.496	0.0009	5.5277	0.1809	5.3945
33	235.563	0.0042	1303.125	0.0008	5.5320	0.1808	5.4149
34	277.964	0.0036	1538.688	0.0006	5.5356	0.1806	5.4328
35	327.997	0.0030	1816.642	0.0006	5.5386	0.1806	5.4485
40	750.378	0.0013	4163.213	0.0002	5.5482	0.1802	5.5022
45	1716.684	0.0006	9531.577	0.0001	5.5523	0.1801	5.5293
50	3927.357	0.0003	21813.094	0.0001	5.5541	0.1801	5.5428

TABLE A.23 19% INTEREST FACTORS FOR DISCRETE COMPOUNDING

t	*Single Payment*		*Equal Payment Series*				*Uniform gradient-series factor*
	Compound-amount factor	*Present-worth factor*	*Compound-amount factor*	*Sinking-fund factor*	*Present-worth factor*	*Capital-recovery factor*	
	To find F Given P F/P, r, t	*To find P Given F P/F, r, t*	*To find F Given A F/A, r, t*	*To find A Given F A/F, r, t*	*To find P Given A P/A, rt*	*To find A Given P A/P, r, t*	*To find A given G A/G, r, t*
1	1.190	0.8403	1.000	1.0000	0.8403	1.1900	0.0000
2	1.416	0.7062	2.190	0.4566	1.5465	0.6466	0.4566
3	1.685	0.5934	3.606	0.2773	2.1399	0.4673	0.8846
4	2.005	0.4987	5.291	0.1890	2.6386	0.3790	1.2844
5	2.386	0.4190	7.297	0.1371	3.0576	0.3271	1.6566
6	2.840	0.3521	8.683	0.1033	3.4098	0.2933	2.0019
7	3.379	0.2959	12.523	0.0799	3.7057	0.2699	2.3211
8	4.021	0.2487	15.902	0.0629	3.9544	0.2529	2.6154
9	4.785	0.2090	19.923	0.0502	4.1633	0.2402	2.8856
10	5.695	0.1756	24.709	0.0405	4.3389	0.2305	3.1331
11	6.777	0.1476	30.404	0.0329	4.4865	0.2229	3.3589
12	8.064	0.1240	37.180	0.0269	4.6105	0.2169	3.5645
13	9.596	0.1042	45.244	0.0221	4.7147	0.2121	3.7509
14	11.420	0.0876	54.841	0.0182	4.8023	0.2082	3.9196
15	13.590	0.0736	66.261	0.0151	4.8759	0.2051	4.0717
16	16.172	0.0618	79.850	0.0125	4.9377	0.2025	4.2088
17	19.244	0.0520	96.022	0.0104	5.9897	0.2004	4.3314
18	22.901	0.0437	115.266	0.0087	5.0333	0.1987	4.4413
19	27.252	0.0367	138.166	0.0072	5.0700	0.1972	4.5394
20	32.429	0.0308	165.418	0.0060	5.1009	0.1960	4.6268
21	38.591	0.0259	197.847	0.0051	5.1268	0.1951	4.7045
22	45.923	0.0218	236.438	0.0042	5.1486	0.1942	4.7734
23	54.649	0.0183	282.362	0.0035	5.1668	0.1935	4.8344
24	65.032	0.0154	337.011	0.0030	5.1822	0.1930	4.8883
25	77.388	0.0129	402.032	0.0025	5.1951	0.1925	4.9359

Contd...

t	*Single Payment*		*Equal Payment Series*				*Uniform gradient-series factor*
	Compound-amount factor	*Present-worth factor*	*Compound-amount factor*	*Sinking-fund factor*	*Present-worth factor*	*Capital-recovery factor*	
	To find F Given P F/P, r, t	*To find P Given F P/F, r, t*	*To find F Given A F/A, r, t*	*To find A Given F A/F, r, t*	*To find P Given A P/A, rt*	*To find A Given P A/P, r, t*	*To find A given G A/G, r, t*
26	92.092	0.0109	479.431	0.0021	5.2060	0.1921	4.9777
27	109.589	0.0091	571.522	0.0017	5.2151	0.1917	5.0145
28	130.411	0.0077	681.112	0.0015	5.2228	0.1915	5.0468
29	155.189	0.0064	811.523	0.0012	5.2292	0.1912	5.0751
30	184.675	0.0054	966.712	0.0010	5.2347	0.1910	5.0998
31	219.764	0.0046	1151.388	0.0009	5.2392	0.1909	5.1215
32	261.519	0.0038	1371.151	0.0007	5.2430	0.1907	5.1403
33	311.207	0.0032	1632.670	0.0006	5.2462	0.1906	5.1568
34	370.337	0.0027	1943.877	0.0005	5.2489	0.1905	5.1711
35	440.701	0.0023	2314.214	0.0004	5.2512	0.1904	5.1836
40	1051.668	0.0010	5529.829	0.0002	5.2582	0.1902	5.2251
45	2509.651	0.0004	13203.424	0.0001	5.2611	0.1901	5.2452
50	5988.914	0.0002	31515.336	0.0000	5.2623	0.1900	5.2548

TABLE A.24 20% INTEREST FACTORS FOR DISCRETE COMPOUNDING

t	*Single Payment*		*Equal Payment Series*				*Uniform gradient-series factor*
	Compound-amount factor	*Present-worth factor*	*Compound-amount factor*	*Sinking-fund factor*	*Present-worth factor*	*Capital-recovery factor*	
	To find F Given P F/P, r, t	*To find P Given F P/F, r, t*	*To find F Given A F/A, r, t*	*To find A Given F A/F, r, t*	*To find P Given A P/A, r, t*	*To find A Given P A/P, r, t*	*To find A Given G A/G, r, t*
1	1.200	0.8333	1.000	1.0000	0.8333	1.2000	0.0000
2	1.440	0.6945	2.200	0.4546	1.5278	0.6546	0.4546
3	1.728	0.5787	3.640	0.2747	2.1065	0.4747	0.8791
4	2.074	0.4823	5.368	0.1863	2.5887	0.3863	1.2742
5	2.488	0.4019	7.442	0.1344	2.9906	0.3344	1.6405
6	2.986	0.3349	9.930	0.1007	3.3255	0.3007	1.9788
7	3.583	0.2791	12.916	0.0774	3.6046	0.2774	2.2902
8	4.300	0.2326	16.499	0.0606	3.8372	0.2606	2.5756
9	5.160	0.1938	20.799	0.0481	4.0310	0.2481	2.8364
10	6.192	0.1615	25.959	0.0385	4.1925	0.2385	3.0739
11	7.430	0.1346	32.150	0.0311	4.3271	0.2311	3.2893
12	8.916	0.1122	39.581	0.0253	4.4392	0.2253	3.4841
13	10.699	0.0935	48.497	0.0206	4.5327	0.2206	3.6597
14	12.839	0.0779	59.196	0.0169	4.6106	0.2169	3.8175
15	15.407	0.0649	72.035	0.0139	4.6755	0.2139	3.9589
16	18.488	0.0541	87.442	0.0114	4.4796	0.2114	4.0851
17	22.186	0.0451	105.931	0.0095	4.7746	0.2095	4.1976
18	26.623	0.0376	128.117	0.0078	4.8122	0.2078	4.2975
19	31.948	0.0313	154.740	0.0065	4.8435	0.2065	4.3861
20	38.338	0.0261	186.688	0.0054	4.8696	0.2054	4.4644
21	46.005	0.0217	225.026	0.0045	4.8913	0.2045	4.5334
22	55.206	0.0181	271.031	0.0037	4.9094	0.2037	4.5942
23	66.247	0.0151	326.237	0.0031	4.9245	0.2031	4.6475
24	79.497	0.0126	392.484	0.0026	4.9371	0.2026	4.6943
25	95.396	0.0105	471.981	0.0021	4.9476	0.2021	4.7352

Contd...

t	*Single Payment*		*Equal Payment Series*				*Uniform gradient-series factor*
	Compound-amount factor	*Present-worth factor*	*Compound-amount factor*	*Sinking-fund factor*	*Present-worth factor*	*Capital-recovery factor*	
	To find F Given P F/P, r, t	*To find P Given F P/F, r, t*	*To find F Given A F/A, r, t*	*To find A Given F A/F, r, t*	*To find P Given A P/A, r, t*	*To find A Given P A/P, r, t*	*To find A Given G A/G, r, t*
26	114.475	0.0087	567.377	0.0018	4.9563	0.2018	4.7709
27	137.371	0.0073	681.853	0.0015	4.9636	0.2015	4.8020
28	164.845	0.0061	819.223	0.0012	4.9697	0.2012	4.8291
29	197.814	0.0051	984.068	0.0010	4.9747	0.2010	4.8527
30	237.376	0.0042	1181.882	0.0009	4.9789	0.2009	4.8731
31	284.852	0.0035	1419.258	0.0007	4.9825	0.2007	4.8908
32	341.822	0.0029	1704.109	0.0006	4.9854	0.2006	4.9061
33	410.186	0.0024	2045.931	0.0005	4.9878	0.2005	4.9194
34	492.224	0.0020	2456.118	0.0004	4.9899	0.2004	4.9308
35	590.668	0.0017	2948.341	0.0003	4.9915	0.2003	4.9407
40	1469.772	0.007	7343.858	0.0002	4.9966	0.2001	4.9728
45	3657.262	0.003	18281.310	0.0001	4.9986	0.2001	4.9877
50	9100.438	0.0001	45497.191	0.0000	4.9995	0.2000	4.9945

TABLE A. 25 25% INTEREST FACTORS FOR DISCRETE COMPOUNDING

t	*Single Payment*		*Equal Payment Series*				*Uniform gradient-factor*
	Compound-amount factor	*Present-worth factor*	*Compound-amount factor*	*Sinking-fund factor*	*Present-worth factor*	*Capital-recovery factor*	
	To find F Given P F/P, r, t	*To find P given F P/F, r, t*	*To find F Given A F/A, r, t*	*To find A Given F A/F, r, t*	*To find P Given A P/A, r, t*	*To find A Given P A/P, r, t*	*To find A Given G A/G, r, t*
1	1.250	0.8000	1.000	1.0000	0.8000	1.2500	0.0000
2	1.563	0.6400	2.250	0.4445	1.4400	0.6945	0.4445
3	1.953	0.5120	3.813	0.2623	1.95200	0.5123	0.8525
4	2.441	0.4096	5.766	0.1735	2.3616	0.4235	1.2249
5	3.052	0.3277	8.207	0.1219	2.6893	0.3719	1.5631
6	3.815	0.2622	11.259	0.0888	2.9514	0.3388	1.8683
7	4.768	0.2097	15.073	0.0664	3.1611	0.3164	2.1424
8	5.960	0.1678	19.842	0.0504	3.3289	0.3004	2.3873
9	7.451	0.1342	25.802	0.0388	3.4631	0.2888	2.6048
10	9.313	0.1074	33.253	0.0301	3.5705	0.2801	2.7971
11	11.642	0.0859	42.566	0.0235	3.6564	0.2735	2.9663
12	14.552	0.0687	54.208	0.0185	3.7251	0.2685	3.1145
13	18.190	0.0550	68.760	0.0146	3.7801	0.2646	3.2438
14	22.737	0.0440	86.949	0.0115	3.8241	0.2615	3.3560
15	28.422	0.0352	109.687	0.0091	3.8593	0.2591	3.4530
16	35.527	0.0282	138.109	0.0073	3.8874	0.2573	3.5366
17	44.409	0.0225	173.636	0.0058	3.9099	0.2558	3.6084
18	55.511	0.0180	218.045	0.0046	3.9280	0.2546	3.6698
19	69.389	0.0144	273.556	0.0037	3.9424	0.2537	3.7222
20	86.736	0.0115	342.945	0.0029	3.9539	0.2529	3.7667
21	108.420	0.0092	429.681	0.0023	3.9631	0.2529	3.8045
22	135.525	0.0074	538.101	0.0019	3.9705	0.2523	3.8365
23	169.407	0.0059	673.626	0.0015	3.9764	0.2519	3.8634
24	211.758	0.0047	843.033	0.0012	3.9811	0.2515	3.8861
25	264.698	0.0038	1054.791	0.0010	3.9849	0.2512	3.9052

Contd...

t	*Single Payment*		*Equal Payment Series*				*Uniform gradient-factor*
	Compound-amount factor	*Present-worth factor*	*Compound-amount factor*	*Sinking-fund factor*	*Present-worth factor*	*Capital-recovery factor*	
	To find F Given P F/P, r, t	*To find P given F P/F, r, t*	*To find F Given A F/A, r, t*	*To find A Given F A/F, r, t*	*To find P Given A P/A, r, t*	*To find A Given P A/P, r, t*	*To find A Given G A/G, r, t*
26	330.872	0.0030	1319.489	0.0008	3.9879	0.2510	3.9212
27	413.590	0.0024	1650.361	0.0006	3.9903	0.2508	3.9346
28	516.988	0.0019	2063.952	0.0005	3.9938	0.2506	3.9457
29	646.235	0.0016	2580.939	0.0004	3.9951	0.2505	3.9561
30	807.794	0.0012	3227.174	0.0003	3.9960	0.2504	3.9628
31	1009.742	0.0010	4034.968	0.0003	3.9968	0.2503	3.9603
32	1262.177	0.0008	5044.710	0.0002	3.9975	0.2502	3.9746
33	1577.722	0.0006	6306.887	0.0002	3.9968	0.2502	3.9791
34	1972.152	0.0005	7884.609	0.0001	3.9980	0.2501	3.9828
35	2465.190	0.0004	9856.761	0.0001	3.9984	0.2501	3.9558

TABLE A.26 30% INTEREST FACTORS FOR DISCRETE COMPOUNDING

t	*Single Payment*		*Equal Payment Series*				*Uniform gradient-series factor*
	Compound-amount factor	*Present-worth factor*	*Compound-amount factor*	*Sinking-fund factor*	*Present-worth factor*	*Capital-recovery factor*	
	To find F Given P F/P, r, t	*To find P given F P/F, r, t*	*To find F Given A F/A, r, t*	*To find A Given F A/F, r, t*	*To find P Given A P/A, r, t*	*To find A Given P A/P, r, t*	*To find A Given G A/G, r, t*
1	1.300	0.7692	1.000	1.0000	0.7692	1.3000	0.0000
2	1.690	0.5917	2.300	0.4348	1.3610	0.7348	0.4348
3	2.197	0.4552	3.990	0.2506	1.6161	0.5506	0.8271
4	2. 856	0.3501	6.187	0.1616	2.1663	0.4616	1.1783
5	3.713	0.2693	9.043	0.1106	2.4356	0.4106	1.4903
6	4.827	0.2042	12.756	0.0784	2.6428	0.3784	1.7655
7	6.276	0.1594	17.583	0.0569	2.8021	0.3569	2.0063
8	8.157	0.1226	23.858	0.0419	2.9247	0.3419	2.2156
9	10.605	0.0943	32.015	0.0312	3.0190	0.3312	2.3963
10	13.786	0.0725	42.620	0.0236	3.0915	0.3235	2.5512
11	17.922	0.0558	56.405	0.0177	3.1473	0.3177	2.6833
12	23.298	0.0429	74.327	0.0135	3.1903	0.3135	2.7952
13	30.288	0.0330	97.625	0.0103	3.2233	0.3103	2.8895
14	29.374	0.0254	127.913	0.0078	3.2487	0.3078	2.9685
15	51.186	0.0195	167.286	0.0060	3.2681	0.3060	3.0345
16	56.542	0.0150	218.472	0.0046	3.2832	0.3046	3.0892
17	86.504	0.0116	285.014	0.0035	3.2948	0.3035	3.1345
18	112.455	0.0089	371.518	0.0027	3.3037	0.3027	3.1718
19	146.192	0.0069	483.973	0.0021	3.3105	0.3021	3.2025
20	190.060	0.00553	630.165	0.0016	3.3158	0.3016	3.2276
21	247.085	0.0041	820.215	0.0012	3.3188	0.3012	3.2480
22	321.184	0.0031	1067.280	0.0009	30.3230	0.3009	3.2646
23	417.539	0.0024	1388.464	0.0007	3.3254	0.6007	3.2781
24	542.801	0.0019	1806.003	0.0006	3.3272	0.3006	2.2890
25	706.641	0.0014	2348.803	0.0004	3.3286	0.3004	3.2979

Contd...

t	*Single Payment*		*Equal Payment Series*				*Uniform gradient-series factor*
	Compound-amount factor	*Present-worth factor*	*Compound-amount factor*	*Sinking-fund factor*	*Present-worth factor*	*Capital-recovery factor*	
	To find F Given P F/P, r, t	*To find P given F P/F, r, t*	*To find F Given A F/A, r, t*	*To find A Given F A/F, r, t*	*To find P Given A P/A, r, t*	*To find A Given P A/P, r, t*	*To find A Given G A/G, r, t*
26	917.333	0.0011	3054.444	0.0003	3.3297	0.3003	3.3050
27	1192.533	0.0008	3971.778	0.0003	3.3305	0.3003	3.3107
28	1550.293	0.0007	5164.311	0.0002	3.3312	0.3002	3.3153
29	2015.381	0.0005	6714.604	0.0002	3.3317	0.3002	3.3189
30	2619.996	0.0004	8729.985	0.0001	3.3321	0.3001	3.3219
31	3405.994	0.0003	11349.981	0.0001	3.3324	0.3001	3.3242
32	4427.793	0.0002	14755.975	0.0001	3.3326	0.3001	3.3261
33	5756.130	0.0002	19183.768	0.0001	3.3328	0.3001	3.3278
34	7482.970	0.0001	25939.899	0.0001	3.3329	0.3001	3.3288
35	9727.860	0.0001	32422.868	0.0000	3.3330	0.3000	3.3297

TABLE A.27 40% INTEREST FACTORS FOR DISCRETE COMPOUNDING

t	*Single Payment*		*Equal Payment Series*				*Uniform gradient-series factor*
	Compound-amount factor	*Present-worth factor*	*Compound-amount factor*	*Sinking-fund factor*	*Present-worth factor*	*Capital-recovery factor*	
	To find F Given P F/P, r, t	*To find P given F P/F, r, t*	*To find F Given A F/A, r, t*	*To find A Given F A/F, r, t*	*To find P Given A P/A, r, t*	*To find A Given P A/P, r, t*	*To find A Given G A/G, r, t*
1	1.400	0.7143	1.000	1.0000	0.7143	1.4001	0.0000
2	1.960	0.5103	2.400	0.4167	1.2245	0.8167	0.4167
3	2.766	0.3645	4.360	0.2294	1.5890	0.8294	0.7799
4	3.842	0.2604	7.104	0.1408	1.8493	0.5408	1.0924
5	5.378	0.1860	10.946	0.0914	2.0352	0.4914	1.3680
6	7.530	0.1329	16.324	0.0613	2.1680	0.4613	1.5811
7	10.541	0.0949	23.853	0.0420	2.2629	0.4420	1.7664
8	14.758	0.0678	34.395	0.0291	2.3306	0.4291	1.9186
9	20.661	0.0485	49.153	0.0204	2.3790	0.4204	4.0423
10	28.925	0.0346	69.814	0.0144	2.4136	0.4144	2.1420
11	40.496	0.0247	98.739	0.0102	2.4383	0.4102	2.2215
12	56.694	0.0177	139.234	0.0072	2.4560	0.4072	2.2840
13	79.371	0.0126	195.928	0.0052	2.4686	0.4062	2.3342
14	111.120	0.0090	275.299	0.0037	2.4775	0.4037	2.3729
15	155.568	0.0065	386.419	0.0026	2.4840	0.4026	2.4030
16	217.794	0.0046	541.986	0.0019	2.4886	0.4019	2.4262
17	304.912	0.0033	759.780	0.0014	2.4918	0.4017	2.4441
18	426.877	0.0024	1064.691	0.0010	2.4942	0.4010	2.4578
19	597.627	0.0017	1491.567	0.0007	2.4959	0.4007	2.4682
20	836.678	0.0012	2089.195	0.0005	2.4971	0.4005	2.4761
21	1147.348	0.0009	2925.871	0.0004	2.4979	0.4004	2.4821
22	1639.887	0.0007	4097.218	0.0003	2.4985	0.4003	2.4866
23	2295.842	0.0005	5737.106	0.0002	2.4990	0.4002	2.4800
24	3217.178	0.0004	8032.945	0.0002	2.4983	0.4002	2.4826
25	4499.847	0.0003	11247.110	0.0001	2.4995	0.4001	2.4946
26	6299.785	0.0002	15756.960	0.0001	2.4997	0.4001	2.4950
27	8819.695	0.0002	22046.730	0.0001	2.4998	0.4001	2.4970
28	12347.570	0.0001	30866.430	0.0001	2.4998	0.4001	2.4978
29	17286.590	0.0001	43213.990	0.0001	2.4999	0.4001	2.4984
30	24201.230	0.0001	60500.580	0.0001	2.4999	0.4001	2.4966

Contd...

TABLE A.28 50% INTEREST FACTORS FOR DISCRETE COMPOUNDING

t	*Single Payment*		*Equal Payment Series*				*Uniform gradient-series factor*
	Compound-amount factor	*Present-worth factor*	*Compound-amount factor*	*Sinking-fund factor*	*Present-worth factor*	*Capital-recovery factor*	
	To find F Given P F/P, r, t	*To find P given F P/F, r, t*	*To find F Given A F/A, r, t*	*To find A Given F A/F, r, t*	*To find P Given A P/A, r, t*	*To find A Given P A/P, r, t*	*To find A Given G A/G, r, t*
1	1.500	0.6667	1.000	1.0000	0.6667	1.5000	0.0001
2	2.250	0.4445	2.500	0.4000	1.1112	0.9001	0.4001
3	3.375	0.2963	4.750	0.2106	1.4075	0.7106	0.7369
4	5.063	0.1976	8.125	0.1231	1.6050	0.6231	1.0154
5	7.594	0.1317	13.188	0.0759	1.7367	0.5759	1.2418
6	11.391	0.0878	20.781	0.0482	1.8245	0.5482	1.4226
7	17.084	0.0656	32.172	0.0311	1.7730	0.5311	1.5649
8	26.629	0.0391	49.258	0.0204	1.9220	0.5204	1.6752
9	38.443	0.0261	74.887	0.0134	1.9480	0.5134	1.7594
10	57.665	0.0174	113.330	0.0089	1.9654	0.5089	1.8136
11	86.498	0.0116	170.995	0.0059	1.9759	0.5059	1.8714
12	129.746	0.0078	257.493	0.0039	1.9846	0.5039	1.9068
13	194.620	0.0052	387.239	0.0026	1.9898	0.5026	1.9329
14	291.929	0.0035	581.858	0.0018	1.9932	0.5018	1.9519
15	437.894	0.0023	873.788	0.0012	1.9955	0.5012	1.9657
16	656.841	0.0016	1311.681	0.0008	1.9970	0.5008	1.9457
17	985.261	0.0011	1368.522	0.0006	1.9980	0.5006	1.9828
18	1477.891	0.0007	2953.783	0.0004	1.9987	0.5004	1.9879
19	2216.837	0.0005	4431.671	0.0003	1.9991	0.5003	1.9915
20	3325.256	0.0004	6648.511	0.0002	1.9994	0.5002	1.9940
21	4987.882	0.0003	9973.765	0.0002	1.9996	0.5002	1.9958
22	7481.824	0.0002	1491.640	0.0001	1.9997	0.5001	1.9971
23	11222.730	0.0001	22443.470	0.0001	1.9999	0.5001	1.9980
24	16834.100	0.0001	33666.210	0.0001	1.9999	0.5001	1.9986
25	25251.160	0.0001	50500.330	0.0001	2.0000	0.5001	1.9991

Index